TRAIN YOUR BRAIN

TRAIN YOUR BRAIN

KINGFISHER

KINGFISHER

First published 2008 by Kingfisher
an imprint of Macmillan Children's Books
a division of Macmillan Publishers Limited
4 Crinan Street, London N1 9XW
Associated companies throughout the world
www.panmacmillan.com

Authors: Clive Gifford, Daniel Gilpin,
Conrad Mason, Helen Varley and Cynthia O'Brien

ISBN 978-0-7534-1591-7

Copyright © Macmillan Children's Books 2008

Authors: Clive Gifford, Daniel Gilpin, Conrad Mason,

9 8 7 6 5 4 3 2
2TR/0708/LFG/PICA(PICA)/128MA/C

A CIP catalogue record for this book is available from
the British Library.

Printed in China

Contents

How this book works

It's as easy as one, two, three! Option one: use the question panels to quiz yourself. Option two: turn the page to read all about the topic – numbered circles show you where to look to work out the answer for yourself. Option three: look up the answers at the back of the book. These are the three ways you can use *Train Your Brain*. Or you can just read the book all the way through!

1. The questions

Look at the question panel on the far right of each page. You will find the questions divided into three levels of difficulty. Level one questions are easy, level two are harder, and level three are real brain-teasers! Stumped? There are two ways to find the answer.

2. Read all about it!

You can turn the page and read all about the quiz topic. Look for the number of each question in the coloured circles – the answer will be somewhere inside the box...

3. The answers

...Or, you can look up the answers at the back of the book. Just turn to the topic and find out whether you got it right.

Picture clues

You can find clues to some of the answers in the pictures. Look at them to try to work out the answer.

Quick quiz

The answer pages have the questions too, so you can ask a friend to give you a quick quiz – another way to use *Train Your Brain*!

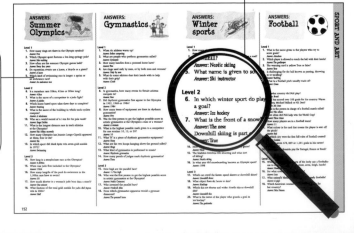

QUIZ ONE
Nature

QUESTIONS:
The rainforest

Level 1

1. Are frogs reptiles or amphibians?
2. Are reptiles cold-blooded or warm-blooded?
3. What 'A' is the world's largest river?
4. How often does it usually rain in the rainforest: daily, weekly or monthly?

Level 2

5. In which continent does the cinchona tree grow?
6. What type of animal is a boa?
7. Which plant has the largest flower in the world?
8. In which part of the rainforest do most of its animals live?
9. What do pitcher plants feed on?
10. What does the flower of the rafflesia plant smell like?
11. GREEN STEM can be rearranged to give the name of which group of tall trees?
12. Where in the world do poison dart frogs live?
13. Is a bromeliad an animal or a plant?
14. A poison dart frog's skin has enough poison to kill a person. True or false?
15. Where does the Atlas moth live?

Level 3

16. Are snakes more closely related to frogs or lizards?
17. How wide is the Amazon river at its mouth: more than 300km, more than 400km or more than 500km?
18. What illness is treated with quinine?
19. What part of geckos' bodies gives them grip?
20. Where do the plants known as epiphytes grow?

The rainforest

Tropical rainforest is the richest of all natural habitats. More animals and plants live here than anywhere else on earth. The rainforest is well named – in most places it rains every day. The mixture of water and warmth is what makes this habitat so full of life.

emergents

parrots

monkey

Canopy   `8` `11`

The canopy is like the roof of the rainforest, formed by the branches of the tallest trees. Most rainforest animals live here, eating leaves, flowers and fruit, or one another. Really tall trees, called emergents, rise above the top of the canopy.

toucan

jaguar

Plants   `13` `20`

Rainforest trees are themselves cloaked with other plants. Climbers such as vines and strangler figs grip their trunks, while ferns and bromeliads grow in their branches. Plants growing on other plants in this way are called epiphytes.

Insects   `15`

Rainforest insects include the world's largest moth – the Atlas moth, which lives in the rainforests of southeast Asia.

Reptiles   `2` `6` `16` `19`

Reptiles are cold-blooded animals, which thrive in the warmth of tropical rainforests. Snakes such as boas and pythons hunt prey in the branches, while gecko lizards scuttle up and down the trunks, gripping with flattened toes, which act a bit like suction pads.

Amphibians   `1` `12` `14`

The dampness of the rainforest suits slimy-skinned amphibians such as the poison dart frog of South America. This type of frog has enough poison in its skin to kill a person.

common lancehead

cheese plant

red-eyed tree frog

heliconia flower

cicada

poison dart frog

Rivers

3 17

Almost all of the world's largest rivers flow through rainforests. Among them is the largest river of all, the Amazon. This massive waterway drains much of the continent of South America. Near its mouth in Brazil, the Amazon river is more than 300km wide.

Plants and animals

7 9 10

Rainforest plants use animals in unusual ways. Pitcher plants lure insects into their 'pitchers' with droplets of nectar. They then digest the insects as food. The rafflesia has the world's largest flower – 1m wide. It smells of rotten meat to attract flies to pollinate it.

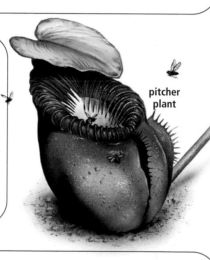

pitcher plant

Water

4

Plants have adapted in different ways to the daily downpours of the rainforests. Many have shiny leaves with downward-pointing tips to channel water away. Some, growing in branches, have trailing roots to gather rain running off the trees.

Plant remedies

5 18

Many medicines were first discovered in rainforest plants. Quinine, for example, is used to treat malaria. It was first taken from the bark of the cinchona tree, which grows in the South American rainforests.

QUESTIONS:
Ants

Level 1

1. Which have the stronger mandibles (jaws): worker or soldier ants?
2. What 'Q' is the large ant that lays all the eggs in a colony?
3. Are aphids worms or insects?
4. Are wood ants bigger or smaller than most other ants?

Level 2

5. Are there any ants that bring aphids into their nests?
6. Most ants build nests underground. True or false?
7. What do aphids feed on?
8. What is the name of the sugary substance that aphids produce?
9. Are honeypot ants most common in dry or wet places?
10. Do leaf-cutter ants live in warm or cold forests?
11. Do wood ants ever bite people?
12. What type of substance can some ants fire at attackers?
13. What do wood ants build their nests from?
14. Do ants ever attack birds?

Level 3

15. Do leaf-cutter ants eat the leaves that they harvest?
16. How many different types of ant are there in a colony?
17. What does the word metamorphose mean?
18. In what kind of forest do most wood ants live?
19. Do all of the workers in a honeypot ant colony store food in their bodies?
20. Name a continent in which both honeypot and leaf-cutter ants live.

FIND THE ANSWER: Ants

Ants live in huge communities of closely related individuals. Most ants are workers, collecting food and looking after the eggs and larvae (young). Soldier ants are slightly larger than workers and protect the nest from intruders. All ants are hatched from eggs laid by a giant ant called the queen.

Farming ③ ⑤ ⑦ ⑧
Some ants farm smaller insects called aphids. Aphids feed on plant sap and produce a sugary substance called honeydew, which the ants eat. Some ants bring aphids into their nests to feed them, so they can eat honeydew.

Eggs ② ⑯ ⑰
All of the eggs in an ants' nest are laid by the queen, and then taken away by worker ants to special chambers. Here they are tended until they hatch. The worker ants feed the newly hatched larvae until they are big enough to metamorphose (change shape) into adult ants themselves.

Leaf-cutter ants ⑩ ⑮ ⑳
These ants live in warm forests in North and South America. They gather leaves as compost to grow mushrooms (fungi), which they eat.

Tunnels ⑥
Most ants build their nests underground for protection from the weather and predators. They dig tunnels and chambers in soft earth.

entrance to the nest

aphids

worker ant

larvae

queen ant

Attack and defence

1 12 14 16

Soldier ants are larger than workers and have stronger mandibles, or jaws, so their job is to protect the colony from attack. Worker ants join in if needed. Some ants also defend themselves by firing acid from the rear sections of their bodies. Ants are fearless and often attack much larger insects for food. They will swarm over birds or mammals if they threaten the ants' nest.

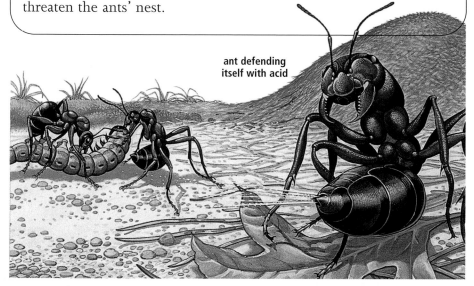

ant defending itself with acid

Honeypot ants

9 19 20

These ants use some of their workers as storage jars. They feed the storage ants with nectar, which is held inside their bodies for future use. Honeypot ants live in dry regions in North and South America, Africa and Australia.

Wood ants

4 11 13 18

Wood ants live in pine forests and make their nests above ground. They build them from dried pine needles, which they collect from the forest floor. Their nests can be over a metre high. Wood ants are bigger than most ant species (types). Their mandibles are so large that they can give even people a painful bite if they are disturbed.

QUESTIONS:
Dinosaurs

Level 1

1. What did *Spinosaurus* have on its back: wings or a sail?
2. What 'S' was the largest stegosaur?
3. Which dinosaur had plates on its back: *Kentrosaurus* or *Tyrannosaurus rex*?
4. Which had larger teeth: plant-eating or meat-eating dinosaurs?

Level 2

5. *Tyrannosaurus rex* teeth could be more than 10cm long. True or false?
6. Do fossils take thousands or millions of years to form?
7. Did sauropods have long necks or short necks?
8. Did any dinosaurs have beaks?
9. What did *Styracosaurus* have on its nose?
10. What did male horned dinosaurs probably use their horns for, apart from defence?
11. Which are more common: scattered fossil bones or entire fossil skeletons?
12. What type of dinosaur was *Kentrosaurus*?
13. How did a *Spinosaurus* cool down?
14. Where can you see dinosaur bones on display?

Level 3

15. What did *Tyrannosaurus rex* eat?
16. Which was bigger: *Seismosaurus* or *Stegosaurus*?
17. Are fossils made of bone or of minerals from rock?
18. *Styracosaurus* ate meat. True or false?
19. Is an *Apatosaurus* more closely related to a *Seismosaurus* or a *Styracosaurus*?
20. How many rows of plates did most stegosaurs have?

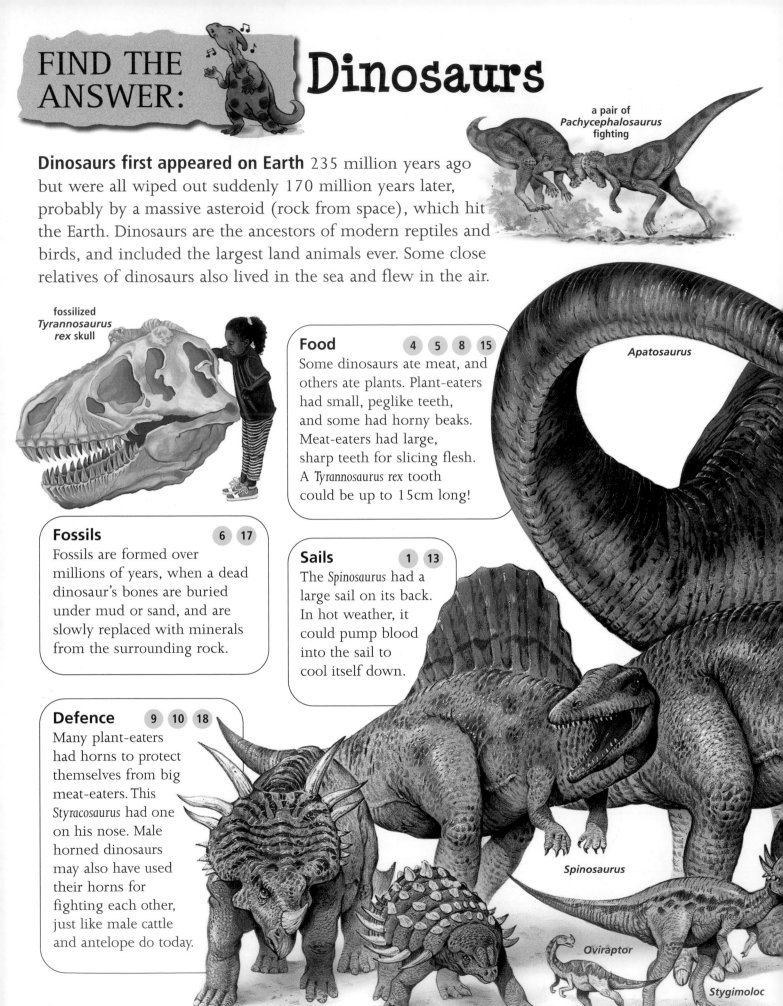

FIND THE ANSWER: Dinosaurs

a pair of *Pachycephalosaurus* fighting

Dinosaurs first appeared on Earth 235 million years ago but were all wiped out suddenly 170 million years later, probably by a massive asteroid (rock from space), which hit the Earth. Dinosaurs are the ancestors of modern reptiles and birds, and included the largest land animals ever. Some close relatives of dinosaurs also lived in the sea and flew in the air.

fossilized *Tyrannosaurus rex* skull

Food   4 5 8 15

Some dinosaurs ate meat, and others ate plants. Plant-eaters had small, peglike teeth, and some had horny beaks. Meat-eaters had large, sharp teeth for slicing flesh. A *Tyrannosaurus rex* tooth could be up to 15cm long!

Apatosaurus

Fossils   6 17

Fossils are formed over millions of years, when a dead dinosaur's bones are buried under mud or sand, and are slowly replaced with minerals from the surrounding rock.

Sails   1 13

The *Spinosaurus* had a large sail on its back. In hot weather, it could pump blood into the sail to cool itself down.

Defence   9 10 18

Many plant-eaters had horns to protect themselves from big meat-eaters. This *Styracosaurus* had one on his nose. Male horned dinosaurs may also have used their horns for fighting each other, just like male cattle and antelope do today.

Spinosaurus

Oviraptor

Stygimoloc

Styracosaurus

Panoplosaurus

Giant dinosaurs ⑦ ⑯ ⑲

The biggest of all dinosaurs were plant-eating sauropods like this *Apatosaurus*. Sauropods all had small heads on long necks. The largest, such as the giant *Seismosaurus*, could sometimes weigh more than 100 tonnes.

Skeletons ⑪ ⑭

Most dinosaur fossils are just a few scattered bones, but sometimes complete skeletons are found. They can then be pieced together on metal frames, to be displayed in museums.

sauropod skeleton on display

Plates ② ③ ⑫ ⑳

Stegosaurs were plant-eaters with twin rows of plates along their backs. These probably worked in a similar way to a sail of a *Spinosaurus*, both for display and to help the dinosaurs cool down. The largest and most famous of the stegosaurs was the *Stegosaurus*. The *Kentrosaurus* was one of the smallest members of the stegosaur family.

Iguanodon

Kentrosaurus

QUESTIONS:
Snakes

Level 1

1. Are pythons snakes?
2. Do snakes have legs?
3. Can snakes see?

Level 2

4. Are there any snakes that eat eggs?
5. Which snakes have a hood that they raise when threatened?
6. Where is a rattlesnake's rattle: in its mouth or on the end of its tail?
7. Are snakes vertebrates or invertebrates?
8. What are snakes' skeletons made from?
9. Do snakes' eggs have hard or flexible shells?
10. Are there any snakes that give birth to live young?
11. Rattlesnakes live in Africa. True or false?
12. Do cobras have solid or hollow fangs?
13. Do anacondas grow to over 50cm long, over 3m long or over 8m long?
14. Does camouflage make a snake harder or easier to see?

Level 3

15. What does a baby snake have on its snout to help it hatch?
16. Why do snakes flick their tongues in and out?
17. How do snakes move?
18. How do pythons kill their prey?
19. What does the African egg-eating snake use to break eggs?

FIND THE ANSWER: Snakes

Snakes are reptiles, like tortoises, turtles and lizards.
Reptiles are cold-blooded animals, which means that their body temperatures change with those of their surroundings. Because they need warmth to be active, most snakes live in hot countries.

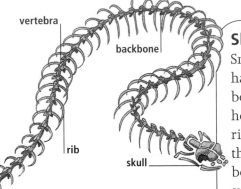

vertebra

backbone

rib

skull

Skeleton 2 7 8 17
Snakes are vertebrates and have skeletons made of bone. Snakes have no legs, however, and move by rippling the muscles on the underside of their bodies. A snake's body is supported by its many ribs.

Eggs 9 10 15
Most snakes lay eggs, although some give birth to live young. Unlike birds' eggs, snakes' eggs have flexible, leathery shells. Baby snakes have a sharp egg tooth on their snouts for breaking out of their eggs.

Food 4 19
Nearly all snakes are predators that catch and eat live animals. A few specialize in eating eggs. The African egg-eating snake dislocates its jaws to swallow birds' eggs three times larger than its head. The egg is swallowed whole and is punctured by sharp spines that stick down from its backbone.

coral snake moving by rippling its muscles

cobra

Cobras 5 12
These large snakes kill their prey with venom. They inject this poisonous liquid into their victims through their hollow fangs. Cobras can easily be told apart from other snakes by the hoods that they have behind their heads. When they feel threatened, they raise themselves up and spread their hoods outwards, just like this cobra is doing.

14

Senses

(3) (16)

Snakes are able to see, but their senses of smell and taste are combined. Snakes flick their tongues in and out because they can taste the air. A snake's forked tongue can pick up particles given off by prey, and these are detected by an organ, called the Jacobson's organ, in the roof of the mouth.

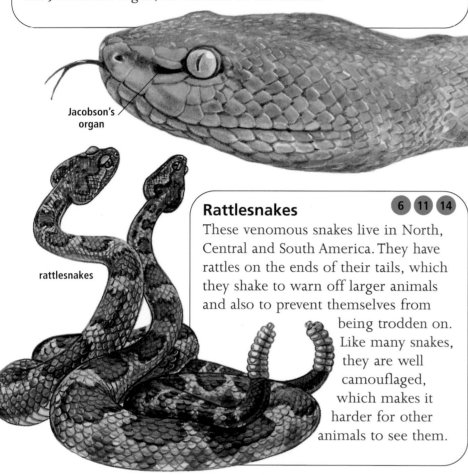

Jacobson's organ

rattlesnakes

Rattlesnakes

(6) (11) (14)

These venomous snakes live in North, Central and South America. They have rattles on the ends of their tails, which they shake to warn off larger animals and also to prevent themselves from being trodden on. Like many snakes, they are well camouflaged, which makes it harder for other animals to see them.

Constrictor

(1) (13) (18)

Some snakes, such as boas and pythons, are called constrictors because they wrap themselves around their prey until it suffocates. Anacondas are constrictors from the Amazon region of South America. They reach more than 8m long.

garter snake

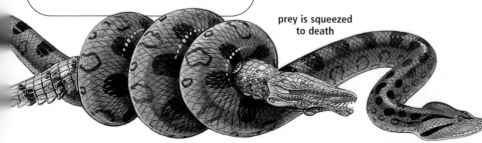

prey is squeezed to death

QUESTIONS:
Sharks

Level 1

1. Are sharks fish or reptiles?
2. The whale shark is the world's biggest fish. True or false?
3. Do great white sharks eat lions or sea lions?
4. Is a shark's egg case called a mermaid's purse or a sailor's purse?

Level 2

5. Do sharks have the same set of teeth all their lives?
6. Do basking sharks live in warmer or cooler waters than whale sharks?
7. The biggest great white sharks can grow up to 6m long. True or false?
8. What is the name given to the tiny sea creatures that are food for whale sharks?
9. Which is bigger: the basking or the great white shark?
10. HE MADE HARM can be rearranged to give the name of which type of shark?
11. How heavy can a whale shark be: 11 tonnes, 21 tonnes or 31 tonnes?
12. Do all sharks lay eggs?
13. The teeth of an individual shark are all the same shape. True or false?
14. Which shark is more likely to attack people: the great white or the hammerhead?
15. Do sharks ever resort to cannibalism (eating each other)?

Level 3

16. What feature of a hammerhead makes it easier to follow a scent trail in the water?
17. What is the largest type of fish seen off the UK?
18. What is the largest shark to actively hunt prey?

Sharks

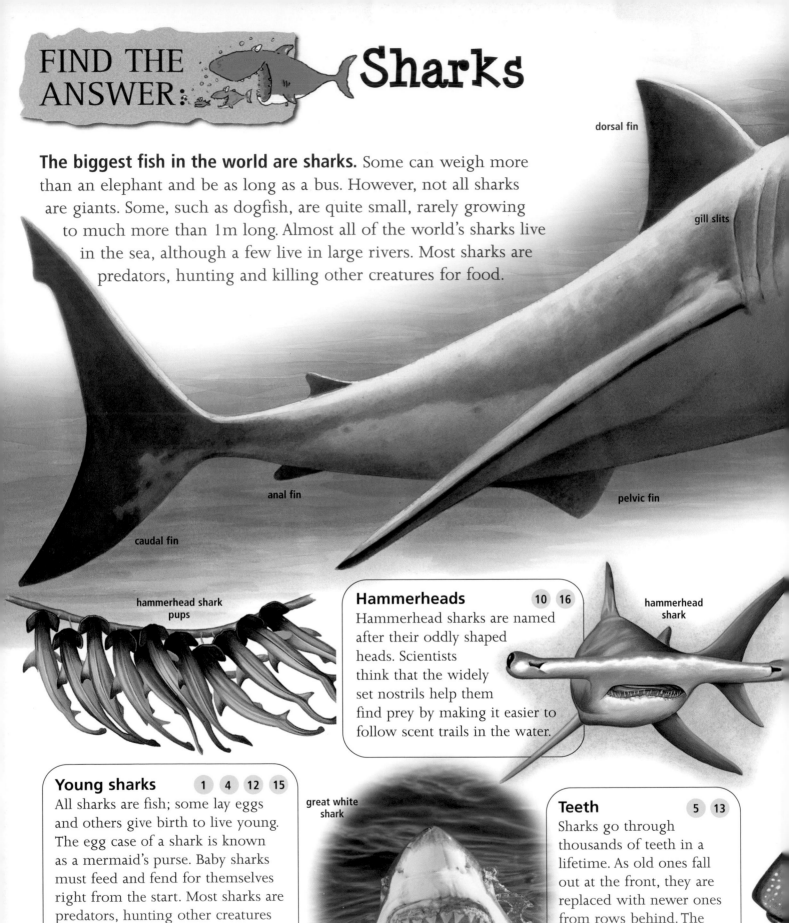

dorsal fin

gill slits

The biggest fish in the world are sharks. Some can weigh more than an elephant and be as long as a bus. However, not all sharks are giants. Some, such as dogfish, are quite small, rarely growing to much more than 1m long. Almost all of the world's sharks live in the sea, although a few live in large rivers. Most sharks are predators, hunting and killing other creatures for food.

anal fin

pelvic fin

caudal fin

hammerhead shark pups

Hammerheads 10 16
Hammerhead sharks are named after their oddly shaped heads. Scientists think that the widely set nostrils help them find prey by making it easier to follow scent trails in the water.

hammerhead shark

Young sharks 1 4 12 15
All sharks are fish; some lay eggs and others give birth to live young. The egg case of a shark is known as a mermaid's purse. Baby sharks must feed and fend for themselves right from the start. Most sharks are predators, hunting other creatures for food. When they are young, they are eaten by other creatures, including other sharks.

great white shark

Teeth 5 13
Sharks go through thousands of teeth in a lifetime. As old ones fall out at the front, they are replaced with newer ones from rows behind. The teeth of an individual shark are all the same shape, but differ in size.

nostril

great white shark

pectoral fin

Great white `3` `7` `14` `18`

The great white is the world's third-largest fish and the biggest shark to actively hunt prey. Some great white sharks grow to around 6m long, although most are smaller. Great white sharks hunt sea lions and other large prey. They kill and injure more people than any other type of shark.

Whale shark `2` `8` `11`

Reaching 18m long and weighing up to 21 tonnes, the whale shark is the world's largest fish. It lives in warm, tropical waters and feeds on tiny sea creatures called plankton.

whale shark

basking shark

Basking shark `6` `9` `17`

The basking shark is the world's second-largest fish. Like the whale shark, it feeds on plankton but it lives in cooler waters such as the seas around the UK.

Level 1

1. How many tentacles does an octopus have?
2. Most of a jellyfish's body is made up of air. True or false?
3. What does SCUBA equipment help people to do?
4. Are seahorses fish or molluscs?

Level 2

5. What is the world's largest species of ray?
6. Are there more than 100 types of shark in the world?
7. How many tentacles does a squid have?
8. What do squid eat: jellyfish, plankton or fish?
9. What do jellyfish use to attack their prey?
10. Are squid invertebrates?
11. Which ocean habitat is home to the most types of fish?
12. How long can divers stay underwater for: 10 minutes or more, 15 minutes or more or 20 minutes or more?
13. What do the tanks in SCUBA equipment contain?
14. Are sharks more closely related to squid or rays?
15. Do squid spend most of their time in open water or on the seabed?

Level 3

16. What 'P' leave behind the hard, stony cases we see in coral reefs?
17. To which of these creatures are corals most closely related: jellyfish, giant clams or sharks?
18. What word is used to describe a tail that can grip things?

Sea creatures

jellyfish

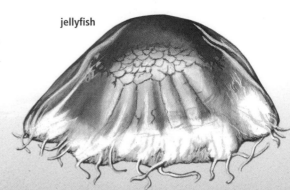

Most of the world's animals live in the sea. The sea itself covers more than two-thirds of the planet's surface. Sea creatures vary greatly in shape, size and form. Most, however, fall into two groups: vertebrates and invertebrates. Vertebrates are animals that have a backbone, like people do. Invertebrates have no bones at all.

Sharks   5   6   14
Altogether, there are more than 360 different species (types) of shark. Sharks are closely related to rays. The world's largest ray, a manta ray, can be seen in this picture just below the squid.

Jellyfish   2   9   17
Jellyfish are invertebrates with simple body structures, closely related to corals. More than 90 per cent of a jellyfish is water. Jellyfish hunt other animals with stinging tentacles.

Squid   1   7   8   10   15
Squid swim in open water and hunt fish and small sea creatures. They are closely related to octopuses but, unlike them, have ten tentacles instead of eight. Both are cephalopods (a type of invertebrate).

hammerhead shark

great white shark

squid

Coral   16
Corals often crowd together to form reefs. The bits we usually see are hard, stony cases laid down by individual polyps: tiny sea anemone-like animals.

coral

giant clam

Diver ③ ⑫ ⑬
People can explore the world of sea creatures by using SCUBA diving gear. Tanks of compressed gas allow them to breathe underwater for 20 minutes or more.

marine biologist

Netting fish ④ ⑪ ⑱
This diver is catching fish for scientific study. More types of fish live on coral reefs than any other sea habitat. Among the strangest-looking fish are seahorses. Their prehensile (gripping) tails help them hold on to coral reefs.

net for collecting sea creatures

seahorses

manta ray

octopus

QUESTIONS:
Marine mammals

Level 1
1. What is the biggest animal on earth: the elephant or the blue whale?
2. Do seals eat fish or seaweed?
3. By what name are orcas more commonly known: killer whales or seals?
4. Baby harp seals are born with grey fur. True or false?

Level 2
5. Which use echolocation to find their prey: dolphins or walruses?
6. What 'K' are shrimp-like creatures that humpback whales eat?
7. Seals give birth in the sea. True or false?
8. Do all walruses have tusks, or only the males?
9. What 'P' is a group of killer whales known as?
10. Why are many large whales rare today?
11. Which marine mammals sometimes kill and eat whales that are larger than they are?
12. Do all whales eat large animals?
13. Which ocean surrounds the North Pole?
14. What 'S' do walruses eat?

Level 3
15. Where on a whale would you find its baleen?
16. What 'C' is the name of the marine mammal group that contains whales and dolphins?
17. Near which pole do walruses live: the North or the South Pole?
18. What part of a blue whale weighs as much as an elephant?
19. How long was the largest blue whale ever measured?

Marine mammals

blue whale's size compared to other animals

Mammals are warm-blooded animals that feed their young on milk. Most of them live on land but some, the marine mammals, live in the sea. Marine mammals include whales, dolphins, seals, sea lions and walruses. All of them breathe air but have adapted to life in the sea, having flippers instead of legs, for example.

Biggest animal (1) (18) (19)

The blue whale is the biggest animal that has ever lived. Its heart is as big as a car and its tongue weighs as much as an elephant. The biggest ever measured was 33.5m long.

Killer whales (3) (9) (11)

Killer whales, or orcas, live and hunt in groups called pods. By working together, they can overpower and kill much larger whales. Some orcas hunt small prey like seals and fish.

killer whale pod attacking a humpback whale

humpback whale

Humpbacks (6) (12) (15)

Like most large whales, humpbacks feed on small fish and shrimp-like krill. They trap whole shoals inside their mouths behind plates of baleen, which hang down from their upper jaws.

whaling ship harpooning a humpback whale

Whaling (10)

Most large whales are rare, because in the past they were hunted. Whalers killed them for their meat, considered a delicacy in some countries. It is now illegal to hunt most large whales, and the huge whaling fleets that once sailed the seas are a thing of the past.

Dolphins 5 16

Like whales, dolphins belong to the mammal group called cetaceans. Dolphins use echolocation to find food, making loud clicks, then listening for echoes that bounce back. They often work together to round up prey.

bottle-nosed dolphins

Seals 2 4 7

Seals eat fish, but they haul themselves out onto ice or land to rest and to give birth to their young. Baby harp seals are born with white coats. Their mothers' milk is very thick and creamy.

baby harp seal with its mother

walrus tusks

Walruses 8 13 14 17

The walrus lives in the Arctic ocean, which surrounds the North Pole. It feeds on shellfish, which it collects from the seabed. All walruses have long tusks, although those of the males are bigger. They use these to spar for mates and also to defend themselves from polar bears. Walruses live together in large groups.

QUESTIONS:
Sea birds

Level 1

1. Do puffins carry food in their mouths, their feet or their wings?
2. Do seagulls ever feed inland?
3. SNIFF UP can be rearranged to give the name of what sea birds?
4. An albatross is a type of sea bird. True or false?
5. What 'F' is the main food of most sea birds?

Level 2

6. Some sea birds carry food for their chicks in their stomachs. True or false?
7. Why do cormorants stand with their wings open after hunting in the water?
8. Do puffins use their wings or feet to swim?
9. Do boobies hunt by diving into the water from the air or by diving in from the surface?
10. Is a male frigate bird's throat-pouch red, yellow or blue?
11. Do cormorants use their wings or feet to swim?
12. Does oil float on water or does it sink?
13. Do frigate birds live in the tropics or near the North Pole?

Level 3

14. What 'G' is a sea bird that nests near the tops of cliffs?
15. What does the word regurgitate mean?
16. How do frigate birds get food?
17. Why do male frigate birds inflate their throat pouches with air?
18. What 'T' is a word for warm air currents that frigate birds use to lift them into the air?

Many birds find their food in the ocean. Birds that do this are known as sea birds. Shore birds, such as the oystercatcher, live beside the sea and find their food on mud flats and beaches. Although sea birds spend their lives out over the ocean, they lay their eggs on land and return every year to coastal cliffs to breed.

Frigate birds 10 13 16 17

Frigate birds live in the tropics, and attack other sea birds in order to steal their food. Males have red throat-pouches which they inflate to attract females.

Colonies 14

Many types of sea bird live and breed in large colonies on cliffs, to help protect each other from predators. The gannet, shown on the right, nests near the tops of cliffs.

Food 1 5 6 15

Most sea birds eat fish, and carry it back to their chicks. Some, such as puffins, stuff their beaks with food. Others swallow it and then regurgitate it (cough it up) when they return.

Hunting 3 8 9

The booby dives from the air into the water to catch its prey. Other sea birds, such as puffins, land on the water and dive in from the surface, paddling with their wings.

gannet

tern

red-billed tropic bird dropping its prey

frigate birds attacking

booby diving

oystercatcher

shearwater

puffin

booby snatching its prey

Cormorant (7) (11)

Cormorants are large sea birds that hunt by diving from the water's surface and using their webbed feet as paddles. After hunting, they stand with their wings held open wide to dry out their feathers.

cormorant drying its wings

Using air currents (4) (18)

Some sea birds, such as frigate birds, use thermals (warm air currents) to lift them into the air. Others, such as albatrosses, use small updraughts that blow off the crests of waves to lift them upwards.

On land and sea (2)

Some sea birds have become successful on land as well as on the ocean. Many seagulls, for instance, have learned to find food in bins and rubbish tips. They also follow fishing boats for discarded fish.

Pollution (12)

Sea birds often suffer because of human waste and pollution. Whenever oil tankers sink, hundreds of sea birds die as the oil floats on water and clogs up their feathers. Only the lucky ones that are found on beaches and cleaned up, survive.

QUESTIONS:
Birds

Level 1

1. Do birds have teeth?
2. Birds are the only animals in the world that have feathers. True or false?
3. Do birds flap their wings when they are gliding?
4. Can swans fly?

Level 2

5. A NEST FILM can be rearranged to give the name of what parts of a feather?
6. What is the world's largest bird?
7. Birds have elbow joints. True or false?
8. Are birds' bones solid or hollow?
9. GLEAM UP can be rearranged to give what name for the feathers that cover a bird?
10. Does a kestrel eat fruit, seeds or meat?
11. Which are usually more brightly coloured: male birds or female birds?
12. Which 'H' means to stay still in mid-air?
13. Which has the longer beak: a curlew or a robin?
14. How many times can hummingbirds flap their wings every second: seven times, 70 times or 700 times?

Level 3

15. What is the chamber between a bird's mouth and its stomach called?
16. How many sections does a bird's stomach have?
17. What do hummingbirds feed on?
18. What 'R' is a large flightless bird?

Birds

Birds are masters of the air. Their ability to fly enables birds to travel long distances in search of food. Some migrate, flying thousands of kilometres each year to breed and take advantage of the abundance of food in spring and summer. All birds lay eggs with hard shells, and most make nests. Some birds sing to attract mates or show they own a territory.

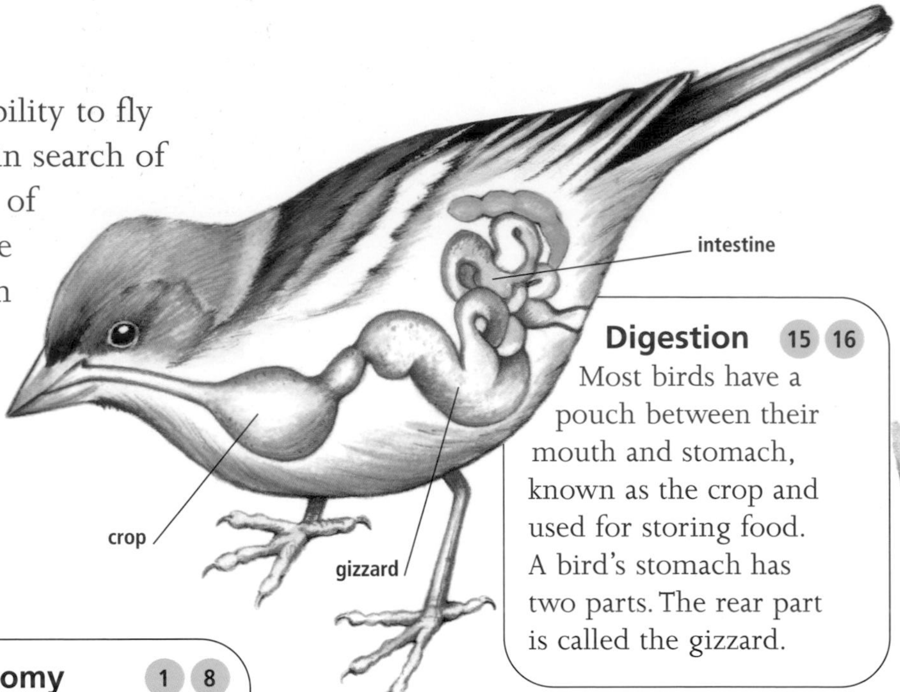

intestine

crop

gizzard

Digestion 15 16

Most birds have a pouch between their mouth and stomach, known as the crop and used for storing food. A bird's stomach has two parts. The rear part is called the gizzard.

Feathers 2 5

Birds are the only animals in the world that have feathers. Feathers are what enable birds to fly. They are lightweight but strong, made of many filaments held together by very small hooks.

Anatomy 1 8

A bird's body has several features to make it lighter and so make flight less of an effort. For example, its bones are hollow and therefore lighter than those of other animals. Birds also have beaks instead of teeth.

rock dove slowing itself down as it lands

filaments

hooks

Flight 3

Most birds fly by flapping their wings, using them to push down on the air and lift their bodies upwards. Some birds glide, holding out their wings and catching updraughts of air – this uses hardly any energy.

Wings 7

A bird's wings are like arms, with shoulder and elbow joints. Bones that formed fingers in birds' ancestors have adapted to form ends of wings.

Large birds (4) (6) (18)
The largest flying birds are pelicans (left), bustards and swans. The largest bird of all is flightless – the ostrich. Other flightless giants include emus and rheas.

Plumage (9) (11)
The feathers that cover a bird are called plumage. Usually, male birds' plumage is colourful, to attract mates, whereas females have dull plumage to hide them when sitting on eggs.

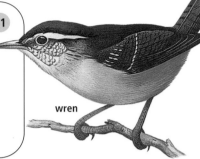
wren

swallow

robin

greenfinch

kestrel

redshank

curlew

Beaks (10) (13)
A bird's beak is adapted for the food that it eats. The curlew's long beak is used for probing in the mud for worms, while the kestrel's hooked beak is used for tearing off meat.

Hummingbirds (12) (14) (17)
hummingbird

Hummingbirds feed on nectar from flowers, and have long beaks and tongues to dip into the blooms. These tiny birds flap their wings over 70 times a second to hover (stay still in mid-air).

QUESTIONS:
African herbivores

Level 1
1. Do zebras have spots or stripes?
2. Are rhinos larger or smaller than rabbits?
3. Are zebras more closely related to horses or sheep?
4. Whereabouts on an elephant's body is its trunk?

Level 2
5. What is the world's largest land animal?
6. What is the world's tallest land animal?
7. What 'B' is the word for a male elephant?
8. How can an elephant use its trunk to cool itself down?
9. African elephants can weigh more than a tonne. True or false?
10. How tall do male giraffes grow: 3m, 6m or 10m?
11. Rhinos have excellent eyesight. True or false?
12. Do giraffes feed mainly on grass, insects or leaves?
13. Which African predator can kill elephants?
14. How many species (types) of zebra are there: three, five or seven?

Level 3
15. What 'P' hunts elephants for their tusks?
16. How many species (types) of rhino are there?
17. What 'J' is a species of rhino that lives in Asia?
18. What are elephants' tusks made of?

FIND THE ANSWER: African herbivores

Herbivores are animals that eat plants but do not eat meat. Many of the world's largest herbivores live on the plains of Africa. Here, there are vast amounts of grass and other vegetation for them to eat, so they exist in large numbers. Some herbivores live quite solitary lives, but most live in small groups or large herds.

Tough skin 13 15 18
Elephants' skin is thick and tough. This makes it hard for predators to kill them, although sometimes lions do attack and kill elephants. Unfortunately, poachers also hunt elephants for their ivory tusks.

Elephants 5 7 9
The African elephant is the world's largest land animal. Adult male, or bull, elephants can weigh up to 12 tonnes.

Trunks 4 8
An elephant uses its trunk to spray water on itself to cool down, and to pick things up. The trunk is formed from the nose and upper lip and contains thousands of muscles.

baby elephant spraying water from its trunk

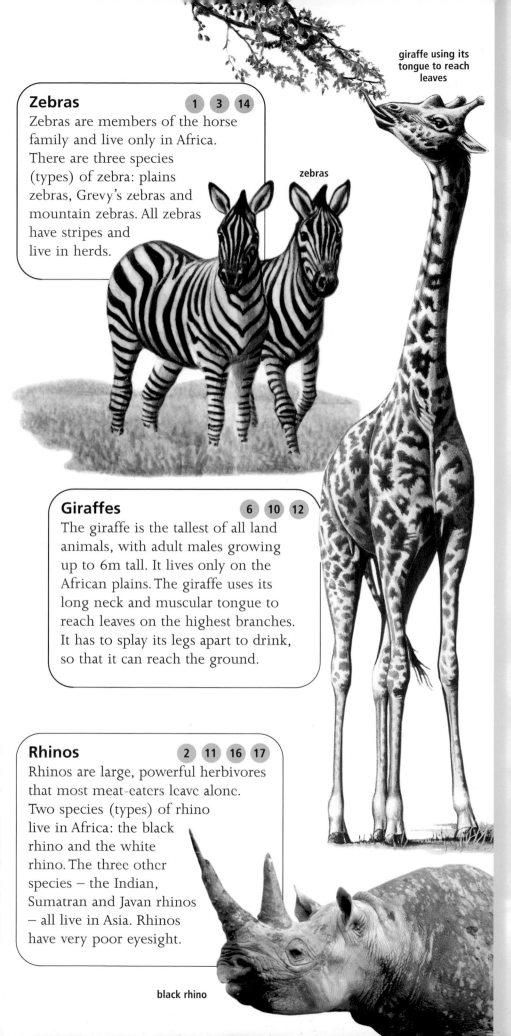

Zebras   ① ③ ⑭

Zebras are members of the horse family and live only in Africa. There are three species (types) of zebra: plains zebras, Grevy's zebras and mountain zebras. All zebras have stripes and live in herds.

zebras

giraffe using its tongue to reach leaves

Giraffes   ⑥ ⑩ ⑫

The giraffe is the tallest of all land animals, with adult males growing up to 6m tall. It lives only on the African plains. The giraffe uses its long neck and muscular tongue to reach leaves on the highest branches. It has to splay its legs apart to drink, so that it can reach the ground.

Rhinos   ② ⑪ ⑯ ⑰

Rhinos are large, powerful herbivores that most meat-eaters leave alone. Two species (types) of rhino live in Africa: the black rhino and the white rhino. The three other species – the Indian, Sumatran and Javan rhinos – all live in Asia. Rhinos have very poor eyesight.

black rhino

QUESTIONS:
Lions

Level 1

1. What is the name for a female lion?
2. RIP ED can be rearranged to give what name for a group of lions?
3. Which lions have manes: the males or the females?
4. Do male or female lions make up most of the pride?
5. Which are bigger: male or female lions?

Level 2

6. Which are the last members of the pride to feed at a kill?
7. Apart from hunting, what do the lionesses do in the pride?
8. Which members of a pride of lions do most of the hunting?
9. Do female lions stay with or leave the pride when they grow up?
10. Do lions usually hunt in groups or on their own?
11. Do lions ever fight to the death?
12. How long do lion cubs stay hidden from the rest of the pride: eight days, eight weeks or eight months?
13. What do lion cubs have on their coats that adult lions do not?
14. How many male lions usually lead a pride?

Level 3

15. What is the name of the area in which a pride of lions lives and hunts?
16. What do lions use to mark the borders of this area?
17. What do male lions do to keep others away?
18. How does a male lion take over a pride?

Lions

The lion is sometimes called the King of Beasts. It is a large, majestic creature, the second biggest of all the cat family after the tiger. Unlike most big cats, lions are social animals, which live and hunt in groups called prides. Most of the world's wild lions live on the African plains, but a few live in north-west India, in an area known as the Gir Forest.

Females   1   2   4   7   8   9

Female lions, called lionesses, make up most of the pride. They stay together throughout their lives. Daughters remain with their mother, aunts and sisters even after they have grown up. As well as caring for the young, they do most of the hunting.

two males fighting

Territory   15   16

Each pride lives and hunts in an area of land known as its territory. The edges are patrolled and marked with urine, droppings and scratch marks on trees.

Fighting   11   18

Rival males without prides may challenge another male for ownership of his pride. These fights can be violent and even end in death.

lioness and her cub

Cubs   12   13

For the first eight weeks, lion cubs stay with their mother away from the pride. Unlike adult lions, lion cubs have spots, which gradually fade as they grow older.

two lionesses hunting

Males 3 5 14 17

Male lions are much bigger than females and have a thick, shaggy mane. Each pride of lions is led by just one or occasionally two or three adult males, who mate with all of the females. Males roar to keep others away.

Hunting 6 10

Lionesses work together when hunting. When an animal is brought down, the kill is shared among the pride. Adult males feed first, followed by the lionesses and, lastly, the cubs.

male lion

QUESTIONS:
Polar animals

Level 1

1. Can penguins fly?
2. Can polar bears swim?
3. Polar bears can weigh over a tonne. True or false?
4. Do polar bears ever lie in wait for their prey?
5. Polar bears eat seals. True or false?

Level 2

6. In which season do migrating birds arrive in the polar regions?
7. Killer whales live in polar waters. True or false?
8. Why do some types of baby seal have white coats?
9. Do polar bears live near to the North Pole or the South Pole?
10. Penguins live in the Antarctic. True or false?
11. ALE BUG can be rearranged to give the name of which whale that lives in Arctic waters?
12. Which sense do polar bears use to find most of their prey: sight, hearing or smell?
13. How do penguins paddle themselves through the water: with their wings or with their feet?
14. What is the world's largest kind of penguin?

Level 3

15. Which bird flies all the way from the Antarctic to the Arctic and back again every year?
16. How can people protect baby seals from humans hunting them for their fur?
17. Do narwhals live near to the North Pole or the South Pole?
18. What word is used for keeping an egg warm until it hatches?

Polar animals

The regions around the poles are tough places to live. In order to survive, animals need to be able to cope with extreme cold and sometimes go for long periods without food. Weather conditions are harsh. In the middle of winter, the sun never rises and it is dark for weeks on end, while in summer the sun is always in the sky, meaning that there are 24 hours of daylight.

Birds 6 15

Many birds migrate to polar regions in spring to lay their eggs. Every year, Arctic terns fly all the way from the Antarctic to the Arctic and then back again. By leaving each pole just before winter, they manage to completely avoid the coldest time of the year.

Polar bears 2 3 9

The polar bear is the world's largest land carnivore (meat-eater). Adult males can weigh over a tonne. Polar bears live in the Arctic, near the North Pole. Their large, padded feet act as paddles when swimming in water.

Life in the water 7 11 17

Many polar animals live in the sea. Seals hunt fish under the ice. Other mammals in the polar seas include killer whales, which live both in the Arctic and Antarctic. Belugas and narwhals are small whales that live only in the Arctic waters.

Hunting 4 5 12

Polar bears hunt on the open ice and find most of their prey by smell. They sometimes feed on walruses, but mainly on seals, chasing them when they are out of the water, or lying in wait beside holes in the ice.

seal

polar bear

Penguins

1 **10** **13**

Penguins are flightless birds that live in the Antarctic. They are totally adapted to life in the sea. Their stiff wings act as paddles for their streamlined bodies.

penguins sliding on the ice

Winter wonder

14 **18**

Emperor penguins are the largest kind of penguin. The males incubate (keep warm) the females' eggs by holding them on their feet through the winter.

male emperor penguin

baby penguin

Seal hunting

8 **16**

Some types of seal are born with beautiful white coats to hide them in the snow. Unfortunately, some people like to wear clothes made from their fur, and many seal pups are killed for this reason. People try to protect the baby seals by spraying them with harmless dye, making their coats useless to the humans who hunt them.

spraying a ringed seal pup

QUESTIONS:
Farm animals

Level 1

1. Are dairy cows kept for their milk or their fur?
2. Is a cockerel a male or a female chicken?
3. What animal do farmers keep to hunt down rats and mice?
4. Which farm animals produce wool?

Level 2

5. What 'K' is a baby goat?
6. Today, dairy cows are milked by hand. True or false?
7. On which part of a cow are its teats?
8. How many teats does a cow have?
9. Which have larger crests on their heads: male or female chickens?
10. Which animal is needed to make butter?
11. EAGER FERN can be rearranged to give the name of what kind of chicken?
12. Which farm animal does gammon come from?
13. What 'L' is a meat from sheep?
14. What 'F' is removed from a sheep by shearing it?

Level 3

15. What is the smallest piglet in a litter called?
16. How many teats does a goat have?
17. What is the most common kind of sheep dog in the UK?
18. What is a male pig called?
19. What is the name for chickens that are kept in cages?

FIND THE ANSWER: Farm animals

Some animals are looked after by people on farms. Most of them are kept to provide us with food, but some give us other useful products, such as wool. Farm animals are domesticated versions of creatures that once lived in the wild. Most of the world's sheep, for example, are descended from the mouflon, which still lives out in the wild in Europe and Asia.

cockerel crowing at sunrise

Dairy cows   1   6   7   10
Farmers keep dairy cows for their milk. Farmers used to milk by hand, but today, machines gently squeeze the teats on the cows' udders to collect the milk. Milk can be used to make butter and cheese.

Cockerels and hens   2   9   11   19
Farmers keep chickens for eggs and meat. Male chickens (cockerels) usually have bigger crests and longer tails than females (hens), and also crow at sunrise. Free-range chickens live outside in the open, while battery chickens are kept indoors in cages.

Friesian cow

milking teats

feed bucket

farmer

Cats   3
Many farmers have cats to hunt down mice and rats. Unlike most pet cats, farm cats spend their lives outdoors and sleep in barns and hayricks. Some farmers have dozens of cats.

Goats   5   8   16
A female goat is called a nanny and a male goat a billy. Baby goats are known as kids. Goats' udders have two teats, unlike those of cows, which have four.

Southdown sheep

Hampshire Down sheep

Romney sheep

Scottish Blackface sheep

Sheep 4 13

Sheep are kept for their wool and also for their meat, which is known as mutton or lamb. Male sheep are called rams and usually have horns. Female sheep are known as ewes.

Sheep shearing 14

Once a year, sheep have their wool cut off, a process known as shearing. The wool from one sheep is called a fleece. Sheep shearing is done by hand, using motorized clippers, and does not hurt the sheep at all.

border collie

Sheep dogs 17

Sheep dogs help farmers round up their sheep from the fields. Most of these dogs are intelligent and easy to train. In the UK, the most common sheep dog is the border collie. The Alsatian was originally bred as a sheep dog.

Pigs 12 15 18

Farmers keep pigs for their meat, which is known as pork, gammon or bacon. A male pig is called a boar and a female a sow. A sow may have ten or more piglets (baby pigs) in a litter. The smallest is called the runt.

mother sow with piglets

QUESTIONS:
Horses

Level 1

1. What are baby horses called?
2. What do cowboys wear to shade them from the sun?
3. In showjumping, do riders try to jump over obstacles or crash into them?
4. Horses are used to pull ploughs. True or false?
5. What 'L' is the looped rope that cowboys use to catch cattle?
6. Are ponies larger or smaller than horses?

Level 2

7. Is an Exmoor a breed of pony or a breed of horse?
8. What is the largest breed of horse?
9. What is the main difference between the skeleton of a horse and the skeleton of a human?
10. When do male horses show their teeth and pull their lips back?
11. HEN CARS can be rearranged to give the name of what large farms on which cowboys work?
12. What is worn by jumping horses to protect their ankles from knocks?
13. BANDY HURDS can be rearranged to give the name of what item, used for removing dirt from a horse's coat?

Level 3

14. What 'C' is a type of pony from Iran?
15. How does a horse show aggression?
16. What is the name of the bones that make up a horse's spine?
17. What kind of brush is used to brush away loose hair on a horse?
18. What 'D' is a horse-riding sport, which tests obedience and rider control?

Horses

rider

People have kept horses for thousands of years. Before the invention of the car and train, they were the main form of transport, carrying people on their backs or towing them in carts and carriages. Horses were also used by farmers to draw ploughs and by cavalry soldiers to carry them into battle. Today, most horses are kept for pleasure, although some are still used as working animals.

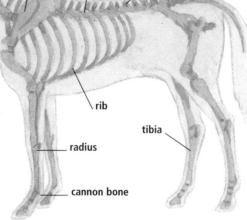

skull (cranium)

shoulder blade (scapula)

spine

vertebra

rib

tibia

radius

cannon bone

clearing a jump in showjumping

Horse skeleton 9 16

Horses have very similar skeletons to humans. The main difference is that they walk on all fours, so their front limbs are legs rather than arms. A horse's skeleton is based around its spine, which is made up of many bones known as vertebrae.

chestnut horse showing aggression

palomino male smelling a female

black horse

bay horse

Horse faces 10 15

Horses have different expressions. Ears held back show aggression. Males pull their lips back when they smell a female.

Training kit 1 12

Training begins when a horse is a year or more old and fully grown. Males are called stallions, females mares and baby horses are known as foals. If they are being trained for jumping, they may wear bandages to protect their ankles from knocks.

Showjumping 3 18

Showjumping is one of three horse-riding sports. The others are dressage, which tests obedience and rider control, and three-day eventing. In show jumping, a competitor has to ride the horse around a course with a series of different jumps.

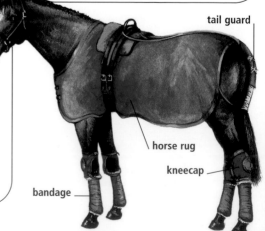

tail guard

horse rug

kneecap

bandage

Cowboys ② ⑤ ⑪

Cowboys ride horses to round up cattle. Today, most work on ranches in the USA, which are like large farms. Cowboys catch cattle with a lasso, a looped rope. They wear wide hats to shade them from the sun.

cowboy with lasso

Working horses ④ ⑧

Police on horseback are often used to control large crowds. Horses are also used to pull carts and ploughs in some places. The largest horse of all is the shire horse, which can weigh a tonne.

Shetland pony

Ponies ⑥ ⑦ ⑭

Ponies are smaller breeds of horse. They are not as fast as large horses, but tougher, and can live outside in all weathers. Caspian ponies from Iran and Exmoor ponies from the UK live out in the wild.

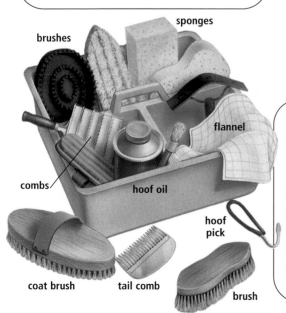

sponges

brushes

flannel

combs

hoof oil

hoof pick

coat brush   tail comb

brush

Grooming ⑬ ⑰

Owners like to keep their horses looking nice and clean by grooming them. Dandy brushes are used for removing dirt, rubber curry combs brush away loose hair and mane combs remove tangles in manes.

QUESTIONS:
Cats

Level 1

1. What are baby cats called?
2. Is catnip a type of plant or a type of animal?
3. Do cats creep up and pounce on their prey or chase it round and round until it is exhausted?
4. Do cat owners use brushes for grooming their cats or for feeding them?
5. Can cats climb?
6. Do young cats prefer playing with balls of wool or with knitting needles?
7. Are cats good at jumping?

Level 2

8. Cats have claws. True or false?
9. What is a scratching post for?
10. Do cats prefer to live on their own or in groups?
11. For how long do a cat's eyes stay closed after it is born?
12. How often should cats be fed?
13. Which fight more often: male cats or female cats?
14. What are male cats called?
15. Why is it a good idea to use a special dish for feeding a cat?

Level 3

16. What part of a cat's body can be retracted?
17. From which animal are domestic cats descended?
18. Why do cats spray and scent-mark things?

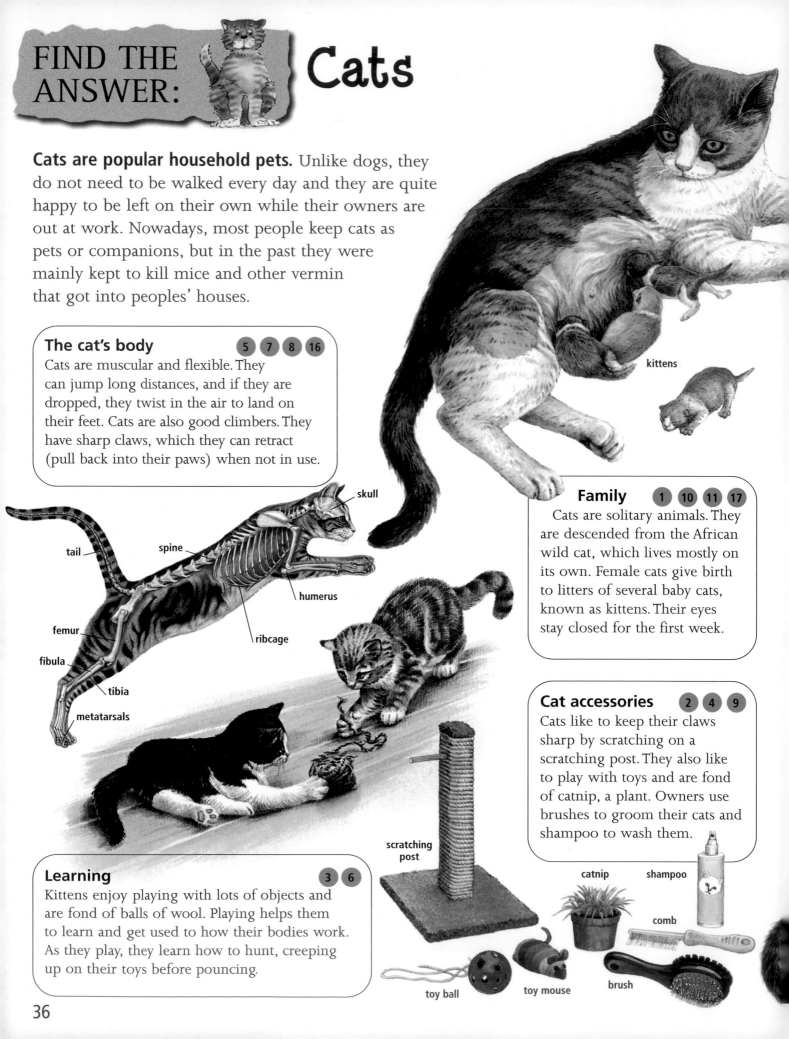

Cats

Cats are popular household pets. Unlike dogs, they do not need to be walked every day and they are quite happy to be left on their own while their owners are out at work. Nowadays, most people keep cats as pets or companions, but in the past they were mainly kept to kill mice and other vermin that got into peoples' houses.

The cat's body **5 7 8 16**

Cats are muscular and flexible. They can jump long distances, and if they are dropped, they twist in the air to land on their feet. Cats are also good climbers. They have sharp claws, which they can retract (pull back into their paws) when not in use.

kittens

skull

tail

spine

humerus

femur

ribcage

fibula

tibia

metatarsals

Family **1 10 11 17**

Cats are solitary animals. They are descended from the African wild cat, which lives mostly on its own. Female cats give birth to litters of several baby cats, known as kittens. Their eyes stay closed for the first week.

Cat accessories **2 4 9**

Cats like to keep their claws sharp by scratching on a scratching post. They also like to play with toys and are fond of catnip, a plant. Owners use brushes to groom their cats and shampoo to wash them.

scratching post

catnip

shampoo

comb

Learning **3 6**

Kittens enjoy playing with lots of objects and are fond of balls of wool. Playing helps them to learn and get used to how their bodies work. As they play, they learn how to hunt, creeping up on their toys before pouncing.

toy ball

toy mouse

brush

Feeding 12 15

Cats are fed at least once a day, either with dry food or moist food from tins or pouches. It is a good idea to put a cat's food in a special dish. Cats learn to associate the dish with feeding and come running when their owners approach it.

moist food

Territory 13 14 18

Both wild and domestic cats defend their home areas, or territories, from others. Male cats, or tom cats, in particular, will fight others that enter their area. Cats spray and scent-mark their territory as a warning to stay away.

defensive cat

scent-marking

cats fighting

QUESTIONS:
Dogs

Level 1

1. What is a baby dog called?
2. Are most police dogs Alsatians or Dalmatians?
3. Were pit bull terriers originally bred for fighting or fetching slippers?
4. Are most Labrador dogs friendly or aggressive?
5. The terrier is the largest breed of dog. True or false?

Level 2

6. What is a group of related puppies, born at the same time, called?
7. How long does it take for a puppy to grow into an adult: six months, a year or three years?
8. Which 'S' is a kind of dog often trained to be a sniffer dog?
9. How might a hearing dog help a deaf owner?
10. If a dog wags its tail, is it happy or angry?
11. Does a sad dog drop its tail or raise it?
12. Which wild animal is the ancestor of all domestic dogs?
13. EDGIER REVEL TORN can be rearranged to spell what breed of dog, often trained as guide dogs?
14. Which would make a better guard dog: a Rottweiler or a Labrador?

Level 3

15. How long should you wait before giving away puppies to new owners?
16. During which year of a dog's life is it easiest to train?
17. What is another word for cutting off a dog's tail?
18. How can you tell when a dog is frightened?
19. What type of dog was bred to hunt large animals?

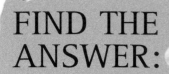
People say that a dog is a man's best friend, and most dog owners agree that this is true. Dogs are friendly, protective and loyal companions. They are descended from wolves, which are pack-living animals, so a dog thinks of its owners as members of its pack. Unlike wolves, most dogs have been bred to be less aggressive and more friendly to humans.

Puppies 1 6 15

A baby dog is called a puppy. Female dogs have a litter of several puppies at a time. Many people sell their dog's puppies to new owners. They have to wait until the puppies are a few weeks old and big enough to be away from their mother.

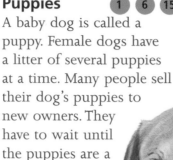

mother and litter

Growing up 7 16

Puppies take about a year to grow up into adults. This first year is the best time to train them, as their brains develop. (Adult dogs need more time for training.) Puppies are playful and enjoy wrestling.

Learning 2 8

You can train dogs to do many things. The police train Alsatians to catch criminals and spaniels as sniffer dogs to find drugs and clues. You can train a pet dog to make it easier to control, using food treats as a reward.

adult golden Labrador

Tails 10 11 17 18

A dog's tail may be straight or curly. A happy dog wags its tail, and a sad dog drops it. A confident dog holds its tail high, while a frightened dog holds its tail between its legs. On some breeds the tails may be cut off (docked) when they are puppies.

frightened dog

docked tail

sad dog

curly tail

Dog breeds ⑤ ⑫ ⑲

All dogs are descended from wolves, but over the centuries many breeds have been created. Dog breeds are grouped by characteristics. Terriers, for example, are small dogs originally bred to hunt rodents. Hounds were bred to hunt larger animals.

Guide dogs ⑨ ⑬

Golden retrievers and black Labradors are trained as guide dogs for blind people. They look out for obstacles on streets. Some dogs are trained as hearing dogs, alerting a deaf owner, for example, if there is a knock at the door.

Temperament ③ ④ ⑭

Dog breeds have different temperaments. Labradors are friendly and eager to please, making them ideal pets. Pit bull terriers and Rottweilers were bred to fight, so they make better guard dogs.

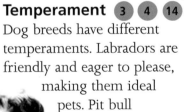

confident dog

straight tail

happy dog

wolf

Alsatian

collie

basenji

basset hound

Dalmatian

bulldog

fox terrier

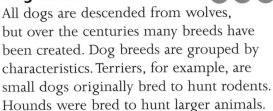

QUESTIONS:
Desert creatures

Level 1

1. What is a coyote: a wild dog or a wild cat?
2. What are the thorny devil and the gila monster: reptiles, birds or insects?
3. Desert foxes have large ears to help keep them cool. True or false?

Level 2

4. Some desert birds build their nests on cacti. True or false?
5. Desert birds of prey eat prickly plants. True or false?
6. Which desert lizard is poisonous: the gila monster or the chameleon?
7. Which bird is not a desert bird of prey: the turkey vulture, lappet-faced vulture or kestrel?
8. What kind of fox lives in the desert: red fox, Arctic fox or fennec fox?
9. Does the thorny devil collect dew from its body or from plants?
10. Which characteristics help desert hunters: swift movement, keen eyesight, claws, or all of the above?
11. Does the Peruvian fox live in the Atacama desert in South America or the Sahara in North Africa?
12. Which does the bobcat eat: rodents or coyotes?

Level 3

13. Which type of lizard lives its whole life in a decaying cactus?
14. Does the desert coyote weigh more or less than a coyote that lives in the mountains?
15. Which feature of a bobcat helps its hearing?
16. Which 'B' is a flying creature that eats the nectar found in cactus flowers?
17. What is another name for the Peruvian fox?
18. Which 'G' lizard can live for months without food?

Desert creatures

bobcat

Deserts are harsh places to live, but many animals have adapted to life there. The biggest problems are finding water and staying cool in hot temperatures. Many desert animals, such as the camel, can live for days without drinking, and get water from the food that they eat, such as insects, reptiles and plants. To stay cool, animals such as the meerkat and the kangaroo rat make burrows underground.

Desert plant life   4   13   16
Animals use desert plants for shelter, food and water. Bats eat their nectar, and some birds build nests on cacti. The yucca night lizard spends its entire life under a decaying cactus.

Bobcats   12   15
The bobcat lives in North America and preys on wild rabbits, hares and rodents. It lives in deserts and scrubland (dry areas with stunted plants) and mountainous regions. The hairs on its ears help to improve the bobcat's already keen hearing.

cactus

Birds of prey   5   7
The lappet-faced vulture of Africa, the turkey vulture of the USA, eagles and other birds of prey eat rodents, rabbits and snakes.

eagle

coyote

hare

kangaroo rat

scorpion

rattlesnake

Hunting   10
Desert hunters run or fly swiftly, have good eyesight and have claws and sharp teeth to catch their prey. Many, such as the desert night lizard, hunt at night when it is cooler.

Foxes
3 **8** **11** **17**

Desert foxes have large ears to keep cool. Fennec foxes are the smallest foxes. They live in the Sahara in North Africa. The Peruvian, or Sechuran, fox lives in the Atacama desert in South America.

Lizards
2 **6** **9** **18**

gila monster

Scaly-skinned lizards are reptiles that have adapted to life in dry desert climates. The thorny devil of Australia is covered in spikes that collect dew for drinking. The poisonous gila monster lives for months without food by storing fat in its tail.

Coyotes
1 **14**

Like other wild dogs, the coyote communicates using barks and yaps. Its howl tells other coyotes where it is. Desert coyotes weigh less than half the weight of coyotes that live in mountains.

QUESTIONS:
Spiders

Level 1

1. Is the spider's body made up of two, three or eight parts?
2. How many wings do spiders have: one pair, two pairs or none?
3. Spiders spin silk to make spider webs. True or false?
4. Most spiders have no eyes. True or false?

Level 2

5. The trapdoor spider catches its prey in a web. True or false?
6. What shape does an orb spider spin after it makes a frame: 'X', 'Y' or 'Z'?
7. A spider's silk-making organs are in its abdomen. True or false?
8. Are a spider's legs attached to the front part of its body or its abdomen?
9. Can some spiders see only shadows and light?
10. How does a spider eat its prey: by chewing it, by turning its insides to liquid and sucking them out, or by eating it whole?
11. In what 'A' part of the body are the organs a spider uses for digesting food?
12. Which spider is the largest in the world?
13. The goliath bird-eating spider eats only birds. True or false?

Level 3

14. A dry silk thread remains on the web when a spider finishes spinning. True or false?
15. What type of spiders are the wolf spider and tarantula?
16. What do a spider's hollow fangs hold?
17. Is it thought that jumping spiders have good or poor eyesight?
18. How does a bird-eating spider detect movement?
19. How does a spider turn its prey's insides into liquid?

Spiders

garden cross spider

Spiders are not insects. They belong to a group of animals called arachnids. This group of over 75,000 species (types) also includes scorpions, mites and ticks. All spiders can make silk with glands in their bodies, but not all spiders spin webs. All spiders have venom glands, but only a few, such as the funnel-web spider, are harmful to people.

Anatomy ① ② ⑧

The spider's body is made up of two parts: the front part (the head and thorax together) and the back part (called the abdomen). The back part is protected by a special plate. Unlike insects, spiders have eight legs. These are attached to the front part of the spider's body. Spiders do not have wings or antennae.

abdomen

thorax and head

Inside ⑦ ⑪ ⑯

The front part of the spider is packed with muscles to move its jaws and legs. Its jaws have hollow fangs, which contain poison made in special venom glands. The spider's abdomen holds the organs for digesting food and making silk, as well as the spider's heart and blood.

Eyes ④ ⑨ ⑰

Most spiders have six or eight eyes. The majority of spiders can see only shadows and light. However some spiders, such as jumping spiders, are thought to have good eyesight.

Spinning webs ③ ⑥ ⑭

To form an orb web, a spider uses silk that comes out of small openings, called spinnerets, at the end of its body. It spins a frame of strong, dry threads, beginning with a bridge thread and a 'Y' shape. After the frame is made, a temporary spiral is spun with the same dry silk. Finally, the spider spins sticky thread in a spiral and removes the dry silk.

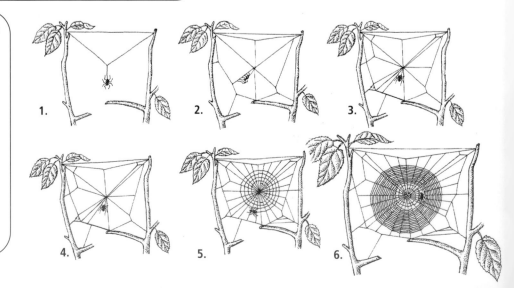

1. 2. 3.

4. 5. 6.

42

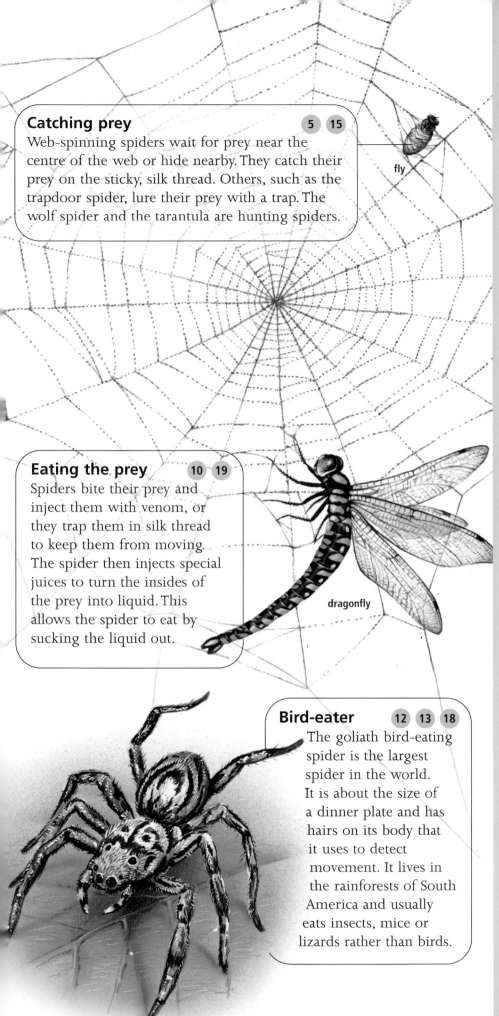

Catching prey   5 15

Web-spinning spiders wait for prey near the centre of the web or hide nearby. They catch their prey on the sticky, silk thread. Others, such as the trapdoor spider, lure their prey with a trap. The wolf spider and the tarantula are hunting spiders.

fly

Eating the prey   10 19

Spiders bite their prey and inject them with venom, or they trap them in silk thread to keep them from moving. The spider then injects special juices to turn the insides of the prey into liquid. This allows the spider to eat by sucking the liquid out.

dragonfly

Bird-eater   12 13 18

The goliath bird-eating spider is the largest spider in the world. It is about the size of a dinner plate and has hairs on its body that it uses to detect movement. It lives in the rainforests of South America and usually eats insects, mice or lizards rather than birds.

QUESTIONS:
Bees

Level 1

1. Honey comes from which creatures: bats, bees or bears?
2. What 'D' are male honey bees called?
3. Wild honey bees build their own nest, called a hive. True or false?
4. Bees do not have an abdomen. True or false?

Level 2

5. Are a bee's wings attached to its thorax (the middle section of its body) or its head?
6. Worker bees collect pollen and nectar. True or false?
7. What 'N' is honey made from?
8. What 'H' shape is a cell in a bee hive?
9. Does a honey bee have two or three types of wings?
10. Do bees' eggs hatch in three days, one week or one month?
11. Bees have special glands that produce what: wax, oil or fat?
12. Some bees have a special 'honey stomach' for storing nectar. True or false?
13. What is the average number of flowers a bee will visit in a single trip: 5–10, 50–100, or 500–1,000 flowers?

Level 3

14. Where do honey bees store pollen when collecting it?
15. Name the special tube that bees use to suck nectar.
16. On average, how many eggs might a queen bee lay in one month?
17. How is honey removed from a honey bee?
18. Name a substance made by worker bees that is fed to future queen bees.
19. What does a honey bee do when it finds a new supply of food?

Bees

Bees are flying insects related to wasps and ants. Honey bees are well known because they pollinate food crops and produce honey and wax. They live in huge colonies. Each colony has a queen and many female worker bees. Male honey bees only enter the hive to mate with the queen.

Flying   9 19

Bees have two types of wings – a pair of forewings and a smaller pair of hind wings. They work together for flying. When a honey bee finds a new supply of food it flies home and does a special 'dance' to tell the other bees about it.

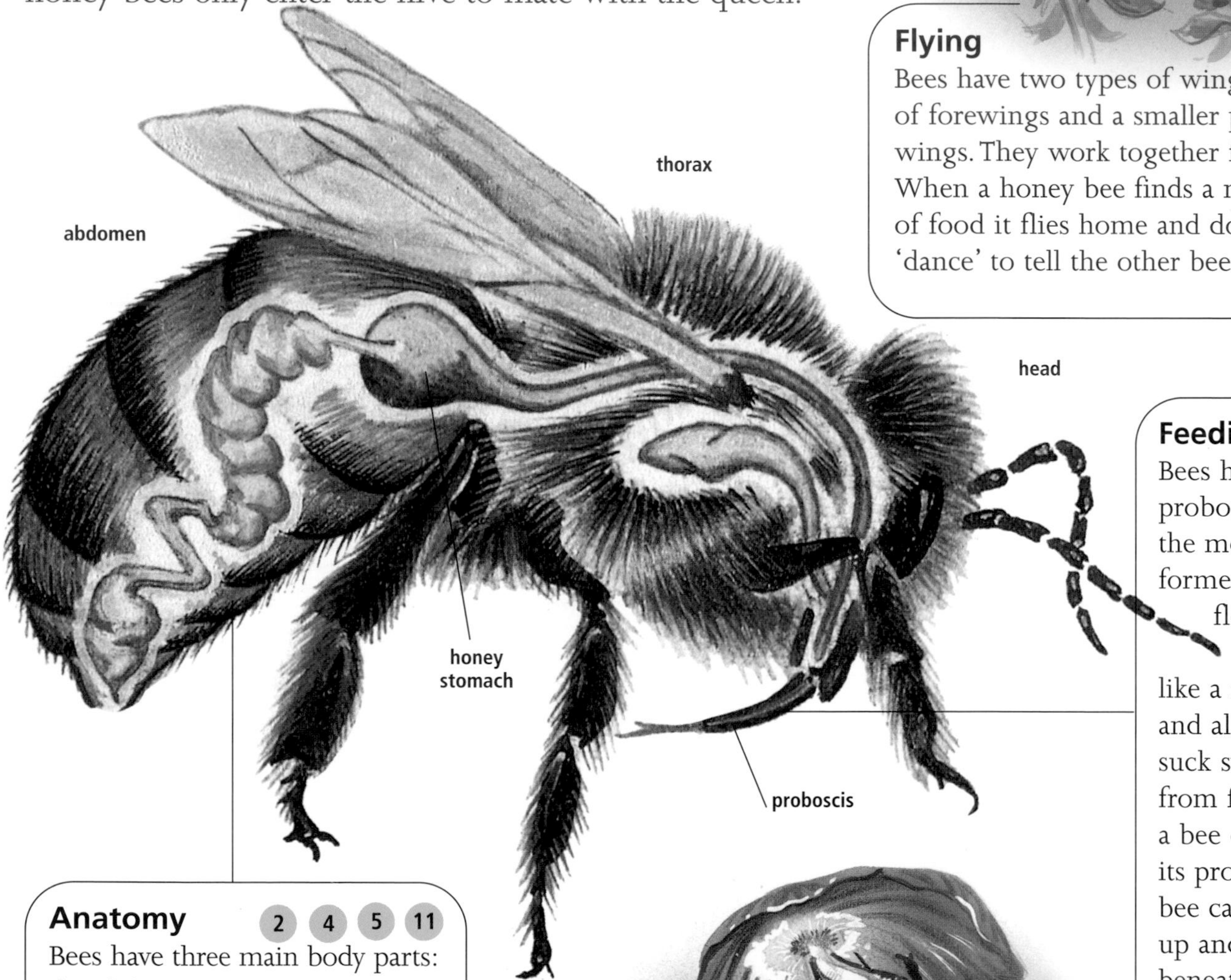

abdomen

thorax

head

honey stomach

proboscis

Feeding 15

Bees have a proboscis, a part of the mouth that is formed into a long, flexible tube. It works like a flexible straw and allows bees to suck sweet nectar from flowers. When a bee does not need its proboscis, the bee can draw it up and fold it beneath its head.

Anatomy 2 4 5 11

Bees have three main body parts: the abdomen, thorax and head. The abdomen has special glands for producing wax (which is used to make honeycomb). The thorax, the middle section of the bee, is where the legs and wings are attached. Unlike male bees, or drones, female bees have stingers at the end of the abdomen that can inject venom. If the stinger breaks off, the bee will die.

Pollen 6 13 14

Worker honey bees leave the nest in summer to visit flowers and gather nectar and pollen. Bees store pollen in pollen 'baskets' on their hind legs. Worker bees will visit between 50 and 100 flowers on a single trip.

Eggs ⑩ ⑯ ⑱

The queen bee lays eggs in individual wax cells, as many as 200,000 in a year. The eggs hatch in three days and larvae are fed pollen and nectar by worker bees. Future queen bees are fed royal jelly, a substance made by worker bees.

Hive ③ ⑧

In the wild, honey bees build their nest, or hive, in the hollow of a tree or in a cave. Beekeepers build a wooden hive. The hive is made from a waxy material, shaped into hexagonal, or six-sided, cells, called honeycomb. A hive can last for 50 years or more.

Honey ① ⑦ ⑫ ⑰

Only honey bees can make honey. The ones that make it have a special 'honey stomach' in which they hold nectar. At the hive, other worker bees suck the nectar out and mix it with special enzymes in their bodies. This mixture is spread on honeycombs. As it dries out it becomes honey.

QUESTIONS:
Deadly creatures

Level 1

1. Some snakes are poisonous. True or false?
2. What creatures do great white sharks hunt: seals, porpoises or both?
3. Female black widow spiders are dangerous to people. True or false?
4. Which creature wraps its body around its victim to kill it: the boa constrictor snake or jellyfish?

Level 2

5. What 'T' do jellyfish have?
6. How does the crocodile kill its prey: by tossing it in the air or drowning it?
7. The cobra snake kills its prey by wrapping its body around it. True or false?
8. How do sharks find prey: by smell, by using special cells that sense movement, or both?
9. What does the jellyfish eat: small fish, worms or both?
10. How heavy is the great white shark: 200kg, 1,000kg or 2,000kg?
11. Is the tiger shark considered safe or dangerous to people?
12. Does the crocodile hide from its prey?

Level 3

13. What is another name for the box jellyfish?
14. How many clusters of tentacles does the box jellyfish have?
15. Which piranha fish is the most dangerous?
16. Which spider is the most dangerous?
17. The crocodile has what type of special feature to stay under the water?
18. What 'B' does a piranha detect with a special sensory system?

Deadly creatures

Many animals have special features that can help them to kill or harm other creatures. Some have venomous bites or stings, while others have razor-sharp teeth or claws.

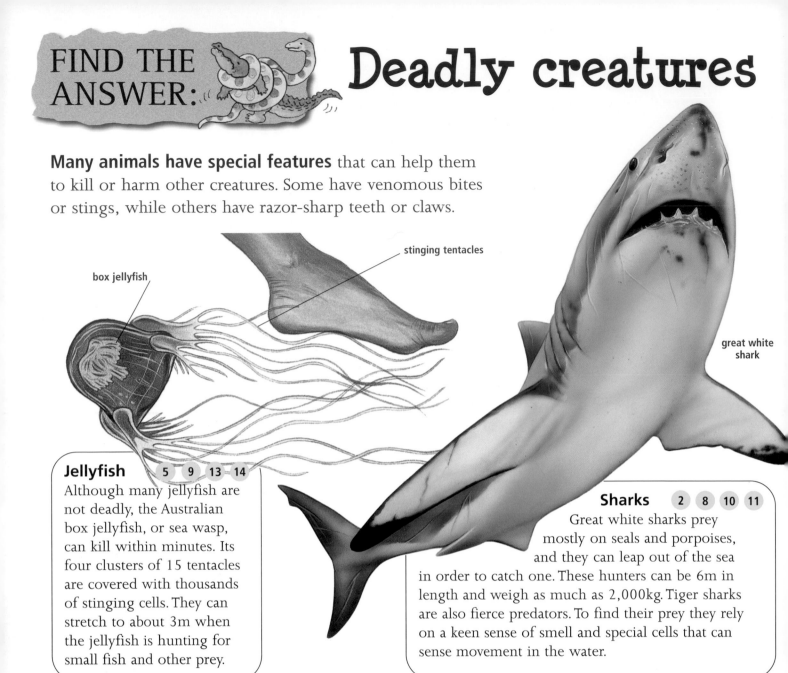

box jellyfish

stinging tentacles

great white shark

Jellyfish 5 9 13 14
Although many jellyfish are not deadly, the Australian box jellyfish, or sea wasp, can kill within minutes. Its four clusters of 15 tentacles are covered with thousands of stinging cells. They can stretch to about 3m when the jellyfish is hunting for small fish and other prey.

Sharks 2 8 10 11
Great white sharks prey mostly on seals and porpoises, and they can leap out of the sea in order to catch one. These hunters can be 6m in length and weigh as much as 2,000kg. Tiger sharks are also fierce predators. To find their prey they rely on a keen sense of smell and special cells that can sense movement in the water.

Crocodiles 6 12 17
To catch its meal, the crocodile has waterproof flaps to seal its eyes, ears, nostrils and throat while it hides under the water. An animal that comes to the water for a drink cannot see or smell the crocodile, who will suddenly explode from the water to snatch and drown its prey.

Spiders `3` `16`

All spiders have poisonous bites. About 30 species are dangerous to people, including the female black widow, the Australian funnel-web and the deadliest: the Brazilian wandering spider.

Snakes `1` `4` `7`

Several snakes have poisonous bites, such as the rattlesnake, the cobra and the brown tree snake. Others, such as pythons and boa constrictors, wrap their bodies around their prey and crush it.

rattlesnake

Piranha fish `15` `18`

The piranha fish lives in rivers in South America. It has sharp teeth and strong jaws for eating meat. It can find its prey by using a special sensory system that can detect the smell of blood. Of the 1,200 species of piranha, the red-bellied piranha is the most dangerous. Piranha fish rarely eat anything larger than themselves.

QUESTIONS:
Frogs

Level 1

1. A baby frog is called a tadpole. True or false?
2. Do flying frogs have feathers, like birds, or flaps of skin?
3. Adult frogs have tails. True or false?
4. Do frogs lay their eggs in water or in nests made in trees?

Level 2

5. Tadpoles have tails, gills and legs. True or false?
6. How often do most frogs shed their skin: once a week, once a year or never?
7. How far can a flying frog glide: 2m, 12m or 22m?
8. All frogs catch food with their tongues. True or false?
9. How many days does it take for a frog's eggs to hatch: 3–5 days, 3–25 days or 25–35 days?
10. FRET LOG can be rearranged to give the name of what stage of frog before it becomes an adult?
11. Are frogs' ears specially tuned in to hear the calls of predators or the calls of their own species?
12. Would a frog puff its throat to call another frog, to scare a predator, or both?
13. What 'A' do tadpoles eat?

Level 3

14. Where do poison dart frogs live?
15. Can a cricket frog jump twice its body length, ten times its body length or more than 30 times its body length?
16. What 'M' is the term used to describe the changes that a tadpole undergoes?
17. Name a species of frog that guards its eggs from predators.
18. The poison from the poison dart frog is used by some tribesmen to do what?
19. Give a reason why frogs need to keep their skin wet.

FIND THE ANSWER: Frogs

frogspawn

A frog is an amphibian

without a tail. It is at home on land and in the water, and can hop and swim. Some climb trees. Frogs have lived on earth for about 190 million years and live on every continent except Antarctica. Both frogs and toads are part of the same animal group, but toads often have drier, rougher skin.

tadpole

1. Eggs (4) (9) (17)

Females lay thousands of eggs, or frogspawn, in fresh water, such as rivers and ponds. The eggs hatch 3 to 25 days later. Some species of frog, such as the Darwin's frog and poison dart frog, guard their eggs from predators.

2. Tadpole (1) (5) (13)

Baby frogs, called tadpoles, have gills for breathing and a tail for swimming but no front or back legs. They feed on plants, such as algae. Many tadpoles are poisonous so birds and beetles don't eat them.

froglet

3. Froglet (10) (16)

After several weeks tadpoles undergo a metamorphosis, which is a change in form. They develop lungs and lose their gills. Their tail also begins to disappear. Froglets develop back and front legs and begin to eat insects rather than plants.

4. Adult (3) (6) (19)

Fully grown frogs do not have tails. They breathe through their skin as well as their lungs, and they keep their skin wet so they can get oxygen from water. Once a week, frogs shed their skin.

adult

Tongue (8)

Some frogs have long and sticky tongues to catch insects or spiders, often in less than a second. Others catch prey with their front feet.

Jumping (15)

A frog's legs are made for leaping. The powerful hind legs have long ankle bones that help them jump. The tiny cricket frog is only about 30mm long, but it is a great jumper, leaping over a metre. A frog's front legs are used for balance when sitting.

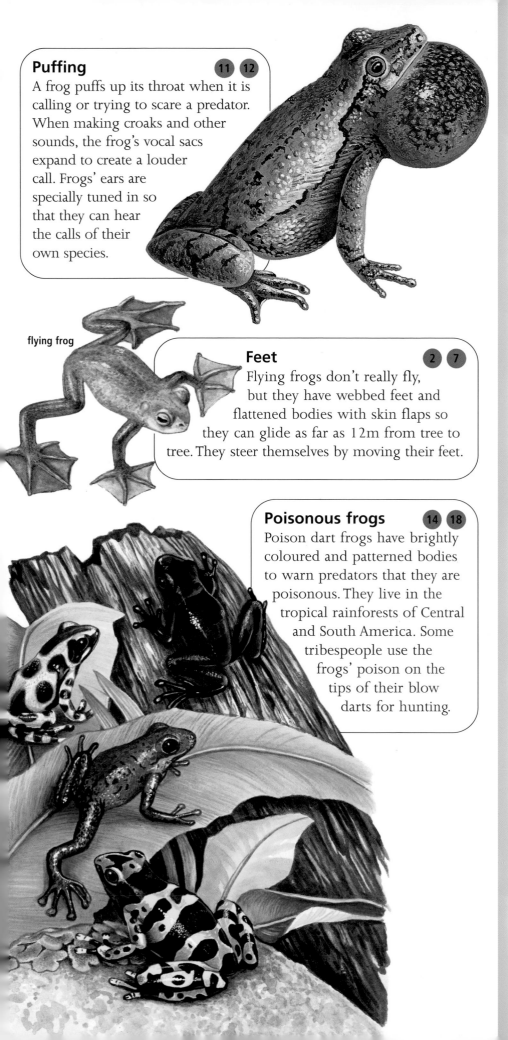

Puffing `11` `12`

A frog puffs up its throat when it is calling or trying to scare a predator. When making croaks and other sounds, the frog's vocal sacs expand to create a louder call. Frogs' ears are specially tuned in so that they can hear the calls of their own species.

flying frog

Feet `2` `7`

Flying frogs don't really fly, but they have webbed feet and flattened bodies with skin flaps so they can glide as far as 12m from tree to tree. They steer themselves by moving their feet.

Poisonous frogs `14` `18`

Poison dart frogs have brightly coloured and patterned bodies to warn predators that they are poisonous. They live in the tropical rainforests of Central and South America. Some tribespeople use the frogs' poison on the tips of their blow darts for hunting.

QUESTIONS:
Coral reef creatures

Level 1

1. Do most corals like warm, shallow water?
2. Is the anemonefish one of the many species of fish that live in the coral reef?
3. Starfish are not really fish. True or false?
4. Do jellyfish have brains?

Level 2

5. Some fish are colourful or patterned so they can recognize each other. True or false?
6. CLEAT NETS can be rearranged to give the name of what part of a jellyfish?
7. What does a jellyfish's nerve net detect: touch or light?
8. How many species of fish inhabit the coral reef: over 3,000, over 4,000 or over 5,000?
9. Which coral reef creature looks as harmless as a rock?
10. Are brain coral and elkhorn types of hard coral or soft coral?
11. What do corals use their tentacles for: to walk along the ocean floor, to feed themselves or to swim?
12. Do sea anemones protect anemonefish or eat them?

Level 3

13. What 'P' do corals eat?
14. What 'S' means 'life together'?
15. What is the name for a large group of jellyfish?
16. How many tentacles do soft corals have?
17. What part of their body do most fish move to swim?
18. Which 'S' creature is an echinoderm?

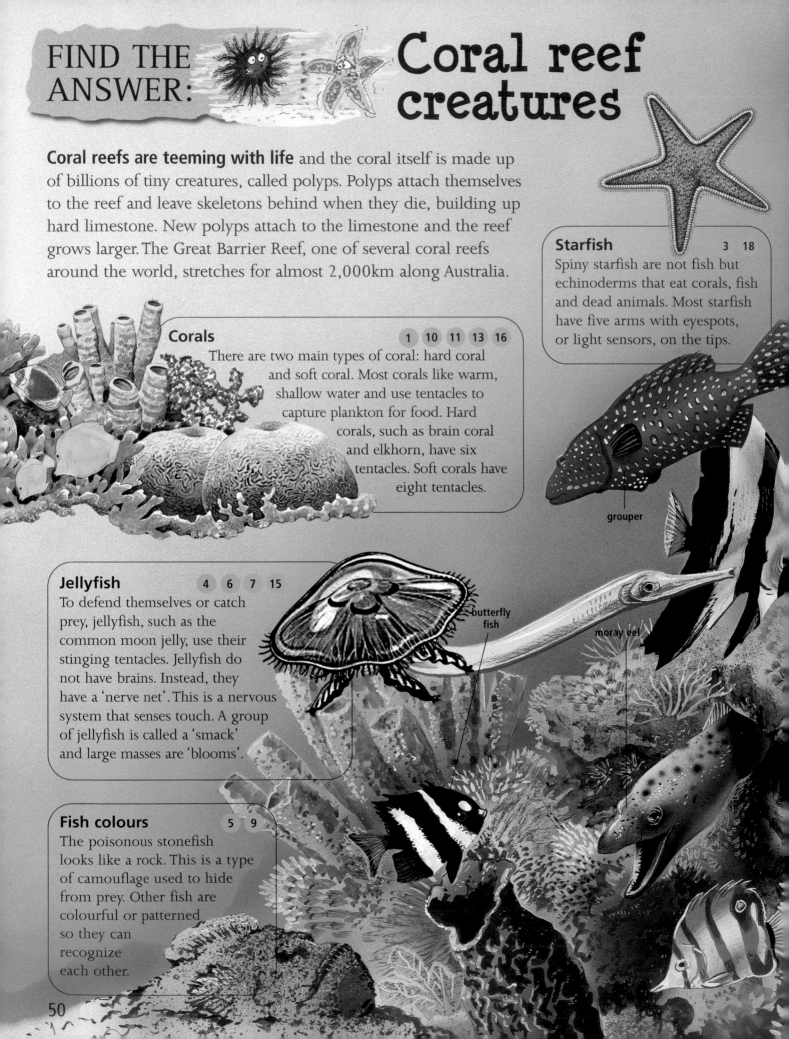

FIND THE ANSWER:

Coral reef creatures

Coral reefs are teeming with life and the coral itself is made up of billions of tiny creatures, called polyps. Polyps attach themselves to the reef and leave skeletons behind when they die, building up hard limestone. New polyps attach to the limestone and the reef grows larger. The Great Barrier Reef, one of several coral reefs around the world, stretches for almost 2,000km along Australia.

Corals **1 10 11 13 16**

There are two main types of coral: hard coral and soft coral. Most corals like warm, shallow water and use tentacles to capture plankton for food. Hard corals, such as brain coral and elkhorn, have six tentacles. Soft corals have eight tentacles.

Starfish **3 18**

Spiny starfish are not fish but echinoderms that eat corals, fish and dead animals. Most starfish have five arms with eyespots, or light sensors, on the tips.

grouper

Jellyfish **4 6 7 15**

To defend themselves or catch prey, jellyfish, such as the common moon jelly, use their stinging tentacles. Jellyfish do not have brains. Instead, they have a 'nerve net'. This is a nervous system that senses touch. A group of jellyfish is called a 'smack' and large masses are 'blooms'.

butterfly fish

moray eel

Fish colours **5 9**

The poisonous stonefish looks like a rock. This is a type of camouflage used to hide from prey. Other fish are colourful or patterned so they can recognize each other.

Fish 2 8 17

There are many types of fish, which use gills for breathing. Most fish swim by moving their tail from side to side. The coral reef is home to over 4,000 species (types) of fish, including the angelfish, anemonefish, butterfly fish, moray eel and grouper.

angelfish

Living together 12 14

Some fish have a symbiotic relationship with other animals. Symbiosis means 'life together', and refers to two creatures relying on each other in a special way. Anemonefish are able to live among the stinging tentacles of sea anemones, which protect them from predators.

anemonefish

QUESTIONS:
Dolphins and porpoises

Level 1

1. Is the bottle-nosed a type of dolphin, crab or lobster?
2. Most porpoises are smaller than dolphins. True or false?
3. What game do dolphins like to play: football, tennis or bow-riding?
4. Which kind of animal is a dolphin: a mammal or a reptile?

Level 2

5. Dolphins have a 'melon' in their head to help them find fish. True or false?
6. Do dolphins make clicks, whistles or both to communicate with each other?
7. Why do porpoises swim upside down: to attract a mate or to eat their food?
8. How fast does Dall's porpoise swim?
9. What 'S' do dolphins like to play with?
10. Does a porpoise or a dolphin have a triangular dorsal fin?
11. Where do female dolphins give birth to their babies: near the seabed or just below the surface of the water?
12. How many games are dolphins thought to play: more than three, more than 30 or more than 300?
13. What is the function of a 'babysitter' dolphin?
14. Do female dolphins give birth to calves, kittens or pups?

Level 3

15. How many species of porpoises are there?
16. Which species is the smallest porpoise?
17. What is a dolphin's beak called?
18. What is bow-riding?
19. What 'C' sound do dolphins use to learn about their surroundings and find fish?

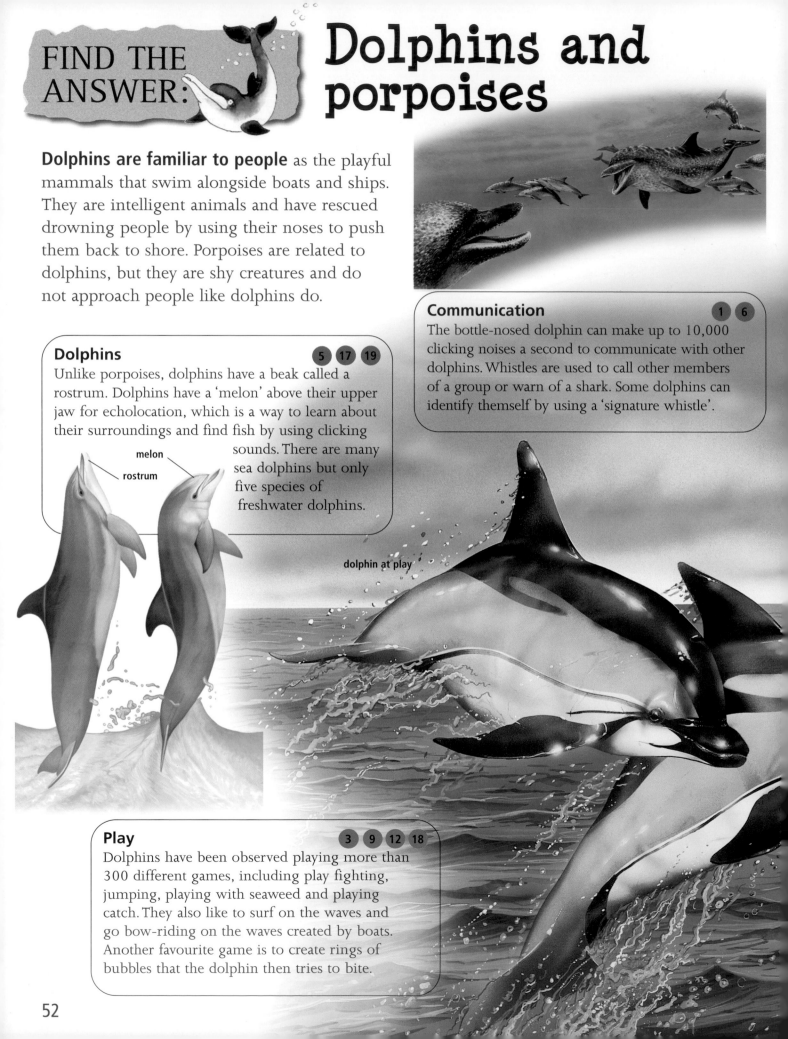

FIND THE ANSWER: Dolphins and porpoises

Dolphins are familiar to people as the playful mammals that swim alongside boats and ships. They are intelligent animals and have rescued drowning people by using their noses to push them back to shore. Porpoises are related to dolphins, but they are shy creatures and do not approach people like dolphins do.

Dolphins   5 17 19

Unlike porpoises, dolphins have a beak called a rostrum. Dolphins have a 'melon' above their upper jaw for echolocation, which is a way to learn about their surroundings and find fish by using clicking sounds. There are many sea dolphins but only five species of freshwater dolphins.

melon

rostrum

Communication   1 6

The bottle-nosed dolphin can make up to 10,000 clicking noises a second to communicate with other dolphins. Whistles are used to call other members of a group or warn of a shark. Some dolphins can identify themself by using a 'signature whistle'.

dolphin at play

Play   3 9 12 18

Dolphins have been observed playing more than 300 different games, including play fighting, jumping, playing with seaweed and playing catch. They also like to surf on the waves and go bow-riding on the waves created by boats. Another favourite game is to create rings of bubbles that the dolphin then tries to bite.

Mothers and calves   ④ ⑪ ⑬ ⑭

Female dolphins give birth to their calves just below the surface of the water. Like other mammals, dolphins feed milk to their young, often for about 18 months. Other female dolphins act like aunts or babysitters. They help the mother to teach the baby feeding and social skills, such as playing and communicating.

Porpoises   ⑧ ⑮

There are six species of porpoises, including the harbour porpoise and Burmeister's porpoise. At 55km/h, Dall's porpoise is one of the fastest swimmers among porpoises, dolphins and whales.

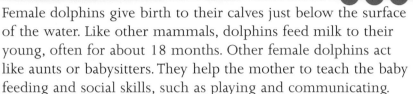

Burmeister's porpoise

dorsal fin

harbour porpoise

Anatomy   ② ⑦ ⑩ ⑯

Most porpoises are smaller than dolphins and have blunt noses. They also have spadelike teeth and triangular-shaped dorsal fins. Some swim upside down to attract a mate. At only 150cm long, the smallest porpoise is the endangered Vaquita.

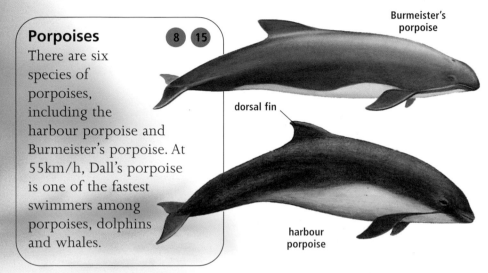

blunt nose

Dall's porpoise

QUESTIONS:
Killer whales

Level 1

1. Do killer whales live in a family group called a pod?
2. Another name for the killer whale is the orca. True or false?
3. Do adult killer whales take care of their young or do they let their young take care of themselves?
4. What is a whale jump called: a breach, a hop or a bungee?

Level 2

5. Is a killer whale also called a shark of the ocean or a wolf of the sea?
6. How long is a male killer whale: up to 4m, 6m or 10m?
7. Killer whales sometimes hunt young blue whales. True or false?
8. Why would a whale breach: to scare prey, warn of danger, attract a mate or all of the above?
9. What 'C' and 'W' noises will a whale use to send messages to another whale?
10. A clan is made up of several pods. True or false?
11. Does a killer whale poke its tail or head out of water when it is spyhopping?
12. Are killer whales mammals or large fish?
13. Do killer whales protect injured and sick members of their pod, attack them or force them away?

Level 3

14. What is a killer whale's cruising speed?
15. What is a lobtail?
16. How much faster does a killer whale swim when it's hunting, not cruising?
17. LEAD CIT can be rearranged to give what name for the common calls shared by a whale pod?
18. For how long can a whale hold itself up while spyhopping?

Killer whales

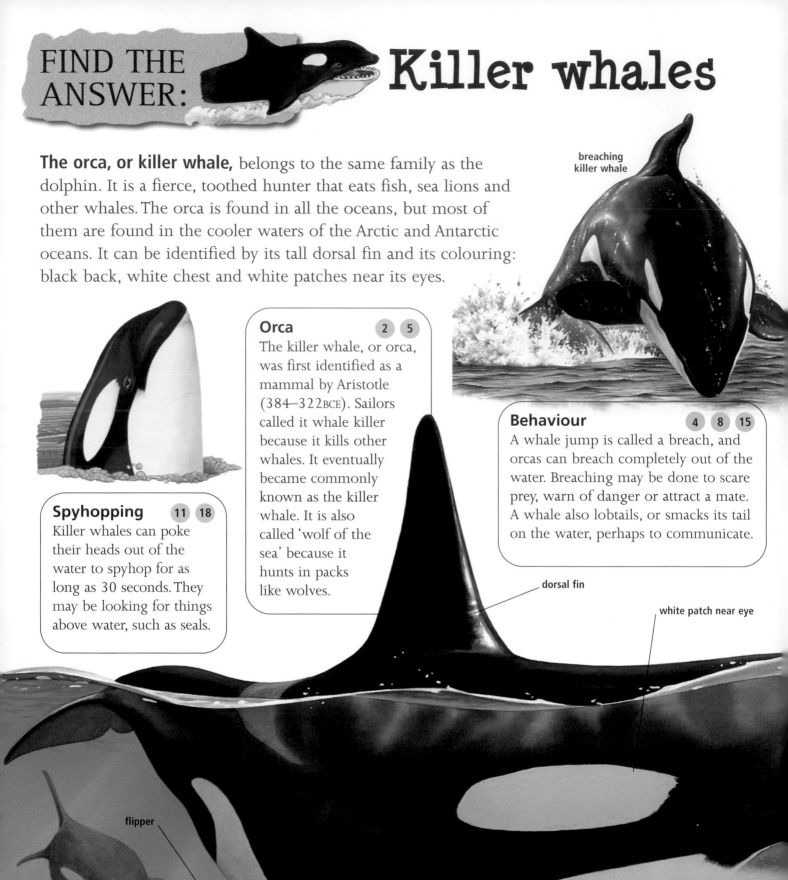

The orca, or killer whale, belongs to the same family as the dolphin. It is a fierce, toothed hunter that eats fish, sea lions and other whales. The orca is found in all the oceans, but most of them are found in the cooler waters of the Arctic and Antarctic oceans. It can be identified by its tall dorsal fin and its colouring: black back, white chest and white patches near its eyes.

breaching killer whale

Orca   2   5
The killer whale, or orca, was first identified as a mammal by Aristotle (384–322BCE). Sailors called it whale killer because it kills other whales. It eventually became commonly known as the killer whale. It is also called 'wolf of the sea' because it hunts in packs like wolves.

Behaviour   4   8   15
A whale jump is called a breach, and orcas can breach completely out of the water. Breaching may be done to scare prey, warn of danger or attract a mate. A whale also lobtails, or smacks its tail on the water, perhaps to communicate.

Spyhopping   11   18
Killer whales can poke their heads out of the water to spyhop for as long as 30 seconds. They may be looking for things above water, such as seals.

dorsal fin

white patch near eye

flipper

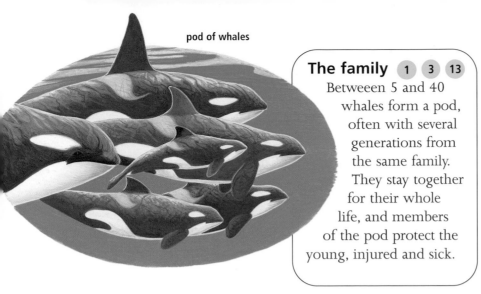

pod of whales

The family ① ③ ⑬

Betweeen 5 and 40 whales form a pod, often with several generations from the same family. They stay together for their whole life, and members of the pod protect the young, injured and sick.

Communication ⑨ ⑩ ⑰

Whales that belong in the same pod share a dialect made up of a set of underwater calls, using whistles and clicking sounds to send messages to each other. Other pods with similar dialects are part of the whale's clan.

Hunting in packs ⑦

Killer whales hunt together in packs, attacking larger prey from different angles. They have even been known to attack young blue whales and other large whales.

Speedy swimmers ⑥ ⑫ ⑭ ⑯

Killer whales are large, fast mammals. Males can be up to 10m long and swim at 48km/h when hunting. They cruise at 10km/h.

QUESTIONS:
Baleen whales

Level 1

1. Is the blue whale the largest mammal on earth?
2. What do baleen whales eat: birds or shrimp-like krill?
3. Whales never migrate with their young. True or false?
4. The blue whale is the loudest animal, much louder than humans. True or false?

Level 2

5. Only the blue whale has two blowholes. True or false?
6. The bowhead whale likes the warm waters of the Mediterranean sea. True or false?
7. The grey whale migrates along which coast of the USA: the eastern or the western coast?
8. What are baleen plates used for: tossing fish, trapping krill or swimming?
9. Do humpback whales use bubbles to trap krill?
10. Name one of two reasons why baleen whales migrate.
11. Why does the bowhead whale have a thick layer of blubber?
12. How far can the grey whale migrate: 1,000km, 5,000km or 10,000km?
13. Rearrange FREET FIELDS to describe how a baleen whale eats.

Level 3

14. How loud is a blue whale call?
15. Do humpback whales eat the food they catch by bubble netting on the seabed or at the surface?
16. What percentage of its total length is the head of the bowhead whale?
17. How many krill can a blue whale eat in a single day?

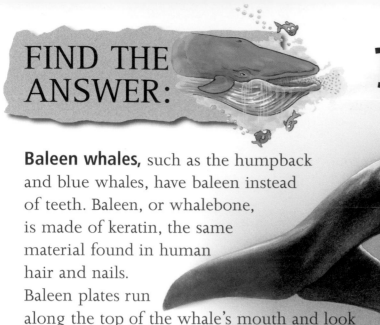

Baleen whales

Baleen whales, such as the humpback and blue whales, have baleen instead of teeth. Baleen, or whalebone, is made of keratin, the same material found in human hair and nails. Baleen plates run along the top of the whale's mouth and look like thick hair, but they are stiffer. Most baleen whales are larger than toothed whales.

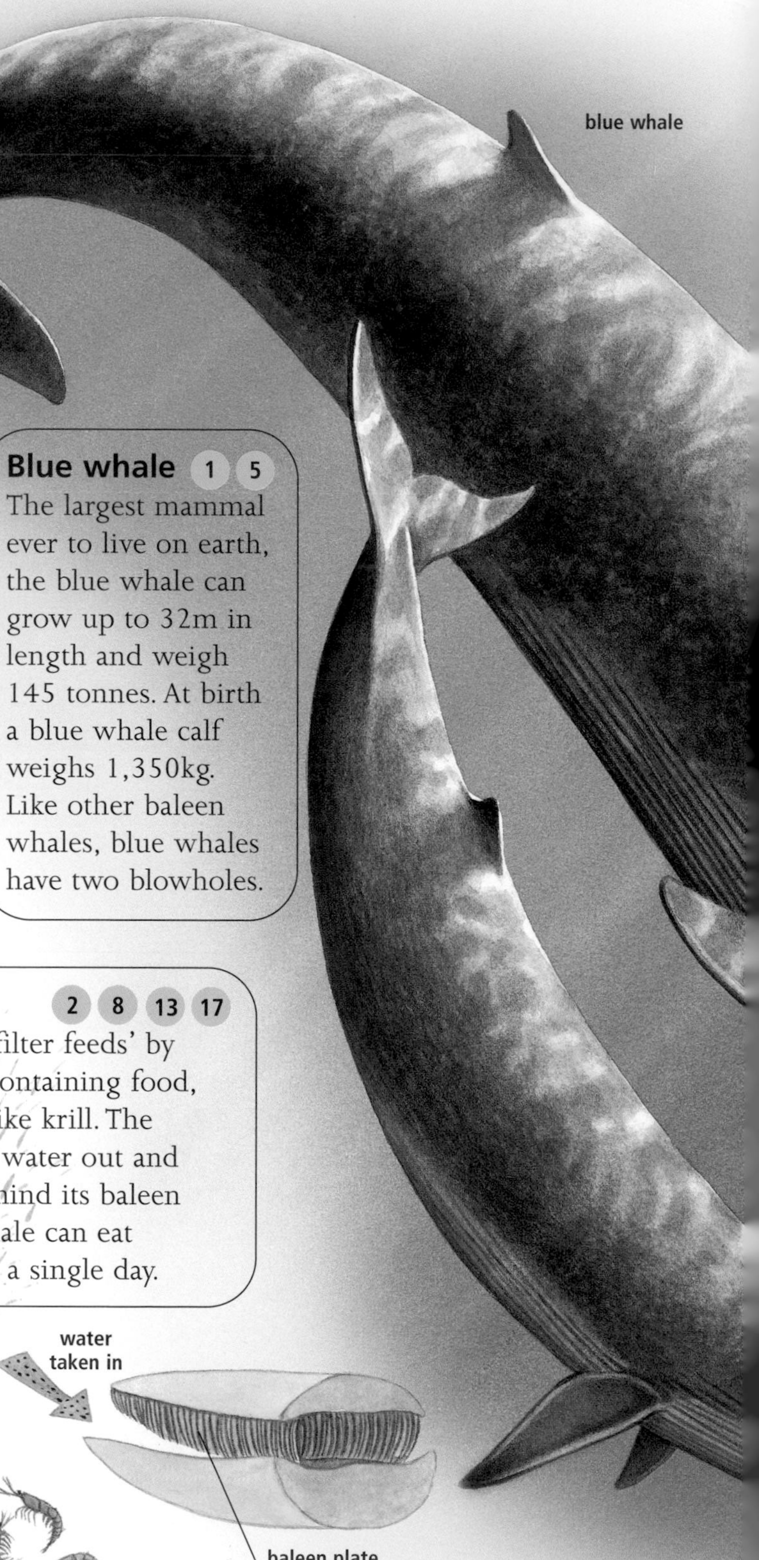

blue whale

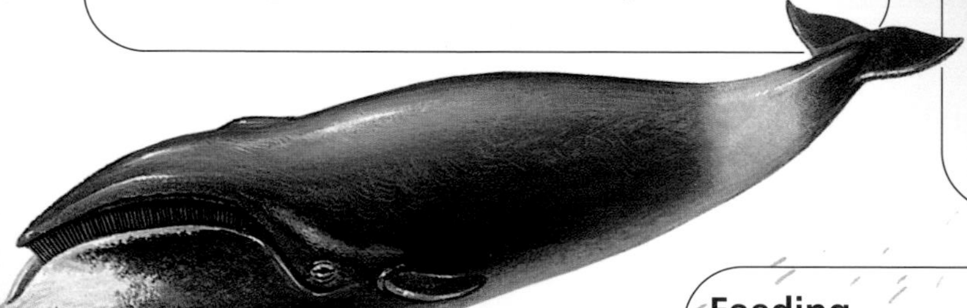

Blue whale 1 5

The largest mammal ever to live on earth, the blue whale can grow up to 32m in length and weigh 145 tonnes. At birth a blue whale calf weighs 1,350kg. Like other baleen whales, blue whales have two blowholes.

Bowhead whale 6 11 16

The endangered bowhead whale lives in Arctic waters. Its large head makes up 40 per cent of its body length. The bowhead has a covering of blubber, up to 70cm thick, to keep it warm.

Feeding 2 8 13 17

A baleen whale 'filter feeds' by taking in water containing food, such as shrimp-like krill. The whale forces the water out and traps the krill behind its baleen plates. A blue whale can eat 4 million krill in a single day.

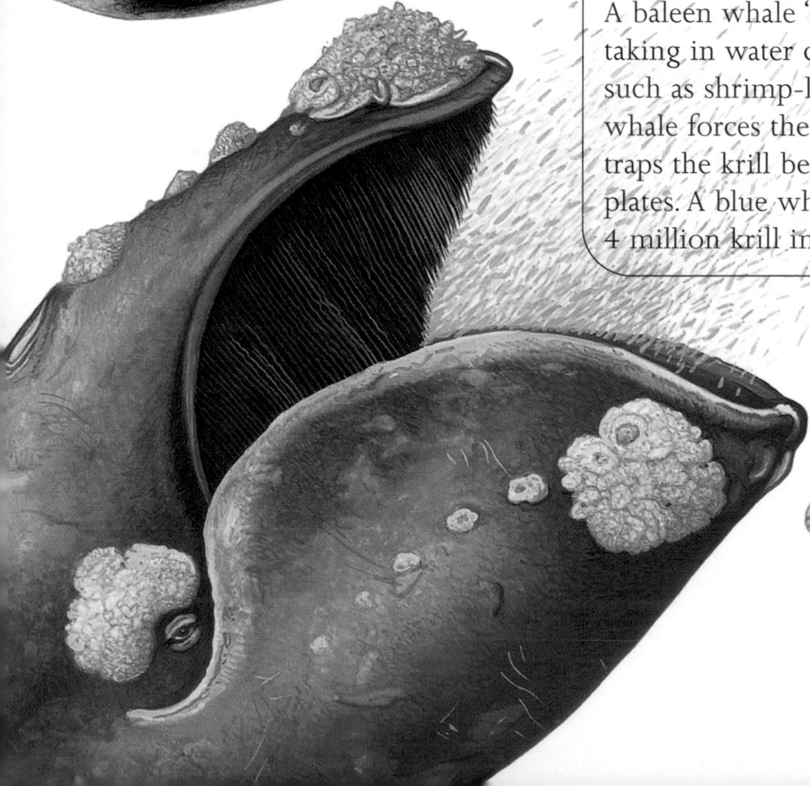

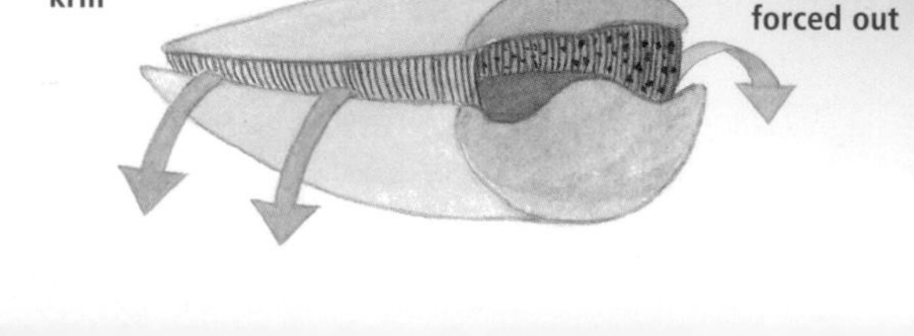

water taken in

baleen plate

krill

water forced out

Bubble netting   9   15

The humpback whale uses bubbles to catch fish and krill. The whale circles beneath them and blows air out of its blowhole. A net of air bubbles rises up and traps the fish or krill, which the whale eats at the surface.

bubble netting

feeding at the surface

Migration   3   7   10   12

Most baleen whales travel long distances to breed and feed, alone or in small groups. A grey whale can travel 10,000km with its young along the USA's western coast, from Mexico to the Bering Strait.

Calls   4   14

Blue whales are the loudest animals with calls up to 188 decibels. A human's shout is 70 decibels. The blue whale's calls can last up to 35 seconds and can travel hundreds of kilometres away.

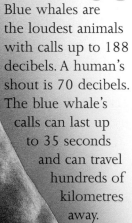

QUESTIONS:
Birds of prey

Level 1

1. Which bird is the national bird of the USA: golden eagle, harpy eagle or bald eagle?
2. Does the osprey live near water or in grasslands?
3. The peregrine falcon is faster than any other creature in the world. True or false?
4. What are talons: claws, wings or legs?

Level 2

5. How many species of falcon are there: about five, 35 or 75?
6. What kind of eagle is the South American harpy: a snake eagle, buzzard-like eagle or sea eagle?
7. How fast can a peregrine falcon dive: 23km/h, 230km/h or 320km/h?
8. Which birds of prey have longer talons: those that catch rabbits or those that catch fish?
9. How many species of eagle are there: about 20, 40 or 60?
10. Which bird of prey has the largest wingspan?
11. What is the world's largest eagle?
12. What does the bald eagle eat: small animals, fish or both?
13. What type of wings enable eagles and buzzards to soar for long periods: broad wings or long, tapered wings?
14. Is the kestrel a type of falcon or eagle?

Level 3

15. Which wing shape allows birds to manoeuvre easily?
16. The golden eagle is which type of eagle?
17. What is unusual about the bottom of an osprey's feet?
18. What happens to a bald eagle at three or four years of age?

Birds of prey

Most birds of prey are diurnal, or daytime, hunters that kill other creatures for food. However, vultures are scavengers that feed on creatures that are already dead. All birds of prey have sharp claws, strong beaks and keen eyesight.

Eagles 6 9 11 16

There are about 60 species of eagle. The main eagle groups are snake eagles, buzzard-like eagles, booted eagles (the golden eagle is one) and sea eagles. The largest eagle is the buzzard-like South American harpy. Some eagles can spot prey such as a rabbit from 3km away.

kestrel

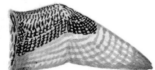

peregrine falcon

buzzard

golden eagle catching rabbit

Bald eagle 1 12 18

The bald eagle, the national bird of the USA since 1782, lives near water and eats fish and small animals. Its white head and yellow beak do not appear until the bird is three or four years of age. Its nest is the largest bird's nest and can be over 6m deep and 2.5m wide.

Wings 10 13 15

Broad wings enable eagles and buzzards to soar for long periods, while hawks and kestrels have short, rounded wings that are ideal for easy manoeuvring. Long, tapered wings, such as those of the peregrine falcon, are made for speed. The Andean condor has the largest wingspan of all birds of prey, up to 3m wide.

Falcons ③ ⑤ ⑦ ⑭

There are about 35 species of falcon, such as the prairie falcon, kestrel and peregrine falcon. The prairie falcon flies fast and low to catch its prey. The peregrine falcon dives up to 320km/h – faster than any other creature in the world.

prairie falcon

talons of harpy eagle

leg

toe

curved talon

Talons ④ ⑧

The claws on birds of prey are called talons. All birds of prey have powerful, curved talons to catch – and kill – their prey. Fish-killing birds of prey have the longest and most curved talons. The osprey's outer toe is reversible, which enables it to grip its prey with two talons in front and two at the back.

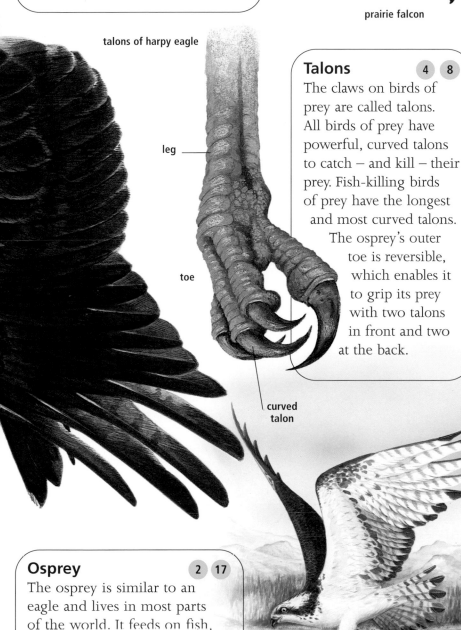

Osprey ② ⑰

The osprey is similar to an eagle and lives in most parts of the world. It feeds on fish, so it lives near fresh or salt water. The bottoms of the osprey's feet are covered with spiny scales, which are designed to help the bird grip and carry its slippery prey.

osprey with fish

QUESTIONS:
Rats and mice

Level 1

1. To what animal group do rats and mice belong: rodents, insects or reptiles?
2. Is the Swiss albino mouse the most common pet mouse?
3. The Norway rat is the most common rat in the world. True or false?
4. What disease were rats blamed for spreading: the plague, flu or colds?

Level 2

5. A mouse has lots of fur when it is born. True or false?
6. The Norway rat killed off many black rats when it arrived in Europe. True or false?
7. Do some rats live in houses and other buildings?
8. Do dormice build nests or live in caves?
9. Where did the Norway rat originate: Europe, Asia or Africa?
10. What 'I' are teeth that both rats and mice have?
11. How many species of mice are there: less than ten, between ten and 100 or more than 100?
12. What is another name for the Norway rat?
13. What 'H' do dormice do during the winter?

Level 3

14. What 'H' is one of the smallest types of mouse?
15. In which areas is the black rat more common than the brown rat?
16. What does the Latin word *rodere* mean?
17. How did the Norway rat arrive in North America?
18. How fast can a mouse run?
19. How many baby mice might a female mouse give birth to in a year?

FIND THE ANSWER:  Rats and mice

Rats and mice are rodents. All rodents have two large front teeth. These continue to grow throughout the animal's life, and gnawing on food and other objects keeps them from growing too long. There are about 900 species of rats and mice living in different areas around the world.

Norway rat `3` `9` `12`
Also called the brown rat, the Norway rat is the most common rat in the world. It spread from Asia across the world in the 18th century. It is a disease carrier.

Norway rat

Types of rat `7` `15` `17`
Norway rats and black rats started living in people's homes and other buildings thousands of years ago. Norway rats arrived in North America in 1755 on the ships of the new settlers. Black rats are more common in tropical areas.

Sharp teeth   `10`
The word 'rodent' comes from the Latin word *rodere* (meaning to gnaw), and rats and mice can chew through very tough materials, such as wire. Rats have molars and incisors. Mice have large incisors.

Brown v black rat `6`
Most black rats were killed off in Europe when their relative, the Norway rat, arrived. The black rat is darker and has a longer tail than the Norway rat.

plague-infested house

The plague `4`
Rats were blamed for spreading the plague, a deadly disease that struck Europe in the 17th century. The plague was spread by fleas that passed from rats to people.

Mice

Mice are small, nocturnal (active at night) rodents. They are quick runners (up to 13km/h), but many animals prey on them. The harvest mouse is one of the world's smallest mice.

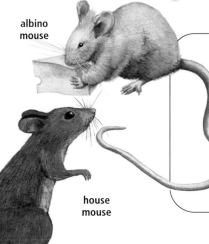

albino mouse

house mouse

Types of mouse `2` `11`

There are hundreds of species of mice. The most common is the house mouse, which lives close to humans all over the world. The Swiss albino mouse is the most popular pet mouse.

baby mouse

Mothers and babies `5` `19`

A mouse gives birth to up to eight young at a time and up to five times a year. At birth, baby mice, called kittens, have no fur and they cannot see or hear. At three weeks old, mice leave the nest. Female mice can give birth as young as seven weeks old.

Dormice `8` `13`

The bushy-tailed dormouse can spend up to three-quarters of its life asleep. When food is scarce, it hibernates – it sleeps for several months in winter. The dormouse will build a nest to keep itself warm and protected.

QUESTIONS:
Bats

Level 1

1. Bats are flying mammals. True or false?
2. Vampire bats drink the blood of which animals: cattle, lizards or snails?
3. Are a bat's bones light in weight to make flying easier?

Level 2

4. What are fruit bats sometimes called: flying cats, flying foxes or flying monkeys?
5. All bats use echolocation to help them to find food. True or false?
6. Some baby bats can fly when they are only two weeks old. True or false?
7. What do bats use the clawed fingers on their wings for: climbing or hanging upside down?
8. How many squeaks per second might a bat use during echolocation: two, 200 or 2 million?
9. Which part of its body does a vampire use to detect heat?
10. TURF BAITS can be rearranged to name which bats found in Asia, Africa and Oceania?
11. Do bats have strong legs or weak legs?
12. What is the wingspan of the largest bat: 1.5m, 1.8m or 2.5m?

Level 3

13. Why does the vampire bat have fewer teeth than other bats?
14. What is another name for the bumblebee bat?
15. How do the fingers of fruit bats differ from other bats?
16. What is the difference in wingspan between the smallest bat and the largest bat?
17. How do some bats find fruit and nectar?
18. Where can a flap of skin be found on a bat?

FIND THE ANSWER: Bats

Bats are small flying mammals that are nocturnal, or active at night. There are around 1,000 species of bats around the world. Many bats eat insects, but there are also fruit-eating bats, fish-eating bats and vampire bats that feed on blood. During the day, bats sleep in colonies, where they hang upside down from their feet.

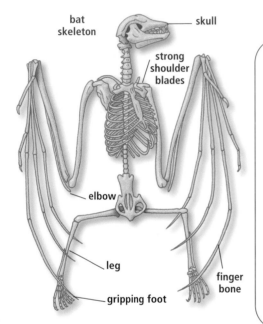

bat skeleton

skull

strong shoulder blades

elbow

leg

gripping foot

finger bone

Bones 3 7 11
A bat's bones are light for easier flying. Finger bones form the wings, but the first finger has a claw for climbing and is not part of the wing. Only one muscle opens and extends the wings. Because bats have weak legs, they do not walk very well.

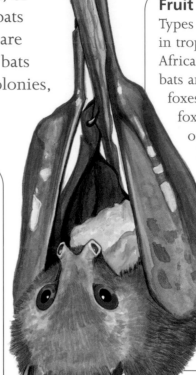

Fruit bats 4 10 15
Types of fruit bat live in tropical parts of Asia, Africa and Oceania. Fruit bats are often called flying foxes because of their fox-like faces. Unlike other bats, fruit bats have claws on both their first and second fingers. Most feed on fruits but some drink flower nectar. They spread seeds and help pollinate the plants that they visit.

fruit bat

Rare breed 14
Kitti's hog-nosed bat, also called the bumblebee bat, lives in Thailand and was discovered in 1973. It is the smallest mammal in the world, being about 3.1cm long and weighing about 2g. Its skull is only 11mm long.

large ears for hearing echoes

Echolocation 5 8 17
Some bats find their prey, such as insects and small animals, by using echolocation. They make up to 200 high-pitched squeaks per second. These bounce, or echo, off their prey, telling the bats where to find them. Other bats use their sense of smell to find fruit and nectar.

sound waves

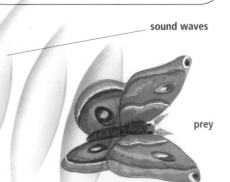

prey

Flying mammal

1 6 12 16 18

Bats are the only flying mammals. Their wings are formed by a double-sided, leathery skin. A flap of skin also joins the legs and tail. Baby bats can fly at just two to five weeks old. The wingspan of the smallest bat is 15cm, while the largest bat has a wingspan of 1.8m.

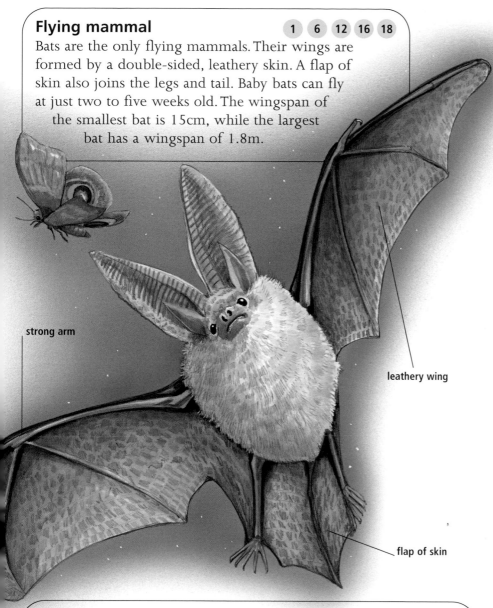

strong arm

leathery wing

flap of skin

Vampire bats

2 9 13

Vampire bats – which are named because of their diet of blood – are found only in Central and South America. These bats drink the blood of mammals such as cattle. A heat sensor on its nose helps the bat to locate warm blood. Vampire bats have fewer teeth than most bats because they do not need to chew their food.

QUESTIONS:
Big cats

Level 1

1. Lions hunt their prey in a group. True or false?
2. What is a group of lions called: a pride or school?
3. Do lions and tigers both roar?
4. All big cats are mammals. True or false?
5. What does a lion eat: zebras, penguins or lobsters?

Level 2

6. The tiger, leopard, jaguar and lynx are all big cats. True or false?
7. How much can a tiger eat in one meal: 10kg, 40kg or 80kg of meat?
8. Which animal is the fastest on land: the jaguar, the lion or the cheetah?
9. Which cat is the largest: lion, tiger or cheetah?
10. Rearrange ROD LEAP to name a big cat that feeds on impala, hares and birds.
11. Each tiger has the same pattern of stripes on both sides of its body. True or false?
12. Which cat will hide its kill in a tree: a lion, tiger or leopard?
13. Which is the only big cat that lives in the Americas: the cheetah, jaguar or ocelot?
14. Which 'S' describes the way lions and tigers hunt?

Level 3

15. Which small tiger is native to Asia?
16. Which mammal group includes lions, tigers, leopards and jaguars?
17. What two things help to hide a big cat when it is hunting?
18. How far can a cheetah travel in just three strides?
19. Which is the only big cat that cannot fully retract its claws?

Big cats

panther leopard

cheetah

lion

domestic cat

lioness

snow leopard wild cat

The big cat family is a group of large mammals. Their numbers have been seriously threatened by hunting and by their habitat being destroyed. The Caspian tiger and Javan tiger have both become extinct within the last 50 years. Even now, big cats, such as the snow leopard, are hunted for fur. Of all the continents, only Australia and Antarctica have no native cats.

Types of cat

The mammal group Panthera includes lions, tigers, leopards and jaguars. Only the jaguar is found in the Americas. All of these cats can roar. The cheetah and puma are not true big cats because they cannot roar. Nor can medium-sized cats such as the lynx and ocelot.

Tigers 7 9 11 15

The largest of the big cats, tigers can eat about 40kg of meat at one meal. Each tiger's pattern of stripes is unique, and is also different on each side of the tiger. The Siberian tiger is the largest, and the Sumatran tiger, from Indonesia, is the smallest. Tigers are strong swimmers.

Lions

A group of lions, a pride, hunts together. Females, or lionesses, do most of the hunting for prey, such as zebras and wildebeests.

Stalking 14 17

Big cats will spend hours watching their prey and waiting for the right moment to pounce. Tall grass and the colour of their fur can camouflage, or hide, the cats.

waiting to pounce

The chase 8 18 19

Cheetahs are the fastest land animals. They can reach 100km/h in three seconds and cover 6m in one stride. They are the only cats that cannot fully retract their claws.

running after prey

Hiding the kill 10 12

Tigers and leopards will hide their kill from other meat-eating animals. The leopard may hide its meal in a tree. It has a varied diet, eating large and small prey, such as impala, hares and birds.

tree-top hiding place

QUESTIONS:
Great apes

Level 1

1. Do chimps live together in groups?
2. What is an adult male gorilla called: a silverback, greyfront or bluetop?
3. Chimps have calls to communicate with each other. True or false?
4. Because rainforests are being destroyed, are all of the great apes in danger of becoming extinct?

Level 2

5. Gorillas and chimps live in both Africa and Asia. True or false?
6. At what age do gorillas learn to 'knuckle walk': three weeks, nine months or nine years?
7. The orang-utan is a sociable creature. True or false?
8. Is blackback another name for a young male gorilla, a young male orang-utan or a young male chimpanzee?
9. Which is an enemy of the gorilla: the leopard, tiger or jaguar?
10. For how long will a juvenile male gorilla stay with his family: until he is three years old, eight years old or 11 years old?
11. How many gorillas do the largest wild groups contain: ten, 30 or 200?
12. What feature identifies an adult male gorilla: a silver, black or brown patch of fur along its back?
13. What is a gorilla group called: a clan, a troop or a family?
14. Where do orang-utans live: in trees, caves or tall grass?

Level 3

15. What 'B' is another word for a pygmy chimp?
16. How many nests can an orang-utan make over seven days?
17. What do opposable thumbs allow a great ape to do?
18. Which member of a gorilla group decides when it is time to move on?
19. What do gorillas eat?

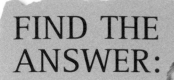

Great apes

Great apes are primates. They include humans, gorillas, chimpanzees, orang-utans and bonobos, the smallest of the great apes. All of these animals are intelligent. Chimps share 98.4 per cent of our DNA. Apes are not monkeys – they are larger, more intelligent and spend more time raising their young.

gorilla with baby in a tree nest

Habitat ④ ⑤
Africa and Asia are home to wild great apes, but gorillas and chimps live only in Africa. All the wild great apes are in danger of becoming extinct because the rainforests in which they live are being destroyed.

Gorilla groups ⑧ ⑪ ⑬
Up to 30 gorillas live in a group, called a troop. Each troop has a male leader, a few juvenile blackback males, many females and their young. Mature males may form a 'bachelor' group before females join them.

adult male

grooming

Young gorillas ⑥ ⑩
Gorillas learn to 'knuckle walk' by nine months old, but they travel on their mothers' backs until they are two or three years old. They leave the group at about 11 years old.

female and young

Gorilla leader ② ⑨ ⑫ ⑱ ⑲
An adult male gorilla is called a silverback because of the silver patch of fur on his back. The dominant silverback decides where the group lives, protects it from enemies, such as the leopard, and decides what the gorillas will eat. Gorillas are mostly vegetarian and eat plant food, but they will also eat insects.

chimpanzee
mother and
baby

Chimpanzees (1) (3) (15)

Chimps live in groups called communities. They have about 30 calls for communicating. Bonobos, or pygmy chimps, live in the Congo, in Africa.

Orang-utans (7) (14) (16)

The word 'orang-utan' is from the Indonesian and Malaysian words for person (*orang*) and forest (*hutan*). The tree-dwelling orang-utan is not a social animal. It lives alone after it leaves its mother at the age of about eight. An orang-utan can make up to 14 nests over seven days.

Using tools (17)

Great apes, like humans, have opposable thumbs, which means they can grasp things. These creatures have the intelligence to use tools to help them with everyday tasks. Gorillas, for example, use sticks to discover the depth of water. When it is raining hard, an orang-utan will keep himself dry by making an umbrella from a large palm leaf.

orang-utan
with a palm-
leaf umbrella

QUESTIONS:
Bears

Level 1

1. Bears hibernate by going into a long sleep. True or false?
2. Where do polar bears live: the Arctic, the Antarctic or South America?
3. Are baby bears called kittens, pups or cubs?
4. Where do mother bears give birth: underwater, by a lake or in a den?
5. Bears are sometimes scavengers. True or false?

Level 2

6. The grizzly bear is a type of brown bear. True or false?
7. For how long can a black bear hibernate: 50, 100 or 200 days?
8. Is the sun bear, Kodiak bear or spectacled bear the smallest bear?
9. Does a polar bear have a 10cm layer, 30cm layer or 50cm layer of fat around its body?
10. At what age does a bear cub leave its mother: one year old, two years old or three years old?
11. What 'S' do Alaskan brown bears love to eat?
12. Where does the spectacled bear live: in mountains, deserts or tundra?

Level 3

13. If a black bear weighs 180kg in spring, how much would it weigh at hibernation?
14. What 'S' is a marine animal that is eaten by polar bears?
15. Name one of two main things cubs learn from their mother.
16. What is an omnivore?
17. Which bear is the largest bear?
18. Which bear eats bromeliad plants?
19. In the autumn, how many hours a week, on average, does a bear spend eating?

Bears are large mammals with furry bodies and short tails. They usually have small, rounded ears and a good sense of smell. Although they walk on all fours, bears can stand on their hind legs. Most bears are fast runners and good swimmers. Only mothers and their babies, called cubs, live together.

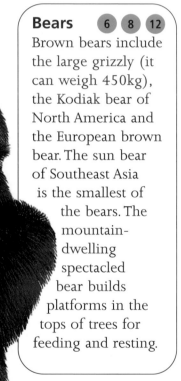

Feeding   11 16 18

Bears are omnivores, which means they eat both plant foods and meat. Alaskan brown bears love salmon, sun bears hunt for termites and spectacled bears eat bromeliad plants.

Bears   6 8 12

Brown bears include the large grizzly (it can weigh 450kg), the Kodiak bear of North America and the European brown bear. The sun bear of Southeast Asia is the smallest of the bears. The mountain-dwelling spectacled bear builds platforms in the tops of trees for feeding and resting.

Young   3 4 10 15

Female bears make dens in which to have their cubs. Bear cubs stay near their mothers for up to three years, while they learn how to hunt and make shelters.

grizzly bear

black bear

polar bear

European brown bear

Hibernation

Many bears go into a winter sleep called hibernation. The black bear can sleep for 100 days without eating or drinking. Before this sleep, bears can increase their weight by 180kg.

1 7 13

Scavenging

5 19

Bears eat for 20 hours a day in the summer and autumn. They are great scavengers and will eat whatever food is available. Black bears sometimes raid rubbish bins.

Polar bears

2 9 14 17

The largest bear is the polar bear. It lives in the Arctic, where it preys on seals. Its fur looks white because it reflects the light, but, in fact, it is translucent. The bear's skin is black to attract heat from the sun. The bear has a 10cm layer of fat under its skin to keep warm.

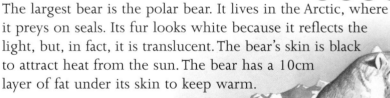

QUESTIONS:
Pets

Level 1

1. Pet fish are kept in a tank called an aquarium. True or false?
2. Cats use their whiskers to find their way around at night. True or false?
3. Are rabbits fast runners or slow animals?
4. Is a cat with its tail held high happy or unhappy?

Level 2

5. Cavies are also called guinea pigs. True or false?
6. Do domestic cats have short hair, long hair or either kind?
7. Are dogs most closely related to rabbits, foxes or wolves?
8. Can a rabbit see almost 90 degrees, 180 degrees or 360 degrees?
9. Which is not a type of parrot: macaw, parakeet or quetzal?
10. What 'H' means an animal that eats plants?
11. The Abyssinian guinea pig has smooth, short hair. True or false?
12. Which animal is also known as a desert rat: the guinea pig, the gerbil or the rabbit?
13. Rearrange DEER BURP to spell a word used to describe cats of a particular type.

Level 3

14. What must a hamster do because its teeth grow all the time?
15. What ability is the African grey parrot known for?
16. What 'S' is another name for the golden hamster?
17. Pet fish owners need to make sure what 'T' in an aquarium is properly controlled to suit the type of fish?
18. How many breeds of dog are there?
19. Rabbits are most active during which times of day?
20. In which states of the USA is it illegal to keep gerbils?

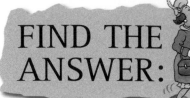

Pets

**Bernese
mountain dog**

Pets are animals kept by people for companionship or amusement. Dogs are often called 'man's best friend' because of their loyal nature. Cats, guinea pigs and hamsters are favourite pets, too. Horses are kept in stables. People also keep all types of exotic fish and birds, reptiles and insects.

Dogs

There are over 400 breeds of dog divided into seven groups: sporting; hounds; working; toy; terriers; non-sporting; and herding. Dogs are related to wolves and have a keen sense of smell. Dogs are the most dependent pets, relying on their owners for company.

Cats 2 4 6 13

Although there are only a few purebred cats, there are many more domestic short- or long-haired cats. Cats use their whiskers to help them get around at night. A cat's tail can show how it is feeling: a high tail means the cat is happy, while a low one means the cat is unhappy.

**domestic
cat**

Labrador

**Yorkshire
terrier**

Guinea pigs 5 11

Cavies, or guinea pigs, are rodents. The American guinea pig has smooth, short hair. The Abyssinian has a rough coat of swirls.

**guinea
pig**

Hamsters 14 16

The Syrian, or golden, hamster is a popular pet, but dwarf hamsters, including the Roborovski, are also common. Like other rodents, a hamster's teeth grow all the time, so they gnaw on whatever is available.

hamster

Gerbils 12 20

'Desert rats', or gerbils, are native to desert regions. They live between two and four years and are sociable. It is illegal to keep them in California and Hawaii, USA.

gerbil

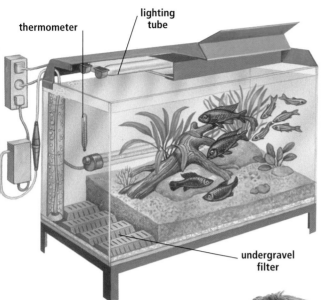

thermometer

lighting tube

undergravel filter

Fish 1 17

Aquariums, or tanks, with filtered fresh or salt water are homes for pet fish. The water temperature is controlled to suit the type of fish. Goldfish like cold water, but tropical fish need heated water to survive.

Rabbits 3 8 10 19

Because rabbits are herbivores, they eat plant foods. Their powerful back legs make rabbits fast-moving animals. They are most active at dawn and dusk. Their eyes are at the sides of their heads, which allows them to see almost 360 degrees.

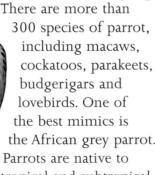

parakeets

Parrots 9 15

There are more than 300 species of parrot, including macaws, cockatoos, parakeets, budgerigars and lovebirds. One of the best mimics is the African grey parrot. Parrots are native to tropical and subtropical areas and feed on fruit and nuts. Parrots taken from their natural habitat in the wild make bad pets.

QUESTIONS:
Where in the world?

Level 1

1. Would you find a European bison in Poland or Madagascar?
2. Do tigers live in Europe or Asia?
3. TAIPAN DANG can be rearranged to give the name of which animal that lives in the bamboo forests of China?

Level 2

4. Are tamarins types of monkey or turtle?
5. Which island off Africa is home to all of the world's wild lemurs?
6. Where in the world does the numbat live?
7. Which country is home to the Iberian lynx?

Level 3

8. What is the world's largest tree-living animal?
9. The Tasmanian wolf is another name for which animal?
10. What is the name of the largest bird in North America?

FIND THE ANSWER: Where in the world?

In many parts of the world, many species of animal have been disappearing at an alarming rate. Some have been hunted to near extinction by man, while others are threatened by damage to their natural habitats or by climate change. Endangered species include not only large mammals, such as the Asian elephant, but also countless birds, fish and insects.

Asia 2 3 8
Asia has many unique species, including many that are endangered, such as giant pandas, tigers, gibbons and orang-utans, the world's largest tree-living animals.

North America 10
The California condor, North America's largest bird, is in danger of extinction. In 2002, there were just 200 left – all in captivity.

Europe 1 7
Endangered species include the European bison, which lives in Poland and the far west of Russia, and the Iberian lynx, which is found only in Spain.

NORTH AMERICA

EUROPE

ASIA

AFRICA

SOUTH AMERICA

Africa 5
The island of Madagascar, off the east coast of Africa, is home to the endangered species of primates called lemurs.

South America 4
The golden lion tamarin, a small monkey, is native to the coastal forests of Brazil and is one of the world's rarest animals.

AUSTRALIA

Australia 6 9
The thylacine, or Tasmanian wolf, is now thought to be extinct. Other endangered species include the numbat, the northern hairy-nosed wombat and the Australian sea lion.

Answers 1) Poland **2)** Asia **3)** Giant panda **4)** Monkey **5)** Madagascar **6)** Australia **7)** Spain **8)** The orang-utan **9)** The thylacine **10)** The California condor

QUIZ TWO
Geography

QUESTIONS:
Continents

Level 1

1. Where is the Nile?
2. Which continent lies to the east of Europe?
3. Is Asia the second-most populated continent?
4. Is Central America part of North or South America?
5. Which is the smallest continent?

Level 2

6. What is the world's largest country?
7. What divides Europe from Africa?
8. What population milestone was reached in 1802?
9. Is Sydney the capital city of Australia?
10. In which continent would you find the world's highest mountains?
11. What larger landmass contains Europe?
12. How many billion did the world's population reach in 1999: one, five, six or 11?
13. Are the Andes on the east or west coast of South America?

Level 3

14. How much of the Amazon rainforest lies outside of Brazil?
15. What are the names of the island groups of the South Pacific?
16. By how many million per year was the world's population increasing in 2004?
17. How many countries are in Africa: 47, 52 or 53?
18. In which continent is the world's largest freshwater lake?
19. How long is the Andes mountain range?

FIND THE ANSWER: Continents

Millions of years ago, the world's land was all connected in a 'supercontinent'. Over time the land shifted and settled into the seven continents we know today. This is known as continental drift. Antarctica is the world's only unpopulated continent because 98 per cent of the land is covered in ice. It is also the coldest, windiest and driest continent.

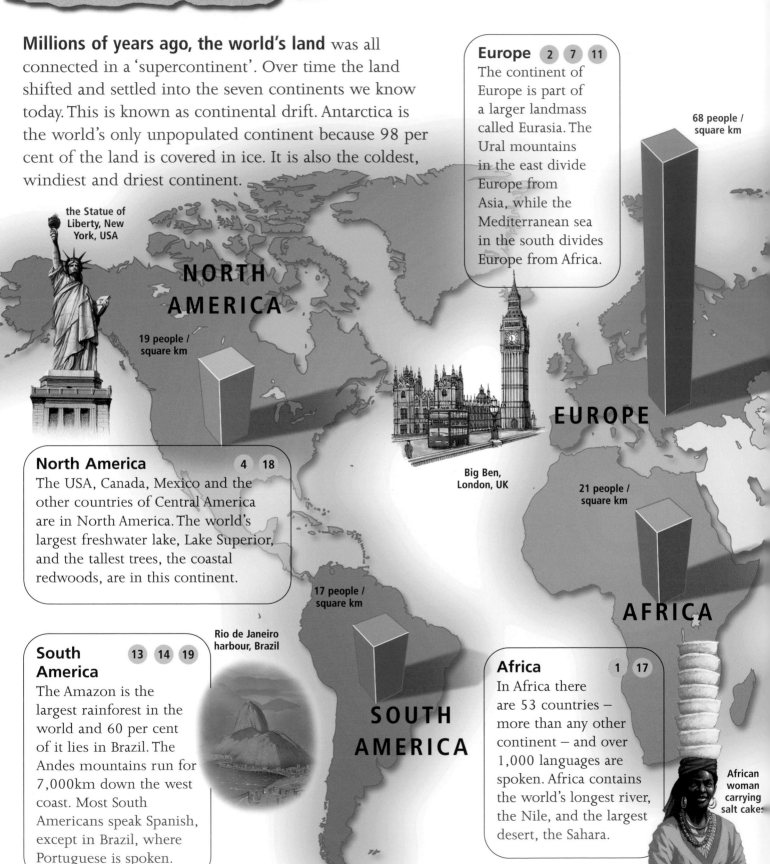

Europe ② ⑦ ⑪
The continent of Europe is part of a larger landmass called Eurasia. The Ural mountains in the east divide Europe from Asia, while the Mediterranean sea in the south divides Europe from Africa.

the Statue of Liberty, New York, USA

NORTH AMERICA

19 people / square km

68 people / square km

EUROPE

Big Ben, London, UK

North America ④ ⑱
The USA, Canada, Mexico and the other countries of Central America are in North America. The world's largest freshwater lake, Lake Superior, and the tallest trees, the coastal redwoods, are in this continent.

21 people / square km

AFRICA

17 people / square km

Rio de Janeiro harbour, Brazil

South America ⑬ ⑭ ⑲
The Amazon is the largest rainforest in the world and 60 per cent of it lies in Brazil. The Andes mountains run for 7,000km down the west coast. Most South Americans speak Spanish, except in Brazil, where Portuguese is spoken.

SOUTH AMERICA

Africa ① ⑰
In Africa there are 53 countries – more than any other continent – and over 1,000 languages are spoken. Africa contains the world's longest river, the Nile, and the largest desert, the Sahara.

African woman carrying salt cakes

Population increase 8 12 16

The world population has grown at an increasingly fast rate, even though birth rates have gone down in many countries. In 1802, the world reached one billion people, and by 1999 it had reached six billion. By 2004, the population increase was 75 million per year.

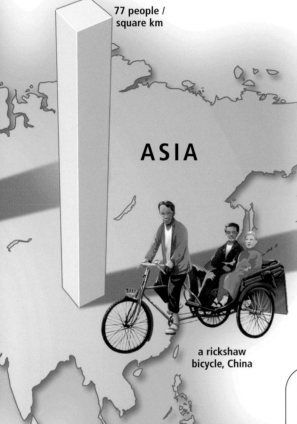

77 people / square km

ASIA

a rickshaw bicycle, China

Asia 3 6 10

Asia is the largest continent and the most populated. It contains the world's largest country, the Russian Federation, as well as the Middle Eastern countries, the Far East and India. The world's highest mountains are in Asia, including 96 in the Himalayas.

Australia 5 9 15

Australia is the smallest continent. It is also a country, with Canberra as its capital and Sydney as its largest city. Australia's neighbours in Oceania include New Zealand, Papua New Guinea and the island groups of the South Pacific: Melanesia, Micronesia and Polynesia.

AUSTRALIA

2 people / square km

the Sydney Opera House, Australia

QUESTIONS:
The international community

Level 1

1. The United Nations was formed during World War I. True or false?
2. What does NATO stand for: the North Atlantic Treaty Organization or the North Antarctic Treaty Organization?
3. All peacekeeping units are armed. True or false?
4. What is the single currency of the European Union?
5. CRESS ROD can be rearranged to give the name of what organization that provides medical aid?

Level 2

6. Why was NATO formed?
7. What convention protects wounded soldiers and prisoners?
8. In what city is the UN headquarters?
9. How many countries are in the UN?
10. What treaty marked the beginning of European union?
11. In what building do member nations of the UN meet?
12. For what purpose can peacekeeping units use their weapons?

Level 3

13. In what year did the UN headquarters officially open?
14. What treaty led to the formation of the European Union?
15. What is the full name of the Red Cross?
16. How much money was donated to buy land for the UN headquarters?
17. What is the name of the central command of NATO's military forces?
18. Who first used the term 'United Nations'?

The international community

The countries of the world have formed many organizations to help each other. These groups provide medical and military aid, as well as opportunities for trade. Many international committees try to make the world into a safer, more peaceful place.

the UN flag

United Nations 1 9 18
The term United Nations (UN) was first used by US President F D Roosevelt during World War II, but the UN was not officially established until 1945. Since then, it has grown from its original 51 members to 192.

Headquarters 8 11 13 16
The UN headquarters officially opened on 9 January 1951, on the banks of the East river in New York City. An American millionaire called John D Rockefeller Jr donated $8.5 million to buy the land. Member nations meet in the General Assembly Building.

Peacekeeping 3 12
When armed fighting breaks out within countries, UN peacekeeping groups may be called in to help. They may set up refugee camps and help to maintain law and order. There are armed and unarmed UN groups. Armed groups are only allowed to use their weapons for self-defence.

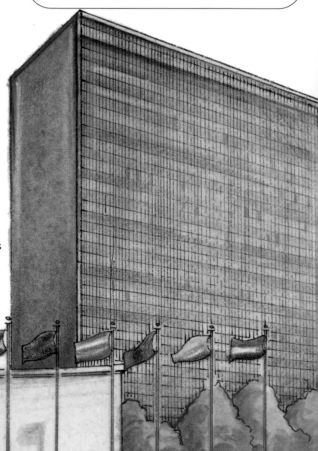

UN headquarters

flags of some UN member states

European Union headquarters

European Union   4   10   14

The Treaty of Paris, in 1951, marked the beginning of European union. The European Community (EC) grew out of this, and the Maastricht Treaty, signed in 1992, led to the formation of the European Union (EU) and the single European currency, the euro.

5 euro note

NATO   2   6   17

The North Atlantic Treaty Organization (NATO) was formed in 1949 to keep peace in its 26 member states. They all help each other if any of their states is attacked. Supreme Headquarters Allied Powers Europe (SHAPE) is the central command of NATO's military forces.

Red Cross   5   7   15

The International Committee of the Red Cross and the Red Crescent Movement provides medical aid in war and peace. The Geneva Convention also helps to protect wounded soldiers and prisoners.

QUESTIONS:
Flags

Level 1

1. What colours could a pirate flag be?
2. Where are naval flags used: at sea or in space?
3. In what kind of sport is a black-and-white chequered flag used?
4. What kind of flag do explorers plant on lands they have discovered?
5. Which has the oldest national flag: Scotland or the USA?

Level 2

6. Which sport uses flags: rugby, cycling, rowing or all three?
7. What are naval flags called?
8. What event prompted the redesign of the French flag?
9. Are signalling flags used alone, together or both?
10. What is semaphore?
11. How many US flags have been placed on the moon: four, five or six?
12. Which colour is not used in naval flags: yellow, black or green?

Level 3

13. What do referees use flags to indicate in an American football game?
14. In semaphore, how is an 'R' signalled?
15. On a pirate flag, what does an hour glass symbolize?
16. What colour flags are used in semaphore?
17. In which century were pirate flags first used?
18. What displayed a US flag on Mars?

FIND THE ANSWER: Flags

Flags have been used for centuries both as identification and to communicate a message. In the Middle Ages, for instance, they were used in battle to identify leaders. Flags vary greatly in colour and style, but they all convey an immediate visual message.

China

Brazil

Sweden

Greece

Germany

Israel

National flags 5 8
National flags are used to identify individual countries. Scotland has the oldest national flag. Sometimes countries change their flags: the French flag was redesigned as the famous tricolour in 1794, after the revolution.

Naval flags 2 7 9 12
Ships at sea communicate with naval flags called signalling flags. These convey different meanings when used alone or together. They use colours that can be seen at sea: blue, white, red, black and yellow.

Sports flags 3 6 13
Flags are used in many sports, including rugby, rowing and cycling, to communicate with the sportsmen. Referees use flags in American football games to indicate an error. The chequered flag is used in auto and motorcycle racing to signal the end of a race.

chequered flag

Semaphore 10 14 16
One signalling system, semaphore, uses two square red and yellow flags held in different positions to indicate letters. Arms and flags straight out means 'R'.

signalling flags

Sudan

Turkey

Australia

United Kingdom

Canada

Argentina

South Korea

Jamaica

Austria

Level 1

1. What is the tallest mountain in the world?
2. What is the tallest waterfall in the world?
3. K2 is in Europe. True or false?
4. The Great Barrier Reef lies off the coast of which country?
5. The Great Barrier Reef can be seen from space. True or false?
6. Which is longer: the Grand Canyon or the Great Barrier Reef?

Level 2

7. Who were the first people to reach the top of Mount Everest?
8. How is the length of the Grand Canyon measured?
9. How many times higher is Angel Falls than Niagara Falls: 10, 15 or 20?
10. What is the Hillary Step?
11. How old are the rocks in the Grand Canyon?
12. In what continent is the widest waterfall in the world?
13. What is another name for *aurora borealis*?

Level 3

14. What causes the Northern Lights?
15. How much older are the Alps than the Himalayas?
16. How high is Mount Everest?
17. What is the Latin name of the Southern Lights?
18. What geographical feature is 10,783m wide?

Pirate flags **1** **15** **17**

A red or black pirate flag was meant to frighten, with images such as a skull, meaning death, or an hourglass, meaning time was running out. These flags were used by British pirates from about 1700.

Black Bart's flag

Christopher Moody's flag

Calico Jack's flag

Explorers' flags **4** **11** **18**

Explorers often plant their national flag on the lands they discover. Six US flags have been placed on the moon. Each US space shuttle is given its own flag. The *Viking* lander displayed a US flag as it explored Mars.

US flag on the moon

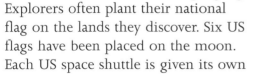

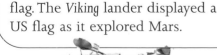

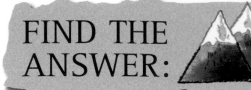

Natural wonders

Spectacular features are found all over the world and include amazing waterfalls, fiery volcanoes and natural phenomena, such as the Northern Lights. Wind and water erosion has created some of these features, such as the canyons, while the movement of the earth's plates has created others, such as the world's highest mountains.

oxygen cylinders

Mount Everest 1 3 15 16
Everest, the tallest mountain in the world, is part of the Himalayan mountain range in Asia. Its peak is 8,850m high. The second highest mountain, K2, is also in the Himalayas. The Himalayas are 60 million years old – younger than the Alps in Europe, which formed 75 million years ago.

Conquering Everest 7 10
In 1953, New Zealander Edmund Hillary and Nepali Tenzing Norgay became the first people to reach the peak of Everest. A steep section of the mountain has since been named Hillary Step.

staghorn coral

angel fish

harlequin tusk fish

jack fish

hard coral

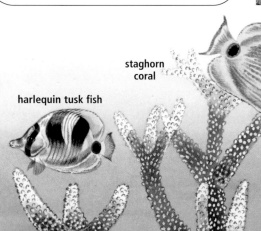

Coral reefs 4 5 6
The Great Barrier Reef, off the coast of Australia, is over 2,000km long and is visible from space. Over 5,000 species of plants and animals live there.

fan coral

Victoria Falls,
Africa

Waterfalls 2 9 12 18

Angel Falls in South America is
the tallest waterfall in the world,
at 979m high. It is 15 times higher
than Niagara Falls in North America.
The widest waterfall is Khône Falls
in Asia. It is 10,783m wide.

Aurora 13 14 17

The Northern Lights (*aurora borealis*)
and the Southern Lights (*aurora
australis*) are dancing displays of
coloured lights in the night sky.
Aurora are caused by high-speed
particles from the sun colliding
with gas molecules to create light.

Canyons 6 8 11

The Grand Canyon,
in Arizona, USA, is
the largest in the
world. It is 446km
long and 1,500m
deep. The canyon's
length is measured
by the Colorado river
that cuts through it.
The oldest rocks there
are 2,000 million
years old, though
the canyon itself
is probably only
about 5 or 6 million
years old.

the Grand
Canyon, USA

QUESTIONS:
Coasts

Level 1

1. A tsunami is caused by the wind.
   True or false?
2. ACE VASE can be rearranged to give
   what name for a cavern in a cliff?
3. What is the wearing down of a
   headland called: erosion or erasure?
4. What two materials do waves deposit
   on beaches?
5. What 'W' causes waves?
6. HELLO BOW can be rearranged to
   give the name of what coastal feature?

Level 2

7. What is special about the Painted Cave?
8. What does the word 'tsunami' mean?
9. What causes water to gush through
   a blow hole?
10. The fetch is the material deposited
    on a beach. True or false?
11. A stack is a mound of sand. True
    or false?
12. Is sea water acidic or alkaline?

Level 3

13. Which is formed first: a cave or
    a blow hole?
14. How fast do tsunami waves move?
15. What coastal process do groynes
    prevent?
16. On what island is the Painted Cave?
17. How high can tsunamis be?
18. A stack is formed from which coastal
    feature?

FIND THE ANSWER: Coasts

The world's coastlines are about 504,000km long, which is long enough to circle the globe 12 times. Primary coasts are formed by changes in the land, such as river deltas. Many of these coastlines were formed as the sea levels changed over thousands of years. Secondary coasts are formed by changes in the ocean, such as coral reefs.

Coastal erosion (3) (12)
Coastlines do not stay the same. They change continually as they are worn down by water throwing pebbles and rocks against the shore, a process called erosion. Sea water is also acidic, helping to wear down coastlines.

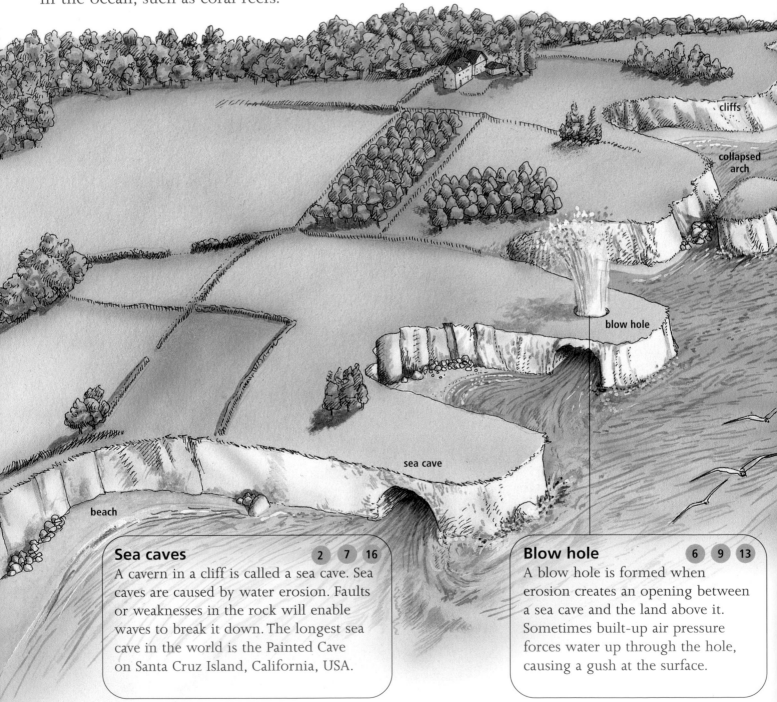

cliffs

collapsed arch

blow hole

sea cave

beach

Sea caves (2) (7) (16)
A cavern in a cliff is called a sea cave. Sea caves are caused by water erosion. Faults or weaknesses in the rock will enable waves to break it down. The longest sea cave in the world is the Painted Cave on Santa Cruz Island, California, USA.

Blow hole (6) (9) (13)
A blow hole is formed when erosion creates an opening between a sea cave and the land above it. Sometimes built-up air pressure forces water up through the hole, causing a gush at the surface.

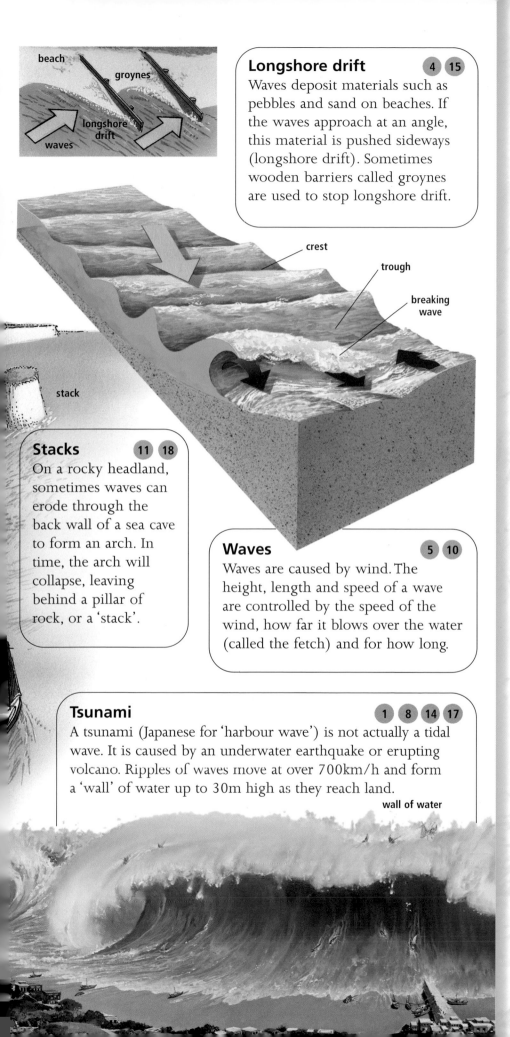

Longshore drift   ④ ⑮

Waves deposit materials such as pebbles and sand on beaches. If the waves approach at an angle, this material is pushed sideways (longshore drift). Sometimes wooden barriers called groynes are used to stop longshore drift.

beach
groynes
longshore drift
waves

crest
trough
breaking wave

stack

Stacks   ⑪ ⑱

On a rocky headland, sometimes waves can erode through the back wall of a sea cave to form an arch. In time, the arch will collapse, leaving behind a pillar of rock, or a 'stack'.

Waves   ⑤ ⑩

Waves are caused by wind. The height, length and speed of a wave are controlled by the speed of the wind, how far it blows over the water (called the fetch) and for how long.

Tsunami   ① ⑧ ⑭ ⑰

A tsunami (Japanese for 'harbour wave') is not actually a tidal wave. It is caused by an underwater earthquake or erupting volcano. Ripples of waves move at over 700km/h and form a 'wall' of water up to 30m high as they reach land.

wall of water

QUESTIONS:
Rivers

Level 1
1. What is the beginning of a river called?
2. In what continent are the Great Lakes?
3. Do waterfalls flow over a ledge of hard or soft rock?
4. What is the name of the process by which water moves between the land and sea and back again?
5. What is the name of the area of flat land on either side of a river?

Level 2
6. What 'R' is precipitation?
7. What kind of lakes are created by ice sheets?
8. What is formed when a river floods shallow lakes or ponds?
9. Do tributaries increase or decrease the water volume of a river?
10. What happens to evaporated water?
11. What other name is used for an estuary?
12. Headwaters are the top of a waterfall. True or false?
13. What prevents water seepage in a marshland?
14. What forms at the bottom of a waterfall?

Level 3
15. What 'Y' is a waterfall in the USA, created by a glacier?
16. What name is given to fertile land formed on a flood plain?
17. What can form from sediment in an estuary?
18. How was Lake Tanganyika formed?

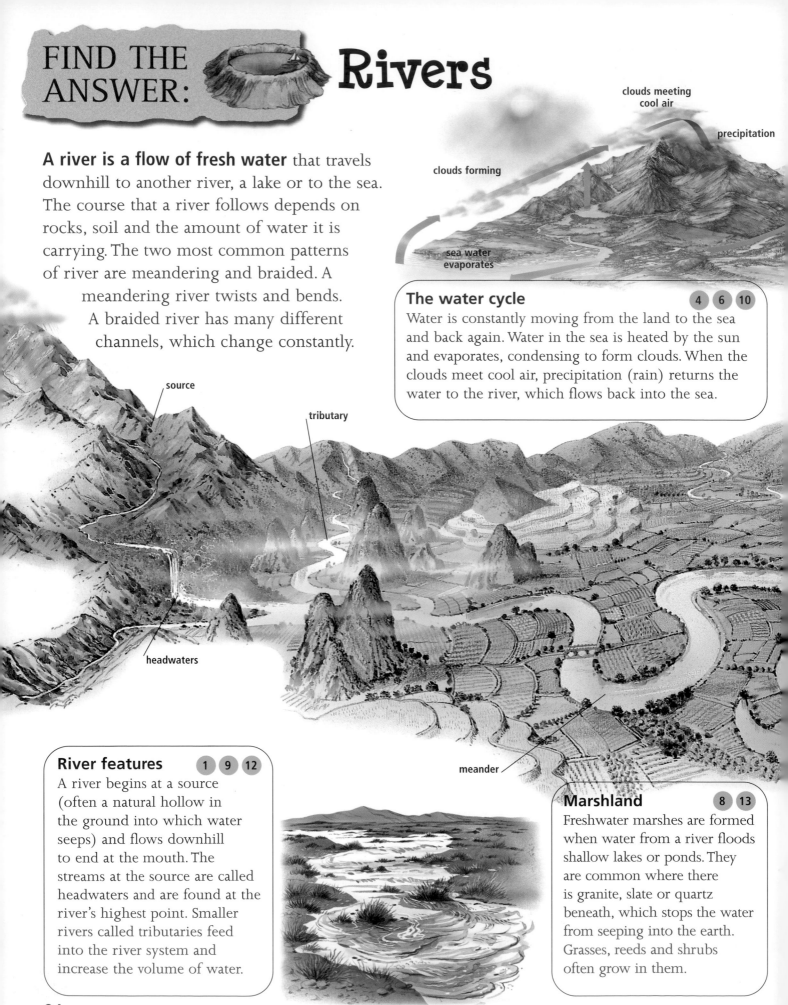

FIND THE ANSWER: Rivers

A river is a flow of fresh water that travels downhill to another river, a lake or to the sea. The course that a river follows depends on rocks, soil and the amount of water it is carrying. The two most common patterns of river are meandering and braided. A meandering river twists and bends. A braided river has many different channels, which change constantly.

clouds meeting cool air

precipitation

clouds forming

sea water evaporates

The water cycle 4 6 10
Water is constantly moving from the land to the sea and back again. Water in the sea is heated by the sun and evaporates, condensing to form clouds. When the clouds meet cool air, precipitation (rain) returns the water to the river, which flows back into the sea.

source

tributary

headwaters

meander

River features 1 9 12
A river begins at a source (often a natural hollow in the ground into which water seeps) and flows downhill to end at the mouth. The streams at the source are called headwaters and are found at the river's highest point. Smaller rivers called tributaries feed into the river system and increase the volume of water.

Marshland 8 13
Freshwater marshes are formed when water from a river floods shallow lakes or ponds. They are common where there is granite, slate or quartz beneath, which stops the water from seeping into the earth. Grasses, reeds and shrubs often grow in them.

84

Waterfalls

Most waterfalls form where an area of soft rock lies in front of an area of hard rock (stage one). The soft rock is quickly worn away by the river, leaving a ledge of hard rock over which the water falls (stage two). The gushing water creates a plunge pool at the bottom (stage three). Other waterfalls, such as Yosemite Falls in California, USA, were made by glaciers.

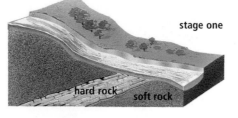

stage one

hard rock   soft rock

stage two

soft rock worn away

stage three

plunge pool

Lakes

Freshwater lakes, such as the Great Lakes in North America, are formed by glaciers or ice sheets. Other lakes, such as Lake Tanganyika in Africa, are made by earth fault movements.

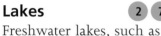

lake

Flood plains

Flat land alongside a river is called a flood plain. If the river overflows, it deposits sand and mud on the land. As the water drains away, this sediment forms fertile land known as alluvium.

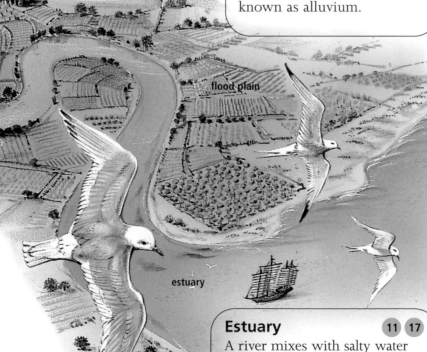

flood plain

estuary

Estuary

A river mixes with salty water from the sea to form an estuary, or harbour. A delta may form from sediment in the river.

QUESTIONS:
Deserts

Level 1

1. What 'D' is a sandy desert feature?
2. Which animal is used to carry people and goods in the desert?
3. Sand holds water. True or false?
4. What plant with spines can survive in a desert?
5. What 'B' is the home of a meerkat?

Level 2

6. Is a Tuareg a type of sand dune or a member of a desert tribe?
7. What type of sand dune forms when the wind blows in all directions?
8. What is a one-humped camel called?
9. What is the name for wind carrying away fine sand?
10. What is the slope of a sand dune called?
11. Wind blowing in two different directions creates which type of sand dune?
12. Is a hoodoo: a type of sand dune, a rock formation or a desert rodent?
13. In which desert would you find a Tuareg?

Level 3

14. What desert plant can be over 200 years old?
15. What 'F' is a kind of fox that lives in the desert?
16. What is a barchan?
17. What substance is formed by cemented sand and gravel?
18. What features of a camel help it survive in deserts?

Deserts

Deserts are dry areas of land with little rainfall or plant and animal life. The driest desert in the world is the Atacama desert in Chile, South America. Deserts may be hot, such as the Sahara in Africa, or cold, such as the Antarctic. Hot deserts can be cold at night because rocks lose their heat quickly and there is little humidity or vegetation to hold in heat.

hoodoo rock

Nomads 6 13
Nomads are people who move from place to place. The nomadic Tuareg tribe live in the Sahara desert in Africa.

Desert winds 9 12
The wind wears away rocks in deserts by deflation (carrying away fine sand) and abrasion (friction). These processes create arches, ridges, flat-topped mesas and pedestal rocks. They also create formations called hoodoo rocks, which look like giant mushrooms.

dromedary camel

Tuareg tribesman

Desert animals 5 15
Many desert animals, such as the fennec fox, are nocturnal (active at night). Others, such as the meerkat, live in burrows to keep themselves cool.

Caravan 2 8 18
The Tuaregs use 'caravans' of camels to carry people and goods. Dromedary (one-humped) camels can go without water for days. Their thick, padded feet can walk on hot sand without pain.

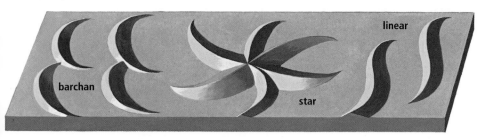

linear

barchan

star

Types of sand dune

A curved barchan dune forms when the wind blows in one direction. A star dune forms when the wind blows in all directions. A linear dune is formed when the wind blows in two different directions.

wind

slip face

Sand dune formation

Dunes, or heaps of sand, form as desert sand is moved and shifted by wind until it creates a slope, called a slip face. A dune's shape depends on the wind speed and direction. Sometimes sand dunes migrate, blown along by wind.

Soil

In deserts water seeps through sand, but can be trapped by soil and rock. Hard layers of cemented sand and gravel (calcrete) are found in many deserts.

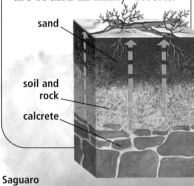
sand

soil and rock

calcrete

Cacti 4 14

Found in the deserts of North and South America, cacti are succulent plants that store water in their stems and branches to survive. Most cacti have spines instead of leaves. The Saguaro cactus can live for over 200 years and grow to 12m tall.

Saguaro cactus

QUESTIONS:
The poles

Level 1

1. On which continent is the South Pole?
2. The explorer Robert Scott reached the South Pole. True or false?
3. LIE CRAG can be rearranged to give the name of what polar feature?
4. Icebergs are lumps of ice that have broken away from glaciers. True or false?

Level 2

5. What is a hollow formed by melting blocks of ice called: a kettle hole or a sink hole?
6. How much of an iceberg is visible above the waterline?
7. Who was the first person to reach the South Pole?
8. Why do glaciers shift?
9. Today, most Inuit use dog sleds to travel over the Arctic ice. True or false?
10. What imaginary line runs between the two poles?
11. What is a moraine?
12. What language is spoken by the Inuit?
13. What 'P' is an item of clothing worn by Arctic people?

Level 3

14. Do the Inuit live near to the North or the South Pole?
15. In which year did a person reach the South Pole for the first time?
16. Near which pole are flat-topped tabular icebergs found?
17. When Scott and his crew fell into difficulties, how far would they have had to travel to safety?
18. What Arctic people live in Greenland?

The poles

The extreme north and south points of the world are called the poles. The polar regions of the Arctic in the north and Antarctica in the south are the coldest places on earth. At the poles themselves, the sun never sets for months in the summer, while in the winter there is complete darkness for several months.

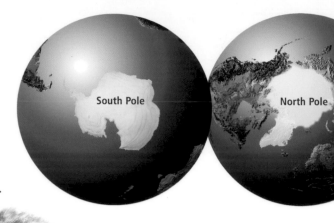

South Pole

North Pole

Native peoples 12 14 18

The Inuit people live in the Arctic regions of Siberia, Alaska, Canada and Greenland. They speak Inuktitut. Other native groups include the Kalaalit of Greenland and the Yupik of the Russian Federation.

North and South 1 10

The axis on which the earth turns runs between the North and South Poles. The North Pole is on the frozen seas of the Arctic ocean. The South Pole is on the continent of Antarctica.

Living in the Arctic 9 13

Arctic people were originally migrating hunters and fishermen, but most now live in modern communities. Parkas made of hide provided warmth, and dog sleds were used to travel across the ice. Snowmobiles are now used.

Scott 2 7 15 17

Robert Falcon Scott tried to become the first person to reach the South Pole. He got there on 17 January 1912, but Norwegian Roald Amundsen had already reached it on 14 December 1911. Scott and his crew starved to death in Antarctica, about 17km away from the supply depot.

traditional-style parka

dog sled

glacier

Glaciers ③ ⑤ ⑧ ⑪

Glaciers are formed when fallen snow packs together over many years and crystallizes into ice. Most glaciers are found in mountainous or polar regions. Glaciers shift over time due to the weight of the ice and gravity. A melting glacier may leave behind ridges of rock called moraines. Blocks of ice that melt may form a hollow called a kettle hole.

castle iceberg

Icebergs ④ ⑥ ⑯

Icebergs are lumps of floating ice that break away from glaciers in a process called calving. Nine-tenths of an iceberg is below water. Pinnacle, or castle, icebergs form in the Arctic. Flat-topped tabular icebergs form in the Antarctic.

QUESTIONS:
Africa

Level 1

1. Is Mount Kilimanjaro Africa's highest point?
2. The Sahara is the largest desert in the world. True or false?
3. Which 'N' in Africa is the longest river in the world?
4. Who built the pyramids: ancient Europeans, ancient Egyptians or ancient Americans?

Level 2

5. The Serengeti is a sandy desert. True or false?
6. Lake Tanganyika is the longest in the world. Is it also the deepest in Africa?
7. Where does the Nile flow to: the Mediterranean sea, Red sea or Atlantic ocean?
8. Is the Serengeti in Tanzania and Kenya or Botswana and South Africa?
9. What happens every year along the Nile: does the river dry up, stay the same or flood its banks?
10. How many blocks of stone make up the Great Pyramid: 23,000, 230,000 or 2,300,000?
11. What 'N' are people who live in the Sahara?
12. How many animals migrate in the Serengeti each year: almost 200,000, 2 million or 5 million?
13. Rearrange MAIN GOLF to name a bird that migrates to Lake Tanganyika.

Level 3

14. How long is Lake Tanganyika?
15. Name the highest point on Mount Kilimanjaro.
16. For which 'C' pharaoh was the Great Pyramid built?
17. What is a stratovolcano?
18. How large is the Sahara?

FIND THE ANSWER:

Africa

The African continent is the second largest in the world (Asia is the largest). It is a land with different habitats, including mountains, grasslands and deserts. Archaeologists believe that humans have lived in Africa for over 7 million years. Few people live in the Sahara, which makes up about a quarter of Africa.

Pyramids 4 10 16

The ancient Egyptians built pyramids as tombs for pharaohs and queens. Three pyramids were built at Giza, near Cairo. The Great Pyramid was built for the pharaoh Cheops. Workers used 2,300,000 stone blocks and built it in 20 years.

The Nile 3 7 9

The world's longest river is the Nile. It starts in mountains and flows downhill, north into the Mediterranean sea. It has two main branches: the White Nile and the Blue Nile. Every year, the Nile floods its banks and deposits rich soil that is ideal for farming.

Grassland migration 5 8 12

In Tanzania and Kenya, the grassland 'Serengeti' (meaning 'the place where the land moves on forever') is home to almost 2 million animals. These include elephants, wildebeest, giraffes and zebras. They go on a circular migration, travelling in search of fresh pastures.

Sahara 2 11 18

The Sahara is the largest desert in the world. It covers 9,000,000km^2. Few people live there, and most of them are nomads, which means they travel from place to place. They must carry all their food, and they rely on camels and sheep that travel with them for meat.

Lake Tanganyika 6 13 14

The longest lake in the world, at 670km, is Lake Tanganyika in the Great Rift Valley. It is also the deepest in Africa at 1,470m. The flamingo is one of the many birds that migrate to the lake.

pink flamingo

Kilimanjaro 1 15 17

Mount Kilimanjaro in Tanzania is a large, inactive stratovolcano – a volcano that is made of hardened lava and volcanic ash. Kilimanjaro is 5,895m high and has three summits. Kibo, which is Africa's highest peak, is the youngest of the three.

QUESTIONS:
The Middle East

Level 1

1. The Blue Mosque is in Istanbul. True or false?
2. Do Muslims make pilgrimages to Mecca?
3. Is the tallest hotel in the world in Dubai or Antarctica?
4. Minarets are tiny Islamic dancers. True or false?

Level 2

5. Diriyah was once the capital of which country: Saudi Arabia, Greece or Spain?
6. How many blue tiles are inside the Blue Mosque: over 200, over 2,000 or over 20,000?
7. Was the Blue Mosque completed in 3600BCE or 1616CE?
8. Was Diriyah destroyed by a flood or an Egyptian-led army?
9. Which is a servant in an Islamic mosque: the muezzin or the serf?
10. In which 'S' country was the Krak des Chevaliers built?
11. The Blue Mosque is also known as the Sultan Ahmed Mosque. True or false?
12. What is a caliph: an Islamic leader or Jewish leader?
13. What 'G' once covered the Dome of the Rock?

Level 3

14. Who ordered the building of the Dome of the Rock?
15. Mecca is in which country?
16. What does Krak des Chevaliers mean?
17. About how much higher than the Burj al-Arab will the Burj Dubai be?
18. When were the Crusades?

FIND THE ANSWER: The Middle East

Southwest Asia and parts of northern Africa make up the Middle East. The countries in this region include Egypt, Iran, Iraq, Israel, Lebanon, Saudi Arabia and Syria. Islam is one of the important religions in the region. Muslims who follow this religion study the Koran and believe that Muhammad is God's prophet.

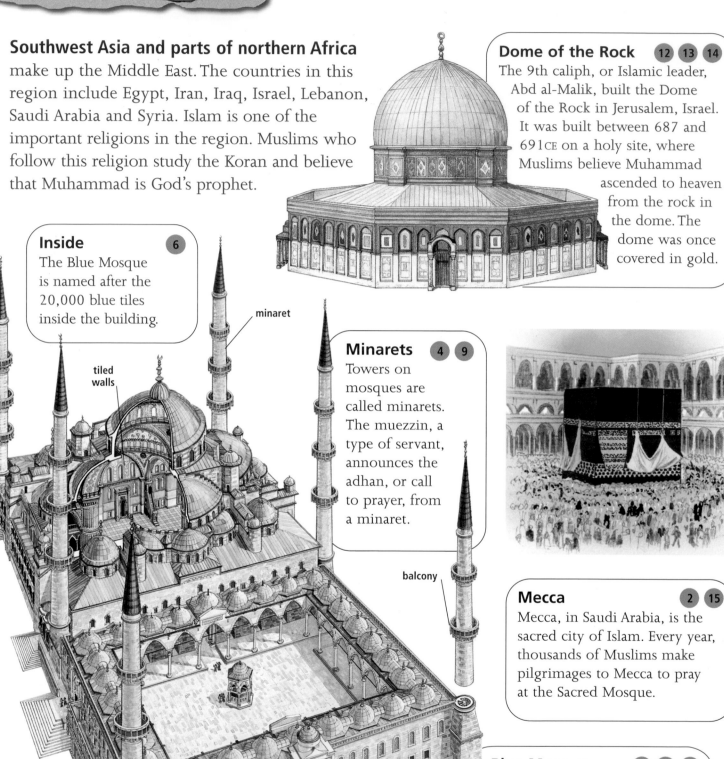

Dome of the Rock (12) (13) (14)
The 9th caliph, or Islamic leader, Abd al-Malik, built the Dome of the Rock in Jerusalem, Israel. It was built between 687 and 691CE on a holy site, where Muslims believe Muhammad ascended to heaven from the rock in the dome. The dome was once covered in gold.

Inside (6)
The Blue Mosque is named after the 20,000 blue tiles inside the building.

minaret

tiled walls

Minarets (4) (9)
Towers on mosques are called minarets. The muezzin, a type of servant, announces the adhan, or call to prayer, from a minaret.

balcony

Mecca (2) (15)
Mecca, in Saudi Arabia, is the sacred city of Islam. Every year, thousands of Muslims make pilgrimages to Mecca to pray at the Sacred Mosque.

Blue Mosque

Blue Mosque (1) (7) (11)
The Blue Mosque in Istanbul, Turkey, is also called Sultan Ahmed Mosque after Ahmed I. He had the mosque built between 1609 and 1616CE.

QUESTIONS:
Asia

Level 1

1. Mount Fuji is the tallest mountain in the world. True or false?
2. Is the Taj Mahal in India, Croatia or Spain?
3. In building the Taj Mahal, over 1,000 elephants were used to haul marble. True or false?
4. Mount Fuji in Japan is a dormant volcano. True or false?

Level 2

5. Shah Jahan built the Taj Mahal for his favourite daughter. True or false?
6. What 'T' does 'wat' mean?
7. Where is the Potala Palace: Japan, Malaysia or Tibet?
8. Which building was built in Kuala Lumpur, the capital of Malaysia: Angkor Wat, the Great Wall or Petronas Twin Towers?
9. How many people climb Mount Fuji's summit to pray each year: 5,000, 50,000 or 500,000?
10. When was Angkor Wat built: in the 11th, 12th or 13th century?
11. The Sarawak Chamber is the world's largest cave chamber. True or false?
12. Name one of the first two people to reach the summit of Mount Everest.
13. In which dynasty did the building of the Great Wall begin?

Level 3

14. For how many years did the Dalai Lamas use the Potala Palace as their winter home?
15. Where can the Sarawak Chamber be found?
16. If Mount Fuji is 3,776m high, how much higher is Everest than Mount Fuji?
17. If the Petronas Twin Towers' skybridge is 170m high, how much taller are the towers themselves?
18. How long is the Great Wall of China?

Saudi Arabia

Diriyah was the capital of Saudi Arabia until 1818. At that time an Egyptian-led army destroyed the buildings and palm groves to make Diriyah uninhabitable.

Syria

Krak des Chevaliers ('Fortress of the Knights'), in Syria, is a castle built between the 11th and 13th centuries. It was used during the Crusades, a series of wars between European Christians and Arab Muslims.

Dubai

Dubai is one of the seven small countries that make up the United Arab Emirates. The Burj al-Arab, built in the shape of a sail, is the tallest hotel in the world at 321m. When completed in 2008, the Burj Dubai will be the tallest skyscraper in the world at about 810m high.

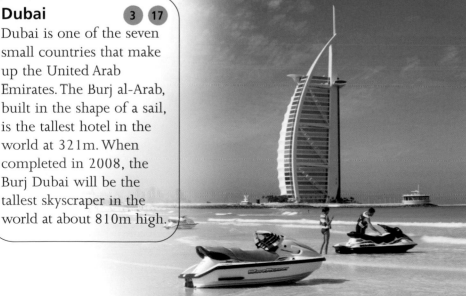

FIND THE ANSWER:  Asia

Mount Fuji

Asia is the largest of Earth's seven continents. It is divided from Europe by the Ural mountains along Asia's western borders. Asia contains the world's two most populated countries: China and India.

Mount Fuji 4 9
Japan's Mount Fuji is the country's highest peak, at 3,776m. It is a dormant volcano that last erupted in 1708. Mount Fuji is sacred to the Japanese — over 500,000 people climb it every year to pray on its summit.

Potala Palace

Tibet 7 14
The Potala Palace in Lhasa, Tibet, was built in the Himalayas on a hill with a sacred cave. It was the winter home of the Dalai Lama from 1648 until 1959, when Tibet was occupied by China. Unlike many other Tibetan religious buildings, the palace was not destroyed.

Taj Mahal 2 3 5
When his wife died in 1631, Shah Jahan employed over 20,000 workmen to build the Taj Mahal, near Agra, India, in her memory. Over 1,000 elephants were used to haul marble from far-away quarries.

Himalayas 1 12 16
The tallest mountain in the world is Mount Everest, in the Himalayas, at 8,848m high. Since Edmund Hillary and Tenzing Norgay first reached the top in 1953, other people have climbed Everest.

mountain climbers

Big cave 11 15
Sarawak Chamber, or Lubang Nasib Bagus, is the world's largest cave chamber, at around 70m high, 700m long and 300m wide. It is in Borneo, Malaysia.

Petronas Twin Towers

8 17

Kuala Lumpur, the capital of Malaysia, is home to the Petronas Twin Towers. It is one of the tallest buildings in the world, at 452m high. There are 88 storeys in each of the towers. A double-decker skybridge, which weighs about 750 tonnes, joins the two towers on the 41st and 42nd floors.

fort

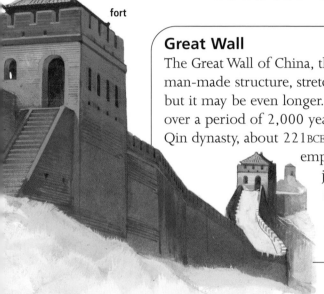

Great Wall

13 18

The Great Wall of China, the world's longest man-made structure, stretches for 6,300km, but it may be even longer. The wall was built over a period of 2,000 years. Work began in the Qin dynasty, about 221BCE, when China's first emperor ordered the joining together of several existing walls, and continued until the early 17th century.

Angkor Wat

6 10

More than 100 wats, or temples, were built at Angkor Wat, Cambodia, between the 9th and 13th centuries. The largest is Angkor Wat, built for the Hindu god Vishnu in the 12th century.

Angkor Wat

QUESTIONS:
Europe

Level 1

1. Where is Red Square: Paris or Moscow?
2. Does the Channel Tunnel go under or over the English Channel?
3. The Leaning Tower of Pisa was designed to lean. True or false?
4. How many tracks are in the Channel Tunnel: one, two or three?

Level 2

5. The Eisriesenwelt ice cave is the largest ice cave in the world. True or false?
6. Is the Guggenheim Museum in Paris, Bilbao or Salzburg?
7. Was the Eiffel Tower built in Paris to celebrate Bastille Day, the end of the Hundred Years' War or the Universal Exhibition?
8. Who commissioned the building of St Basil's Cathedral: Ivan the Terrible, Rasputin or Catherine the Great?
9. What does 'Eisriesenwelt' mean: tiny ice world, giant cave or giant ice world?
10. Which famous Alpine mountain is pyramid-shaped?
11. What features appear on the top of St Basil's Cathedral?
12. How high is Mont Blanc: 4,808m, 5,808m or 7,808m?
13. What is a campanile: a bell tower, a dome or a steeple?
14. How much does the Eiffel Tower's structure weigh: about 5,330, 7,300 or 10,300 tonnes?

Level 3

15. How long is the Channel Tunnel?
16. How long did it take to construct the Leaning Tower of Pisa?
17. What forms the bottom of the Eiffel Tower?
18. What material covers the curved panels in the Guggenheim Museum?

Europe is the world's second-smallest continent.

It lies west of the Ural mountains, which divide it from Asia. Europe consists of many countries and several microstates. Despite being small, these microstates are independent states. Vatican City is the smallest microstate in the world. This tiny state lies within Rome, Italy.

onion dome

bell tower

Pisa   3 13 16

The Leaning Tower of Pisa, in Pisa, Italy, is the city's campanile, or bell tower. The tower began to lean during its construction, which began in 1173 and ended in 1370. There are 294 steps to the bell tower, which has seven bells.

Moscow   1 8 11

Ivan the Terrible ordered the building of St Basil's Cathedral in Moscow's Red Square. The cathedral was built between 1555 and 1561. Each of the towers has a unique onion-shaped dome.

Channel Tunnel   2 4 15

Eleven giant tunnel-boring machines were used to dig the Channel Tunnel under the English Channel, between Britain and France. The tunnel was completed in 1994 after seven years' work. It is 50km long, with 39km running under the sea. The tunnel contains three tracks: two tracks for trains and one that is used as a service track.

Eiffel Tower (7) (14) (17)

The Eiffel Tower, in Paris, France, was built in 1889 for the Universal Exhibition. Its structure weighs about 7,300 tonnes. It is 324m high and stands on a base held by four pillars.

Modern museum (6) (18)

The architect Frank O. Gehry designed the Guggenheim Museum in Bilbao, Spain. It opened in 1997. The curved panels are covered in titanium.

The Alps (10) (12)

This mountain range is in Germany, Austria, France, Italy, Liechtenstein, Slovenia and Switzerland. Mont Blanc is the highest peak at 4,808m high. The Matterhorn is known for its pyramid shape.

Ice cave (5) (9)

The largest ice cave in the world is the Eisriesenwelt, or 'giant ice world', near Salzburg, Austria. It is part of a cave system that is about 42km in length, with 1km of the cave covered in ice. Although local hunters knew about the cave, Eisriesenwelt was officially 'discovered' in 1879 by Anton Posselt.

QUESTIONS:
North America

Level 1

1. The Statue of Liberty is in Washington, D.C. True or false?
2. How many falls is Niagara Falls made up of?
3. The Grand Canyon is in Arizona. True or false?
4. Which is the world's tallest tree: the coast redwood or the Scots pine?
5. Does the Golden Gate Bridge cross San Francisco Bay?

Level 2

6. Which US president's face is not carved on Mount Rushmore: Lincoln, Kennedy or Theodore Roosevelt?
7. How many main sections make up the Grand Canyon: three, five or seven?
8. How many faces of US presidents were carved into Mount Rushmore: three, four or five?
9. How high is the Statue of Liberty: 82.5m, 93.5m or 95m?
10. How old is the oldest giant sequoia: 1,000, 3,200 or 5,500 years old?
11. Do the vertical ribs on the Golden Gate Bridge stand out on a sunny day?
12. What 'S' on the Statue of Liberty's crown represent the world's seven seas and continents?
13. Rearrange COWES TOAST to name where redwoods grow.

Level 3

14. Why do the towers on the Golden Gate Bridge appear taller than they are?
15. What changes about the plants you can find as you go further down the Grand Canyon?
16. How much wider is Horseshoe Falls than American Falls?
17. How long did it take to carve the monument at Mount Rushmore?
18. How long is the Golden Gate Bridge?

North America

The continent of **North America** includes Greenland and dozens of small islands in the Caribbean, as well as the United States, Canada, Mexico and the Central American countries. The name 'America' is probably in honour of Amerigo Vespucci, who first wrote about it as a separate 'New World'.

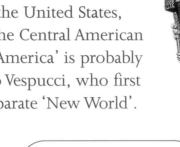

Statue of Liberty

Liberty ① ⑨ ⑫

The 93.5m-tall Statue of Liberty, in New York Harbor, was a gift from France in 1884. It was designed by Gustave Eiffel. The seven spikes on the crown represent the world's seven seas and continents.

Redwoods ④ ⑩ ⑬

The USA's West Coast is home to impressive redwood trees. The coast redwood is the tallest tree, at 112m high. The oldest giant sequoia is 3,200 years old.

Golden Gate Bridge ⑤ ⑪ ⑭ ⑱

The San Francisco Bay in California can be crossed by the Golden Gate Bridge, which is 2,737m long. The longest span between the main posts is 1,280m. The towers are smaller at the top than the base to make the towers appear taller. The vertical ribs stand out on a sunny day when the sun's rays light the bridge.

coast redwood

Grand Canyon

3 7 15

There are three main sections of the Grand Canyon in Arizona: the South Rim, the North Rim and the Inner Canyon. Each has a different climate and plant life. Plants become shorter and sparser as they grow further down the canyon, and desert scrub lives on the canyon floor.

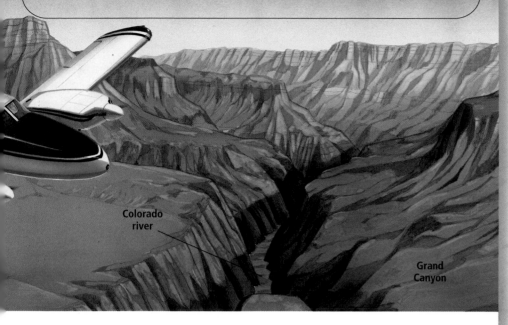

Colorado river

Grand Canyon

Niagara Falls

2 16

There are three falls that together form Niagara Falls: American Falls (323m wide), Horseshoe Falls (792m wide) and Bridal Veils Falls (17m wide). The falls and Niagara river flow between Ontario, Canada, and New York, USA.

Mount Rushmore

6 8 17

The faces of four US presidents – Lincoln, Jefferson, Washington and Roosevelt – were carved into Mount Rushmore, South Dakota, by Gutzon Borglum and 400 workers from 1927 to 1941.

George Washington

Thomas Jefferson

Theodore Roosevelt

Abraham Lincoln

QUESTIONS:
South America

Level 1

1. Did the Incas build Machu Picchu in the Andes?
2. Angel Falls is the highest waterfall in the world. True or false?
3. The Amazon is the world's largest river, but not the longest. True or false?
4. Which city is famous for its beaches: Lima or Rio de Janeiro?
5. The llama is a kind of wild cat. True or false?

Level 2

6. Can a statue of Jesus be found at the top or base of Sugar Loaf Mountain in Brazil?
7. What percentage of the earth's oxygen does the Amazon rainforest produce: two per cent, ten per cent or 20 per cent?
8. Angel Falls is named after which American pilot?
9. Machu Picchu was built in which century: the 13th, 14th or 15th?
10. Is Lake Titicaca a freshwater lake or saltwater lake?
11. How many structures made up Machu Picchu: about ten, 100 or 200?
12. What 'A' in Argentina has fine fleece?
13. In the Quechua language, does Machu Picchu mean high mountain, old mountain or young mountain?
14. Can the source for the Amazon river be found in the Andes, Himalayas or Rocky mountains?

Level 3

15. How long is the Amazon river?
16. Where can most of the remaining rainforests be found?
17. What are the artificial islands in Lake Titicaca made from?
18. What material did the Incas use to build their structures?

South America

The continent of South America is divided into 12 countries, the largest of which is Brazil. It is joined to North America by the Isthmus of Panama, a tiny strip of land. As well as Spanish and Portuguese, there are many native languages spoken in South America, such as Aymara, Guarani and Quechua – the language used by the Incas.

tropical rainforest

Rainforest 7 16

Over half of the world's remaining rainforests can be found in the Amazon basin. The Amazon rainforest contains more species than any other rainforest. It also produces around 20 per cent of the Earth's oxygen.

Rio 4 6

Rio de Janeiro, Brazil, is set at the foot of Sugar Loaf Mountain. It is famous for its Copacabana beach and the statue of Jesus, known as Christ the Redeemer. The statue is at the top of the mountain.

Copacabana beach

Amazon 3 14 15

The Amazon river is the world's largest river by volume of water. At 6,387km, it is the second longest river, after the Nile. The source of the Amazon is a stream on Nevado Mismi, high in the Andes mountains.

Machu Picchu 1 9 13

In about 1450, the Incas built Machu Picchu in the Andes in Peru, on a site that was probably a sacred place. Machu Picchu means 'Old Mountain' in the Quechua language. Its ruins were rediscovered by Hiram Bingham in about 1911.

Angel Falls 2 8

The world's highest waterfall, at 979m high, is Angel Falls in Venezuela. It is 15 times higher than Niagara Falls. It is named after James Crawford Angel, an American pilot who flew over the falls in 1933.

Lake Titicaca  10 17

South America's largest freshwater lake is Lake Titicaca. It lies in the Andes of Peru and Bolivia. The Uros are people who live on artificial islands in the lake. They make them from totora reeds that grow in the lake, and they last about 30 years.

the Andes

grassland

Pampas 5 12

The Argentinian pampas extends from the Atlantic Ocean to the Andes. Llamas graze the grassland. The Incas used this camelid for its wool and meat. Its cousin, the alpaca, has finer fleece.

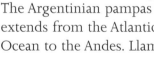

Structure 11 18

The Incas built Machu Picchu using ashlar blocks – polished, rectangular stones. The city had about 200 structures, including temples to the Sun god, Inti.

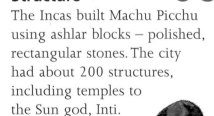

remains of Inca structure

QUESTIONS: Australia and Oceania

Level 1

1. Is Sydney Australia's largest city or one of its smaller cities?
2. Easter Island (or Rapa Nui) is home to statues carved by Polynesian settlers. True or false?
3. Does the kangaroo live in Australia?
4. Road trains are really trucks that pull trailers. True or false?

Level 2

5. Uluru in Australia is also called Ayers Rock. True or false?
6. How many statues are there on Easter Island (or Rapa Nui): six, 60 or 600?
7. Uluru is sacred to: British convicts, Australian Aborigines or marsupials?
8. What is fitted to the front of an Australian road train: a roo bar, bull bar or marsupial bar?
9. What can be found on New Zealand's North Island: volcanoes, geysers, hot springs or all of the above?
10. How long was the longest road train: 13 trailers, 33 trailers or 113 trailers?
11. What 'F' are the Naracoorte Caves in Australia known for?
12. Was Sydney founded as a new colony for sheep farmers, for sugar plantations or as a convict settlement?

Level 3

13. What is the name for the Easter Island (or Rapa Nui) statues?
14. What 'M' is a type of animal group, with the largest one living in Australia?
15. In what year did palaeontologists first visit Victoria Fossil Cave, one of the Naracoorte Caves in Australia?
16. Where was the Sydney Opera House built?
17. What is the Maori name for New Zealand?
18. How far is Easter Island from South America?

FIND THE ANSWER: Australia and Oceania

The continent of Australia is an island surrounded by the Pacific and Indian oceans. It is the flattest continent and one of the driest. Australia is also the name of the country on the island. Oceania is a term used for a region of over 25,000 islands, including Australia, New Zealand and the Polynesian islands, found in the Pacific ocean and nearby seas.

Sydney 1 12 16
Captain Arthur Philip founded Sydney, Australia's largest city, in 1788 as a British convict settlement. It was built around Sydney Harbour. The famous Sydney Opera House was built on Bennelong Point in the harbour.

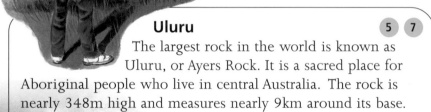

Uluru 5 7
The largest rock in the world is known as Uluru, or Ayers Rock. It is a sacred place for Aboriginal people who live in central Australia. The rock is nearly 348m high and measures nearly 9km around its base.

Hot springs 9 17
New Zealand, called Aotearoa by the native Maori people, is made up of two islands: North Island and South Island. They lie on the edge of the Pacific Plate and the Indo-Australian plate. The area around Rotorua, in the North Island, has active volcanoes, geysers, hot springs and mud pools.

hot springs

Naracoorte caves 11 15
The small town of Naracoorte, in South Australia, has a series of 26 limestone caves. In 1969, paleontologists discovered tens of thousands of fossils inside Victoria Fossil Cave. Holes had opened in the top of the caves, which are weak because they are just below ground. The fossils are from animals that fell into the holes and were trapped.

Marsupials 3 14

Animals in the marsupial group give birth to young that are underdeveloped and are often carried in their mother's pouches. The largest marsupial, the kangaroo, lives in Australia, as do koalas and the sugar glider, a possum.

koala

sugar glider

Easter Island 2 6 13 18

Chile's Easter Island, or Rapa Nui, is a Polynesian island in the Pacific Ocean, 4,000km from South America. Early Polynesian settlers carved 600 statues, or moai, on the island about 1,000 years ago.

Easter Island statues

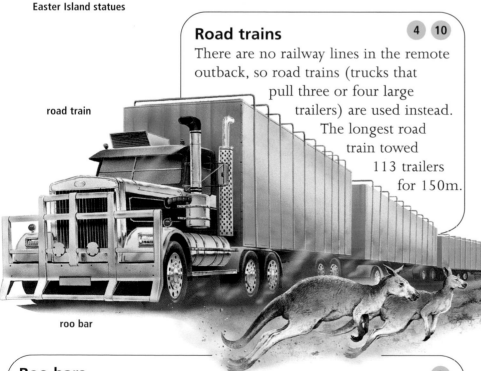

Road trains 4 10

There are no railway lines in the remote outback, so road trains (trucks that pull three or four large trailers) are used instead. The longest road train towed 113 trailers for 150m.

road train

roo bar

Roo bars 8

Because there are so many vehicle collisions with kangaroos in Australia, a 'roo' bar is fitted to the front of a road train to protect the vehicle and driver. In areas where cattle roam, a 'bull' bar is used.

QUESTIONS:
Antarctica

Level 1

1. Penguins live in Antarctica. True or false?
2. How do people travel on the ice in Antarctica: by skidoo, car or bus?
3. There are permanent research stations in Antarctica. True or false?
4. What are groups of elephant seals called: harems or groupies?
5. A penguin is a bird. True or false?

Level 2

6. How many scientists live and work in Anatarctica during the summer: 400, 4,000, or 40,000?
7. What does the Global Positioning System link to: the internet, mobile phones or satellites?
8. Is the Lambert Glacier Antarctica's largest, smallest or youngest glacier?
9. How deep can an elephant seal dive: down to 15m, 150m or 1,500m?
10. Why do whales migrate north: to breed, to feed or to follow ships?
11. When do whales migrate south: in the spring, summer, autumn or winter?
12. What is a Dornier 228: a plane, skidoo or bulldozer?
13. Ranulph Fiennes and Mike Stroud pulled their own sledges as they crossed Antarctica in 1993. True or false?

Level 3

14. What are rookeries?
15. What is the name of the earth's most southern point?
16. Which vehicle has tracks like a bulldozer?
17. What might a beachmaster have in his harem?
18. Why are special tents used by scientists?

FIND THE ANSWER: Antarctica

Antarctica measures 14 million km², almost one-and-a-half times the size of the USA. Its landscape is made up of only 2 per cent barren rock – the remaining 98 per cent is ice. It is the coldest, windiest and driest continent in the world. No one lives there all year round, but scientists travel there to study, and they live in specially equipped research stations.

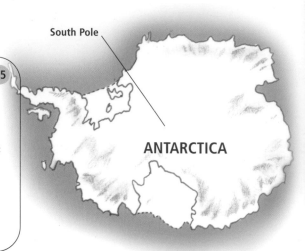

South Pole

ANTARCTICA

South Pole `15`
The South Pole on Antarctica is the Earth's most southern point. The ice cap is always shifting, so the South Pole moves a little every year.

Whales `10` `11`
Antarctic whales, such as the sperm whale, minke and humpback, migrate to the southern oceans for the summer to feed on swarms of shrimp-like krill. Then they travel north to breed.

minke whale

Transport `2` `12` `16`
The Dornier 228 plane is used to carry passengers and cargo. Land travel is by skidoo or the Hagglund – it has tracks like a bulldozer.

Dornier 228

POLAR 2 I.

Explorers `13`
Roald Amundsen was the first person to reach the South Pole, but in 1993 Ranulph Fiennes and Mike Stroud made the first unsupported walk across Antarctica, each pulling a 225kg sledge.

Penguins `1` `5` `14`
Antarctica's penguins include the emperor, adélie and gentoo. Penguins do not fly but they are good swimmers and can leap to avoid predators. The birds breed in large colonies called rookeries.

Scientists `3` `6`
Permanent and summer research stations are run in Antarctica by 27 different nations. During the summer, about 4,000 scientists live and work there. Fewer than 1,000 people live in Antarctica during the winter.

Glaciers (8)

Lambert Glacier is the largest glacier in the world at 80km wide and 500km long. Fisher Massif is a 1,700m-high nunatak, or mountain, that runs along the western side of the glacier.

Seals (4) (9) (17)

Elephant seals are powerful swimmers and can dive down to 1,500m. They live in breeding groups called harems. Male bulls fight over breeding rights. The winner, the beachmaster, may have up to 50 cows in his harem.

Scientific study (7) (18)

The Global Positioning System (GPS) links to satellites above the Earth to give scientists an accurate reading of their position in Antarctica. Special tents are made to resist the strong icy winds that can reach 145km/h.

QUESTIONS:
Where in the world?

Level 1

1. What city is nicknamed 'The Big Apple'?
2. In which country is Rio de Janeiro?
3. What city is the biggest tourist destination in Europe?

Level 2

4. What famous event is held in Rio de Janeiro every year?
5. What did Mumbai, India, used to be called?
6. What is the oldest city in South Africa?
7. What is the biggest island in Japan?

Level 3

8. What percentage of Japan's population lives in its capital city?
9. What is a person who lives in Sydney, Australia, called?
10. Where is the biggest underground train network in the world?

Where in the world?

Cities are large settlements, bigger or more populated than towns and villages. Most cities grew from small farming or hunting settlements, although others are planned from scratch. The world's most famous cities can be larger or richer than some nations – if New York were a nation, it would be the 16th richest in the world.

Tokyo 7 8 10
Tokyo is the capital city of Japan, 'The Land of the Rising Sun'. It is on the largest of Japan's four main islands, Honshu, and is home to around 10 per cent of the country's population. Tokyo has the biggest underground train network anywhere in the world.

New York 1
New York, 'The Big Apple', is the most populated city and the financial heart of the USA, although Washington, D.C. is the capital.

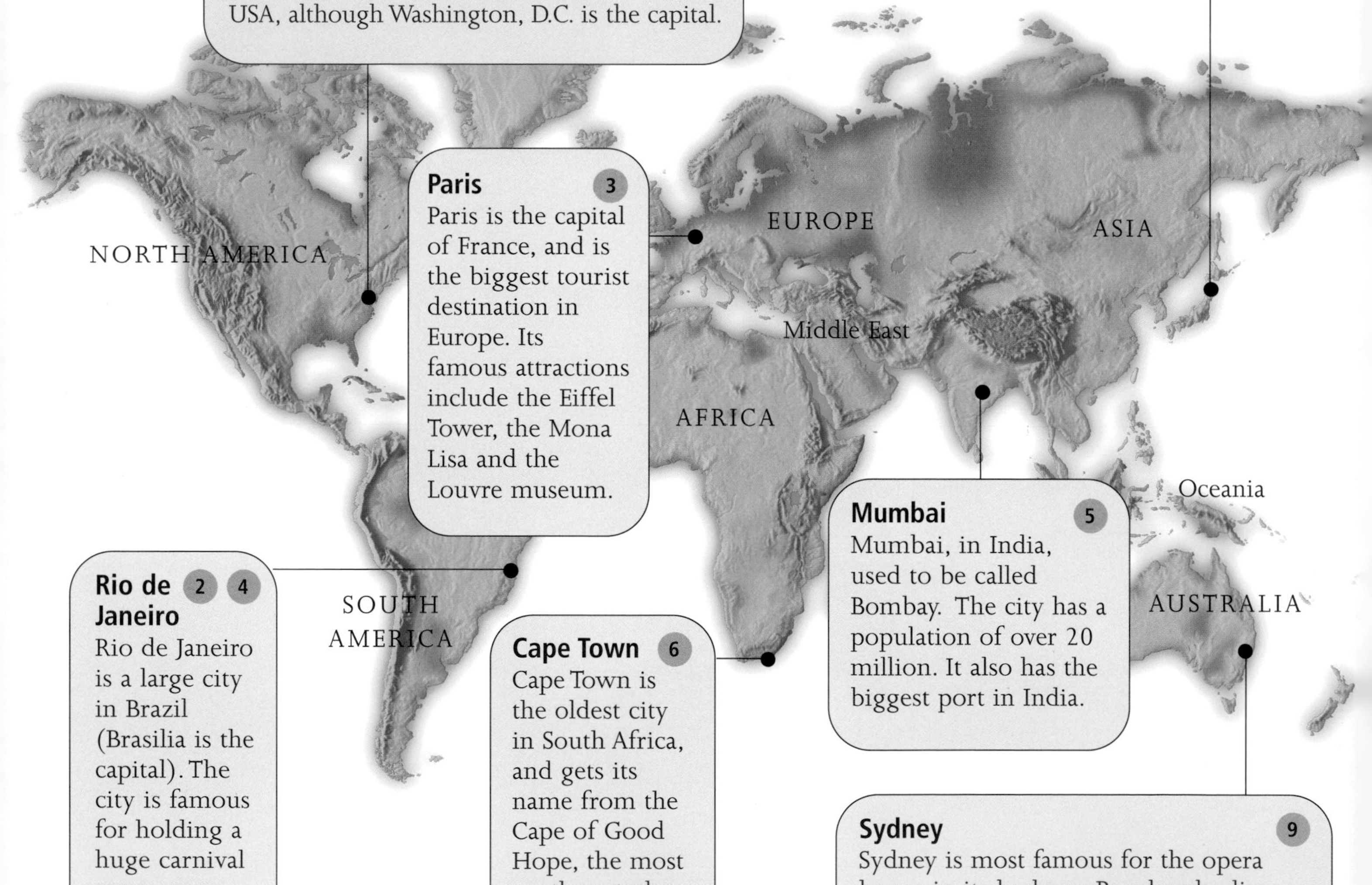

Paris 3
Paris is the capital of France, and is the biggest tourist destination in Europe. Its famous attractions include the Eiffel Tower, the Mona Lisa and the Louvre museum.

NORTH AMERICA

EUROPE

ASIA

Middle East

AFRICA

Rio de Janeiro 2 4
Rio de Janeiro is a large city in Brazil (Brasilia is the capital). The city is famous for holding a huge carnival every year.

SOUTH AMERICA

Cape Town 6
Cape Town is the oldest city in South Africa, and gets its name from the Cape of Good Hope, the most southwesterly point of Africa.

Mumbai 5
Mumbai, in India, used to be called Bombay. The city has a population of over 20 million. It also has the biggest port in India.

Oceania

AUSTRALIA

Sydney 9
Sydney is most famous for the opera house in its harbour. People who live in Sydney are known as 'Sydneysiders'.

Answers 1) New York, USA **2)** Brazil **3)** Paris, France **4)** A carnival **5)** Bombay **6)** Cape Town **7)** Honshu **8)** 10% **9)** Sydneysiders **10)** Tokyo, Japan

QUIZ THREE
Science and inventions

QUESTIONS: Exploring space

Level 1

1. The first living creature in space was a mouse. True or false?
2. Who was the first person on the Moon: Neil Armstrong, Nelly Armstrong or Norman Armstrong?
3. ENVISION OUT can be rearranged to give the name of what group of republics?
4. What 'S' is an object that orbits Earth?

Level 2

5. What 'L' was the name of the first living creature in space?
6. What 'S' was the first artificial satellite?
7. AN AIR RIG GUY can be rearranged to give the name of what astronaut, the first person to go into space?
8. In which year did people first walk on the Moon: 1959, 1969 or 1979?
9. In which year did a person first go into space: 1941, 1951 or 1961?
10. Who said 'That's one small step for man, one giant leap for mankind'?
11. VAN OR RULER can be rearranged to give the name of what vehicle used on the surface of the moon?
12. For how long did the first person to go into space stay there: 89 minutes, 89 hours or 89 days?

Level 3

13. Which was the last *Apollo* mission to land people on the Moon?
14. In what year did it reach the Moon?
15. What were Soviet astronauts called?
16. What 'V' was the first manned spacecraft?
17. What was launched on 12 April 1981?
18. Where is the Baikonur Cosmodrome: in Kazakhstan, Ukraine or the Russian Federation?

FIND THE ANSWER: Exploring space

Sputnik

It seems strange to think that 50 years ago no one had been into space. Nowadays, an International Space Station constantly circles the Earth, manned by a crew of people from different countries. The history of space flight has happened within the lifetimes of many people alive today. It is an exciting story – and one that is far from being over.

Laika ① ⑤ 18
The first living thing to enter space was Laika the dog. Laika was launched in 1957 aboard the satellite *Sputnik 2*, from Baikonur Cosmodrome in Kazakhstan.

Laika the dog

Sputnik ③ ④ ⑥
Sputnik 1 was the world's first-ever man-made satellite (an object travelling around Earth). It was launched from Kazakhstan on 4 October 1957 by a group of republics called the Soviet Union.

Moon landing ② ⑧ 10
In 1969, Neil Armstrong of the US mission *Apollo 11* became the first person to walk on the Moon, with the famous words 'That's one small step for man, one giant leap for mankind'.

Yuri Gagarin

rocket boosters

shuttle

USA

Man in space ⑦ ⑨ 12 16
On 12 April 1961, Yuri Gagarin became the first person ever to travel into space, aboard the spacecraft *Vostock 1*. A pilot from the Soviet Air Force, he travelled around the Earth for 89 minutes.

space shuttle launch

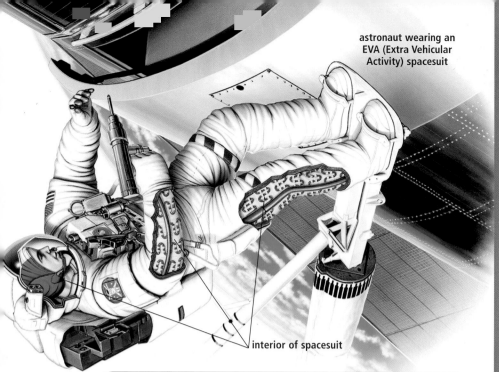

astronaut wearing an
EVA (Extra Vehicular
Activity) spacesuit

interior of spacesuit

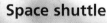
external tank

Spacesuits (15)

Spacesuits are designed to keep people alive in space. At first, they were worn by astronauts and cosmonauts (Soviet astronauts) inside their spacecraft. Nowadays, they are mainly used for operating outside in space itself – making repairs to a space shuttle, for instance.

Moon missions (11) (13) (14)

In total, Americans have made six successful missions to the Moon. The fourth, *Apollo 15*, carried a vehicle called a lunar rover to drive astronauts around on the surface. The last manned mission was *Apollo 17*, which landed on 7 December 1972. Since then, no one has visited the Moon.

Space shuttle (17)

Early missions into space used massive, expensive rockets, which could only be used once. On 5 January 1972, the American government announced it was going to develop a reusable spacecraft. The result was the space shuttle, which first launched on 12 April 1981. Since then, there have been over 100 launches.

QUESTIONS:
Solar System

Level 1

1. Which planet do people live on?
2. How many main planets are in the Solar System: five, eight or 15?
3. MY CURER can be rearranged to give the name of what planet?

Level 2

4. On the part of a planet facing away from the Sun, is it night or day?
5. How many planets in our Solar System have names beginning with the letter 'M'?
6. Which planet is the nearest to the Sun?
7. A GANG SITS can be rearranged to give the name of what group of large planets?
8. Which are the four rocky planets?
9. The Sun is a star. True or false?
10. Are any planets in the Solar System bigger than the Sun?
11. Did the planets form at around the same time as the Sun or long before?
12. Which 'S' is a planet made mostly of hydrogen and helium?
13. How long does the Earth take to circle the Sun: a day, a month or a year?
14. What 'O' is the path planets take around the Sun?
15. Which takes longer to circle the Sun: Earth or Pluto?
16. How many planets in the Solar System have oceans of water?

Level 3

17. What 'N' is a swirling cloud of particles from which planets form?
18. Which is farther from the Sun: Uranus or Saturn?
19. Which is larger: Earth or Mars?

The Solar System is the group of planets, including Earth, that circle the Sun. Some of these planets are smaller than Earth and others are many times larger. The Solar System has existed for around 4,600 million years, first appearing about 10,400 million years after the 'Big Bang' that began the Universe.

Neptune

Uranus

(Pluto)

The planets   **2 3 5 6 18**

There are eight main planets in the Solar System. The closest to the Sun is Mercury, followed by Venus, Earth, Mars, Jupiter, Saturn, Uranus and Neptune. Pluto used to be known as a planet, but in 2006 it was reclassified as a dwarf planet.

Jupiter

Venus

Mars

Earth

Mercury

Saturn

The Sun   **9 10**
The Sun is a star, far bigger than any of the planets. It is 1,392,000km wide and more than a million times bigger than Earth. For a star, it is relatively small.

Gas giants   **7 12**
Jupiter, Saturn, Uranus and Neptune are called the gas giants. Their small, rocky cores are surrounded by thick gases, mostly hydrogen and helium.

The smaller planets   **8 19**
The smaller planets are Mercury, Venus, Earth and Mars. All of them are rocky planets with solid surfaces. Earth is the largest of this group.

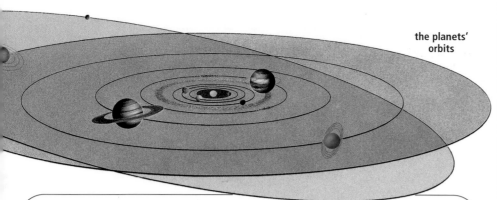

the planets' orbits

Orbits

All of the planets orbit the Sun (travel in a circle around it). The closer the planet is to the Sun, the shorter its orbit. Earth's orbit takes exactly a year. The dwarf planet Pluto takes more than 248 years to complete its orbit.

nebula

gas and dust particles drawn together

Planets forming

The planets formed at about the same time as the Sun, from a nebula (a swirling cloud of gas and dust particles). Over time, the particles of the nebula slowly gathered together to form planets, drawn together by the force of gravity.

newly formed planet

The Earth

People live on the planet Earth, the only one known to support life. It is the fifth largest in the Solar System, and the only one with oceans of water. As well as circling the sun once a year, Earth spins round once every 24 hours. It is day on the part of Earth facing the Sun, and night on the part facing away.

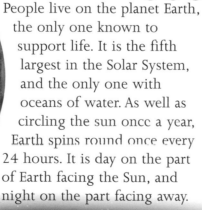

surface of the Earth

QUESTIONS:
Volcanoes and earthquakes

Level 1

1. Is the surface of the Earth made of solid or liquid rock?
2. What is another name for the Earth's surface: the skin, crust or coat?
3. RUIN POET can be rearranged to give what word for a volcano exploding?
4. A seismologist is a kind of earthquake. True or false?

Level 2

5. What 'R' is the scale used to measure the strength of earthquakes?
6. Which are thicker: continental plates or oceanic plates?
7. Are most earthquakes strong enough to destroy buildings?
8. How thick is the Earth's mantle: 290km or 2,900km?
9. Do ridges form where plates move together or where they move apart?
10. Earthquakes are common where plates slide past one another. True or false?
11. Japan is situated where two plates meet. True or false?
12. What 'L' is the molten rock released by a volcanic eruption?
13. What 'F' is the force produced by plates sliding past each other?
14. CUBOID NUTS can be rearranged to give the name of which kind of plate movement?
15. Volcanoes may occur where two plates are moving apart. True or false?

Level 3

16. What is the most common substance in the Earth's core?
17. Which makes up a greater proportion of the Earth: the crust or mantle?
18. On which plate do volcanoes occur when an oceanic plate and a continental plate meet?

Volcanoes and earthquakes

volcano erupting

The Earth's crust is in constant motion. Volcanoes and earthquakes arise as sections of crust ('plates') push together or pull apart. Volcanoes and earthquakes are more common in certain parts of the world. By monitoring ground vibrations ('seismic activity'), scientists can sometimes predict a massive earthquake or volcanic eruption and warn people.

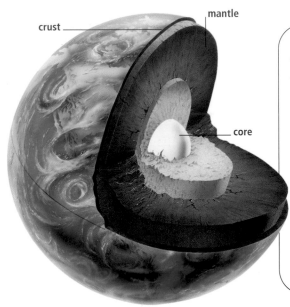

crust
mantle
core

Earth 1 2 8 16 17
The solid surface layer of the Earth is known as the crust, and ranges from 5km to 80km in thickness. Beneath the crust is the mantle, which is 2,900km thick and made up of molten rock. The centre of the Earth, the core, is mostly made of iron. It has a liquid outer core and a solid inner core, and is around 4,500°C hot.

Volcanoes 3 12 18
Volcanoes form when molten rock is pushed up through the crust. When subduction occurs, the oceanic plate melts underground, creating a vast supply of molten rock. The rock is then released as lava in a volcanic eruption.

Moving apart 9 15
When plates move apart, ridges form. Often volcanoes occur there as molten rock moves up from the mantle to fill the gaps.

Subduction 6 14
When continental and oceanic plates move towards each other, the oceanic plate often slides underneath the thicker continental plate – this is called subduction.

oceanic plate

plates moving apart

plate melting

effects of an earthquake

moving plates

Earthquakes   4   5   7   11

Earthquakes are most common where two plates meet, such as under Japan. Most earthquakes are mild, but some can destroy buildings. Special scientists called seismologists can measure the strength of earthquakes, using the Richter Scale.

Friction   10   13

Earthquakes are the result of frictional forces as two plates move side by side. The plates judder as they slide past each other, and each judder causes an earthquake.

lava

volcanoes

molten rock

continental plate

QUESTIONS:
Rocks and minerals

Level 1
1. Emeralds are purple. True or false?
2. What colour are rubies?
3. Gold is a metal. True or false?
4. How many sides does a hexagon have: one, three or six?

Level 2
5. TEARING can be rearranged to give the name of what igneous rock, often used for building?
6. Crystals form underground. True or false?
7. Do sedimentary rocks form on the bottoms of seas, lakes and rivers or deep within the earth?
8. What word is used for rocks which form under great pressure or heat: metamorphic, mathematic or metaphysical?
9. Is basalt an igneous or a sedimentary rock?
10. Gems are cut and polished to make gemstones. True or false?
11. What 'C' is the substance from which diamond is formed?
12. Which are the most valuable: diamonds, emeralds or garnets?
13. HIS PAPER can be rearranged to give the name of what valuable gemstone?
14. A START can be rearranged to give what word for layers of rock?

Level 3
15. In which country is the Giant's Causeway?
16. What 'M' is molten rock, which cools to form igneous rocks?
17. What is the name for a stone which has had its edges worn smooth by the action of water?
18. What 'E' cannot be broken down into any simpler substance?

Rocks and minerals

Rocks are the building blocks of Earth's crust, and the substances of which they are composed are called minerals. The appearance and qualities of a rock are determined by the way it was formed. Humans use rocks and minerals to make everything from jewellery to houses.

basalt columns

Metamorphic rocks 8

The three main types of rock are metamorphic, sedimentary and igneous. Metamorphic rocks such as marble form underground, when existing rock is exposed to great pressure or heat.

erupting volcano

Igneous rocks 4 9 15 16

The Giant's Causeway in Northern Ireland is made up of hexagonal (six-sided) columns of basalt, an igneous rock. Like all igneous rocks, it formed from volcanic magma (melted rock), which erupted and then cooled down.

igneous rock

Sedimentary rocks 7 14

These rocks form from sediments such as sand and mud at the bottoms of seas, lakes and rivers, building up over long periods of time. Gradually, the weight of water compresses them into rock. Sedimentary rocks form in strata (layers).

Stones 5 17

A stone is a small piece of rock, and a pebble is a stone that has had its edges smoothed over time by the action of water. The hardest stones are those from igneous rocks such as granite, or from metamorphic rocks such as slate.

granite

pumice

obsidian

serpentinite

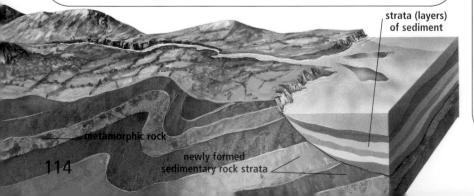

strata (layers) of sediment

metamorphic rock

newly formed sedimentary rock strata

amethyst

Minerals 3 18
There are two types of mineral: those with crystalline structures, and naturally occurring metals such as gold. These metals are elements – they cannot be broken down into any simpler substance.

Crystals 6
Crystalline minerals form in underground rocks under great heat or pressure. Crystals have flat sides and can be extremely beautiful.

realgar	azurite	quartz	diamond

galena   malachite   pyrite   fluorite

Gemstones 10
Some crystalline minerals are known as gemstones. They are precious or semiprecious stones that can be cut and polished to make gems, which are used in jewellery. The rarest ones are considered the most valuable.

1. gemstone in rock

2. rough gemstone

3. glittering jewel

turquoise

garnet

amethyst

topaz

aquamarine

opal

diamond

sapphire

emerald

peridot   ruby   pearl

Types of 1 2 11 12 13 gemstone
The most famous and expensive gemstone is diamond. It is unusual in being a crystal made from a single element – carbon. Other very rare and precious gemstones include emeralds, which are green, rubies, which are red, and sapphires, which are blue.

QUESTIONS:
Weather

Level 1
1. Does weather happen in the atmosphere or under the sea?
2. Are clouds made of cotton wool or water vapour?
3. What 'O' is the gas we must breathe in order to live?
4. What 'L' is the word for an electrical charge released from a storm cloud?
5. A weather balloon is a type of cloud. True or false?

Level 2
6. Where does the majority of the water vapour in clouds originally come from?
7. Does a weather vane measure wind speed or wind direction?
8. Which is usually associated with fine weather: high pressure or low pressure?
9. What 'R' is sometimes formed as sunlight passes through raindrops?
10. Do rainbows appear when it rains or when there is no rain?
11. Do raindrops become bigger or smaller as they fall through a cloud?
12. What 'H' is a word for frozen raindrops?
13. Do clouds become cooler or hotter as they rise?
14. REACH RUIN can be rearranged to give the name of what powerful storm?
15. RING TONE can be rearranged to give the name of what very common gas?

Level 3
16. What is a scientist who studies the weather called?
17. How many colours are there in a rainbow?
18. What 'S' do weather forecasters use to watch storms building up in the atmosphere?

FIND THE ANSWER: Weather

The weather affects all of us. It makes us decide what clothes to put on in the morning and whether we go outside or stay indoors. In some places, the weather can be very hard to predict. As we learn more about our planet, however, we are gradually getting better at working out what the weather is going to do next.

weather satellite

Watching weather　14　18
Nowadays, satellites watch the weather from above. They help weather forecasters to see storms building up in the atmosphere. Large storms and hurricanes appear as massive swirls of cloud.

Storm cloud　4　13
As clouds rise, they cool and the water vapour turns into droplets. The droplets bump into each other, causing an electric charge to build up. If the charge becomes large enough, it is released as lightning.

storm cloud

Atmosphere　1　3　15
Weather occurs in the atmosphere – the layer of gases surrounding the earth. The most common gas is nitrogen, followed by oxygen, which we breathe in order to stay alive.

Clouds　2　6
Clouds are collections of water vapour. The vapour forms as the sun's energy evaporates liquid water, mostly from the surface of the sea.

rain

116

Weather research ⑤ ⑯

Scientists who study the weather are known as meteorologists. Weather balloons are just one of the tools meteorologists use to gain information about the weather. The balloons carry devices that measure weather conditions far above the ground.

anemometer

weather vane

thermometers

barometer

Measuring the weather ⑦ ⑧

There are many devices for measuring the weather. Thermometers measure temperature, while barometers measure air pressure – high pressure means fine weather, and low pressure signals storms. An anemometer measures wind speed, while a weather vane shows wind direction.

weather balloon

Rain ⑪ ⑫

Rain falls when the droplets in clouds become too large and heavy to remain aloft. As they fall through the air, they hit other droplets and grow bigger. Sometimes they freeze and fall as hail or snow.

rain cloud

Rainbows ⑨ ⑩ ⑰

Rainbows form when it rains on sunny days. They are the result of the light from the sun being split into its seven colours as it passes through raindrops.

rainbow

QUESTIONS:
Bones and muscles

Level 1
1. BELOW can be rearranged to give the name of what joint in the middle of the arm?
2. Are there muscles in the human leg?
3. What 'S' is the name for all the bones in the body put together?

Level 2
4. Do people have joints in their fingers?
5. Muscles contain millions of cells called fibres. True or false?
6. What 'B' is a muscle in the arm that helps to raise the forearm?
7. Which bones form a cage that protects the internal organs?
8. What 'C' is the proper name for the gristle in human bodies?
9. Which bone links the legs to the backbone?
10. The patella is another name for which bone?
11. The muscles in the heart work automatically. True or false?
12. When a person raises their forearm does their triceps contract or relax?
13. How many bones are there in an adult's skull: two, 12 or 22?
14. Do people have more muscles or more bones in their bodies?
15. Is the shoulder joint a hinge joint or a ball-and-socket joint?
16. Which is the largest bone in the human body?
17. What is the name of the eight bones that, together, encase the brain?

Level 3
18. The mandible is another name for which part of the body?
19. In which part of the body is the smallest bone?
20. How many bones are there in the human skeleton?

Bones and muscles

The human body is an incredible natural machine. It can perform a huge variety of different movements and operations – far more than any robot or other man-made machine. Like those of other mammals, the human body is based on a complex system of muscles attached to a strong but flexible bony skeleton.

knee

elbow

shoulder

hip

Joints   1   4   15

Joints are the areas in the skeleton where different bones meet. They are what make the skeleton flexible, and allow limbs and other parts of the body to move. The shoulder and the hip joints are called ball-and-socket joints. The elbow, knee and finger joints are known as hinge joints.

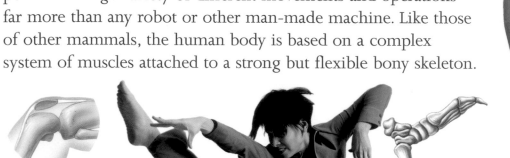

Skull   13   17   18

The skull of an adult is made up of 22 bones. Eight form the cranium, the bony box that surrounds the brain. Only the lower jaw (mandible) is able to move, allowing the person to eat and speak.

kneecap (patella)

thigh bone (femur)

upper arm bone (humerus)

hip bone (pelvis)

ribcage

spine

skull

collarbone (clavicle)

radius

ulna

shin bone (tibia)

fibula

Knees   8   10

These joints separate the upper and lower halves of the legs. The ends of the bones are covered with a layer of cartilage (gristle) to stop them rubbing together. The patella (kneecap) is a small bone that protects the knee from injury.

Skeleton   3   7   9   14   16   19   20

The human skeleton is made up of 206 bones. The largest are the two thigh bones (femurs), linked to the backbone by the pelvis. The smallest are the stirrup bones, which help transmit sounds from the eardrums to the brain. The ribs mostly remain in the same position, forming a protective cage around the organs.

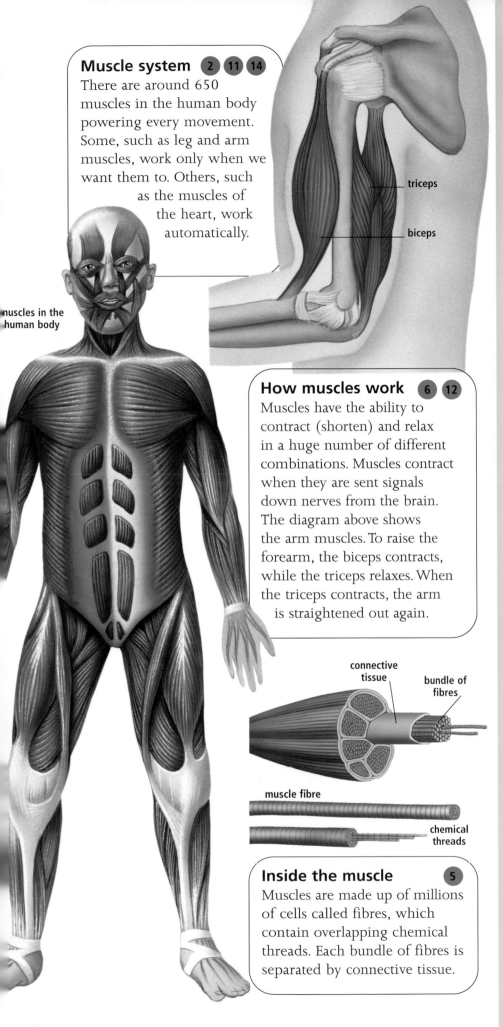

Muscle system ②①①④

There are around 650 muscles in the human body powering every movement. Some, such as leg and arm muscles, work only when we want them to. Others, such as the muscles of the heart, work automatically.

muscles in the human body

triceps

biceps

How muscles work ⑥⑫

Muscles have the ability to contract (shorten) and relax in a huge number of different combinations. Muscles contract when they are sent signals down nerves from the brain. The diagram above shows the arm muscles. To raise the forearm, the biceps contracts, while the triceps relaxes. When the triceps contracts, the arm is straightened out again.

connective tissue

bundle of fibres

muscle fibre

chemical threads

Inside the muscle ⑤

Muscles are made up of millions of cells called fibres, which contain overlapping chemical threads. Each bundle of fibres is separated by connective tissue.

QUESTIONS:
Medicine

Level 1
1. What 'D' is the person people visit when they are feeling ill?
2. What vehicles take people to hospital: ambulances, fire engines or tractors?
3. Are ambulances part of the emergency services?
4. Do nurses work in hospitals or shops?

Level 2
5. Broken bones mend themselves. True or false?
6. What 'S' is used to listen to a person's heartbeat?
7. What does a thermometer measure?
8. Is intensive care given to people who are very ill or to people who are better, just before they leave hospital?
9. What 'S' is the word for a person who carries out operations?
10. What 'T' means to replace a damaged body part with a new, healthy one?
11. Would you wear a plaster cast if you had flu or if you had a broken leg?
12. Rearrange A SCARED IMP to make the name of the people who look after patients on the way to hospital.
13. A symptom is a kind of medicine. True or false?
14. What 'S' is a large machine that looks inside people's bodies?

Level 3
15. What 'D' means 'to work out what is wrong with a patient'?
16. What sort of injury can be treated by traction?
17. What is used to transfer nutrients straight into a person's bloodstream?
18. What 'M' is a kind of wave that scanners use to look inside a body?

Medicine

The word medicine has two meanings. When someone is ill, a doctor may give them medicine to make them feel better; but medicine is also a branch of science that studies diseases and injuries. Doctors, nurses and surgeons work in the field of medicine, and so do the pharmacists and researchers who develop new drugs and cures.

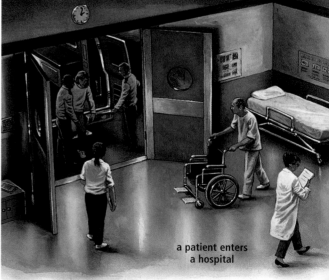

the scene of an accident

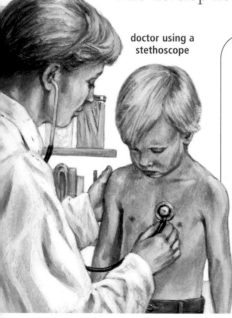

doctor using a stethoscope

Doctors   1   6   7   13   15

The doctor is the first person you go to see if you are feeling ill. Doctors look for symptoms (signs) of different illnesses and diagnose (work out) what is wrong. This doctor is using a stethoscope to listen to the boy's heartbeat. Doctors also use thermometers to measure body temperature.

Emergency services   2   3   12

Ambulances are vehicles that carry sick or injured people to hospital. They are part of the emergency services. Most ambulances have paramedics on board, who are trained to treat patients as they are taken to hospital.

Treating broken bones   5   11   16

Broken bones mend themselves, but to make sure they join back together in the right way, doctors wrap the affected limbs in rigid plaster casts. Sometimes they use 'traction' (shown below) – a system of pulleys and wires that keep the bones in the correct position.

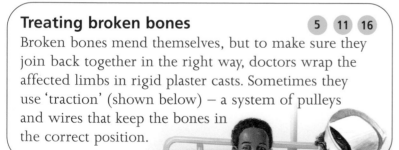

girl with her leg in traction

a patient enters a hospital

Hospitals   4

Hospitals are where sick and injured people go to be treated and get better. They are also the places where many doctors and most surgeons and nurses work. Most large towns and cities have at least one hospital.

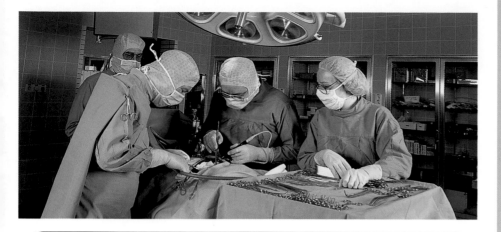

Operations ⑨ ⑩

Surgeons carry out operations to make people better. Some operations involve removing diseased parts of the body. Others, known as transplants, involve taking out an old or damaged part and replacing it with a healthy new one.

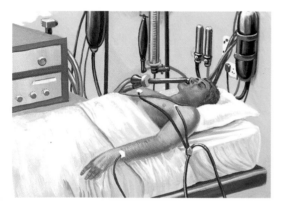

Intensive care ⑧ ⑰

Very ill people need intensive care. They are watched closely by nurses and are assisted by machines. They may have a drip, which feeds nutrients through a tube straight into the blood.

Body scans ⑭ ⑱

Scanners are machines that can look inside the body. They do this using X-rays or magnetic waves, which pass through the body and are picked up by sensors. The pictures generated may reveal signs of injury or disease that would otherwise be invisible.

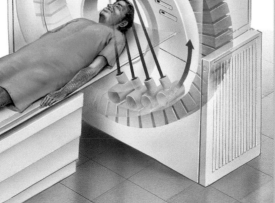

a patient has a CT (computerized tomography) scan

Level 1

1. Which came first: steam engines or electric trains?
2. Do all trains carry passengers?
3. Is diesel a type of fuel or a type of food?
4. Who built the train that ran on the first-ever steam railway: Richard Trevithick, Richard Branson or Richard the Lionheart?
5. What 'C' was burned in steam engines?

Level 2

6. Was the Wild West in Europe or in the USA?
7. Is steam created by heating water or by heating petrol?
8. Which country has bullet trains and super expresses?
9. What 'R' was a famous steam engine built by George Stephenson?
10. Which country has TGVs?
11. Are there any trains that can go faster than 200km/h?
12. What 'C' on Wild West trains was used for moving cattle off the line?
13. Were steam trains cleaner or dirtier than modern trains?

Level 3

14. In which country was the world's first-ever steam railway?
15. In which century was the first railway to cross North America built?
16. What 'F' is the word used for the goods carried by some trains?
17. How long was the world's longest ever train: 5km, 6km or 7km?
18. What 'P' were exploring settlers who travelled into the Wild West by train?

FIND THE ANSWER: Trains

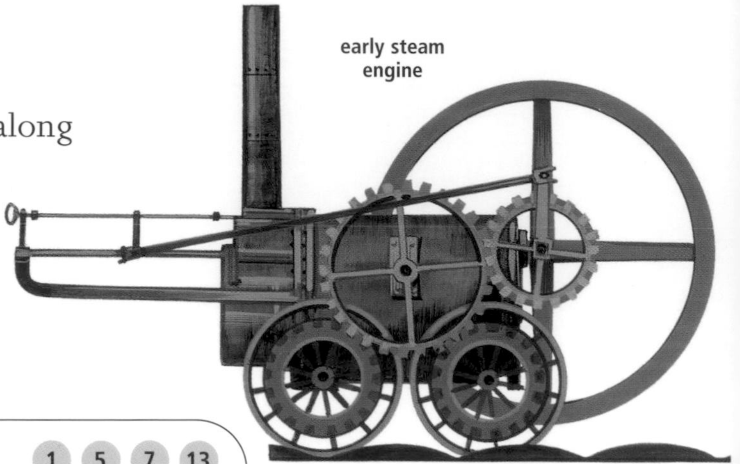

Trains are great for getting around. They travel along networks of railway tracks. As well as being fast, they are comfortable and usually quiet. Trains have been around for about 200 years, longer than there have been cars on the roads. They can carry lots of people while using a relatively small amount of fuel, which is good for the environment.

early steam engine

George Stephenson's *Rocket*

Steam   1 5 7 13
The first trains were powered by steam. This was created by burning coal to heat tanks of water to very high temperatures. Because they were burning coal, steam trains were much dirtier than modern electric trains.

Rails   4 9 14
Richard Trevithick was the first to put a steam engine on rails, and in doing so invented the railway. His first engine set off in south Wales in February 1804 – 25 years before George Stephenson's famous engine, the *Rocket*.

bullet train

JR500 WEST JAPAN

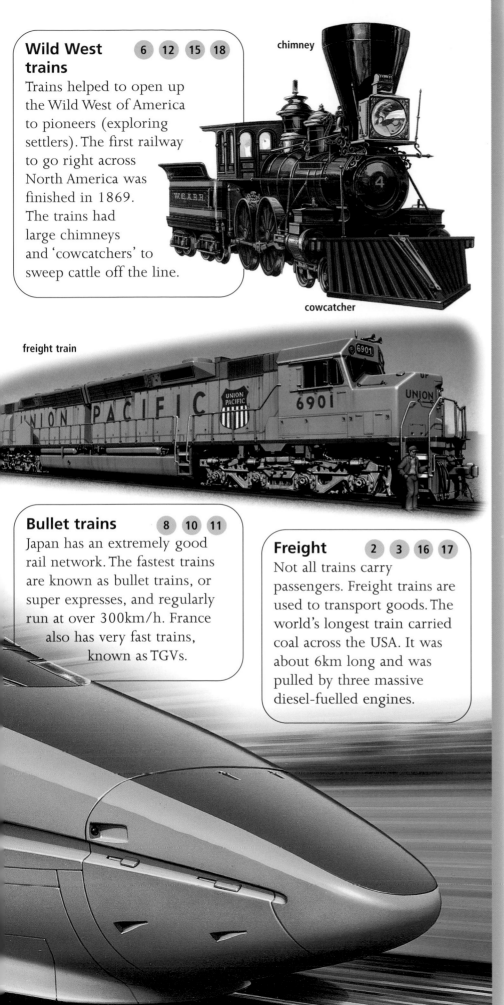

Wild West trains

⑥ ⑫ ⑮ ⑱

chimney

Trains helped to open up the Wild West of America to pioneers (exploring settlers). The first railway to go right across North America was finished in 1869. The trains had large chimneys and 'cowcatchers' to sweep cattle off the line.

cowcatcher

freight train

Bullet trains

⑧ ⑩ ⑪

Japan has an extremely good rail network. The fastest trains are known as bullet trains, or super expresses, and regularly run at over 300km/h. France also has very fast trains, known as TGVs.

Freight

② ③ ⑯ ⑰

Not all trains carry passengers. Freight trains are used to transport goods. The world's longest train carried coal across the USA. It was about 6km long and was pulled by three massive diesel-fuelled engines.

QUESTIONS:
Early flight

Level 1

1. GIRDLE can be rearranged to give the name of what type of unpowered aircraft?
2. The first manned flight was in a hot-air balloon. True or false?
3. Is a dirigible a steerable airship or an Australian musical instrument?

Level 2

4. What 'H' is a type of aircraft with rotating blades?
5. Which body of water was Louis Blériot first to fly across in 1909: the English Channel or Atlantic ocean?
6. In which century did Otto Lilienthal make the first controlled glider flights: the 9th or 19th century?
7. How many wings does a monoplane have: two or four?
8. Which 'G' is a country, home to Otto Lilienthal?
9. Jean-François Pilâtre was the first man to fly. True or false?
10. Was the first powered aeroplane flight in Europe or the USA?
11. Which great 16th-century Italian artist and thinker designed a glider that was never built?
12. Which 'M' were brothers who built the first manned aircraft?

Level 3

13. What was the surname of Wilbur and Orville, who designed the first ever heavier-than-air powered aircraft?
14. What was their aircraft called?
15. What did the first heavier-than-air powered aircraft use as fuel?
16. In which century did the first-ever manned aircraft take off: the 16th, 17th or 18th century?
17. Who made the first-ever powered flight?
18. What was his nationality?

Early flight

Nowadays, many people take flight for granted. Every day thousands of aeroplanes carry passengers all over the world. Yet it was only around a hundred years ago that the first petrol-driven aircraft took to the skies. The very first flights were made in hot-air balloons, airships and unpowered winged gliders.

Montgolfier 2 9 12 16

The first-ever manned aircraft was a hot-air balloon built by the French Montgolfier brothers. On 15 October 1783, it lifted Jean-François Pilâtre 25m above the city of Paris, France. It was anchored with rope to stop it floating away.

the Montgolfier hot-air balloon

da Vinci's glider

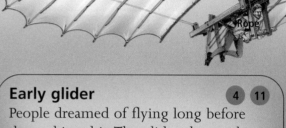

Rope

Early glider 4 11

People dreamed of flying long before they achieved it. The glider shown above was designed by Italian thinker and artist Leonardo da Vinci around the year 1500. He also designed a type of helicopter with rotating blades, but neither of his flying machines was actually built.

Powered flight 3 10 14 17 18

The first heavier-than-air powered aircraft, the *Wright Flyer*, took off on 17 December 1903 in the USA. The first powered flight had already been made 50 years earlier by the Frenchman Henri Giffard in a steam-powered dirigible (steerable airship).

the *Wright Flyer*

Lilienthal (1) (6) (8)

German engineer Otto Lilienthal built gliders (unpowered winged aircraft). He made the first controlled glider flights in 1861. Others had flown gliders but had not been able to control them.

Lilienthal's glider

monoplane

Blériot (5) (7)

In 1909, Frenchman Louis Blériot became the first person to fly an aeroplane across the English Channel. Blériot also designed and built some of the world's first successful monoplanes (aeroplanes with just two wings, instead of four or six).

The Wright brothers (13) (15)

Wilbur and Orville Wright designed and built the first heavier-than-air powered aircraft. It had a special lightweight petrol engine. The brothers went on to build aircraft for other people.

QUESTIONS:
Sailing

Level 1

1. Sailing boats use the wind to push them along. True or false?
2. Are boats kept moored in a marina, a merino or a mariner?
3. What kind of jackets do people wear to keep them afloat in the water?
4. Do any sailing boats have engines?
5. What suit keeps windsurfers warm?
6. A rudder is used to help a boat steer. True or false?
7. What 'Y' is a large sailing boat used for pleasure?

Level 2

8. Which were invented first: square sails or triangular sails?
9. What 'P' is the left-hand side of a boat and a place where ships dock?
10. What is the word for the rear of a boat?
11. BROAD ARTS can be rearranged to give what word for the right-hand side of a boat?
12. Boats with square sails can only go in the same direction as the wind. True or false?
13. How many hulls do trimarans have?
14. What is a boat with two hulls called?
15. What are small, open boats without cabins called?
16. What 'W' are people who sail standing up on a board?

Level 3

17. What part of a boat helps keep it from tipping over?
18. Which Mediterranean island was home to the sea-faring Minoans?
19. When did ancient sailing ships use their oars?

FIND THE ANSWER: Sailing

Before the 19th century, most of the world's boats and ships had sails. Sailing ships carried the explorers to America and Australia, and carried the Europeans who later settled those continents. Today, most people who sail do so for pleasure or sport, although in some parts of the world boats with sails are still used to transport goods.

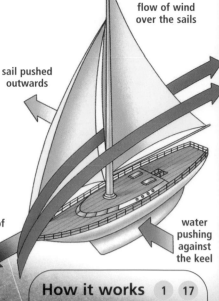

flow of wind over the sails

sail pushed outwards

direction of travel

water pushing against the keel

spinaker

cabin

How it works   1   17
The force of the wind pushes against the sails to move a boat through the water. Modern sailing boats can travel in any direction except directly into the wind. Changing direction is called 'tacking'. A keel under the boat prevents it tipping over if the wind is too strong.

The first sailing ships   8   12   18   19
Built around 2500BCE by the Minoans of Crete and the ancient Greeks, the first sailing boats had square sails, which meant that they could only sail in the same direction as the wind. They used oars to go forwards against the wind. When triangular sails appeared around 1200BCE, people could move them to sail in any direction.

Sailing for pleasure   2   4   7
Most people who own sailing boats use them for fun and keep them docked in harbours or marinas. Larger sailing boats are known as yachts. Some sailing boats also have engines for travelling when there is no wind.

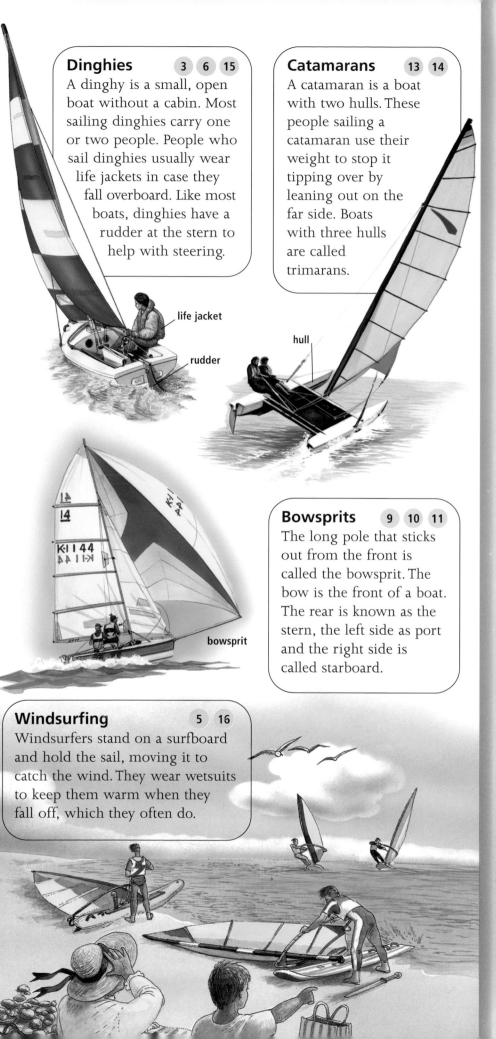

Dinghies   (3) (6) (15)

A dinghy is a small, open boat without a cabin. Most sailing dinghies carry one or two people. People who sail dinghies usually wear life jackets in case they fall overboard. Like most boats, dinghies have a rudder at the stern to help with steering.

life jacket

rudder

Catamarans   (13) (14)

A catamaran is a boat with two hulls. These people sailing a catamaran use their weight to stop it tipping over by leaning out on the far side. Boats with three hulls are called trimarans.

hull

Bowsprits   (9) (10) (11)

The long pole that sticks out from the front is called the bowsprit. The bow is the front of a boat. The rear is known as the stern, the left side as port and the right side is called starboard.

bowsprit

Windsurfing   (5) (16)

Windsurfers stand on a surfboard and hold the sail, moving it to catch the wind. They wear wetsuits to keep them warm when they fall off, which they often do.

QUESTIONS:
Submarines

Level 1

1. Does the word submarine literally mean 'under the sea' or 'above the mountains'?
2. Is a torpedo a type of weapon or a running shoe?
3. What 'D' is the word for people who explore underwater?
4. LATIN CAT can be rearranged to give the name of what ocean?

Level 2

5. Which country's submarines were known as U-boats?
6. Are there any submarines that are driven by nuclear power?
7. What is the name for the spinning objects that push submarines through the water?
8. Can submarines attack boats that are on the surface?
9. Are research submarines called submersibles or submissives?
10. What 'D' is a kind of fuel commonly used in submarines?
11. What is the name for the tanks that fill with seawater when a submarine descends?
12. A bathyscaphe is a type of radar system. True or false?
13. What do the letters ROV stand for?
14. SPICE ROPE can be rearranged to give the name of what device, used by submarine crews to see above the water?

Level 3

15. Where is the Mariana Trench, the deepest point on earth?
16. What was the name of the bathyscaphe that first carried people to the bottom of the Mariana Trench?
17. What was the name of the manned submersible that first explored the wreck of the *Titanic*?
18. Which ocean liner was torpedoed and sunk by a German U-boat on 7 May 1915?

FIND THE ANSWER: Submarines

Submarines are used to explore the world under the sea. They are also used in the navies of some countries for defence in times of war. Although people long dreamed of voyaging under the sea, submarines have been around for less than 400 years. Today's submarines are a far cry from the earliest designs, most of which were made of wood and were powered by the people who rode in them.

Power   6   7   10
Modern submarines are driven by propellers, like most ships. These propellers are turned by massive engines. Some submarines have diesel engines, while others are driven by nuclear power.

Warfare   5   8   18
During the World Wars, the German navy made great use of their submarines, which were called U-boats. They used them to fire torpedoes at enemy warships, such as the RMS *Lusitania*, which was sunk on 7 May 1915.

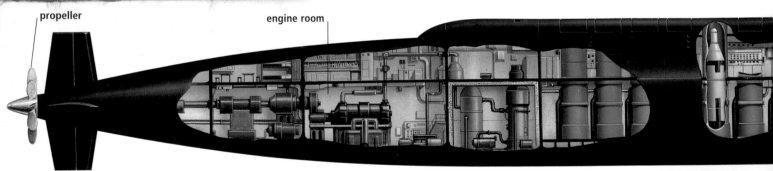

propeller   engine room

Diving and resurfacing   1   11
Submarine literally means 'under the water'. When a submarine dives, special tanks (ballast tanks) fill up with seawater. To resurface, compressed air is pumped into the tanks. This forces water out, making the submarine lighter.

Subsuits   3
Divers sometimes use subsuits like a one-person submarine for exploration in deep water. These have arms with pincers that the diver can operate, allowing him or her to pick things up and manipulate objects deep beneath the sea.

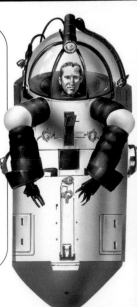

diving – seawater in

up – air in, water out

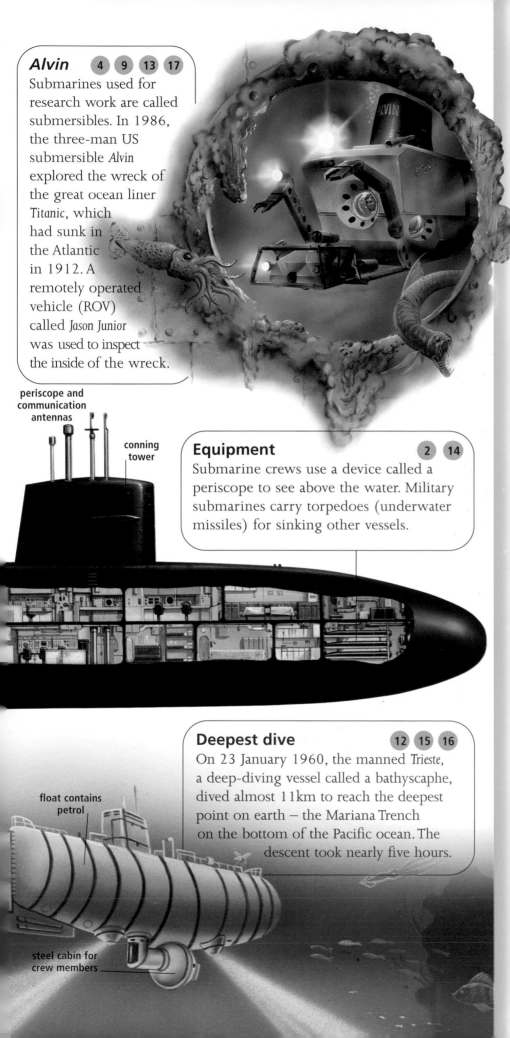

Alvin (4) (9) (13) (17)

Submarines used for research work are called submersibles. In 1986, the three-man US submersible *Alvin* explored the wreck of the great ocean liner *Titanic*, which had sunk in the Atlantic in 1912. A remotely operated vehicle (ROV) called *Jason Junior* was used to inspect the inside of the wreck.

periscope and communication antennas

conning tower

Equipment (2) (14)

Submarine crews use a device called a periscope to see above the water. Military submarines carry torpedoes (underwater missiles) for sinking other vessels.

Deepest dive (12) (15) (16)

On 23 January 1960, the manned *Trieste*, a deep-diving vessel called a bathyscaphe, dived almost 11km to reach the deepest point on earth – the Mariana Trench on the bottom of the Pacific ocean. The descent took nearly five hours.

float contains petrol

steel cabin for crew members

QUESTIONS:
Household inventions

Level 1

1. Would you put bread in a toaster or a dishwasher?
2. What 'K' is used for heating water?
3. Is a Hoover a type of vacuum cleaner or a type of zip?

Level 2

4. Which invention is usually credited to John Logie Baird?
5. SHARED WISH can be rearranged to give the name of what household appliance?
6. Did the automatic cut-out on an electric kettle appear in 1890, 1930 or 1989?
7. Which was invented first: the electric washing machine or the dishwasher?
8. Which household object is usually associated with Thomas Edison?
9. People only started to use zips in the 1940s. True or false?
10. Which handy implement was invented by Laszlo Biro?
11. The aero-foam extinguisher is used on what kind of fires?
12. SCOOPS RED ROOF can be rearranged to give the name of what kitchen appliance?
13. In which decade of the 20th century did microwave ovens first go on sale?

Level 3

14. In what year was the first television picture transmitted?
15. James Murray Spangler invented the first portable what?
16. What did Alexandre Godefoy invent?
17. Which kitchen appliance was developed from an earlier invention called the magnetron?
18. Who invented the sewing machine?

Household inventions

Most homes are full of man-made objects designed to make people's lives easier or get jobs done faster. Technological advances in the 20th century brought dramatic changes, with the introduction of labour-saving appliances, such as the washing machine, the dishwasher and the vacuum cleaner.

The kettle `2` `6`

The electric kettle was invented by Arthur Leslie Large in 1922. A safety device called an automatic cut-out appeared in 1930, to prevent electric shocks.

kettle

Living room `4` `8` `14` `16`

Thomas Edison made the first light bulb for sale in 1879. The first television picture was transmitted in 1925 by the engineer John Logie Baird. The electric hairdryer was invented in the 1920s by Alexandre Godefoy.

Microwave `13` `17`

The first microwave ovens went on sale in 1967. They were developed from an earlier invention called the magnetron.

In the kitchen `1` `5` `7` `12`

The electric washing machine was invented in 1908, the electric dishwasher in 1913 and the electric toaster in 1909. The food processor was invented later, in 1971.

telephone

food processor

microwave

radio

toaster

washing machine

fridge-freezer

oven

dishwasher

130

Fire extinguisher 11
The first-ever fire extinguisher was patented in 1872 by Thomas Martin. The aero-foam extinguisher, for use against gas and oil fires, was invented by Dr Percy Julian, during World War II.

fire extinguisher

Ball-point pen 10
The ball-point pen was invented in 1938 by the Hungarian journalist Laszlo Biro. He invented the ball-point so that the same quick-drying, thick ink, which was used in newspaper printing, could also be used in a pen.

ball-point pen

The zip 9 18
The zip was invented in 1851 by Elias Howe, who also invented the sewing machine. However, it was not until the end of the 19th century that they began to be manufactured.

zip

vacuum cleaner

The vacuum cleaner 3 15
Early vacuum cleaners made in the 19th century were huge. The first portable version was invented in 1907 by James Murray Spangler. The Hoover is a type of vacuum cleaner.

QUESTIONS:
Robots

Level 1
1. Are there any robots that work in factories?
2. Do robots ever get tired?
3. Are there any robots that can work underwater?
4. ODD SIR can be rearranged to give what name for robots such as R2-D2?
5. Robots can only do one thing at a time. True or false?

Level 2
6. Are there any robots that can play the piano?
7. Which series of films starred the robot C-3PO?
8. What 'C' is programmed with the information that is needed to make robots operate?
9. LEWDING can be rearranged to give the name of what task performed by robots?
10. Which have travelled farthest from earth: robots or humans?
11. Solar panels are used to capture energy from which source?
12. HOW TO CORD can be rearranged to give the name of what popular TV programme?
13. Which planet is currently being explored by robots?
14. What 'M' is the word for doing more than one job at a time?
15. Can robots be programmed to detonate bombs?

Level 3
16. The word robot comes from which language?
17. Which country developed the WABOT-2 robot?
18. In what year was the animated film *Robots* released?

FIND THE ANSWER: Robots

Robots are machines that can perform some of the physical tasks that would normally be carried out by humans. A lot of robots are now used in factories, particularly where large objects, such as cars, are made. They are also used to explore where people cannot go, such as the seabed and the surface of other planets.

robotic arm

Industry ① ② ⑧ ⑨
Many factories nowadays use robots for heavy, repetitive or difficult jobs. Unlike people, robots do not become tired or bored. Industrial robots are directed by computers to carry out particular tasks, such as spraying car bodywork or welding pieces together.

Multitasking ⑤ ⑭
Some robots can carry out more than one job at once. They are known as multitasking robots. Each robot arm does a different job or a similar job in a different direction.

Human-like robots ⑥ ⑰
The Japanese robot WABOT-2 can play the piano much faster than a human. It can either read new music, or choose a song it has played before and stored in its memory. WABOT-2 can also play gently or furiously. Other robots can perform sign language, and others can behave like pets.

UPHAUT 2 explored a narrow shaft in the Great Pyramid of Giza in 1993

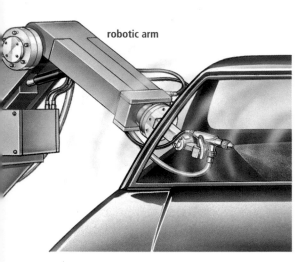

Difficult access ③ ⑮ ⑯
The word robot comes from the Czech word *robota*, meaning 'forced labour'. Robots are very useful for doing dangerous jobs. Some are used to defuse or safely detonate bombs. Others can work deep underwater to explore shipwrecks or dangerous areas of the seabed.

Mars robots 10 11 13

Robots have travelled farther than any human being. Since January 2004, robots known as the Mars rovers have been exploring the surface of Mars. The robots, which carry cameras, are powered by solar panels, which capture energy from sunshine.

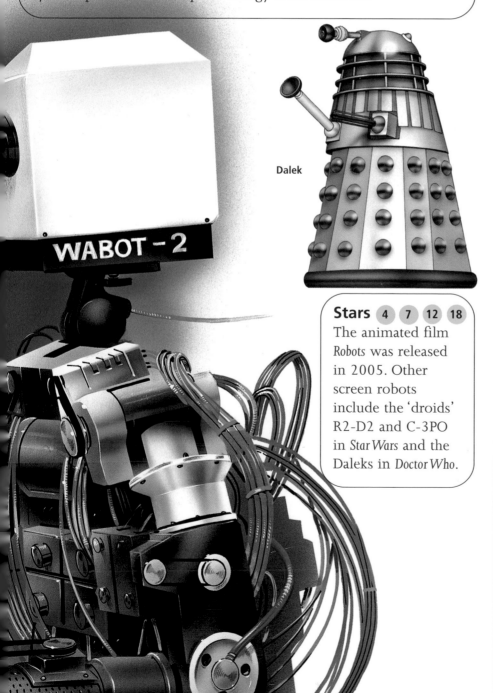

WABOT-2

Dalek

Stars 4 7 12 18

The animated film *Robots* was released in 2005. Other screen robots include the 'droids' R2-D2 and C-3PO in *Star Wars* and the Daleks in *Doctor Who*.

QUESTIONS:
Computers and gaming

Level 1

1. What 'I' is the network that links computers all over the world?
2. Does PC stand for Perfect Computer or Personal Computer?
3. What is a computer that is small enough to fit in the hand called: a handbag, a handheld or a handshake?
4. What 'M' is a small furry animal, and a thing that attaches to a computer?
5. What is stored in MP3 files?

Level 2

6. Where were computer games played before people had home computers?
7. Can people play computer games while they are on the move?
8. What kind of computer is the word Mac short for?
9. Do most handheld gaming machines take cartridges or discs?
10. Is the information in a computer held in the hard drive, printer or mouse?
11. What 'B' is the computer equipment used to put information onto a CD?
12. Is a computer keyboard a peripheral or a profiterole?
13. What 'H' do you wear when playing a virtual-reality game?
14. What 'V' is put in front of the word 'reality' to describe lifelike situations produced by computers?
15. TOP PAL can be rearranged to give what name for a portable computer?

Level 3

16. Which would you use to store data: a CD-RAM, a CD-REM or a CD-ROM?
17. What connects a home computer to the internet?
18. What kind of files would you put on to an iPod?

FIND THE ANSWER: Computers and gaming

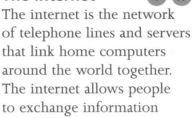

In the past few decades, computers have completely changed the way that people work. They have also changed the way that we play, bringing a new world of entertainment into our homes. There are now gaming machines that plug into televisions, while small, portable machines (handhelds) allow us to play games anywhere.

The internet ① ⑰
The internet is the network of telephone lines and servers that link home computers around the world together. The internet allows people to exchange information quickly and freely.

girl using laptop computer

Home computers ② ⑧ ⑮
Many people have PCs (Personal Computers). Others have Macs, or Macintoshes, like the one shown below. Smaller, portable computers are called laptops.

Hard drive ⑩
The hard drive holds all the information that a computer needs to be able to work. It is the most important part of the machine.

Digital accessories ⑤ ⑱
All sorts of equipment can be plugged into computers. Pictures from digital cameras can be copied on to a computer's hard drive. Music can also be stored on a computer, and can be passed to and from MP3 players such as the iPod.

hard drive

Macintosh computer

CD drive

iPod MP3 player

digital camera

keyboard

gaming handset

Peripherals ④ ⑫
A peripheral is any device that plugs into a computer or gaming machine. Peripherals include the keyboard and mouse, as well as gaming handsets.

CD burning ⑪ ⑯
CD-ROMs store data (information). Digital music files (or MP3s) can be put on to a CD using a CD burner. Most modern computers have built-in CD burners.

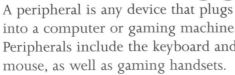

Handhelds ③ ⑦ ⑨

With small gaming machines known as handhelds, people can play video games while on the move. Most handhelds take small cartridges, which store the information for individual games.

computer graphics

Gaming ⑥

Every year, computer games become more and more complex and realistic, as computers become more powerful. Before home computers and gaming machines, the games were played in video arcades.

Virtual reality ⑬ ⑭

Special headsets, gloves and suits can allow people to experience virtual-reality games. These are computer programs that generate situations that look and feel virtually (almost) real.

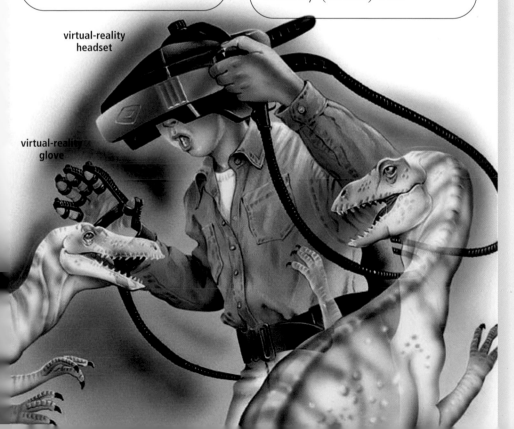

virtual-reality headset

virtual-reality glove

QUESTIONS:
Telephones

Level 1

1. What 'T' is a written message sent by a mobile phone?
2. Were the first mobile phones bigger or smaller than mobile phones today?
3. Do most modern telephones have rotating dials or buttons?
4. Do mobile phones send messages using microwaves, water waves or Mexican waves?
5. Are there mobile phones that can connect to the internet?

Level 2

6. Did the world's first telephone have touch-tone dialling?
7. In what century was the telephone invented: 9th, 19th or 21st?
8. SAME CAR can be rearranged to spell what feature of some mobile phones?
9. HOME CUT PIE can be rearranged to spell what part of a telephone, that you speak into?
10. What 'E' is the place where telephone calls are connected?
11. What name is given to people who used to connect the calls?
12. How many names were in the first-ever telephone directory: 50, 500 or 5,000?
13. What 'T' was a kind of coded message used before telephones were invented?

Level 3

14. How did people generate the electricity to power early phones?
15. Who invented the telephone?
16. In which country was Alexander Graham Bell born?
17. Who invented the carbon-granule microphone?
18. Which was invented first: the fax or the telephone?
19. In what year did rotating dials appear: 1886, 1896 or 1906?

FIND THE ANSWER: Telephones

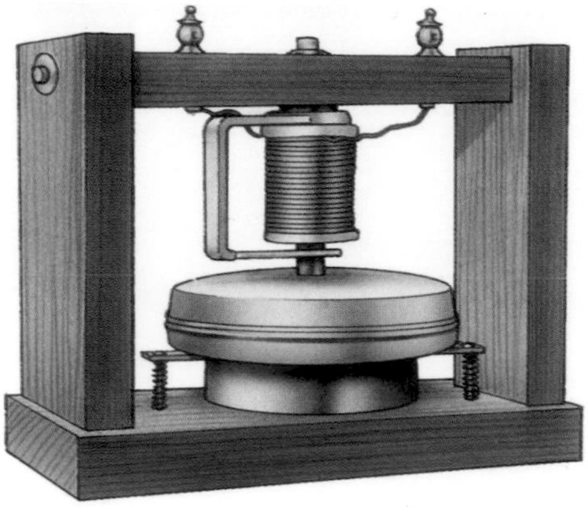

The telephone is the world's most popular means of communication. Telephones connect friends and families all over the world, and are a vital tool for most businesses. In recent decades, the telephone has given birth to a new invention that has totally changed the world: the internet.

Early years **14 17**

Early telephones had handles that were wound to generate electricity to power them. In 1878, the American Thomas Edison invented the carbon-granule microphone, which transmitted voices more clearly.

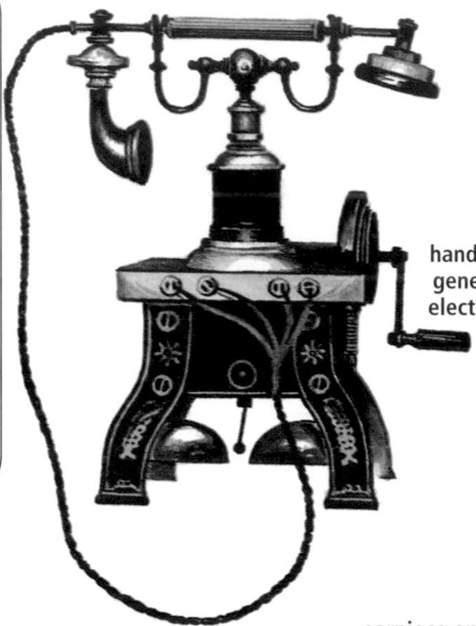

receiver

handle to generate electricity

earpiece on a wire

Inventing the telephone **7 15 16 18**

The Scotsman Alexander Graham Bell invented the telephone in 1876, with help from Thomas Watson. The first words were Bell's: 'Mr Watson, come here – I want you'.

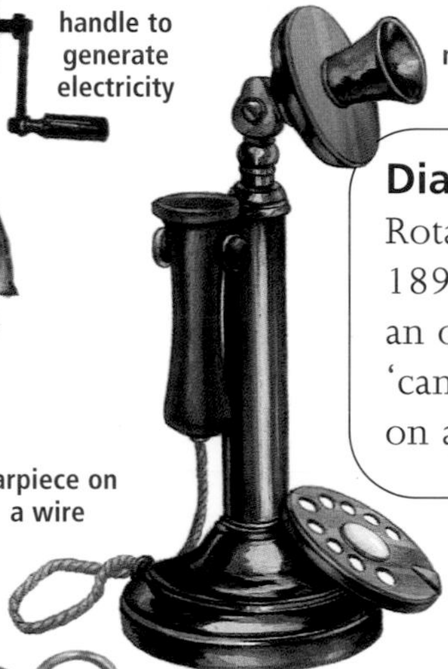

mouthpiece

Dialling numbers **9 19**

Rotating dials first appeared in 1896. Previously, people had to ask an operator to connect them. Early 'candlestick' phones had earpieces on a wire and mouthpieces on top.

'candlestick' telephone

operators connecting calls

Exchanges **10 11 12**

A telephone exchange is where wires from different telephones are connected together, enabling calls to be made. For many years, operators worked in exchanges. They connected calls by plugging wires into the correct sockets. Today, most exchanges are automated. The first telephone directory was printed in 1878. It had just 50 names in it.

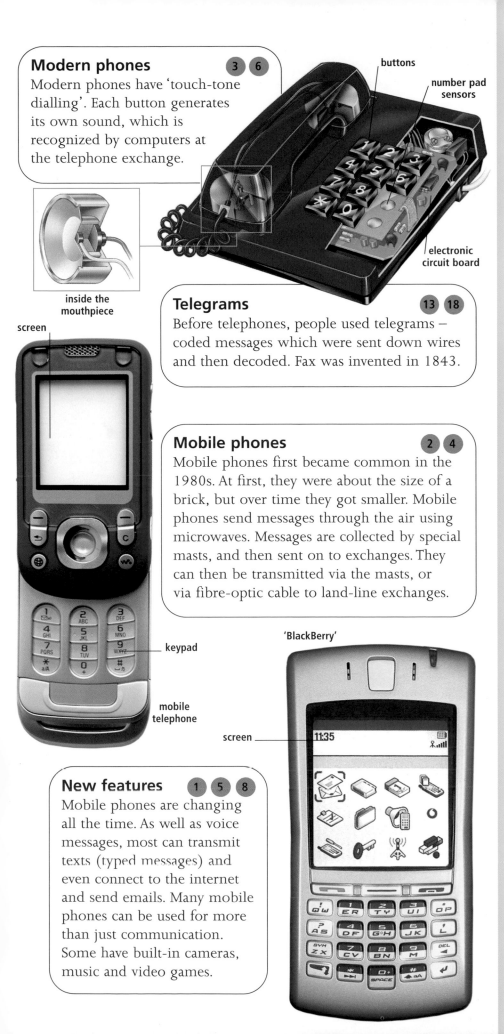

Modern phones ③ ⑥

Modern phones have 'touch-tone dialling'. Each button generates its own sound, which is recognized by computers at the telephone exchange.

buttons

number pad sensors

electronic circuit board

inside the mouthpiece

screen

Telegrams ⑬ ⑱

Before telephones, people used telegrams – coded messages which were sent down wires and then decoded. Fax was invented in 1843.

Mobile phones ② ④

Mobile phones first became common in the 1980s. At first, they were about the size of a brick, but over time they got smaller. Mobile phones send messages through the air using microwaves. Messages are collected by special masts, and then sent on to exchanges. They can then be transmitted via the masts, or via fibre-optic cable to land-line exchanges.

keypad

mobile telephone

'BlackBerry'

screen

11:35

New features ① ⑤ ⑧

Mobile phones are changing all the time. As well as voice messages, most can transmit texts (typed messages) and even connect to the internet and send emails. Many mobile phones can be used for more than just communication. Some have built-in cameras, music and video games.

QUESTIONS:
Discoveries

Level 1

1. What type of food is said to have fallen on Isaac Newton's head, giving him the idea for his most famous theory?
2. What 'W' turns around and around, allowing vehicles to move?
3. IT GRAVY can be rearranged to give the name of what force that pulls objects towards the ground?

Level 2

4. Which mathematician living in ancient Greece shouted 'Eureka' when he was in his bath?
5. What nationality was Isaac Newton?
6. In which century did the first cars with petrol engines appear?
7. Michael Faraday was an American scientist. True or false?
8. What 'S' was used to drive the earliest cars?
9. Karl Benz was a pioneer of the motor car. True or false?
10. SPICY HITS can be rearranged to give the name of what type of scientist?
11. Who came up with the theory of relativity?
12. Was the wheel invented more than 3,000 years ago?
13. What 'M' did Michael Faraday help us to understand better?
14. What nationality was Nicolas Cugnot, who built the first car?
15. By what three letters is deoxyribonucleic acid usually known?

Level 3

16. In which modern country are the ruins of the city of Uruk?
17. Which two scientists are usually credited with discovering the double helix of deoxyribonucleic acid?
18. In the formula $E = mc^2$, what does 'E' stand for?

Discoveries

The history of science is a history of discoveries. The reason we know so much about the world is because of the great thinkers who had ideas and then tested them to see if they were true. Some of these ideas led to useful inventions. Others helped us better understand the universe around us.

Sir Isaac Newton

The wheel 2 12 16

Nobody knows who invented the wheel. The earliest images of wheels come from Iraq and date back around 5,500 years. At that time, a great civilization lived there, based around the city of Uruk. It is possible that the wheel was invented before this date, however.

Newton 1 3 5

The English scientist Sir Isaac Newton (1642–1727) discovered gravity. The idea came to him when he was sitting under a tree, and an apple fell on his head.

Archimedes 4

This ancient Greek scientist made an important discovery about water displacement one day, when he was in his bath and noticed water spilling out. At the moment the idea came to him, he shouted 'Eureka!'

Faraday 7 13

Michael Faraday (1791–1867) was an English chemist and physicist, who helped us to understand the nature of electricity and magnetism.

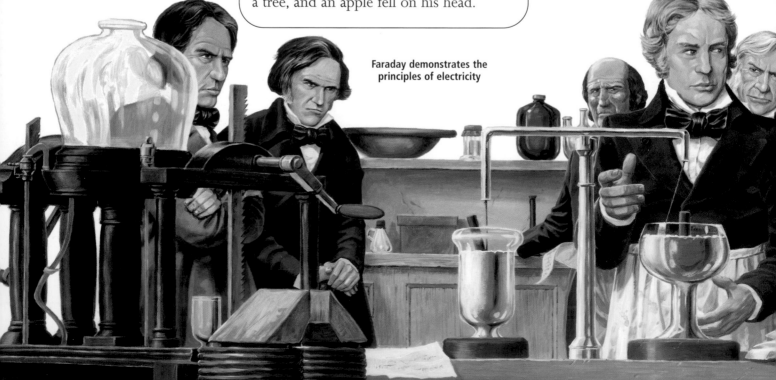

Faraday demonstrates the principles of electricity

The car   6   8   9   14

The first self-propelled road vehicle was built by the Frenchman Nicolas Cugnot in 1769 and was driven by steam. In the 1880s, Karl Benz and Gottlieb Daimler worked independently to produce the first petrol engine. In 1885, Benz built his motorized three-wheel car, the first to be powered by petrol.

Relativity   10   11   18

The theory of relativity was the brainchild of the German-born physicist Albert Einstein (1879–1955). Einstein's theory showed that time, space and mass are not fixed, but change according to the position from which they are seen or measured. His theory also showed that mass and energy are interchangeable. He summed this up with a single equation: $E = mc^2$ (E is energy, m is mass and c is the speed of light).

the double helix

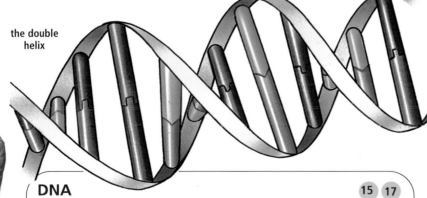

DNA   15   17

All plants and animals contain molecules of DNA (deoxyribonucleic acid) – the blueprint for life. DNA consists of chains of paired units called bases. The structure of DNA, known as the double helix, was first described in 1953 by James Watson and Francis Crick.

QUESTIONS:
The Sun

Level 1

1. The Sun has a core. True or false?
2. While it is daytime in one part of the Earth can it be night-time in another part of the Earth?
3. What 'S' is the name we give to the different times of year?
4. Rearrange RINSE US to spell the time of day when the Earth turns towards the Sun, and the Sun first appears above the horizon.

Level 2

5. Energy released from the Sun affects electronic systems, such as telephone networks, on Earth. True or False?
6. At sunset is the Earth turning towards or away from the Sun?
7. Bright patches that appear in the Sun's corona are called solar prominences. True or false?
8. How long does a sunspot cycle usually last?
9. What comes between the Earth and the Sun in a solar eclipse: the Moon, Mars or Venus?
10. What 'R' does the Earth do as it orbits around the Sun?
11. What are magnetic storms on the Sun called: coronas, sunspots or eclipses?
12. What 'H' does the Sun seem to sink below at sunset?
13. What is visible during a solar eclipse: sunspots, the Sun's corona or neither?
14. Do the solstices occur when the Earth is most or least tilted on its axis?

Level 3

15. How hot is the hottest part of the Sun?
16. What 'T' is the dividing line between daytime and night-time?
17. How large can sunspots be?
18. Name three things that are released from a build-up of energy in the Sun's corona.

The Sun

The Sun is a medium-sized star made up of a huge, rotating ball of hot gas. It is located in the galaxy (a group of star systems) called the Milky Way. The Sun is at the centre of the Solar System, and an average of 150,000,000km from Earth. Its powerful gravity keeps all the planets in the Solar System in orbit. Most life on Earth depends on heat and light from the Sun.

The core `1` `15`

The Sun's hottest part, its core, may be over 15,000,000°C. Huge amounts of energy are released from the core and carried outwards.

sunspot

core

The seasons `3` `14`

The Earth has seasons – spring, summer, autumn and winter – because its axis (an imaginary line through its centre) tilts at an angle. This brings different areas of the Earth closer to the Sun at various times during the year, which affects the weather. The solstices occur when Earth's axis is most tilted.

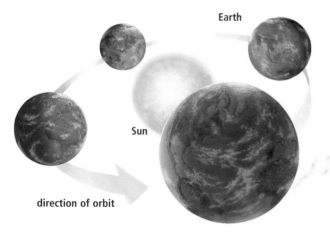

Earth

Sun

direction of orbit

Night and day `2` `10` `16`

While the Earth orbits (travels around) the Sun, it also rotates, or spins. The half of the Earth that faces the Sun is in daylight, while the half that faces away from the Sun is in darkness. A line called the 'terminator' separates daytime from night-time. A supersonic jet can overtake it.

Sunset and sunrise `4` `6` `12`

The Sun seems to sink below the horizon at sunset. In fact, the sky darkens as the Earth rotates away from the Sun. At sunrise, the Earth is turning towards the Sun.

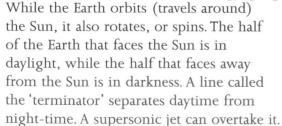

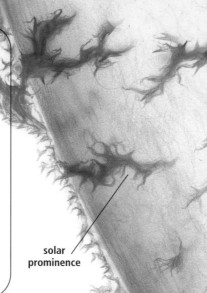

The corona   5 7 18

Temperatures in the Sun's outer atmosphere, called the corona, are over 1,000,000°C. Streams of gas called solar prominences shoot out millions of kilometres into space. Huge bright patches called solar flares appear in the corona, caused by a build-up of energy. This is released into space as radio waves, ultraviolet light and X-rays. These cause chaos in telephone networks on Earth.

solar prominence

year 1

year 5

year 11

Sunspots   8 11 17

Dark patches seen in the Sun's photosphere (its outer surface) are called sunspots. These are magnetic storms that occur on the Sun. Although they look small from Earth, sunspots can be as large as 50,000km in diameter. Their temperature of 4,073°C is considered cool for the Sun. Sunspots regularly appear and disappear in 11-year cycles.

Eclipse of the Sun   9 13

During a solar eclipse the Moon comes between the Earth and the Sun. From Earth, the Moon blocks the Sun from view and only the corona is seen. This plunges the Earth into twilight. Because the Earth is spinning, the eclipse is visible along a path that crosses the planet.

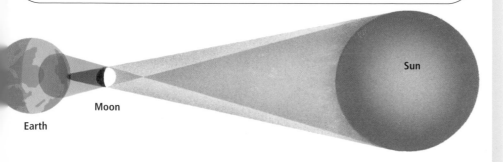

Earth

Moon

Sun

QUESTIONS:
The Moon

Level 1

1. Does the Sun or the Earth light the Moon?
2. The Moon doesn't have any gravity. True or false?
3. Does the Moon orbit around the Earth or the Sun?
4. When the sea falls back from the shore it is low tide. True or false?

Level 2

5. The new moon is sunny on the side we cannot see. True or false?
6. There is a face of the Moon we never see. True or false?
7. What 'G' causes tides?
8. Which type of tide occurs when the Moon is overhead: high tide or low tide?
9. How long does the Moon take to orbit Earth: 24 hours, 27.3 days or 39.5 days?
10. Who was the first astronaut to set foot on the Moon: Al Shepard, Buzz Aldrin or Neil Armstrong?
11. Does the Earth's or the Sun's shadow pass over the Moon during a lunar eclipse?
12. Which 'W' means that the Moon is getting thinner?
13. Are high tides higher or lower during spring tides?
14. Do neap tides occur when the Earth, Moon and Sun are in line?

Level 3

15. What is the diameter of the Moon?
16. How long does the Moon take to pass through all its phases?
17. Where are the Sun and Moon when there is a full moon?
18. When does a lunar eclipse occur?
19. What was the date of the first American Moon landing?

The Moon

The Moon is a satellite that orbits around Earth. It is bigger than the dwarf planet Pluto, but it has no atmosphere. The 'seas' seen on the face of the Moon are craters made by asteroids that crashed there 3,000 to 4,000 years ago. The Moon's gravity causes the tides – the rising and falling of the Earth's oceans and seas.

Tides 4 7 8

high tide   low tide

When the Moon is overhead, its gravity pulls the sea up to the shore. This is high tide. As Earth turns, the Moon's pull weakens and the sea falls back to low tide.

The Moon 2 15

The diameter of the Moon is 3,476km and its orbit is 384,400km from Earth. Its gravity is only one-sixth of the force of gravity produced by Earth.

Neap tides 14

When the Earth, Moon and Sun shift apart, high tides are lower and low tides are higher. These are called neap tides.

Spring tides 13

When the Earth, Sun and Moon are in line, high tides are higher and low tides are lower. These are called spring tides.

Earth

The Moon's face 3 6 9

The Moon rotates on its axis, but we see only one face. This is because Earth's pull keeps one side of the Moon always in sight. The Moon rotates and orbits Earth in the same amount of time: 27.3 days.

Moon orbiting around Earth

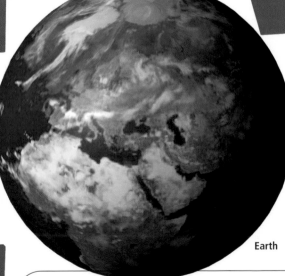

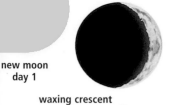
new moon
day 1

waxing crescent
day 4

first quarter
day 7

Phases of the moon `1` `5` `16`

The Sun lights the orbiting Moon from different directions. At new moon it lights the side we never see. The Moon passes through eight phases over 29.3 days. Six are shown here.

full moon
day 14

Full moon `12` `17`

When a full moon occurs, the Sun and Moon are on opposite sides of Earth. A new moon 'waxes' – more of it is seen each day – until the full moon on day 14. Then it 'wanes', or grows thinner each day.

last quarter
day 22

waning crescent
day 26

Lunar eclipse `11` `18`

When a full Moon passes exactly behind the Earth, the Earth blocks sunlight from reaching the Moon. We see the Earth's shadow pass over the Moon. This is called a lunar eclipse.

On the Moon `10` `19`

US space missions landed on the Moon six times between 1969 and 1972. Neil Armstrong was the first astronaut to walk on the Moon, on 21 July 1969. The Moon's gravitational force is less than Earth's, so the astronauts could easily jump across the landscape.

QUESTIONS:
Constellations

Level 1

1. You must always use binoculars or a telescope to see stars. True or false?
2. The constellation Scorpius is also known as Scorpio. True or false?
3. How many halves can the celestial sky be split into: two or three?
4. Can the Southern Cross be seen in the northern hemisphere?
5. Centaurus is a constellation named after a creature from Greek mythology. True or false?

Level 2

6. Pegasus is named after which animal from Greek mythology: a winged horse, bull or goat?
7. Columba is named after which bird sent from the Ark by Noah to look for land: a dove, pigeon or eagle?
8. Which constellation did sailors use to navigate in the southern hemisphere?
9. Rearrange BRUIN COLAS to name an instrument used for stargazing.
10. Which star is the brightest: Sirius, Orion or Cygnus?
11. Which 'O' is the constellation with the largest number of bright stars?
12. Rearrange BEE GLUE SET to spell the name of the bright red star that marks Orion's shoulder.
13. Which 'C' is a southern constellation that can be seen in the northern hemisphere in February?

Level 3

14. What object does the constellation Libra depict?
15. What is the name of the 13th brightest star in the sky?
16. When in history do we know that the Southern Cross could be seen from the Middle East?
17. Name the bright star that marks the tail of Cygnus.

FIND THE ANSWER: Constellations

Constellations are groups of stars that form a shape, such as a creature from mythology. There are 88 constellations in total, and they are best seen on dark nights. Farmers and astronomers have used constellations for over 6,000 years to identify the stars.

Centaurus · 5

This constellation is in the shape of a centaur – a creature from Greek mythology that is half man and half horse. It can be seen in the southern hemisphere.

Hemispheres · 3

An imaginary line, called the celestial equator, divides the sky into northern and southern hemispheres. Some constellations and stars appear to move between the hemispheres throughout the year.

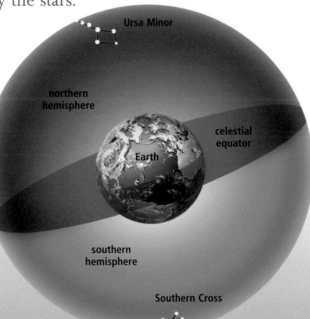

Ursa Minor

northern hemisphere

celestial equator

Earth

southern hemisphere

Southern Cross

looking into the celestial sky

Southern Cross · 4 · 8 · 16

Sailors in the southern oceans use this constellation to navigate when sailing. In Biblical times it could be seen in the Middle East, but now it can be seen only in the southern hemisphere.

Stargazing · 1 · 9 · 10 · 11

Binoculars or a telescope are used to see faint stars, but some stars are bright enough to be seen with only your eyes. The brightest star in the night sky is Sirius. It is in the constellation of Canis Major. Orion is the constellation with the largest number of bright stars.

Libra · 14

The ancient Greeks saw Libra as the scales held by Virgo, the goddess of justice, whose constellation is nearby. Libra is in the southern hemisphere and its stars are faint.

Cygnus

The swan, or Cygnus, appears to fly south along the Milky Way. Deneb is the bright star in its tail. With binoculars, you can see millions of faint stars in Cygnus.

Scorpio

Scorpius, or Scorpio, rises near the horizon as Orion sets in the summer sky. In its body is Antares, a giant red star and the thirteenth brightest star in the sky.

Pegasus

This northern hemisphere constellation is named after Pegasus, a winged horse in Greek myth. It shares a star called Delta Pegasi with the constellation Andromeda.

Columba

Although a southern constellation, Columba moves into northern skies in February. It was named after the Biblical dove that Noah sent to look for land.

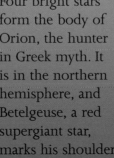

Orion

Four bright stars form the body of Orion, the hunter in Greek myth. It is in the northern hemisphere, and Betelgeuse, a red supergiant star, marks his shoulder.

QUESTIONS:
Outer space

Level 1

1. Which can you find in outer space: a green hole, a black hole or an orange hole?
2. Who was a famous astronomer: Rubble, Bubble or Hubble?
3. The galaxy that contains Earth is called the Creamy Way. True or false?
4. Does a star begin life in a nest or in a nebula?

Level 2

5. A galaxy is a large group of black holes. True or false?
6. Stars usually last for billions of years. True or false?
7. Which is an American space agency: LASA, MASA or NASA?
8. When a nebula shrinks and condenses, does it heat up or cool down?
9. Does the Milky Way appear to be pale, colourful or dark in the night sky?
10. Rearrange RAVEN SOUP to name a type of space explosion.
11. How many galaxies are in the Local Group: about three, about 30 or about 300?
12. A nebula is a large star. True or false?
13. Is the Milky Way a large galaxy or a small galaxy?
14. How many known types of galaxy are there: four, five or seven?
15. Which forms first: a red giant or a white dwarf?

Level 3

16. In which part of the Milky Way is Earth's solar system?
17. What do some scientists believe lies at the centre of our galaxy?
18. What is the main gas in the Eagle Nebula?

Outer space

The universe is so vast that astronomers (scientists who study space) measure distances in light years – the distance that light travels in one year. The solar system that includes Earth is only a tiny part of the universe. The area outside the solar system is called outer space. Astronomers are always learning more about outer space, as technology becomes more and more advanced.

The Milky Way   3 9 11 13 16

The Earth's solar system lies in one of the arms of the Milky Way, which is a large barred spiral galaxy. This galaxy gets its name from its pale appearance in the night sky. The Milky Way is part of a group of about 30 galaxies that is known as the Local Group.

Milky Way
(barred spiral galaxy)

Types of galaxy   2 5 12 14

A huge group of stars is called a galaxy. Astronomer Edwin Hubble showed that galaxies conform to a set of basic shapes. The four main shapes are elliptical, spiral, barred spiral and irregular. Each galaxy has billions of stars and nebulae – clouds of dust or gas.

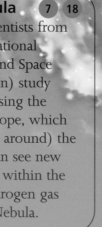

irregular galaxy

spiral galaxy

elliptical galaxy

Eagle Nebula   7 18

American scientists from NASA (the National Aeronautics and Space Administration) study outer space using the Hubble telescope, which orbits (travels around) the Earth. They can see new stars forming within the clouds of hydrogen gas of the Eagle Nebula.

Life cycle of a star ④ ⑥ ⑧ ⑮

A star begins life as part of a nebula, which shrinks and condenses. As this happens, the nebula heats up. When it is hot enough, a newborn star will begin to shine. Over billions of years, the star grows and swells up into a red giant. At this point, the star will expel its outer layers, leaving the white-hot core. This is a white dwarf star.

Black hole ① ⑩ ⑰

Sometimes an especially large star at the end of its life swells enough to become a supergiant and then explodes. This is a supernova. When this happens, the star collapses in on itself and creates a black hole – a bottomless pit that sucks in anything nearby, even light. Some scientists think that there is a giant black hole in the centre of the Milky Way.

QUESTIONS:
Gold

Level 1

1. What 'Y' colour is gold?
2. Where in the USA was there a famous gold rush that began in 1848: California or Ohio?
3. Gold is a hard metal. True or false?
4. What is gold dust: chunks of gold or tiny particles of gold?

Level 2

5. Rearrange GET GUNS to name the gold pieces found by mining.
6. Were there gold rushes in the 19th century in South Africa, Russia or Japan?
7. Which 'O' is the word for rock that contains metals such as gold?
8. Rearrange ANN PING to name a way of searching for gold in rivers using a wide pan.
9. What 'G' do we call a person who can make jewellery from gold?
10. What 'I' is the word for the bars of gold that countries keep as part of their money reserves?
11. Exposing gold to air can make it dull. True or false?
12. What 'P' is the name for someone who searches for gold?
13. Gold can be drawn out to make thin wire. True or false?

Level 3

14. Which country is the world's largest gold producer?
15. What were used to wash gold pieces from river beds?
16. Where is the largest gold mine?
17. For how long has gold been used as money?
18. What 'E' is a substance that cannot be broken down, such as gold?

FIND THE ANSWER: Gold

Pure gold is an orangey-yellow metal that forms underground in layers called lodes, or veins. Its purity is measured in carats, and pure gold is 24 carats. Because gold is soft, it is usually mixed with another metal. This mixture, called an alloy, becomes a paler yellow, reddish or white.

Gold (11) (18)

Pure gold is a chemical element, which means that it cannot be broken down into other elements. Leaving it in water or exposed to air does not destroy it or dull its shine.

Gold rush (2) (6)

In the 19th century, gold deposits were found in North America, Australia and South Africa. Men rushed to these places to 'stake a claim'. A famous gold rush began in 1848 in California, USA.

Mining (7) (12) (15)

Mines are sunk to dig up ore (rocks containing gold). Most 19th-century prospectors (searchers) looked for gold that was carried to the surface by underground rivers or volcanic lava flows. They washed gravel from river beds in sluice boxes, which trapped gold pieces called nuggets.

Panning (4) (5) (8)

Some miners put river mud in a shallow metal pan filled with water and swirled it around. Sand and pebbles were washed away, but the heavier gold sank to the bottom. Panning collected gold nuggets, flakes and tiny particles of gold dust.

mud washed in large metal pans

Modern gold mining (14)(16)

Today, miners blast and drill tunnels into rock to find veins of gold ore. The ore is refined to separate the gold from the rock. South Africa is the world's largest gold producer. The largest gold mine is in West Papua, Indonesia.

camp hut

sluice box

Currency (10)(17)

Gold has been used as money for 4,000 years. Merchants paid for goods with gold bars called ingots. Today, most countries store gold ingots as part of their reserve of money.

gold ingots

Jewellery (1)(3)(9)(13)

Gold is valued for its yellow colour and shine. Goldsmiths make jewellery from gold. Because gold is a soft metal, they can beat it into many shapes and draw it out into thin wire.

gold ring

QUESTIONS:
Caves

Level 1

1. Worms sometimes live in caves. True or false?
2. Do bats or eagles roost in cave roofs?
3. Do bacteria and insects feed on fungi or potatoes growing in caves?
4. Plants such as ferns and mosses cannot grow in a cave entrance. True or false?

Level 2

5. Rearrange NOODLE WRAPS to name a big cat that shelters in caves in winter.
6. What is volcanic lava when it is red hot, soft and runny: molten, malted or moulded?
7. Name one of two 'S' birds that nest on ledges in the ceiling of a cave's entrance.
8. Rearrange LEAST STIGMA to name the rock formations that grow up from a cave floor.
9. Fungi growing in caves need little light, water or nutrients. True or false?
10. Do cockroaches or swallows feed on bat droppings in caves?
11. Which is the name of a zone of a cave system: the sunrise zone, twilight zone or midnight zone?
12. Which rock formations hang like icicles from cave roofs: stalagmites or stalactites?
13. Name two 'S' types of creepy-crawly that can live in caves.

Level 3

14. Which 'C' is a mineral that is formed when limestone is dissolved?
15. Temperatures remain constant in which cave zone?
16. Underground rivers carve out what features?
17. What happened to the soft lava that once filled a lava tube?
18. Rearrange BLAME EMPIRE to form another word meaning 'watertight'.

Caves

Some caves are hollow spaces along the bottom of cliffs, carved out by waves. Others form underground when rainwater eats away soft limestone rock. In many caves there are beautiful columns and pinnacles, mineral deposits, lakes and rivers.

Rock formations 8 12 14

Rainwater drips into underground caves. The drips contain dissolved limestone (calcite), which slowly hardens. It forms stalactites, which hang like icicles from the cave roof. Some drips fall to the floor. They harden and grow upwards, forming spires that are called stalagmites.

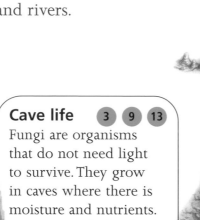

Cave life 3 9 13

Fungi are organisms that do not need light to survive. They grow in caves where there is moisture and nutrients. Fungi provide food for bacteria and insects. Spiders, bats, salamanders and fish also live in caves.

Cave systems 1 2 10 11 15

Beyond the cave entrance is the twilight zone. There, bats may roost in the roof and cockroaches, worms and bacteria live on their droppings. Deeper inside is the dark zone, where the temperature is always about 13°C

Cave entrances 4 5 7

Bears and snow leopards may shelter from harsh weather in a cave entrance. If the entrance gets sunlight and rain, ferns and mosses grow there. They provide food for insects and other small animals. Swallows and swiftlets build their nests on high ledges.

limestone

entrance zone

Cave rivers 16 18

Rivers form below ground after rain sinks through rock that has cracks and holes, such as limestone. The rain seeps down until it reaches impermeable, or watertight, rock. A river forms and flows towards the sea, carving out tunnels and caves.

Lava tubes 6 17

These tunnels form in lava from a volcano. Lava flowing in a channel down a volcano's side may cool and harden on the outside, but it remains molten (soft) underneath. In time, the soft lava drains or flows away, leaving a long cave inside a hard outer crust.

hard outer crust

lava tube

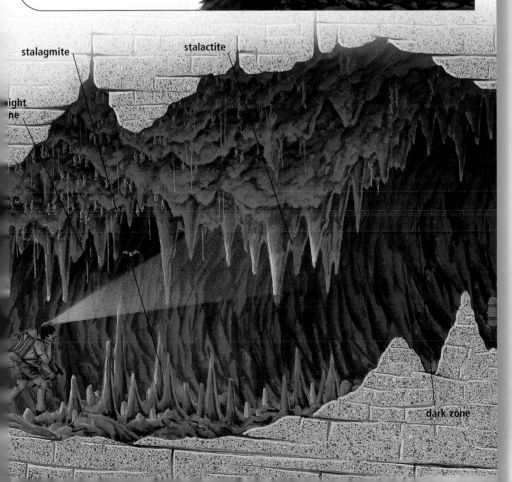

stalagmite

stalactite

light ne

dark zone

QUESTIONS:
Climate

Level 1

1. During a drought is there less or more rainfall than usual?
2. What are clouds made of: water vapour or icy water?
3. Cirrus is the name for a type of cloud. True or false?

Level 2

4. Which 'S' is the largest desert in the world?
5. Which is a greenhouse gas: oxygen or carbon dioxide?
6. In how many years do meteorologists think that all the glaciers could melt away: ten, 20 or 30?
7. Is an arid climate hot and wet, hot and dry, or cold and icy?
8. Where did scientists find a hole in the ozone layer: over Antarctica, the Arctic or both?
9. How much rainfall do deserts receive in a year: less than 25cm, less than 50cm or more than 1m?
10. Which of these two cloud types brings rain: cirrus or cumulonimbus?
11. Rearrange ACE GIRL to name a source of water entering rivers.
12. What 'L's have been drying up in recent years?
13. Are cumulus clouds wispy or puffy clouds?
14. How much of the land on Earth is desert: one-third, one-quarter or one-fifth?

Level 3

15. During a drought, why do crops die?
16. The ozone layer shields the Earth from what kind of harmful rays?
17. What never thaws in the tundra?
18. When did the recent drought in the Sahel, northern Africa, begin?
19. How high up in the atmosphere is the ozone layer?

Climate

The atmosphere is a protective layer of gases around the Earth. It lets in the Sun's light and heat, but sends harmful ultraviolet (UV) rays back into space. There are different climate zones around the world. However, changes in the atmosphere are making the Earth overheat. This is making weather change.

dried-up river

Clouds 2 3 10 13
Clouds are water vapour in the sky. High clouds such as the wispy cirrus and the puffy cumulus are seen on dry days. Grey stratus clouds that blanket the sky, and big, black, cumulonimbus thunderclouds, bring rain.

Drought 1 15 18
A long period when rainfall is below the usual level is called a drought. In a drought, water supplies dry up and crops die. Without food and water, animals and people die. There has been a drought in the Sahel region of northern Africa since 1968.

Rain and water 12
Rain feeds streams, rivers and lakes. Humans use increasing amounts of water in their homes, cities, farms and industries. Many rivers and lakes have been drying up in recent years.

mountain snow

river fed by mountain streams

Mountains and glaciers 6 11
The springtime melting of mountain snow and glaciers (rivers of ice) and summer rains feed the rivers where people fish, drink and grow food. Because of climate change, less snow and ice falls on mountains and glaciers may melt away within 30 years.

The zones (7)(17)

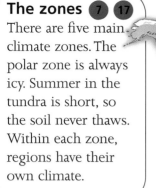

There are five main climate zones. The polar zone is always icy. Summer in the tundra is short, so the soil never thaws. Within each zone, regions have their own climate.

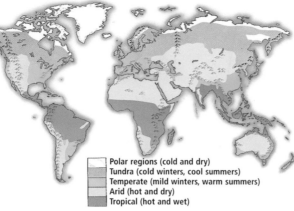

Polar regions (cold and dry)
Tundra (cold winters, cool summers)
Temperate (mild winters, warm summers)
Arid (hot and dry)
Tropical (hot and wet)

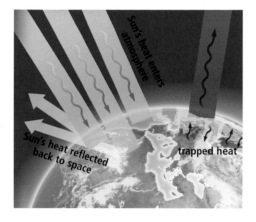

Sun's heat enters atmosphere
Sun's heat reflected back to space
trapped heat

Greenhouse effect (5)

The atmosphere includes gases, such as carbon dioxide, that trap heat like the glass in a greenhouse. When we burn coal, oil, and gas we release more of these gases, which causes the Earth to overheat.

Ozone hole (8)(16)(19)

A 22km-high layer of ozone gas around the Earth reflects ultraviolet rays back into space. The rays harm people, animals and plants. Scientists have found holes in the ozone layer above Antarctica and over the Arctic.

hole in the ozone layer

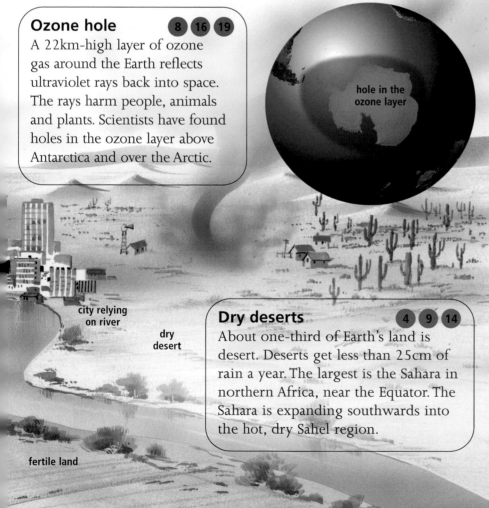

city relying on river

dry desert

fertile land

Dry deserts (4)(9)(14)

About one-third of Earth's land is desert. Deserts get less than 25cm of rain a year. The largest is the Sahara in northern Africa, near the Equator. The Sahara is expanding southwards into the hot, dry Sahel region.

QUESTIONS:
Storms

Level 1

1. Lightning is a spark of electricity in a cloud. True or false?
2. Is a blizzard a snowstorm or a dust storm with strong winds?
3. Where do sandstorms happen: in deserts or rainforests?
4. What time of year do thunderstorms usually happen: summer or winter?

Level 2

5. If a wave tips a lifeboat over, does it always sink?
6. Rearrange FIND LOGO into a word that describes what happens when seawater spills over on to dry land.
7. How many people are killed by lightning in the USA every year: about ten, 100 or 1,000?
8. How many thunderstorms take place on Earth at any time: about 20, 200 or 2,000?
9. Electricity is made in what type of cloud: nimbostratus, cumulonimbus or cumulus?
10. Lightning always takes the form of a long bright streak that follows a zigzag path. True or false?
11. What 'M' is the word for a weather expert?
12. What happens to a tree struck by lightning: does it get soggy, or glow in the dark, or is it blown apart?
13. What 'G' is a system that can be found on lifeboats?

Level 3

14. A huge North Sea storm surge in 1953 hit which countries?
15. What is thunder?
16. What is the effect of warm air from the ground rising quickly into the cold atmosphere?
17. What is a lightning rod?
18. How high can wind blow sand during a sandstorm?

Storms

Different types of storm occur depending on the climate. Hot air at the Equator rises, then colder air rushes in, causing strong winds. Across northern Europe and the USA, rain and snowstorms occur in winter when icy air from the North Pole meets warmer air from the south. The warm air chills, sinks and blows outwards as wind.

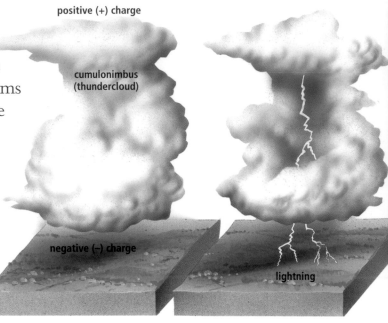

positive (+) charge

cumulonimbus (thundercloud)

negative (–) charge

lightning

How storms form `4` `8` `16`

Thunderstorms often occur in summer, when warm air rises fast from ground level into the cold atmosphere. This causes rain, wind, lightning and thunder. At any time, about 2,000 thunderstorms are happening on Earth.

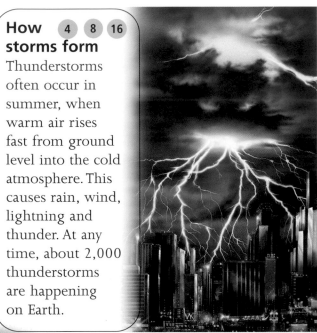

Thunder and lightning `1` `9` `15`

Lightning is a huge spark of electricity made in a cloud. Cumulonimbus clouds have a positive electrical charge above and a negative charge beneath. This electricity builds up. The electricity heats the air so fast it vibrates, making thunder. Negatively charged electricity streams to the ground and a positive charge rises up to meet it, making a channel for the lightning to streak through.

Lightning damage `7` `12` `17`

As well as blowing trees apart, lightning kills about 100 people a year in the USA. Tall buildings have metal lightning rods fitted to the top. They conduct, or direct, the lightning down a cable to the ground, where it won't cause damage.

Ball lightning `10` `11`

Meteorologists (weather experts) cannot explain the ball-shaped lightning that is sometimes seen. It can be as small as a golf ball or as large as a basketball.

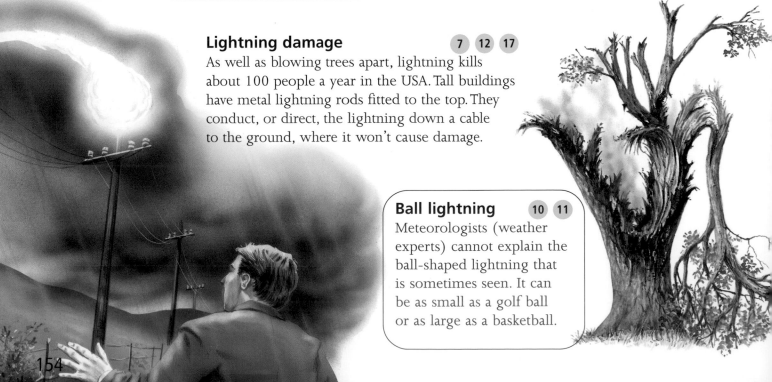

Sandstorms and snowstorms   2 3 18

In desert areas, winds blow sand into clouds 1,500m high. In cold northern regions, the wind whips snow and ice into clouds that blot out the Sun. A large snowstorm with strong winds is called a blizzard.

Storm surges   6

High winds blowing across the ocean for many days can cause a storm surge. The winds whip up the waters above normal sea level and high waves hit the coast, causing flooding. This often occurs when high tides pull the seas to their highest level.

Rescue at sea   5 13 14

A North Sea storm surge in 1953 drove waves up to 3.36m higher than normal onto the UK and Netherlands coasts. Thousands died in the floods. Hundreds more died at sea when lifeboat crews could not find them in the storm. Today's lifeboats have Global Positioning System receivers and good communications. The boats can operate in wild weather. If a huge wave tips one over, it flips back upright.

QUESTIONS:
Hurricanes and tornadoes

Level 1
1. Are planes ever flown into the centre of a hurricane?
2. There is torrential rain during a hurricane. True or false?
3. Do hurricanes usually happen during the warmer or colder months?
4. Are hurricanes strong enough to lift up boats and trucks?
5. What is the term for studying storms up close: storm chasing, storm checking or storm charting?

Level 2
6. Tornadoes are not much more than 10m in diameter. True or false?
7. What is the name of the truck used for studying storms up close?
8. Do hurricanes form over land or ocean?
9. Where is Tornado Alley: in China, India or the USA?
10. What 'D' is a kind of radar used to investigate storms?
11. How many tornadoes can the USA have in a year: ten, 100 or more than 1,000?
12. What is the minimum water temperature needed for a hurricane to form: 22°C, 27°C or 30°C?
13. What 'R' equipment can be found on a weather-tracking plane?
14. Do hurricanes move faster or slower as they near land?

Level 3
15. What two things do weather-tracking aircraft measure about a hurricane?
16. Inside what type of cloud do tornadoes form?
17. What are hurricane surges?

Hurricanes and tornadoes

Hurricanes are huge whirling storms that rise over warm tropical oceans north and south of the Equator. Tornadoes are powerful whirlwinds, faster and more violent than hurricanes. Meteorologists use satellites, ships, air balloons and aircraft to build a picture of hurricanes and tornadoes and broadcast warnings.

Tracking a hurricane 1 13 15
Weather-tracking planes are equipped with radar and probes. They fly into the eye, or centre, of hurricanes to measure the wind speed and pressure.

clouds spin in upward spiral

warm ocean

Hurricanes 3 8 12
In the warmer months hurricanes occur when two air masses meet over an ocean with a temperature above 27°C. Warm, moist air is drawn up from the ocean in a slow, circular motion. This is caused by Earth's spin.

The storm hits 2 4 14 17
Hurricanes can be more than 400km in diameter, with wind speeds of 120–350km/h. Many last for several days. At sea, they can build up giant waves, causing surges that flood coasts. They often grow bigger and faster as they move towards land. When they hit the coast they lift boats and trucks, rip up trees and roofs, and blow down buildings. They bring torrential rain, which can cause flooding.

Tornadoes 6 16

The inside of huge thunderclouds called supercells are where tornadoes form. They are fed by currents of warm air that rise into the clouds from below. These currents start spinning and grow into a funnel shape, up to 1.5km wide. As tornadoes grow, they descend and touch land or ocean.

Storm chasing 5 7 10

Scientists can use Doppler radar to investigate storms. Special 'Dopplers on wheels' (trucks with satellite dishes) are used to closely follow tornadoes and hurricanes and study them. This dangerous job is called storm chasing.

Tornado land 9 11

The USA has more than 1,000 tornadoes a year. Most hit Tornado Alley, between the Gulf of Mexico and the Great Lakes. Russia and East Asia also get tornadoes.

Doppler on wheels

QUESTIONS:
Tsunamis

Level 1

1. A tsunami can travel thousands of kilometres. True or false?
2. A tsunami is only about 1m high when travelling across the ocean. True or false?
3. Can ships pass over tsunamis before they reach the coast?
4. A tsunami is one massive wave. True or false?
5. Does a tsunami start on land or at sea?

Level 2

6. Rearrange HE ATE QUARK to name an undersea event that can cause a tsunami.
7. What 'A' is a rock hurtling in space, which may crash into the sea and set off a tsunami?
8. Tsunamis can be formed by rock slides. True or false?
9. What is the average height above sea level of a tsunami wave as it hits a coast: 3m, 45m or 500m?
10. There are usually two to four hours between two tsunami waves in a train. True or false?
11. How fast can a train of waves travel: 70km/h, 170km/h or 700km/h?
12. Do waves from tsunamis look curved or squarish when seen from the side?
13. Are mega-tsunami waves less than 4m, 14m or more than 40m high?

Level 3

14. Name the parts of the Earth's crust that move, causing an earthquake.
15. Why do tsunamis slow down as they approach a shore?
16. How many people were killed in the 2004 Asian tsunami?
17. Which volcano in Indonesia erupted in 1883, causing massive waves that killed 36,000 people?
18. What does the word 'wavelength' mean?

FIND THE ANSWER: Tsunamis

A sign that a tsunami is coming is the sea sucking back from the shore. A huge wall of water then races to the shore, growing higher and higher. The wave floods inland, causing terrible damage. The 2004 Asian tsunami was caused by earthquakes beneath the Indian ocean. The Pacific ocean, where 85 per cent of tsunamis occur, has tsunami warning systems.

Waves (2)(3)(12)

Tsunamis racing across the ocean, about 1m high, are so small that ships pass over them. When they pile up at the coast, they look squarish from the side. Waves made by hurricanes will look curved.

Mega-tsunamis (13)(17)

The waves of a mega-tsunami are 40m high or more. In 1883, Krakatoa, a volcano near Java, Indonesia, erupted. Its lava chamber emptied and collapsed. The sea then rushed in, creating massive waves that killed 36,000 people.

Trains (4)(9)(15)

A tsunami is really a train, or series, of waves. The waves grow only when they reach land. A rising seabed close to the coast slows the waves to about 100km/h. They then pile up, one on top of the other. They reach an average of 3m above sea level, but they can be much higher. The sea pulls back from shore before each wave in the train surges inland.

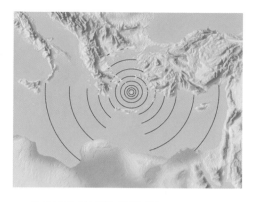

A tsunami's journey   1   5   6   11

An undersea earthquake pushes seawater up and out. A train of waves, about 1m high, forms. They can race up to 700km/h across the ocean for thousands of kilometres.

How tsunamis form   7   8   14

Most tsunamis occur when two parts of the Earth's crust – tectonic plates – move below the seabed. They jolt or go under each other. Tsunamis can also be formed by huge rock slides, or asteroids falling into the sea.

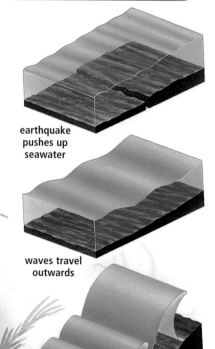

earthquake pushes up seawater

waves travel outwards

waves at shoreline increase in size

The aftermath   10   16   18

Tsunamis can have a 100m wavelength (distance between waves). They surge onto the coast every 15–60 minutes and travel up to 1km inland. They are very destructive. In the 2004 Indian ocean tsunami, about 230,000 people were killed.

QUESTIONS:
The senses

Level 1

1. Which 'T' is the part of the mouth you use to taste food?
2. To smell something, you have to breathe the smell in through your nose. True or false?
3. Do sensors in the ear send information about sound to the other ear or to the brain?
4. If a person needs glasses, are the objects he sees without them focused or blurry?

Level 2

5. Rearrange FINEST GRIP to name a part of the body that is sensitive to touch.
6. Does light enter the eye through the pupil, the lens or the retina?
7. Do sound waves first enter the ear through the outer ear, middle ear or inner ear?
8. Rearrange LIBERAL to name a method that people can use to read with their fingertips.
9. Is the middle ear made up of tiny bones, cilia or sensor cells?
10. Name four basic types of taste your tongue can detect.
11. Which 'C' is the word for the tiny hairs in the nose?
12. How many taste buds can be found on your tongue and throat: less than 100, 1,000 or up to 10,000?
13. What 'G' would you wear to correct blurry vision?
14. Which part of the ear vibrates: the ear drum, middle ear or cochlea?

Level 3

15. Where on your body are the sensors that detect temperature?
16. Upside-down images form on which part of the eye?
17. Rearrange CHEER TOP TROOPS into a word for cells in the retina.
18. Do the sounds made by flutes have long wavelengths?

The senses

We have five senses – hearing, sight, smell, taste and touch – to communicate with the world around us. Millions of sensor cells all over the body send information about what we sense to the brain. The senses work together. Smell and taste are so closely linked that if you have a cold and cannot smell, food tastes bland.

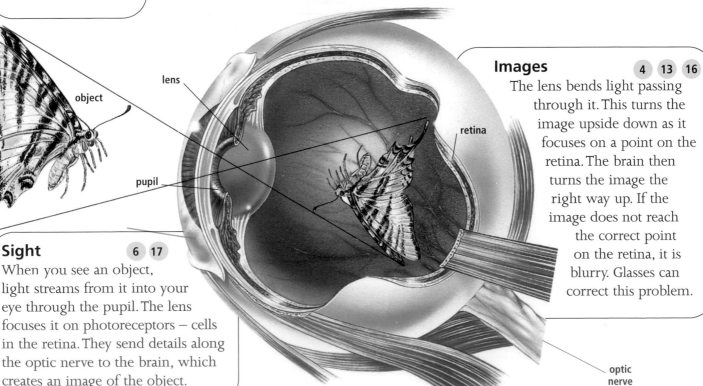

hot water

cold water

Smell   2 11

When you smell something, you breathe in tiny chemical particles. They dissolve in the mucus in your nose and are sensed by tiny hairs in the nose, called cilia. The cilia are attached to smell receptor cells.

Touch   5 8 15

There are millions of touch sensors in your skin. People can read Braille by feeling raised dots with their sensitive fingertips. Some sensors can detect temperature. If you move your hands from hot water into cold water, your brain will notice the difference.

object

lens

pupil

retina

Images   4 13 16

The lens bends light passing through it. This turns the image upside down as it focuses on a point on the retina. The brain then turns the image the right way up. If the image does not reach the correct point on the retina, it is blurry. Glasses can correct this problem.

Sight   6 17

When you see an object, light streams from it into your eye through the pupil. The lens focuses it on photoreceptors – cells in the retina. They send details along the optic nerve to the brain, which creates an image of the object.

optic nerve

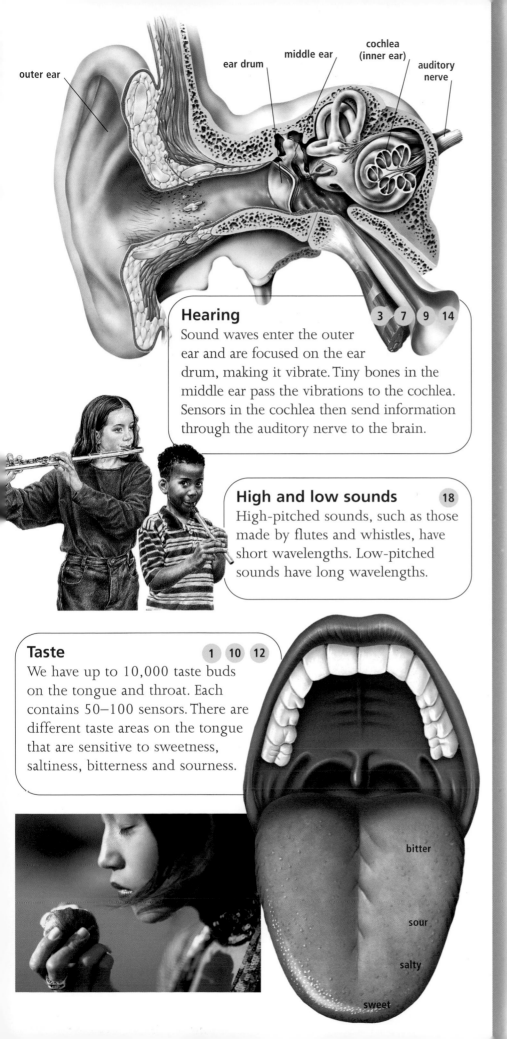

Hearing

3 7 9 14

Sound waves enter the outer ear and are focused on the ear drum, making it vibrate. Tiny bones in the middle ear pass the vibrations to the cochlea. Sensors in the cochlea then send information through the auditory nerve to the brain.

High and low sounds

18

High-pitched sounds, such as those made by flutes and whistles, have short wavelengths. Low-pitched sounds have long wavelengths.

Taste

1 10 12

We have up to 10,000 taste buds on the tongue and throat. Each contains 50–100 sensors. There are different taste areas on the tongue that are sensitive to sweetness, saltiness, bitterness and sourness.

outer ear

ear drum

middle ear

cochlea (inner ear)

auditory nerve

bitter

sour

salty

sweet

QUESTIONS:
Digestion

Level 1

1. Waste passes from the large intestine to the anus. True or false?
2. What should you do when you feel thirsty: eat ice cream or drink water?
3. Where is saliva produced: in the mouth or liver?
4. What 'T' rolls food into a ball before swallowing?

Level 2

5. Most sugars and fats are broken down in the large intestine. True or false?
6. Are finger-shaped villi found in the small intestine?
7. Why do we need proteins: to prevent heart disease, provide energy or for body-building?
8. Rearrange BOTCHED ARRAYS to name something in food.
9. Is urine held in the stomach, bladder or lungs?
10. Where is bile stored: in the small intestine, stomach or gall bladder?
11. Does digestion in the stomach take one, two or four hours?
12. What 'B' is the name of the ball of food that is pushed down to the stomach when you swallow?
13. How long does digestion usually take in the intestines: eight, 20 or 30 hours?
14. How much of our bodies is water: one-third, two-thirds or four-fifths?

Level 3

15. What role does saliva play in digestion?
16. What are enzymes?
17. What does bile do?
18. What 'P' is the name for the muscle movements that push food down the oesophagus?

Digestion

The mouth ③ ⑮
The teeth chop food into small pieces. Glands inside the mouth make saliva. It starts to break down sugars.

Digestion is what the body does to get the energy it needs from food. As food travels from your mouth to your stomach and then to your intestines, it is broken down by acids and digestive chemicals called enzymes. The body can use the proteins, sugars, fats, vitamins and other nutrients it contains. The body also needs water.

Stomach ⑪ ⑯
Food is churned in the stomach for at least four hours. It is mixed with an acid to kill germs. An enzyme (digestive chemical) begins to break down proteins.

Swallowing ④ ⑫ ⑱
The tongue moistens chewed food with saliva and rolls it into a bolus, or ball. Swallowing pushes the bolus into the oesophagus. This tube has muscles that relax ahead of the bolus and tighten behind it. These movements, called peristalsis, push the bolus into the stomach in less than a minute.

muscle

oesophagus

bolus

liver

The intestines ① ⑤ ⑥ ⑬
Partially digested food travels by peristalsis along the small intestine. There, enzymes break up sugars and fats. Finger-shaped villi absorb these with water and pass them to the blood vessels. Waste passes into the large intestine and is pushed out of the anus as faeces (poo). This stage takes about 20 hours.

villus

small intestine

stomach

large intes

blood vessel

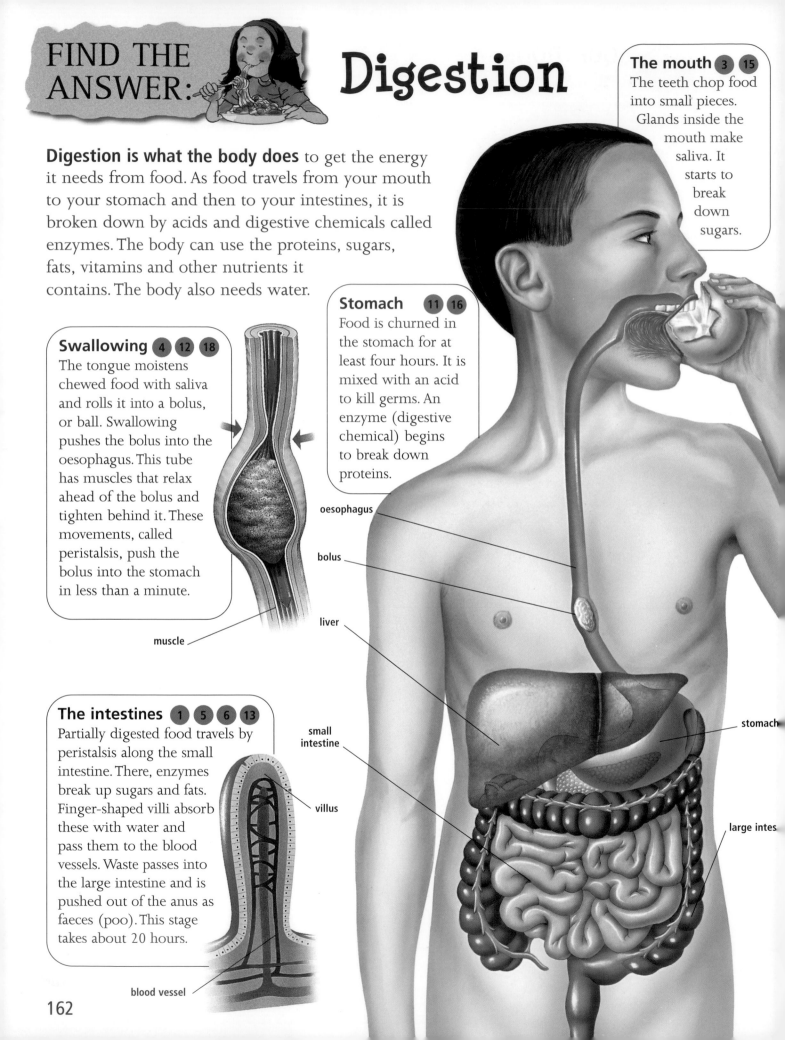

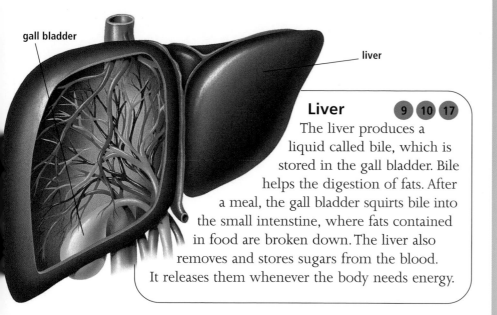

Liver 9 10 17

The liver produces a liquid called bile, which is stored in the gall bladder. Bile helps the digestion of fats. After a meal, the gall bladder squirts bile into the small intenstine, where fats contained in food are broken down. The liver also removes and stores sugars from the blood. It releases them whenever the body needs energy.

gall bladder

liver

Water 2 14

Our bodies are about two-thirds water. It is used for many functions, such as digestion, and for blood and other fluids. If you feel thirsty, your body is telling you to drink more water.

Good food guide 7 8

To stay healthy, eat different types of food every day. You need carbohydrates (sugars and starchy food) and fats for energy; protein for body-building; minerals for strong bones and teeth; and vitamins to prevent illnesses.

bread provides carbohydrates

eggs have minerals and protein

fish provides protein

fruit and vegetables provide vitamins

cheese and dairy provide calcium

meat is good for iron and protein

QUESTIONS:
Inventors

Level 1

1. Is a telescope or a microscope used to see planets?
2. Are microscopes used by scientists or musicians to carry out experiments?
3. The Greek philosopher and scientist Aristotle studied plants and animals. True or false?
4. What is believed to have been the first writing instrument: a stylus made from reed or a pencil?

Level 2

5. The other planets in the Solar System orbit the Earth. True or false?
6. Rearrange MARINES US to name the ancient people who are believed to have invented the first writing system.
7. Which 'O' is a building where astronomers study the sky?
8. When did Aristotle begin to study nature: about 3000BCE, 350BCE or 1350CE?
9. Who built the first telescope: Galileo or Isaac Newton?
10. Rearrange REMOTE BAR to name a scientific instrument.
11. Which scientist worked out the movement of planets: Aristotle, Galileo or Isaac Newton?
12. Which scientist studied plants and animals: Aristotle, Galileo or Isaac Newton?
13. Benjamin Franklin installed a lightning rod on his house. True or false?
14. Were the first writings made on clay, paper or plant leaves?

Level 3

15. In which year did Alexander Graham Bell first successfully try his telephone?
16. Who discovered that electricity has positive and negative charges?
17. Who made the first star maps?
18. What shapes form the letters in cuneiform writing?

FIND THE ANSWER: Inventors

tradesman with stylus and clay tablet

The first observatories and calendars appeared in Egypt and Mesopotamia (modern-day Iraq), about 3000BCE. Telescopes were invented in Europe in the 17th century, and helped scientists to observe planets that had not been seen before. Observations made by Galileo and Newton laid the foundations of modern science.

Astronomy 7 17

Observatories were built by ancient people to study the stars and planets. Chinese astronomers made the first maps of the stars. They recorded a solar eclipse in 2136BCE.

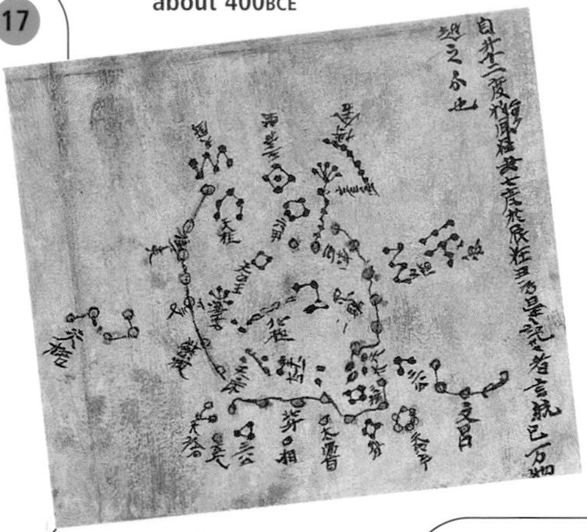

Chinese star map, about 400BCE

Sumerians and writing 4 6 14 18

The Sumerians in Mesopotamia are thought to have invented writing in about 3500BCE. They used a stylus (a piece of reed) to press shapes in clay. They made lists of the goods they traded, using triangles and lines to make images that stood for things, such as fish, sheep, numbers and days. This system is called cuneiform (wedge-shaped) writing.

Aristotle

The first scientist 3 8 12

In around 350BCE, the Greek Aristotle (384–322BCE) became the first philosopher to observe nature and do experiments on plants and animals. He wrote descriptions about them and tried to work out what their different parts – brains, hearts, leaves, stems – were for.

Galileo 1 5 9

Galileo (1564–1642) observed weights being dropped from the Leaning Tower of Pisa, in Italy. When the heaviest and lightest hit the ground at the same time, he realized that the speed of moving objects is not affected by weight. He built the first telescope, and discovered that the planets orbit the Sun.

Newton's telescope (11)

Isaac Newton (1642–1727) designed a telescope more powerful than Galileo's. He worked out the laws behind the movement of planets.

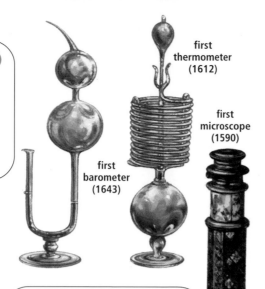

first thermometer (1612)

first microscope (1590)

first barometer (1643)

Instruments (2) (10)

The inventions of the microscope, thermometer and barometer helped scientists to carry out more accurate experiments.

Benjamin Franklin (13) (16)

Electricity was studied by Benjamin Franklin (1706–90). It is said that in 1752 he flew a kite with metal in its tail into a thundercloud to prove that lightning is electricity. He discovered that electricity has positive and negative charges. He invented the lightning rod and installed one on his own house.

Alexander Graham Bell

Alexander Graham Bell (15)

Mass communications began when Alexander Graham Bell (1847–1922) had the idea of transmitting the human voice along waves of electricity. In March 1876, he spoke to his assistant on a telephone he had invented. In 1877, he began the Bell Telephone Company.

QUESTIONS:
Cars

Level 1

1. What 'P' do most cars run on?
2. The Ford Model-T was the first affordable car. True or false?
3. The Mini was originally designed for driving around where: in the city or in the countryside?
4. From where do solar-powered cars get energy?

Level 2

5. How many wheels did Karl Benz's Motorwagen have: two, three or four?
6. Rearrange ARE RELAX to name a part found in a car.
7. What nationality was Henry Ford: British, American or Australian?
8. How many doors did the original Mini have?
9. Which type of car is better for the environment: a petrol-powered car or solar-powered car?
10. What 'E' drives a car forward?
11. Was the Ford Model-T also known as Thin Lizzie, Tin Lizzie or Tin Dizzy?
12. Which was the first vehicle to use a petrol-powered engine?
13. In which decade was the Mini introduced: the 1950s, 1960s or 1970s?
14. In 1914, a Ford Model-T could be assembled in 93 minutes. True or false?
15. Solar-powered cars can run all the time. True or false?

Level 3

16. Is a propeller shaft a type of long rod, a series of gears or a type of steering mechanism?
17. What 'A' means the way that air flows over a moving car?
18. What 'G' helps control the engine's speed?

FIND THE ANSWER: Cars

The car is one of the most popular forms of transport in the world today. Before motorized vehicles were invented, people travelled by horse-drawn carriage. Engineers still refer to the 'horsepower' of a car. Cars are one of the biggest causes of pollution in the world, so scientists are looking for ways to make them cleaner and safer for the environment.

Karl Benz (5) (12)

In 1885, the German inventor Karl Benz produced the three-wheeled Motorwagen, the first vehicle with a petrol-powered engine. It could travel at about 15km/h. The back wheels carried the engine and travellers. The front wheel was for steering.

Early cars (2) (7) (11) (14)

In 1908, the American Henry Ford introduced the Ford Model-T (or 'Tin Lizzie'). It was the first affordable car and was mass-produced on an assembly line. By 1914, a car could be assembled in only 93 minutes.

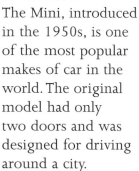

Mini revolution (3) (8) (13)

The Mini, introduced in the 1950s, is one of the most popular makes of car in the world. The original model had only two doors and was designed for driving around a city.

Modern cars

Today's cars are shaped so that air flows more easily over the car. The car can then travel faster using less energy. This is called aerodynamics.

aerodynamic car

Inside a car

The engine in a car drives it forward. A long rod called a propeller shaft transfers power from the engine to the rear axle and its wheels. A gearbox helps control the engine's speed.

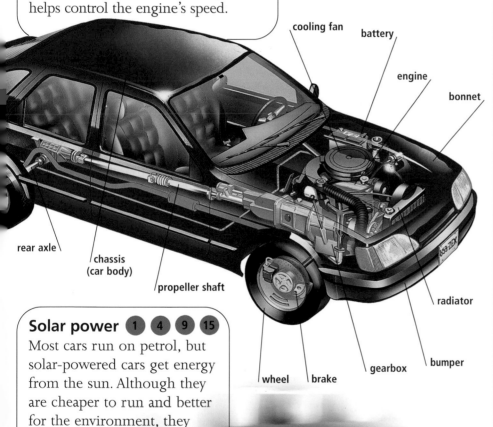

cooling fan

battery

engine

bonnet

rear axle

chassis (car body)

propeller shaft

radiator

gearbox

bumper

wheel

brake

Solar power ① ④ ⑨ ⑮

Most cars run on petrol, but solar-powered cars get energy from the sun. Although they are cheaper to run and better for the environment, they may not run in bad weather.

QUESTIONS:
Motorcycles

Level 1

1. Is the Lambretta a scooter?
2. A chopper is a motorcycle that was changed by chopping bits off its frame. True or false?
3. Rearrange EMPOD to name a very small type of motorcycle.
4. The first motorcycle was made in Germany. True or false?

Level 2

5. In racing, do motorcycles have the same or different engine capacities?
6. Are the handlebars on choppers higher or lower than on other motorcycles?
7. What 'S' is a bike that motocross racers use?
8. Was the Vespa introduced in 1946, 1956 or 1966?
9. What 'S' is the name for a motorcycle carriage with one wheel?
10. Did the Hildebrand brothers' 1889 trial motorcycle have a steam-driven or petrol-driven engine?
11. Superbikes are not road bikes. True or false?
12. Scramblers race for how long: 10 to 40 minutes or 1 to 2 hours?
13. Is Harley Davidson known for scooters or choppers?

Level 3

14. Name two of the three engine classes for Grand Prix motorcycle circuit racing.
15. In which year did Eric Oliver first win the World Motorcycle Sidecar Championship?
16. What 'P' is another word for a trial model?
17. What was the top speed of the motorcycle made by the Hildebrand brothers and Alois Wolfmuller?
18. What is the name of the largest sidecar maker?

The motorcycle was invented in 1885, when German engineer Gottlieb Daimler fixed a petrol engine to a bicycle. Motorcycles are cheaper to buy and run than cars, which made them popular in the 1920s and 1930s, and after World War II. World championship motorcycle racing began in 1949. Motorcycle sports, from road-racing to speedway and hill-climb, are popular worldwide.

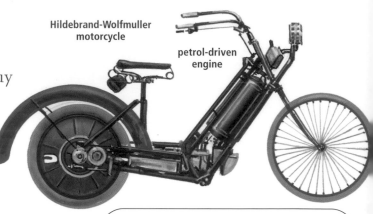

Hildebrand-Wolfmuller motorcycle

petrol-driven engine

Sidecars 9 15 18
One-wheeled motorcycle carriages are called sidecars. Watsonian-Squire, which began in the UK in 1912, is the largest sidecar maker. Eric Oliver won the first racing sidecar World Championship in 1949.

Early motorcycle 4 10 16 17
In 1889, the Hildebrand brothers of Munich, Germany, made a prototype (trial model) motorcycle with a steam engine. They made a petrol-driven motorcycle with Alois Wolfmuller in 1894. Its top speed was 40km/h.

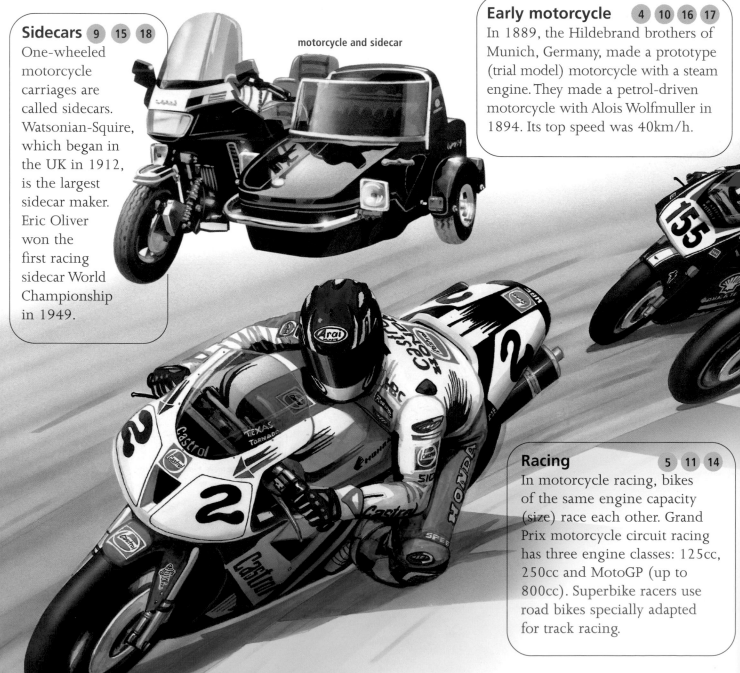

motorcycle and sidecar

Racing 5 11 14
In motorcycle racing, bikes of the same engine capacity (size) race each other. Grand Prix motorcycle circuit racing has three engine classes: 125cc, 250cc and MotoGP (up to 800cc). Superbike racers use road bikes specially adapted for track racing.

1960s scooter

engine under seat

'step-through' frame

Scooters (1) (3) (8)

Mopeds have engines of up to 50cc, and scooters up to 250cc – smaller than most motorcycles. They have been popular since the Vespa was introduced in 1946 and the Lambretta in 1947.

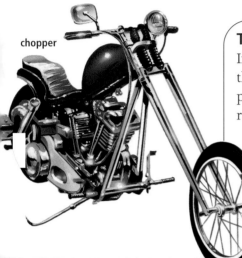

chopper

The chopper (2) (6) (13)

In the 1950s, US bikers lightened their motorcycles by chopping parts off the frame. They added raked (low-angled) front wheel forks and high handlebars. These motorcycles are called choppers. Harley Davidson now makes popular choppers.

Scrambling (7) (12)

Riding scrambler bikes with tough suspension, brakes and tyres, bikers race along a course lasting between 10 and 40 minutes. The course often involves jumps, and twisting uphill and downhill tracks. Motocross is one of the five types of off-road (dirt-track) racing for motorcyclists.

QUESTIONS:
Aeroplanes

Level 1

1. Are the economy-class seats in an aeroplane usually in the back part of the cabin or the front?
2. Do aircraft taxi or train as they move along the ground?
3. Is cargo packed into containers before being loaded on a plane?
4. Rearrange NICER SOUPS to make a word that describes really fast aircraft.

Level 2

5. At an airport, passengers might be driven in a bus to aircraft parked on the tarmac. True or false?
6. Which 'T' is the name of a building in an airport?
7. What 'F' is the name of the part of an aeroplane where digital screens provide flight information?
8. Cargo decks can be found under the cabins. True or false?
9. What was the first wide-body jet plane: the Boeing 747 or the Airbus A380?
10. Do scissor trucks lift cargo containers into the cargo hold or lift passengers to the passenger cabins?
11. Did Concorde fly from London, Paris, New York or all of the above?
12. Which is quieter: the Boeing 747 or the Airbus A380?
13. What 'B' is the term used when a plane turns left or right in the air?
14. Where in an airport do passengers go when they want to board a plane?

Level 3

15. What do flaps on the wings do when they are open?
16. In which year did Concorde begin a passenger service?
17. What are the metal strips on the wings that make the plane turn called?
18. What is Mach 2.2 expressed as kilometres per hour?

Aeroplanes

The development of the aeroplane took a huge step forward in 1939 when the first jet aircraft was flown by a German pilot. Planes that have jet engines can fly more people greater distances than the first powered aircraft flown in 1903. Today's aeroplanes are designed to be quieter, use less fuel and carry more people.

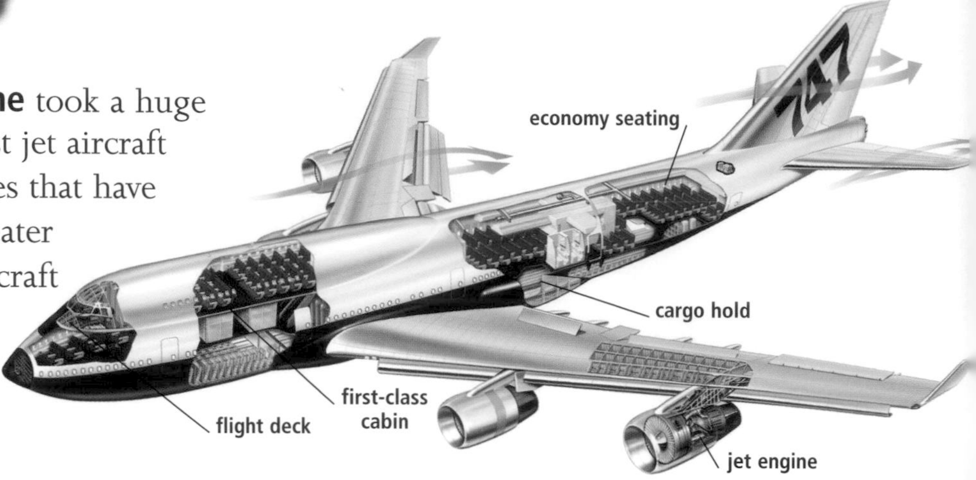

economy seating

cargo hold

jet engine

first-class cabin

flight deck

Inside an aeroplane (1) (7)

Digital screens in the flight deck provide flight information. There is also an instrument panel with over 350 switches. The passengers sit in a first-class cabin behind the flight deck or in economy further back.

upper deck lounge

cargo containers

Airports (2) (6) (14)

At major airports, aeroplanes taxi to and from docking bays outside terminal buildings. The departure lounge is where passengers go to board a plane. They enter and leave the aircraft through gangways.

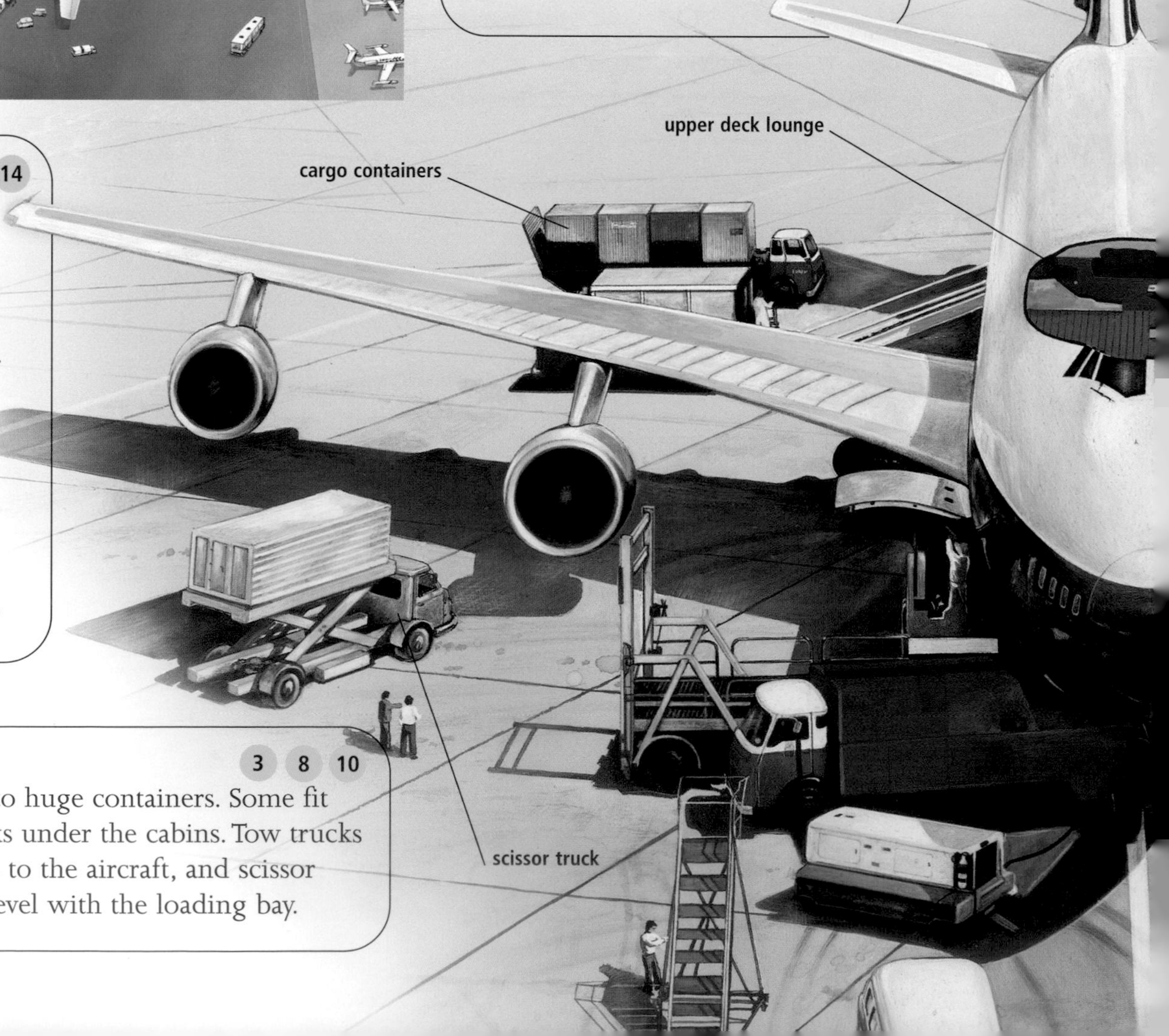

Air freight (3) (8) (10)

Cargo is packed into huge containers. Some fit into the cargo decks under the cabins. Tow trucks haul the containers to the aircraft, and scissor trucks raise them level with the loading bay.

scissor truck

Jumbo jets 9 12
In 1970, the Boeing 747 was the first wide-body jet plane. It can carry up to 500 passengers. The Airbus A380 is now the largest jet plane. It is quieter and more fuel-efficient.

Supersonic jet 4 11 16 18
Concorde, the first supersonic passenger jet plane, was built by Britain and France. Its fastest speed was Mach 2.2 (2,200km/h), over twice that of any other passenger jet. It flew between London, Paris and New York from 1976 until 2003.

Concorde

Wings and flaps 13 15 17
When flaps and slats along the wing open, they act like a brake. Ailerons are metal strips that move up and down to make the plane bank (turn).

portable passenger gangway

Steps 5
If an aircraft parks on the tarmac away from the terminal, steps and gangways are brought to the aircraft. Passengers may be transported in an airport bus.

QUESTIONS:
Where in the world?

Level 1
1. Is Cambridge in England or in Egypt?
2. Scissors were invented by Toshiba. True or false?
3. What 'A' is an American computer company and also a piece of fruit?

Level 2
4. Was gunpowder invented in China, France or Russia?
5. ARROW SLOPE can be rearranged to give the name of what form of power, used in Australia?
6. Is the company Sony from Europe, the USA or Asia?
7. In which state of the USA is Silicon Valley: Kentucky, Vermont or California?

Level 3
8. What 'E' do Brazilian cars use instead of petrol?
9. What 'S' is the plant from which this fuel is extracted?
10. In which year did the first human heart transplant take place: 1967, 1977 or 1987?

FIND THE ANSWER: Where in the world?

Advances in science and technology have caused changes all over the world. In some cases they have made countries rich. In others, they have improved all of our lives. Every year, scientists make new discoveries and inventors come up with new ideas and products. In 50 years' time, many more exciting advances will have totally changed the way that people live.

Japan 4 6
Asia has a long history of invention. Gunpowder, for instance, was invented in China. Today, Japan is known for high-tech companies, such as Sony, Toshiba and Hitachi. The Japanese car manufacturers Honda and Toyota are currently developing cars that use electricity instead of petrol.

England 1
England's famous universities, Oxford and Cambridge, have been home to many groundbreaking scientists, including Sir Isaac Newton and Sir Stephen Hawking.

Brazil 8 9
In Brazil, cars run on ethanol (alcohol) instead of petrol. This protects the environment and uses up waste sugarcane, from which the ethanol is extracted.

Egypt 2
Ancient Egypt first produced many of the household objects that are common today, including paper and scissors.

NORTH AMERICA

ASIA

EUROPE

AFRICA

SOUTH AMERICA

AUSTRALIA

The USA 3 7
California in the USA is home to Silicon Valley, where many of the world's biggest computer companies, such as Apple and Microsoft, have their headquarters.

South Africa 10
In 1967, Christian Baarnard performed the first-ever human heart transplant in South Africa, revolutionizing the field of medicine.

Australia 5
With its baked outback and deserts, Australia is one of the world's biggest users of solar power. The country hosts a giant solar-powered car race every year, with teams from all over the world competing.

Answers 1) England **2)** False (they were invented in ancient Egypt) **3)** Apple **4)** China **5)** Solar power **6)** Asia **7)** California **8)** Ethanol **9)** Sugarcane **10)** 1967

QUIZ FOUR
History

QUESTIONS:
Ancient Egypt

Level 1

1. Which river flows through Egypt?
2. What did the ancient Egyptians call their leader?
3. Did Egyptians believe in life after death?
4. What was made of wool or human hair?
5. What were Egyptian clothes made from?

Level 2

6. What form of writing did the Egyptians use?
7. What was papyrus made from?
8. What was usually buried with an Egyptian's body?
9. How did the Egyptians usually decorate their coffins?
10. What was 'Opening the mouth'?
11. What is the biggest pyramid called?
12. What flower was the symbol of the Nile?

Level 3

13. Which part of the body was used to measure a cubit: the leg, the foot or the forearm?
14. How did the Egyptians transport a pharaoh's body?
15. What did Egyptians use to dry the body when embalming?
16. What animal is associated with the Egyptian god of kings?
17. What did the priest say during a death ceremony?
18. For how long did the pharaohs rule Egypt?
19. Who is buried in the Great Pyramid of Giza?

Ancient Egypt

Over 5,000 years ago, a great civilization was born on the banks of the River Nile in Egypt. Egyptians were ruled by one king, obeyed one set of laws and worshipped one group of gods. Their civilization lasted for thousands of years. People's lives depended on the Nile, which overflowed each year and enriched the land.

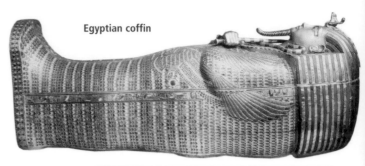

Egyptian coffin

Afterlife 3 8

The Egyptians believed that when a person died, they would live again in a kind of heaven. There they needed the same things they needed in Egypt, including their body. A person's clothes and furniture were buried in their tomb, together with food and drink.

Writing 6 7

The Egyptians wrote on papyrus (paper made from reed). They used red or black ink and a reed pen or a brush. Their writing consisted of pictures, called hieroglyphics, that stood for objects and sounds.

The Nile 1 12

The lotus blossom was the symbol of the River Nile in Egypt. Every year the river flooded its banks, leaving a layer of rich soil in which farmers grew crops.

Art 9

The Egyptians painted their coffins and the walls of their tombs beautifully. The coffin was usually painted with a portrait of the dead person.

Pharaohs 2 16 18

The pharaohs (powerful kings) ruled Egypt for 3,000 years. The Egyptians believed pharaohs were gods, linked with Horus (god of kings), who took the form of a hawk.

symbol of Horus

Mummies 15

After death, Egyptians preserved bodies by embalming them. They used salt to dry the body, then wrapped it in linen. The head was covered with a mask.

Tombs 10 11 14 17 19

Pyramids were tombs for pharaohs. The largest is the Great Pyramid of Giza, built for the pharaoh Cheops. The pharaoh's body was taken to his tomb in a funeral boat. Priests then performed a ceremony called 'Opening the mouth', saying 'You live again, you live again forever.'

pharaoh's coffin on a funeral boat

Measurement 13

A cubit is 52.5cm – the average distance between a person's middle finger and their elbow. Egyptians made special rods to measure cubits exactly.

Clothes 4 5

Egyptians, even the pharaoh, usually walked barefoot or wore sandals made of reeds. People wore simple linen clothes and sometimes wore wigs made of wool or human hair. Egyptians wore lots of jewellery to keep away evil spirits.

wall painting of a duck

QUESTIONS:
Ancient Greece

Level 1

1. What 'M' is one of the seas around Greece?
2. Who was the ruler of the Greek gods?
3. Where were the ancient Olympic games held?
4. Was the Trojan horse made of stone or wood?
5. The Greeks had slaves. True or false?

Level 2

6. A SPRAT can be rearranged to give the name of what Greek city-state?
7. What did women use to weave fabric for clothes?
8. At about what age did women marry?
9. Who hid inside the Trojan horse?
10. SNOOD PIE can be rearranged to give the name of what Greek god?
11. What material did the Greeks use to make bricks?
12. How did wealthy Greeks travel on land: by horse or by carriage?
13. The Greek empire included many islands. True or false?
14. When travelling in Greece, people slept outside. True or false?
15. Where were the gods said to live?

Level 3

16. In which modern country was the ancient city of Troy?
17. What did a winner receive at the Olympic games?
18. What was a *chiton*?
19. Where in the home did the Greeks have an altar?
20. Who was the goddess of the home?

Ancient Greece

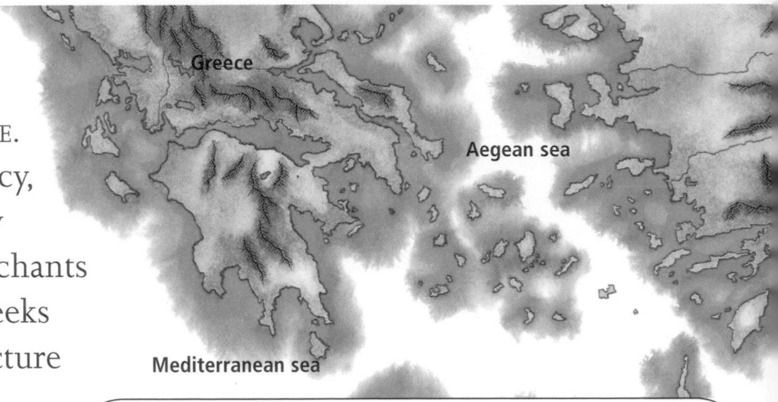

The Greek civilization first emerged around 1200BCE, and reached its height in about 500BCE. The Greeks were the first to introduce democracy, when men in Athens were given the vote. Many people were farmers, but a middle class of merchants and craftspeople emerged in the towns. The Greeks developed forms of philosophy, art and architecture that have endured through the centuries.

Greece

Aegean sea

Mediterranean sea

Geography   1 6 13
Greece is surrounded by the Mediterranean and Aegean seas. The Greek empire included city-states in Greece itself, such as Athens (the largest) and Sparta, and many islands.

Houses   5 11 19
Greek houses were made from mud bricks and wood. They were usually built around a courtyard, which contained an altar. There were separate quarters for men, women and slaves.

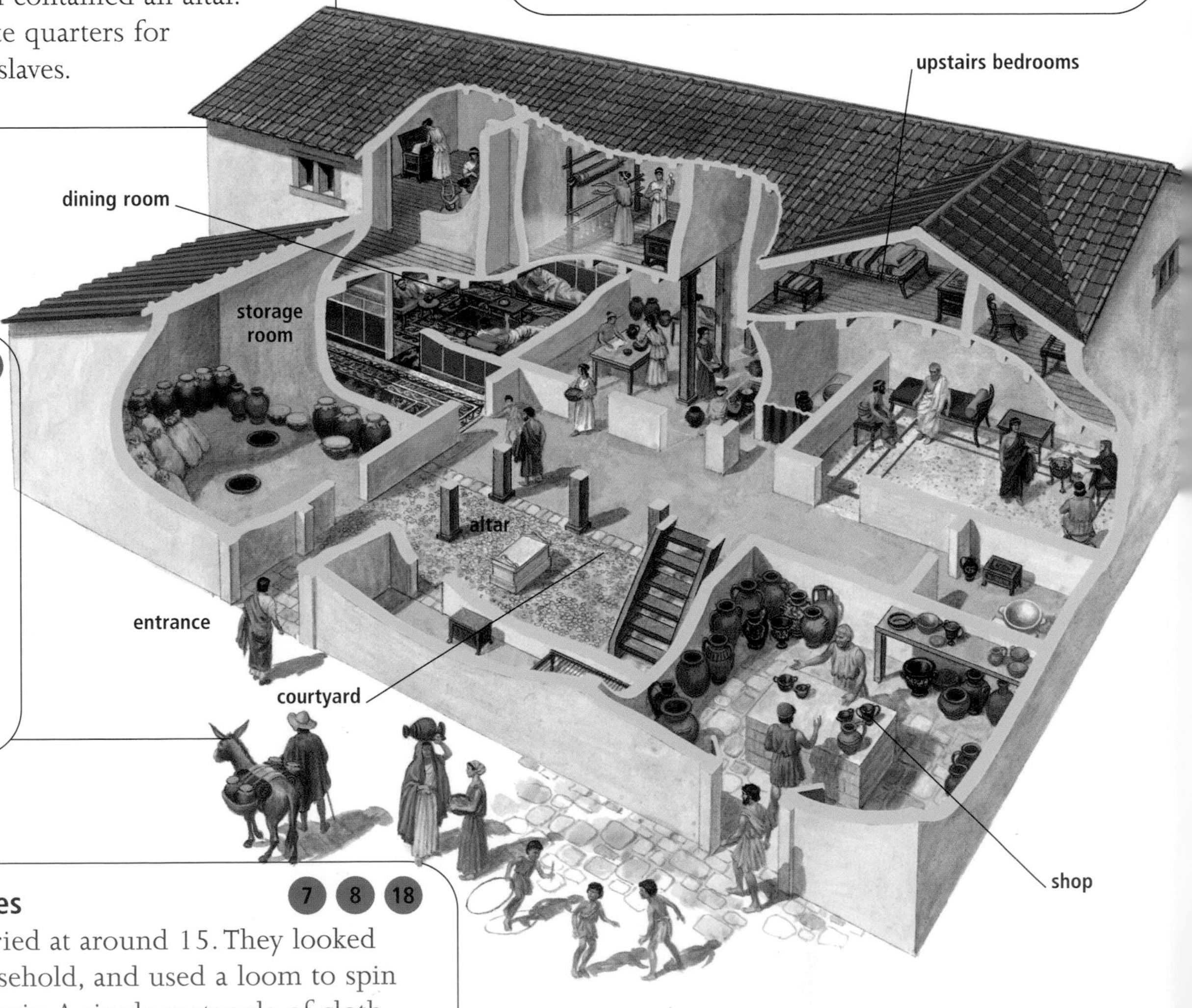

upstairs bedrooms

dining room

storage room

Travelling 12 14
On land, wealthy citizens travelled on horseback. Others walked. People often slept outside or in the porch of a public building when away from home.

altar

entrance

courtyard

shop

Women's lives   7 8 18
Women married at around 15. They looked after the household, and used a loom to spin and weave fabric. A single rectangle of cloth made a basic woman's dress, called a *chiton*.

Hermes   Diana   Zeus   Hera   Athena   Apollo

Greek gods

10 15 20

Greeks believed in many different gods, who represented every aspect of their lives: from music (Apollo) to love (Aphrodite); from the sea (Poseidon) to the home (Hestia). The gods were said to live on Mount Olympus, on the mainland of Greece.

Olympic games

2 3 17

The Olympics were held every four years at Olympia to honour Zeus, the ruler of the gods. Events included running and chariot races. The winner of each event was rewarded with a crown of olive leaves.

Trojan horse

4 9 16

Troy was a city in what we now call Turkey. The Greeks wanted to capture Troy, so they presented the Trojans with a large wooden horse, in which Greek soldiers were hiding. After nightfall, the soldiers left the horse and captured the city.

QUESTIONS:
The Colosseum

Level 1

1. What famous gladiator led a revolt of slaves?
2. There were elephants in the Colosseum. True or false?
3. What signal did the crowd give for a gladiator to die?
4. CUT ROSE can be rearranged to give the name of what type of gladiator?

Level 2

5. In what part of the Colosseum were the gladiators and animals kept?
6. Which emperor often fought at the Colosseum?
7. What was a *bestiarius*?
8. What did a *retiarius* use to catch his opponent?
9. Who was thrown to the animals?
10. What kind of gladiator wore a helmet decorated with a fish?
11. How many years did it take to build the Colosseum: ten, 20 or 30?
12. The *venationes* were Roman soldiers. True or false?

Level 3

13. What did a freed gladiator receive?
14. How many people could attend games at the Colosseum?
15. When were the first gladiator games held?
16. How did the Colosseum get its name?
17. How many times did Commodus fight at the Colosseum?
18. How many animals were killed in the first celebrations at the Colosseum?

The Colosseum

The ancient Romans built huge arenas called amphitheatres to stage their entertainments. The Colosseum in Rome was one of the grandest, commissioned by the Emperor Vespasian. The first ceremonies lasted for 100 days and included a mock sea battle. Romans enjoyed watching bloodthirsty games at the Colosseum for over 400 years.

Punishment   7   9
Christians, criminals and slaves were thrown into the arena with wild animals. The *bestiarius*, on the other hand, was trained to fight animals.

Gladiators   3   15
The first gladiator games were held in 264BCE. Most gladiators were prisoners, slaves or criminals who were trained to fight. If a gladiator was wounded, the crowd decided his fate by giving the thumbs up (to live) or the thumbs down (to die).

gladiator's helmet

wounded gladiator appealing to crowd

retiarius

Types of gladiator   4   8   10
There were several different kinds of gladiator. The *secutor* was heavily armed. The *murmillo* wore a helmet decorated with a fish. The *retiarius* tried to catch his opponent with a net and a three-pronged spear.

Commodus   6   17
Emperor Commodus reigned 180–192CE. During his reign, he dressed as a gladiator and fought at the Colosseum 735 times. He never lost. This behaviour shocked many Romans, who thought that gladiators were the lowest members of society. Eventually, Commodus was murdered.

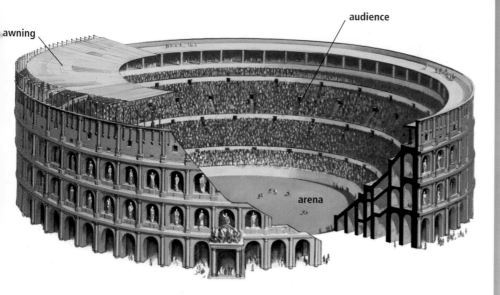

awning

audience

arena

The Colosseum 5 11 14 16

It took about ten years to build the Colosseum, which got its name from the nearby colossus (statue) of Nero. It had 80 entrances and was divided into the podium, arena and *cavea* (seating area) for 50,000 people. Underground chambers held gladiators and animals.

Spartacus 1

Spartacus, a Thracian soldier, was sold into slavery and became a gladiator in Capua. In 73 BCE, Spartacus led a revolt of slaves, but he was eventually defeated and killed.

Exotic animals 2 12 18

Venationes (staged hunts) were held in the morning. Exotic animals, such as elephants and tigers, were imported from overseas. During the first shows at the Colosseum, 5,000 animals were killed.

bone tablet and coins

Freedom 13

If a gladiator fought well, he could be set free. His master gave him a bone tablet, inscribed with his name, and a gift of coins.

QUESTIONS: Medieval life

Level 1

1. A banquet is a type of battle. True or false?
2. People ate meals in the great hall. True or false?
3. Was a *jongleur* a person or a musical instrument?
4. Who owned the land in medieval times?
5. Who taught the children of noblemen: priests or servants?

Level 2

6. Who rented land from noblemen?
7. What were *jongleurs* called in England?
8. What was the name of the system by which land was given out?
9. What was the centre of the castle called?
10. Where did important people sit during a banquet?
11. How were castle floors kept warm?
12. Where were medieval girls taught?
13. What was the cup board for?
14. What was used to help rid the castle floor of bad smells?

Level 3

15. What language did sons of nobles learn?
16. Why did people like to hear music while they were eating?
17. Where did village boys learn trades?
18. What were trenchers?

Medieval life

Society in the middle ages was strictly ordered. The king, at the head, owned all of the land but allowed certain noblemen to use it in return for their loyalties and services in war. Peasants led a hard life and had few rights. Social events were important for all medieval people – lords held banquets in their castles, while villagers attended weddings and fairs.

travelling musicians

The great hall   2 10 13 18

People dined and were entertained in the great hall. The lord and other important people sat at 'high table' near a display of cups and plates on the 'cup board' that showed off the lord's wealth. Diners ate off wooden boards called trenchers.

Music   3 7 16

Travelling musicians, called *jongleurs* in France and gleemen in England, entertained guests by singing and playing musical instruments, such as the lute and the harp. People believed that music aided digestion.

Banquets   1

Banquets (feasts) were held to show a lord's generosity and wealth, as well as for celebration. Food included beef, lamb, venison, fish, cheeses, eggs, bread, vegetables and fruit, as well as wines and ales. Lavish banquets included figs, dates and citrus fruit.

spiral staircase

bed chambers

The castle (9) (11) (14)

A spiral staircase led to the main tower, which was used for defence. The centre of the castle, the 'keep', held the great hall, kitchen, chapel and upstairs bed chambers. The stone floors were covered with reeds for warmth and were sprinkled with spices to reduce the stench.

great hall

priest teaching sons of nobles

Learning (5) (12) (15) (17)

Children of nobles were taught by priests. They learnt grammar, logic, Latin and mathematics. Village boys learned trades such as masonry (stone work) at local guilds, while girls were taught cooking and sewing at home.

Feudal system (4) (6) (8)

In feudal society, the king, who owned the land, granted 'fiefs' of land to nobles. This land was then rented by knights and lords, who had peasants to farm it. The peasants, or 'serfs', were allowed to farm a small area to feed their families.

QUESTIONS:
Knights

Level 1
1. What 'L' was a weapon used by knights on horseback?
2. What was a battering ram used for?
3. RED GAG can be rearranged to give the name of what weapon, used by knights?
4. Knights only ever fought on horseback. True or false?

Level 2
5. What did an esquire become during a dubbing ceremony?
6. What was a mace?
7. How did a jousting knight knock his opponent off his horse?
8. What kind of missiles did a mangonel shoot?
9. Did a knight use a crossbow or a longbow?
10. Why did jousting begin?
11. What weapon was used to shoot bolts at a castle?
12. How could knights tell each other apart in battle?
13. What is a trebuchet?
14. How could attackers force the defenders of a castle to surrender?

Level 3
15. What was the name of the fee paid by knights who did not want to fight?
16. What was a bevor?
17. How was an esquire dubbed?
18. By which century had knights begun wearing plated armour?

Knights

Knights were sons of noblemen who trained to become soldiers of the king. A knight began training as a page at the age of seven. He then became an esquire, and an assistant to a knight, before finally becoming a knight himself at the age of 21. Knights were bound by the rules of chivalry, and fought to the death to protect their king and country.

Jousting   7 10

Although it began as battle training, jousting became popular entertainment to show off knights' skills at riding and fighting. Pairs of knights used blunted lances to try to knock their opponent off his horse.

Armour   16 18

By the 15th century, knights wore plated armour, which offered better protection than mail armour. Large metal plates were joined by smaller plates called 'lames'. The knight's neck was protected by a 'bevor', which was attached to the breast plate.

defenders with bows

scaling ladders

Dubbing   5 17

Esquires became knights in a ceremony called dubbing. The knight's lord tapped him on the shoulder with the flat blade of his sword.

Defence   14

Defenders shot arrows from window slits, and threw rocks, boiling water and red-hot irons at the enemy. Many sieges ended when the defenders were starved into surrendering.

Siege weapons (8) (11) (13)

A trebuchet hurled stones at castle walls. A ballista, like a giant crossbow, shot bolts. The mangonel was a catapult used for throwing rocks.

trebuchet

ballista

mangonel

Battle (1) (4) (12) (15)

Knights fought on horseback with lances and on foot with other weapons. A knight was identified by the coat of arms he wore on his surcoat. Knights who did not want to fight had to pay a 'scutage' fee to the king.

broadsword

mace

crossbow

dagger

shield

axe

longbow

Weaponry (3) (6) (9)

A knight's weapons included a crossbow, axe, mace (heavy club), longbow, broadsword, dagger and a shield.

Castle siege (2)

Attackers used battering rams and catapults to weaken castle walls. They also tunnelled under the castle and shot at it from a siege tower. Meanwhile, archers on the ground kept a steady stream of arrows aimed at the defenders.

siege tower

siege catapult

QUESTIONS:
The Renaissance

Level 1
1. Does the word Renaissance mean 'rebirth' or 'revolting'?
2. BLAMER can be rearranged to give the name of what material, used by Renaissance sculptors?
3. Was Donatello a painter or a sculptor?
4. The lute is a musical instrument. True or false?

Level 2
5. Ghiberti was a Renaissance philosopher. True or false?
6. Where was block printing invented?
7. What was the *lira da braccio* used for?
8. What painting featured the ancient philosophers Plato and Aristotle?
9. What was the first-ever mass-produced book?
10. HARE PAL can be rearranged to give the name of what Renaissance artist?
11. Of what nationality was Erasmus?
12. Which two civilizations influenced Renaissance artists?
13. What is the name of the leather pad, which applied the ink in the first European printing press?
14. What kind of philosophers thought that moral lessons could be learned from ancient texts?

Level 3
15. What 'B' was a famous Renaissance architect?
16. In what year was the printing press invented in Europe?
17. The Renaissance lasted until which century?
18. Who invented the printing press in Europe?

The Renaissance

The Renaissance was an era of great change that brought Europe out of the Middle, or Dark, Ages. It began in the 14th century in the Italian cities of Florence and Venice, and later spread across Europe. Artists, musicians, architects and thinkers flourished with the support of wealthy patrons, such as the Medici family. Fine libraries, academies and universities were established.

psaltery

lira da braccio

Music ④ ⑦
Renaissance instruments included the psaltery and the *lira da braccio*, used by poets to accompany their poems. The lute, the recorder and the *organetto*, which used pipes, were also popular.

Ideas ① ⑪ ⑭ ⑰
Renaissance means 'rebirth'. There was a reawakened interest in science, art and literature. The period lasted until the 17th century. Humanism was one important movement. Humanists, such as the Dutch philosopher Erasmus, thought moral lessons could be learned from Greek and Latin texts.

Painting ⑧ ⑩ ⑫
Artists were drawn to the human form, nature and the art of ancient Greece and Rome. Raphael painted Greek philosophers like Aristotle and Plato in *The School of Athens*.

bronze sculpture

Renaissance artists

Sculpture

Sculptors such as Donatello and Ghiberti created amazingly realistic work that was inspired by classical sculpture, although they did not necessarily depict classical themes. Donatello carved saints and prophets clothed in Roman or Greek styles. Sculptors used materials such as bronze and marble.

classical-style arch

Architecture

Early Italian architects, such as Brunelleschi and Palladio, looked to classical styles for their designs, using Greek columns and Roman arches on many buildings.

Invention

Block printing was invented in China, but Johannes Gutenberg, a German, invented the printing press in Europe in 1440. It had moveable type held in a wooden frame, and ink was applied using a leather pad called an 'inkball'. In 1455, Gutenberg printed a Bible that became the world's first-ever mass-produced book.

Gutenberg's printing press

QUESTIONS: Age of exploration

Level 1

1. Was Sir Francis Drake an Englishman or a Spaniard?
2. What was Columbus' largest ship called: the *Santa Maria*, the *Santa Anna* or the *Santa Barbara*?
3. Francisco Pizarro conquered the Incas. True or false?
4. From which country was Bartholomew Diaz?

Level 2

5. Which did Magellan discover: the Indian ocean or the Pacific ocean?
6. How many men were in the crew of Columbus' largest ship: 30, 40 or 60?
7. Who sent Columbus to find a route to China?
8. Did Diaz or da Gama sail around the southern tip of Africa?
9. Who reached India in 1498?
10. What was Zheng He the first to do?
11. What were the names of Columbus' two caravels?
12. What was a backstaff used for?
13. Why did Ferdinand Magellan not reach his final destination?
14. What did Columbus believe he had reached?
15. What part of the world did the Incas rule?

Level 3

16. On which island did Columbus land?
17. What was discovered in 1911?
18. What is a *nao*?
19. When did a ship first sail all the way round the world?

Age of exploration

During the 15th and 16th centuries, Europeans became increasingly curious about the world. Explorers made bold strides in their efforts to increase trade, find wealth and discover new worlds. By the end of this era, Portuguese, Spanish and English explorers had made their way to Africa, India, China, America and around the globe.

compass

Navigation `10` `12`

Compasses, star charts and a backstaff, which measured the angle of the sun, helped explorers find their way. Zheng He was the first person to use a compass on his sea voyages.

Columbus `7` `14` `16`

Christopher Columbus was sent by the Spanish king to find a route to China. When Columbus arrived at the Caribbean island of San Salvador in 1492, he thought he had reached the Far East.

NORTH AMERICA

SOUTH AMERICA

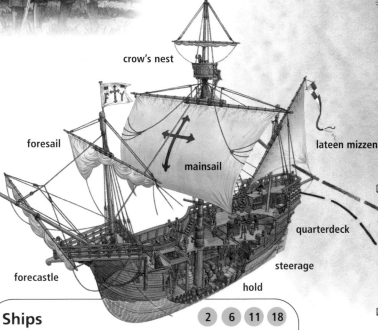

crow's nest

foresail

mainsail

lateen mizzen

quarterdeck

steerage

forecastle

hold

Key
Diaz's route
.... da Gama's route
Magellan's route
Columbus' route
Drake's route

Ships `2` `6` `11` `18`

Christopher Columbus' largest ship was the *Santa Maria*, a *nao*, or merchant ship, usually used for cargo. The others, called the *Niña* and the *Pinta*, were caravels, which were much lighter ships. The *Santa Maria* held a crew of 40 men and had large square sails that gave it a lot of power at sea.

Great exploration routes `1` `4` `8` `9`

In 1488, Portuguese explorer Bartholomew Diaz sailed around the southern tip of Africa. In 1497–8, Vasco da Gama travelled to India. A century later, Sir Francis Drake, an Englishman, travelled around the world.

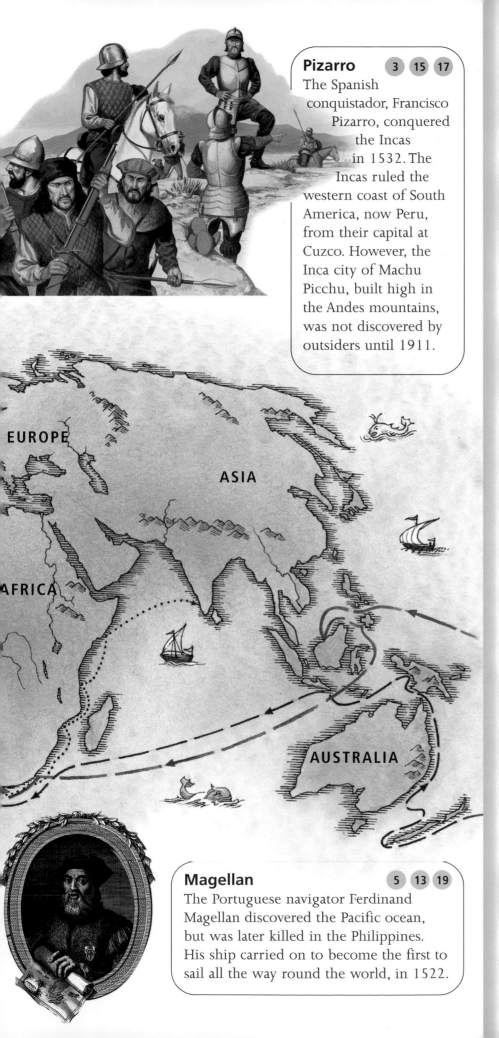

Pizarro ③ ⑮ ⑰
The Spanish conquistador, Francisco Pizarro, conquered the Incas in 1532. The Incas ruled the western coast of South America, now Peru, from their capital at Cuzco. However, the Inca city of Machu Picchu, built high in the Andes mountains, was not discovered by outsiders until 1911.

Magellan ⑤ ⑬ ⑲
The Portuguese navigator Ferdinand Magellan discovered the Pacific ocean, but was later killed in the Philippines. His ship carried on to become the first to sail all the way round the world, in 1522.

QUESTIONS:
World War I

Level 1
1. What large machine was used for the first time in World War I?
2. What is a dogfight?
3. What was the area between enemy trenches called?
4. A grenade is a weapon. True or false?

Level 2
5. What kind of protection did soldiers have against gas?
6. For what purpose were horses used?
7. Which 'J' was a major battle fought at sea?
8. Where was the Western Front?
9. What name is used for a trained marksman who tries to pick off lone soldiers?
10. What weapon could be attached to a rifle?
11. How many lives were lost in the war: over 7.5 million, over 8.5 million or over 10 million?
12. In which country is Jutland?
13. What lined the tops of the trenches?
14. What weapons were fighter planes fitted with?

Level 3
15. In what year was poison gas first used?
16. Which model of tank was the first one strong enough to withstand anti-tank rifles?
17. What was the name given to the British soldiers who trained horses?
18. What German fighter plane was considered to be the best fighter plane of the war?

World War I

World War I, often called 'The Great War', was thought to be the 'war to end all wars'. The war began with the assassination of Archduke Franz Ferdinand in 1914. The Central Powers of Germany, Bulgaria, Austro-Hungary and Turkey fought against the Allied forces, which included Britain, France and Russia, as well as a number of other countries. The war ended in 1918 when the Central Powers surrendered to the Allies.

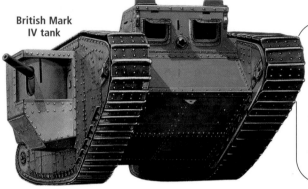

British Mark IV tank

Tanks   1   16

During WWI, tanks were used for the first time in battle. The British Mark IV, introduced in 1918, was the first tank strong enough to withstand anti-tank rifles.

Battle of Jutland   7   12

The largest sea battle fought during WWI occurred in the North sea near Jutland, Denmark. Both the Allies and the Central Powers claimed that they had won.

The Western Front   8   11

Fighting was fiercest in the trenches, built through Belgium and France and known as the Western Front. The war claimed over 8.5 million lives.

Trench warfare   3   13

Trench systems were made up of interconnecting dugouts. The land between the two opposing trenches was called 'no-man's-land'. The tops of the trenches were lined with sandbags to absorb enemy fire. Soldiers in the muddy, cold and unsanitary trenches suffered from trench foot, dysentery and body lice.

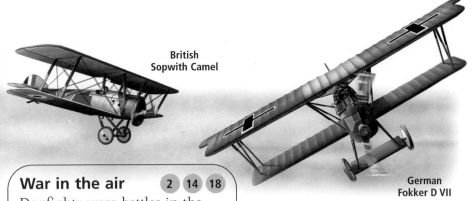
British
Sopwith Camel

German
Fokker D VII

War in the air 2 14 18
Dogfights were battles in the air between two or more aircraft, fitted with machine guns. The German Fokker D VII was considered to be the best fighter plane of the war.

Poison gas 5 15
Poison gas was used for the first time in 1915 at Ypres. Although soldiers had masks for protection, over 90,000 men died from the poison.

soldier wearing gas mask

Horses 6 17
British soldiers called 'roughriders' trained tough horse breeds, such as the Australian Waler, to haul ambulances and weaponry.

Snipers 9
Snipers were trained marksmen who looked for movement in the enemy trench, trying to pick off lone soldiers.

Weaponry 4 10
Grenades are bombs thrown by hand. Soldiers were also supplied with bayonets, short blades which could be attached to rifles. These were used in close combat.

bayonet

rifle

QUESTIONS:
Ancient Egyptian daily life

Level 1
1. What animals did the Egyptians hunt: hippopotamuses, horses or hamsters?
2. From what material did Egyptians build boats: plastic, plywood or papyrus?
3. Egyptians did not farm the land next to the River Nile. True or false?
4. Egyptians built houses out of mud bricks. True or false?

Level 2
5. Were Egyptian peasants ever beaten?
6. OH APRON can be rearranged to give what weapon used in hunting?
7. At what age did Egyptian children begin going to school: three, four or five?
8. Egyptians drank beer. True or false?
9. When did the River Nile flood: spring, summer or winter?
10. Who baked bread in ancient Egypt: the men or the women?
11. Only Egyptian boys went to school. True or false?
12. In what season did the Egyptian harvest take place?
13. What was a mertu: a type of person, a type of food or a type of house?
14. What animals did the Egyptians use to help plough the land?
15. What 'F' is used to make linen clothing?

Level 3
16. What did Egyptians call a team of five labourers?
17. What 'S' was an Egyptian hairstyle worn by children?
18. What 'B' is a crop used by Egyptians to make a popular drink?

For most ancient Egyptian farmers life was tough.
They worked hard for nine days out of ten on fields owned by wealthy nobles, and were paid in beer, corn or bread instead of money. How much they were paid depended on how successful the harvest was. Ordinary Egyptians also had to spend part of the year helping to build enormous tombs for the pharaohs (rulers) of Egypt.

oxen tread out grain on the threshing floor

Peasants 5 9 13 14

Egyptian mertu (peasants) were the lowest members of society. Their working year began after the summer flooding of the Nile. Some drove oxen to plough the land, while others scattered seed. If the mertu did not work hard enough, their masters would beat them.

Hippos 1 2 6

Egyptians hunted hippopotamuses because they trampled crops and ruined the harvest. Hunters travelled in boats made of papyrus and carried harpoons (spears).

hunters using harpoons

Education 7 11 17

The children of farmers began going to school at the age of four and left to start work when they were 12. At school, boys and girls learned to read and write. They wore their hair in 'side locks'.

Harvest time

The ancient Egyptian harvest took place during the spring. The labourers worked in teams of five men, called 'hands', gathering in wheat to make bread, barley to make beer, and flax to make linen clothing. Oxen trod out the grain on the threshing floor. Egyptians farmed only the land next to the River Nile, which was kept fertile by the flooding.

the River Nile

Housing

Labourers built small houses from bricks of mud that had been dried out in the sun. Often they had no more than two or three rooms. Many familics had a bread oven, which the women used to bake bread.

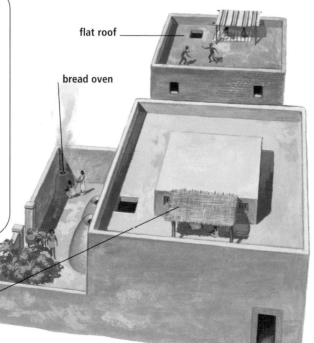

flat roof

bread oven

canopy for shade

QUESTIONS:
Ancient Egyptian gods and goddesses

Level 1

1. Egyptians believed in magic. True or false?
2. Who was a ruler of the gods: Ma, Ra or Pa?
3. What name is given to evil magic: red, black or blue?
4. Egyptians made statues of their gods. True or false?

Level 2

5. What was a 'coming forth': a birth, a death or a type of procession?
6. Only priests took part in daily rituals at the great temples. True or false?
7. ALE TUM can be rearranged to give the name of what item supposed to protect against magic?
8. What kind of animal bit the god Ra: a tiger, a cobra or a spider?
9. Anubis had the head of which animal: a snake, a jackal or a rhino?
10. Was Amun a god of fire or of air?
11. On what item of jewellery would an Egyptian wear a model of a hand?
12. Which god was guardian of the underworld?
13. Who was the husband of Isis?

Level 3

14. Who learned Ra's secret name?
15. What mask would priests wear when preparing a body for burial?
16. Which Egyptian god had a name that meant 'The Hidden One'?
17. What 'K' is the location of a great temple to Amun?
18. In which city was Amun originally worshipped?

Ancient Egyptian gods and goddesses

The ancient Egyptians worshipped many different gods and goddesses. Some looked like men and women, but others took the forms of animals, such as the crocodile god Sobek. The Egyptians built huge temples to their gods, which were looked after by priests. Everyone took part in religious festivals and processions.

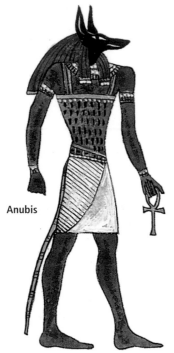

Anubis

Anubis 9 12 15

Anubis was the guardian of the underworld. He protected the souls of dead people on their way to the afterlife. He had the body of a man and the head of a jackal. Priests often wore a jackal mask while preparing a body for burial.

Ra's secret name 2 8 13 14

Isis wanted her husband, Osiris, to rule Egypt, so she sent a cobra to bite Ra, king of the gods. When Ra had been bitten, Isis promised to cure him if he told her his secret name, which was the key to his power. Ra gave in and surrendered his power to Osiris.

cobra

Isis

Ra

Isis

Osiris

Horus

Amun (10) (16) (17) (18)

In Thebes, the god Amun ('The Hidden One') was originally worshipped as a god of air, but eventually he came to be seen as the king of all gods. His great temple at Karnak took many centuries to build.

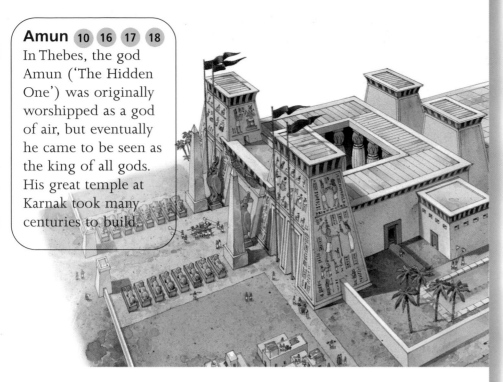

Magic (1) (3) (7) (11)

Egyptians believed magic could help or harm them. Jewellery known as amulets protected the wearers from evil ('black') magic. Amulets of a hand were worn on bracelets and amulets of a foot, on anklets.

eye of Horus amulet   hand amulet   foot amulet

Inside the temple (4) (5) (6)

Only priests took part in daily rituals at the great temples. On some days there was a 'coming forth' procession, during which a statue of the god was paraded outside the temple.

morning ritual in a temple of Amun

QUESTIONS:
Ancient Greek warfare

Level 1

1. What were Greek shields made of: linen, paper or wood?
2. REAPS can be rearranged to give what weapon used by the Greeks?
3. Where did the battle of Salamis take place: on land or at sea?
4. What did Greeks make helmets from: bronze, copper or aluminium?

Level 2

5. The main tactic of Greek warships was to ram the enemy. True or false?
6. What was a phalanx: a weapon, a formation or an oar?
7. RIM TREE can be rearranged to give the name of what Greek warship?
8. Spartans were Greeks. True or false?
9. At what age did boys start training in Sparta: seven, nine or 11?
10. What colour did Spartans use to paint on their shields: red or yellow?
11. Who won the battle of Salamis: the Greeks or the Persians?
12. Rearrange I PASS to name a Greek shield.
13. What 'H' was the most common kind of soldier in ancient Greece?
14. What part of the human body did a greave protect?
15. Who was Xerxes: a Persian king, a Spartan general or a Theban god?

Level 3

16. What letter did Spartans paint on their shields?
17. What did Spartans call their country?
18. From what city were the Greeks who fought at Salamis?
19. What kind of weapon was a xiphos?

FIND THE ANSWER: Ancient Greek warfare

The ancient Greeks fought many wars, both among themselves and against foreign invaders, such as the Persians. In the city of Athens, every man had to fight in the army and provide his own weapons and armour. The Macedonians conquered all of Greece in the 4th century BCE.

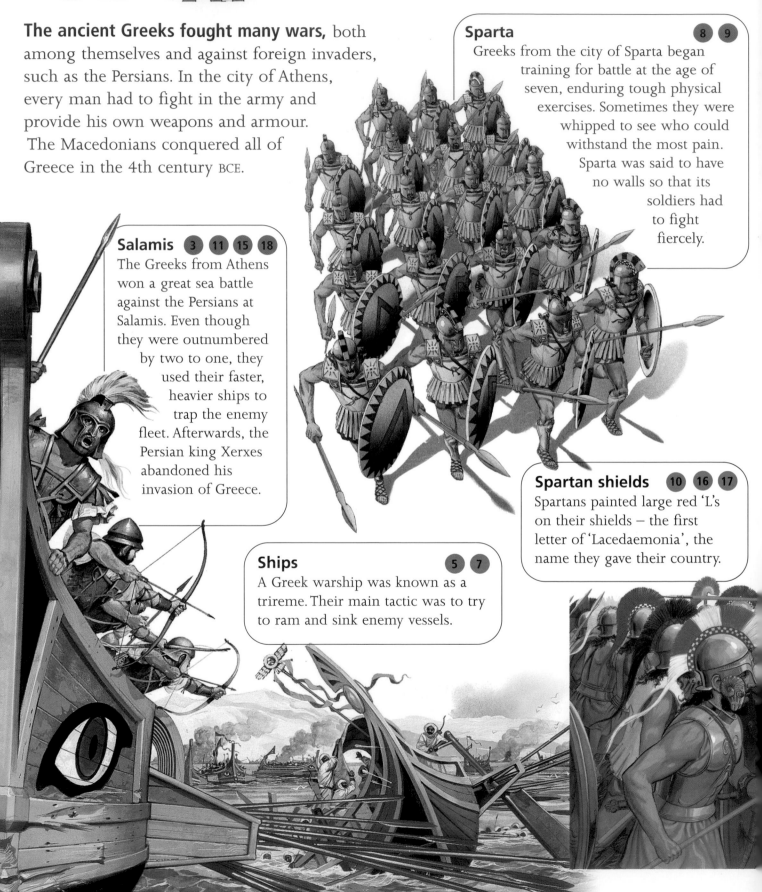

Sparta `8` `9`
Greeks from the city of Sparta began training for battle at the age of seven, enduring tough physical exercises. Sometimes they were whipped to see who could withstand the most pain. Sparta was said to have no walls so that its soldiers had to fight fiercely.

Salamis `3` `11` `15` `18`
The Greeks from Athens won a great sea battle against the Persians at Salamis. Even though they were outnumbered by two to one, they used their faster, heavier ships to trap the enemy fleet. Afterwards, the Persian king Xerxes abandoned his invasion of Greece.

Spartan shields `10` `16` `17`
Spartans painted large red 'L's on their shields – the first letter of 'Lacedaemonia', the name they gave their country.

Ships `5` `7`
A Greek warship was known as a trireme. Their main tactic was to try to ram and sink enemy vessels.

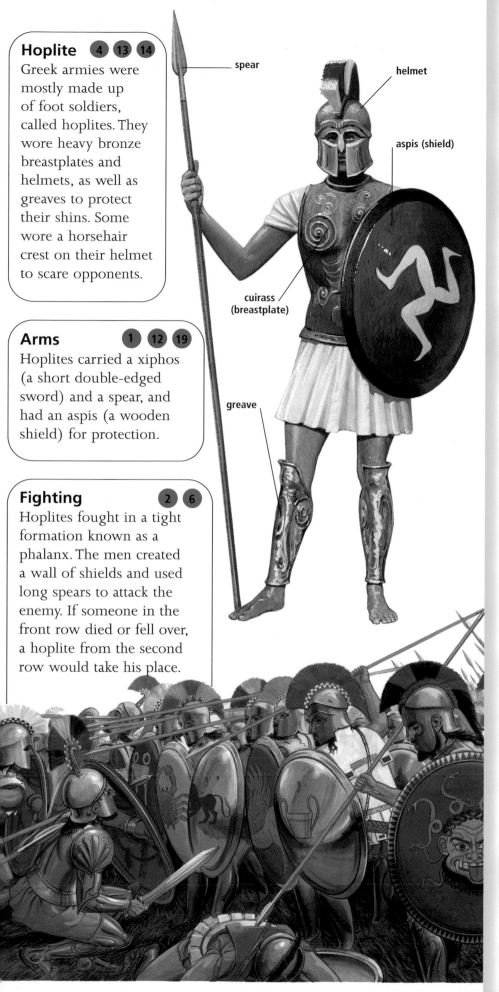

Hoplite   ④ ⑬ ⑭

Greek armies were mostly made up of foot soldiers, called hoplites. They wore heavy bronze breastplates and helmets, as well as greaves to protect their shins. Some wore a horsehair crest on their helmet to scare opponents.

Arms   ① ⑫ ⑲

Hoplites carried a xiphos (a short double-edged sword) and a spear, and had an aspis (a wooden shield) for protection.

Fighting   ② ⑥

Hoplites fought in a tight formation known as a phalanx. The men created a wall of shields and used long spears to attack the enemy. If someone in the front row died or fell over, a hoplite from the second row would take his place.

spear

helmet

aspis (shield)

cuirass (breastplate)

greave

QUESTIONS:
Ancient Greek gods and goddesses

Level 1

1. What 'Z' was the king of the gods?
2. The Greeks sacrificed bulls to the gods. True or false?
3. Was Aphrodite the goddess of love and beauty or of hatred and ugliness?

Level 2

4. What 'A' was the Greek god of war?
5. What was the symbol of Athene: the owl, the eagle or the crow?
6. WORN RUDDLE can be rearranged to give the name of what place that Greeks went to after death?
7. Was Asclepius the god of law or of medicine?
8. Who was the Greek god of the sun: Artemis, Poseidon or Apollo?
9. Who went to the Elysian Fields: those who had led good lives or those who had led bad lives?
10. What 'L' was a gift of wine, poured onto an altar?
11. What 'S' was a river that the Greeks crossed when they died?
12. Athene was the goddess of hunting. True or false?
13. Where was the Panathenaea held?
14. Rearrange STAR RUT to name a burning pit.
15. What animal appeared in the symbol of Asclepius: a snake, a spider or a scorpion?
16. What 'O' was a temple in which people could ask questions about the future?

Level 3

17. What gift did Athene give to Athens?
18. Who was the husband of Aphrodite?
19. Which temple in Athens contained a vast gold and ivory statue of Athene?

Ancient Greek gods and goddesses

The ancient Greeks thought that powerful gods and goddesses watched over the world and interfered in the affairs of men. These gods behaved just like humans, falling in love, having arguments and trying to trick each other. The Greeks held festivals in honour of their gods and always took care not to make them angry.

statue of Athene

Aphrodite 3 4 18

Although Aphrodite was the goddess of love and beauty, her husband was the ugly god Hephaestos and she was in love with Ares, god of war. She was often jealous of beautiful girls, and punished them severely.

Aphrodite

Hades

Hades' wife Persephone

Asphodel Meadows

Elysian Fields

Tartarus

Athene 1 5 12 17 19

Zeus, king of the gods, was the father of Athene, who was the goddess of wisdom and craft. Athene's symbol was the owl. Athene gave Athens its first olive tree. The tree provided food, wood and olive oil, and so the grateful citizens chose Athene to be patron of their city. They built a vast gold and ivory statue of the goddess, which stood in the Parthenon, a great temple in Athens.

The afterlife 6 9 11 14

The Greeks believed that after death they crossed the River Styx into the underworld. Hades, king of the dead, judged how well they had lived their lives. Those who had led good lives went to the Elysian Fields. Those who had led bad lives went to the burning pit of Tartarus. People who had been neither good nor bad went to the Asphodel Meadows, a land of shadows.

Offerings

7 15

The Greeks left offerings at the statues of gods, hoping for their help. Here (see right), sick people would ask to be healed by Asclepius, the god of medicine and healing. The god grasps his symbol in his left hand, a snake coiling around a rod.

Oracles

8 16

The sun god Apollo had an oracle (a temple where people asked questions about the future) at Delphi. Apollo replied through a priestess, the pythia.

Worship and sacrifice

2 10 13

The Greeks sacrificed animals to the gods. They considered a bull to be the best offering. They also gave the gods libations (gifts of wine poured onto an altar). There were large public festivals, such as the Panathenaea, held every four years in Athens, and almost every home had an altar for private worship.

QUESTIONS:
The Roman empire

Level 1

1. What could no one wear except the emperor: polka dots, purple or hats?
2. The Romans built winding roads. True or false?
3. SEA NET can be rearranged to give the name of what group of citizens?

Level 2

4. What were aqueducts used to transport: water, men or food?
5. Was Rome founded by a pair of twins or a pair of lovers?
6. Which famous Roman was murdered: Hadrian, Augustus or Julius Caesar?
7. What 'V' looted Rome?
8. The name Augustulus meant 'father of Augustus'. True or false?
9. Augustus conquered the Dacians. True or false?
10. What was a toga: a crown, a shoe or a robe?
11. How long is Zaghouan Aqueduct: more than 74km, more than 92km or more than 109km?
12. Was Odoacer a German or a Greek?
13. SOUL RUM can be rearranged to give the name of what founder of Rome?
14. Julius Caesar was the first emperor. True or false?
15. Augustus was the son of Julius Caesar. True or false?
16. Under which emperor was the empire at its largest: Nero, Trajan or Vespasian?

Level 3

17. Who was the first Christian emperor?
18. Who said 'I found Rome brick, and left it marble'?
19. Who killed himself so that Trajan would not capture him?

The Roman empire

The ancient Romans built up a vast empire that reached across Europe and into Asia and Africa. Its influence can still be seen today in languages, laws and architecture. The Romans used their powerful armies to keep control in their provinces (countries they had conquered). They called foreigners 'barbarians', and they believed Romans had a duty to bring peace and civilization to the world.

Senate   1 3 10

The senate was a group of the most important citizens who helped to govern Rome. They wore long white robes called togas, which showed their status. Only the emperor could wear purple.

Empire   9 16 19

The empire reached its largest size under Emperor Trajan. A brilliant general, Trajan conquered the Dacians in the southeast of Europe. The Dacian king Decebalus killed himself so that he would not be captured.

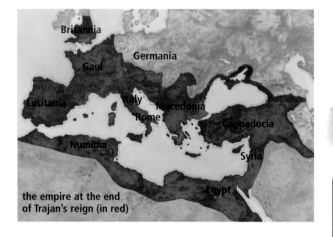

Britannia
Germania
Gaul
Lusitania
Italy
Macedonia
Rome
Cappadocia
Numidia
Syria
Egypt

the empire at the end of Trajan's reign (in red)

The city   5 13 18

The Romans claimed their city was founded by a pair of twins named Romulus and Remus. Over the years, Rome grew into a huge metropolis. Emperor Augustus spent lots of money making the city look beautiful. He boasted: 'I found Rome brick, and left it marble'.

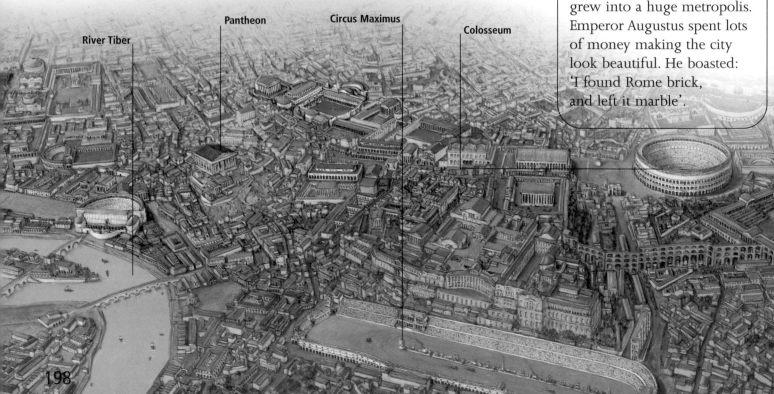

River Tiber   Pantheon   Circus Maximus   Colosseum

Julius Caesar

Augustus

Hadrian

Constantine

Rulers

Julius Caesar was murdered in 44BCE. His grand-nephew Augustus became the first emperor. Emperor Hadrian built huge walls around the empire. Constantine was the first Christian emperor.

Engineering

The Roman empire brought new technologies and architecture to the lands they conquered. They built long straight roads and massive aqueducts to transport water. Some countries still use these today. Zaghouan Aqueduct, the longest that the Romans built, ran for more than 92km through north Africa.

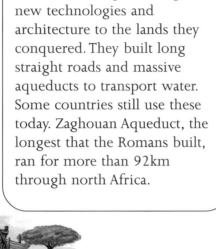

building an aqueduct

The end of Rome

In 455CE, an army of Vandals from Germany looted Rome. The last emperor, a 13-year-old boy named Augustulus ('little Augustus'), surrendered to the German chief Odoacer 20 years later. It was the end of the empire.

QUESTIONS:
Roman warfare

Level 1

1. Roman soldiers fought together in formations. True or false?
2. What was the symbol of the Roman army: a mouse, an eagle or a giraffe?
3. Would Roman soldiers be more likely to form a tiger, a tortoise or a toad?

Level 2

4. What was an aquilifer: a general, a doctor or a standard-bearer?
5. What 'L' was the name for a Roman foot soldier?
6. Was a ballista used to throw spears or rocks?
7. COIN TUNER can be rearranged to give the name of what army officer?
8. What was an onager: a war machine, a soldier or a shield?
9. The Romans conquered the German tribes. True or false?
10. What 'G' was a land conquered by Julius Caesar?
11. What name was given to soldiers from the provinces?
12. TOE STUD can be rearranged to give the name of what formation?
13. Roughly how many men were there in a legion: 50, 500 or 5,000?
14. What 'P' was an empire to the east of Rome?
15. How many years did an auxiliary have to spend in the army before they were given citizenship?

Level 3

16. How many soldiers were there in a century?
17. Who fought Julius Caesar in a great civil war?
18. Which Roman general was killed at the battle of Carrhae?

Roman warfare

The Roman army was hardly ever defeated. As well as inventing many new battle tactics, the ancient Romans trained their soldiers to be disciplined and tough, and never to run away. When they were not conquering new territories, the Roman army had to maintain the *pax romana* (Roman peace) throughout the empire, making sure that no one fought back against Roman rule.

Julius Caesar (10) (17)
Julius Caesar was a brilliant general who conquered Gaul (France). He later defeated his rival Pompey in a great civil war and became ruler of Rome.

centurion   legionary

Soldiers (5) (7) (13) (16)
Legionaries (foot soldiers) fought in legions of about 5,000 men. A centurion led a century consisting of 100 men.

The standard (2) (4)
The eagle was the symbol of the army, carried by a man called the aquilifer (standard bearer). Soldiers fought hard to protect the eagle, as it was seen as dishonourable to lose it in battle.

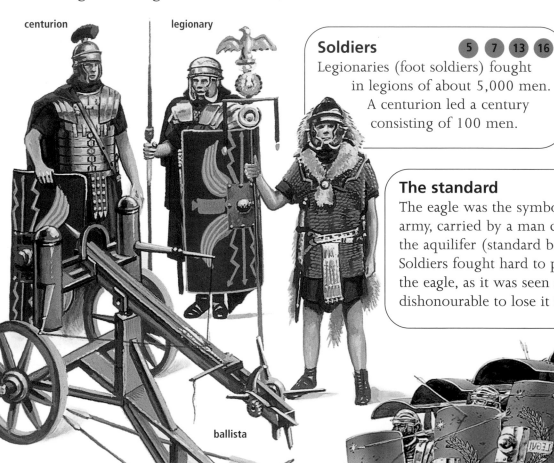

ballista

War machines (6) (8)
The Romans used powerful war machines when attacking towns or forts. The ballista could throw large spears like a giant bow and arrows. Catapults known as onagers were used to throw huge rocks.

Romans fighting German tribesmen

auxiliaries

Auxiliaries   11 15
Soldiers from the provinces – who often carried specialist weapons, such as slings or bows – were called auxiliaries. After 25 years in the army, they were allowed to retire and become Roman citizens.

Foes   9 14 18
The Romans never conquered the tribes of Germany or the Parthian empire in the east. The Germans fought in forests and never risked open battles. The Parthians fought with bows and once won a great battle against the Romans at Carrhae, killing the Roman general Crassus.

Testudo   1 3 12
Legionaries fought in formations. The testudo (tortoise) formation protected them on all sides. Soldiers in the centre held shields above their heads; those at the sides held them in front.

QUESTIONS:
The Aztecs

Level 1
1. The Aztecs sometimes demanded prisoners for human sacrifices. True or false?
2. What did scribes do: write things down or fight in battles?
3. Most Aztec houses were made of concrete. True or false?

Level 2
4. The Aztecs had a team of men who collected household rubbish. True or false?
5. What does the name 'tlatoani' mean: speaker or listener?
6. I BUTTER can be rearranged to give the name of what kind of payment made to the Aztecs?
7. Where was the Aztec capital built: on Lake Texcoco, on Mount Texcoco or on the Texcoco river?
8. The Aztec capital had no streets. True or false?
9. Who conquered the Aztecs: the Spanish, the French or the Portuguese?
10. The Aztec word 'hueyi' means 'small'. True or false?
11. Aztec houses had no toilets. True or false?
12. A chinampa was a kind of floating house. True or false?
13. What was a 'snake woman': a warrior, a doctor or an adviser?
14. What 'G' did Aztecs use in writing?
15. How many days were there in the Aztec sacred calendar: 160, 260 or 360?

Level 3
16. How many types of calendar did the Aztecs have?
17. What was the Aztec capital city?

The Aztecs

The Aztecs settled in what is now Mexico in about 1325CE, and quickly became the leaders of a large empire. They developed a carefully ordered community with strict rules on how to behave, from the tlatoani, the ruler, right down to the slaves at the bottom of society. Their empire lasted until the 16th century, when Spanish conquistadors ('conquerors') invaded and destroyed their civilization.

Homes   3 4 11

Most Aztec homes were made of wood, but some houses had stone walls and a central courtyard. The Aztecs were clean. Each house had a toilet, and a team of men collected household rubbish.

Tenochtitlán   7 8 12 17

Around 200,000 people lived in the city of Tenochtitlán, the Aztec capital, built in the middle of Lake Texcoco. People travelled along canals instead of streets, while farmers grew crops on floating gardens called chinampas. Causeways were used to link the city with the mainland.

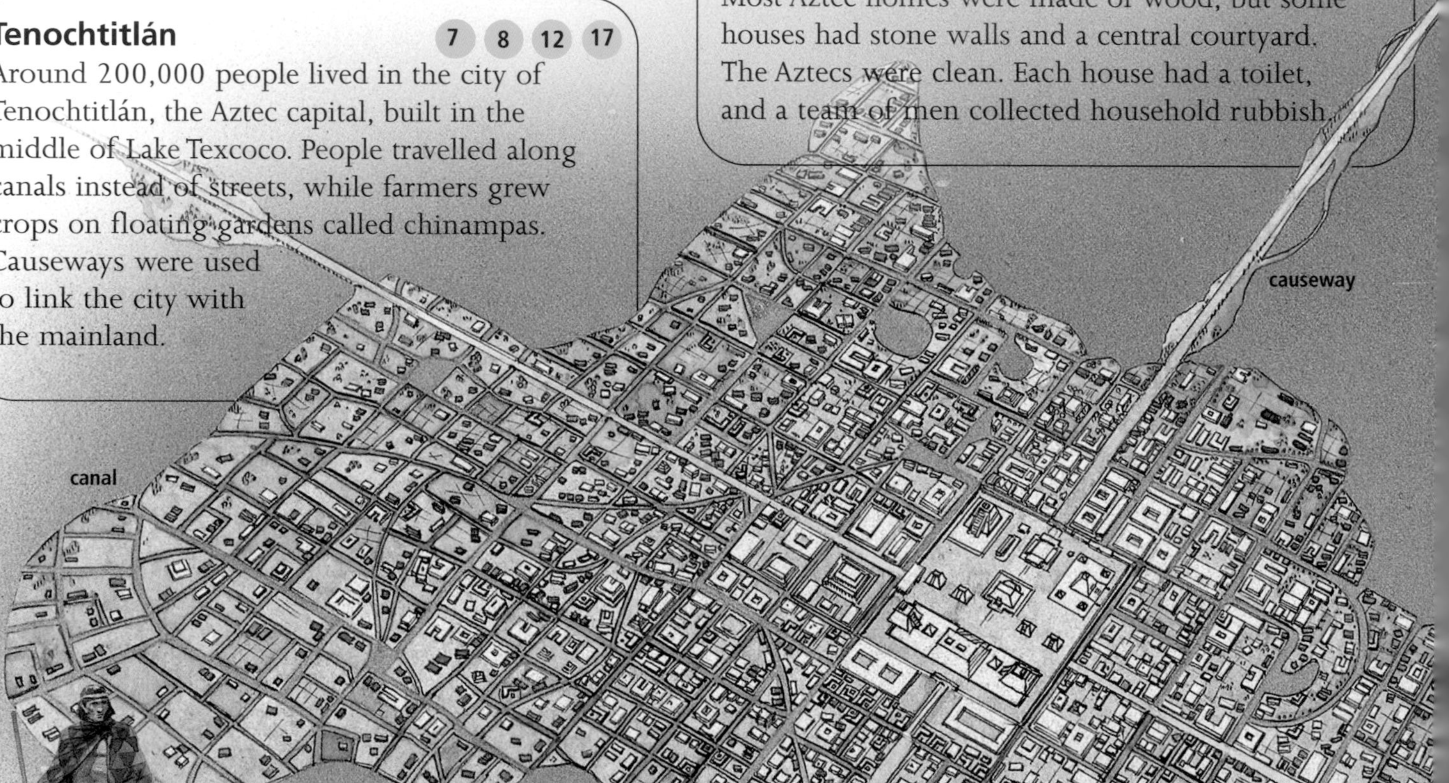

causeway

canal

The calendar   15 16

This Aztec calendar is shaped like the sun and has the face of the sun god carved in the centre. The Aztecs had a solar calendar of 365 days, and the tonalpohualli, a sacred calendar of 260 days, divided up between the Aztec gods. Priests used it to decide whether it would be lucky to do something on a certain day.

Tribute

1 **6**

The Aztecs demanded tribute (a yearly payment of goods) from the people who lived in their empire. Hundreds of foreign rulers came to the palace to deliver treasures of all kinds. The Aztecs punished those who did not pay with raids or demands for human prisoners to sacrifice.

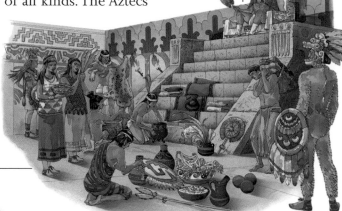

Writing

2 **9** **14**

Scribes kept track of the tribute paid to the Aztec rulers. They wrote lists using glyphs (small pictures) instead of words. When the Spanish conquered Tenochtitlán, they burnt most of these papers.

Tlatoanis

5 **10** **13**

Aztec nobles elected their ruler, whom they called the tlatoani ('the speaker'). The supreme ruler of all the Aztecs was called the hueyi tlatoani ('great speaker'), and the people worshipped him as a god. The hueyi tlatoani had a head adviser, a man called the cihuacoatl ('snake woman'), who looked after most of the day-to-day running of Tenochtitlán.

QUESTIONS:
Aztec religion

Level 1

1. The Aztecs only sacrificed animals. True or false?
2. What did Aztecs use to make balls used in tlachtli: rubber, iron or wood?
3. Was Huitzilopochtli the god of the sun or the god of the night?

Level 2

4. Where did Aztecs perform sacrifices: on top of a temple, inside a temple or in front of a temple?
5. What was the Aztec colour of sacrifice: red, yellow or blue?
6. Aztec priests shaved their hair off. True or false?
7. What was cut out during sacrifice: the tongue, the liver or the heart?
8. Was Tlaloc the god of rain or the god of the moon?
9. Where did Huitzilopochtli have a shrine: in all temples or at the Great Temple in the capital city?
10. Which Aztecs filed their teeth into points: warriors, priests or rulers?
11. How often did the Aztecs sacrifice to Huitzilopochtli: every hour, every day or every five years?
12. What was the penalty for losing a game of tlachtli?
13. How long did the Aztecs claim it took to sacrifice 84,400 victims: four days, four months or four years?

Level 3

14. BISON AID can be rearranged to give the name of what volcanic rock, used by the Aztecs to make knives?
15. Players in tlachtli could only use their hands. True or false?
16. Which animal eating a snake was a sign to Aztecs to build a city?
17. What did Aztec priests use to paint their skin black?

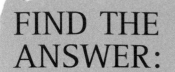

Aztec religion

victim

priest

The Aztecs of Mexico and Central America believed they had to sacrifice humans to the gods in order to keep the world in balance. Their priests killed about 10,000 people every year. Aztecs believed that there were five different eras (periods) of life on earth, and that they were living in the final era before the end of all time.

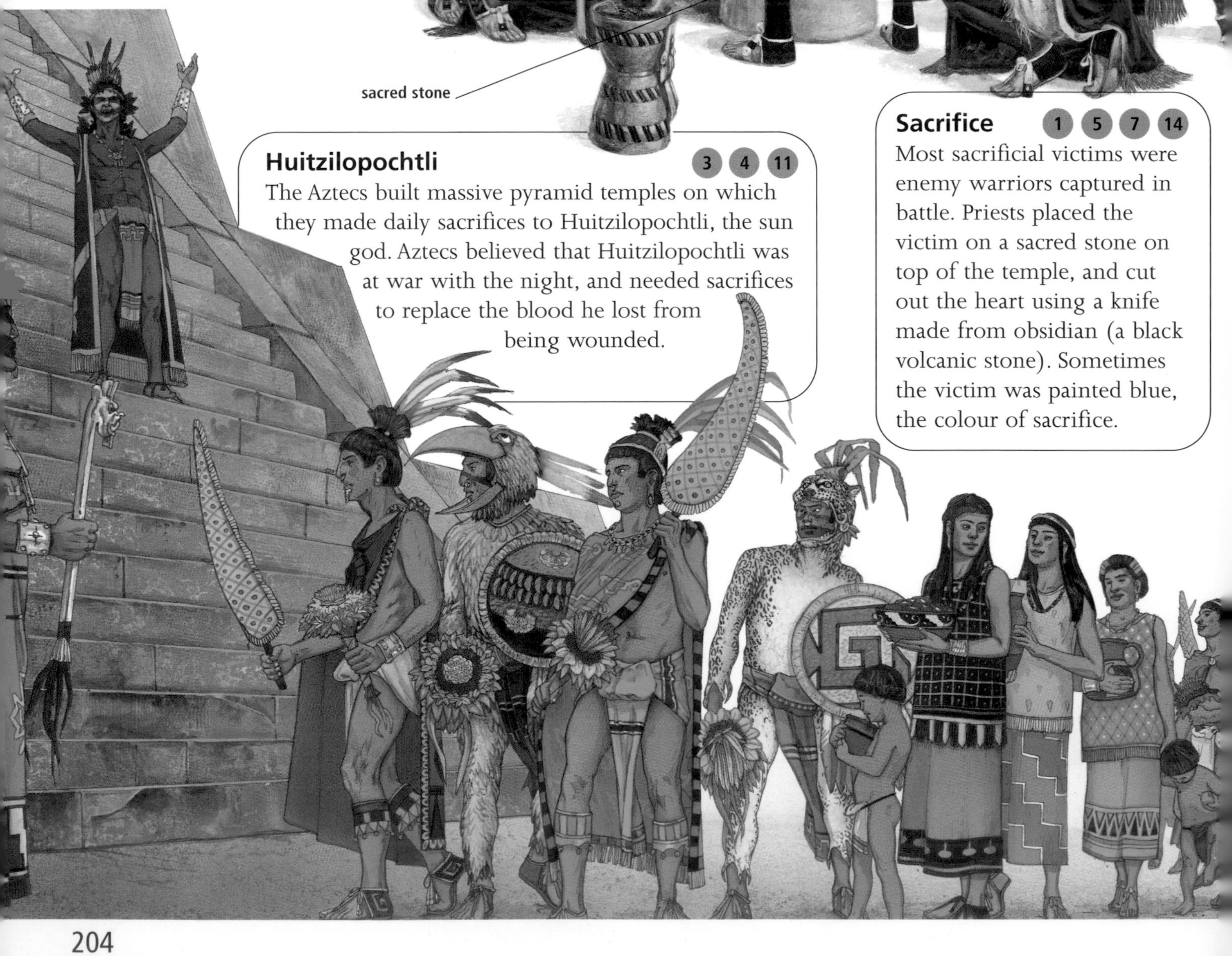

sacred stone

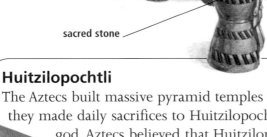

Huitzilopochtli   **3** **4** **11**
The Aztecs built massive pyramid temples on which they made daily sacrifices to Huitzilopochtli, the sun god. Aztecs believed that Huitzilopochtli was at war with the night, and needed sacrifices to replace the blood he lost from being wounded.

Sacrifice   **1** **5** **7** **14**
Most sacrificial victims were enemy warriors captured in battle. Priests placed the victim on a sacred stone on top of the temple, and cut out the heart using a knife made from obsidian (a black volcanic stone). Sometimes the victim was painted blue, the colour of sacrifice.

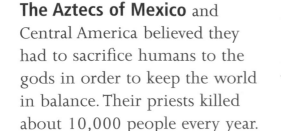

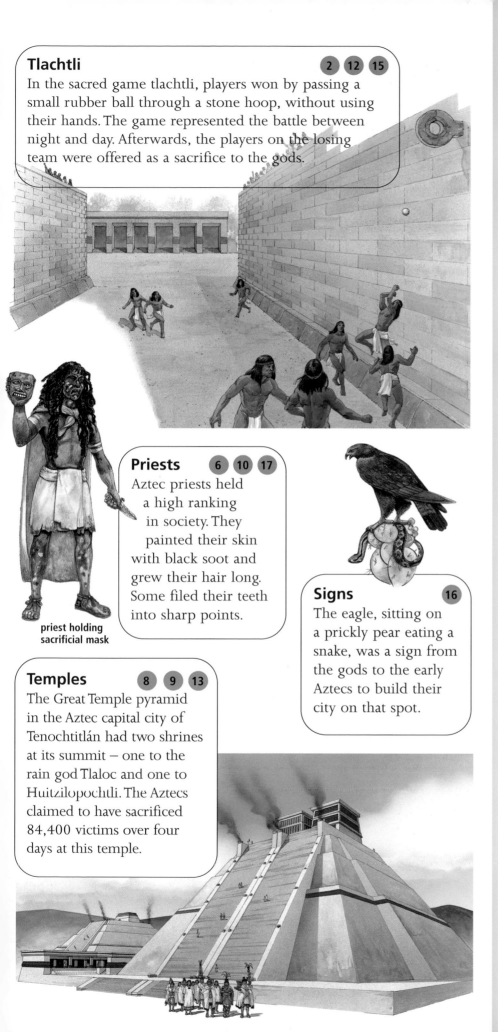

Tlachtli ② ⑫ ⑮

In the sacred game tlachtli, players won by passing a small rubber ball through a stone hoop, without using their hands. The game represented the battle between night and day. Afterwards, the players on the losing team were offered as a sacrifice to the gods.

Priests ⑥ ⑩ ⑰

Aztec priests held a high ranking in society. They painted their skin with black soot and grew their hair long. Some filed their teeth into sharp points.

priest holding sacrificial mask

Signs ⑯

The eagle, sitting on a prickly pear eating a snake, was a sign from the gods to the early Aztecs to build their city on that spot.

Temples ⑧ ⑨ ⑬

The Great Temple pyramid in the Aztec capital city of Tenochtitlán had two shrines at its summit — one to the rain god Tlaloc and one to Huitzilopochtli. The Aztecs claimed to have sacrificed 84,400 victims over four days at this temple.

QUESTIONS:
Where in the world?

Level 1

1. Where did the ancient Greek civilization begin: in Rome or in Athens?
2. The Olmec was the first Mexican civilization, before the Aztecs. True or false?
3. Did people first travel to islands in the Pacific ocean by swimming, in boats or in planes?

Level 2

4. What kind of political organization did the ancient Greeks pioneer: dictatorships or democracy?
5. China's Terracotta Army has statues of soldiers and which 'H' animal?
6. Which 'I' people were expert engineers but could not write?
7. Which ancient civilization built temples, cities and pyramids about 3000BCE?
8. Which ancient Mexican civilization carved gigantic heads of stone: the Incas or the Olmecs?

Level 3

9. Who was the first Chinese emperor?
10. When did Greek civilization begin?

Where in the world?

Civilizations emerged in different regions at different times. The first great civilization began about 5,000 years ago in Mesopotamia (modern-day Iraq). There, the Sumerians built temples, invented wheeled transport, made pottery and invented writing. The Roman civilization began 3,000 years ago and spread from Greece and Mesopotamia north to Britain.

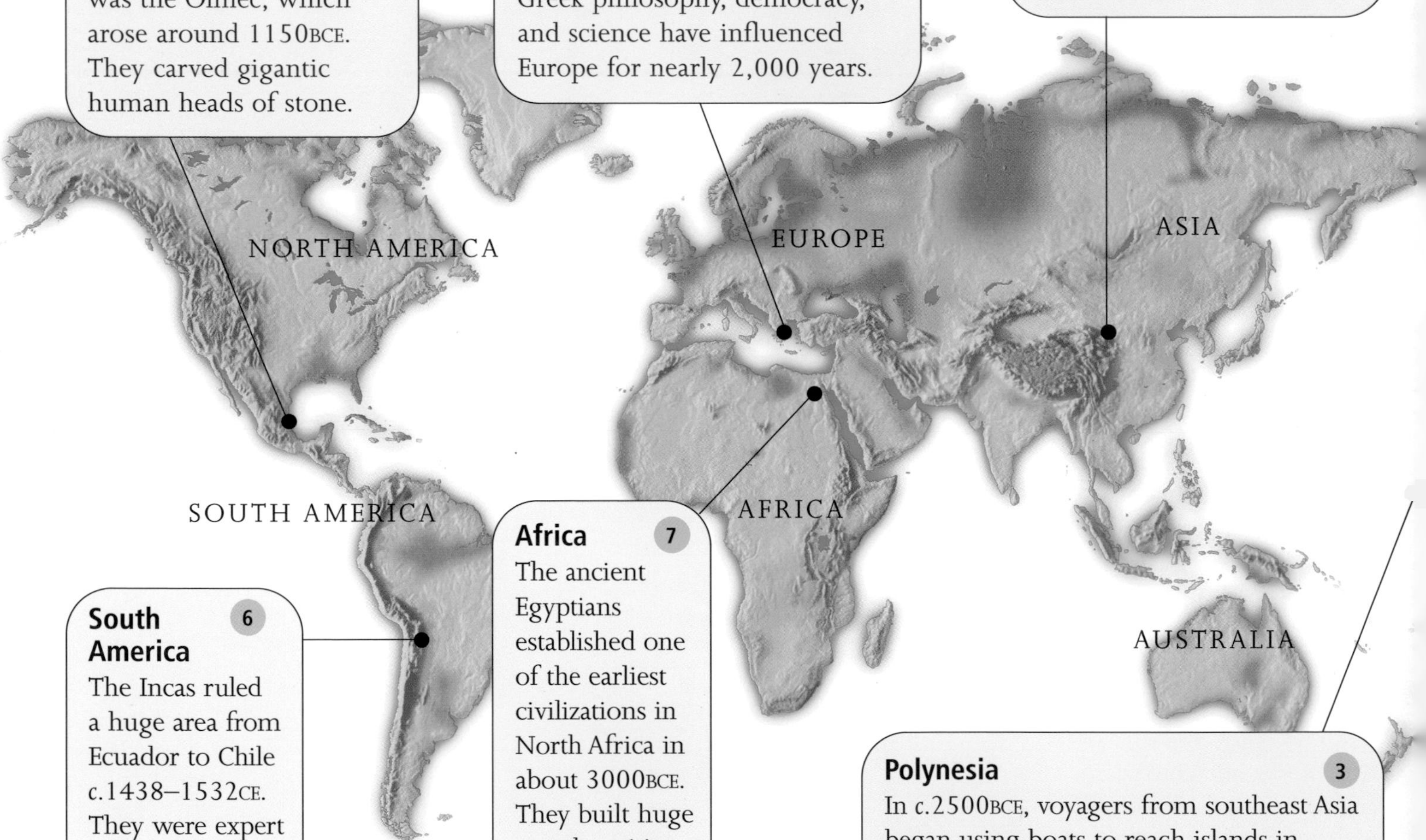

Asia `5` `9`
Qin Shi Huangdi, the first Chinese emperor, ruled 221–210BCE. He built the Great Wall of China and was buried with the Terracotta Army – huge statues of soldiers and horses.

North America `2` `8`
The first civilization in Mexico, before the Aztecs, was the Olmec, which arose around 1150BCE. They carved gigantic human heads of stone.

Europe `1` `4` `10`
The ancient Greek civilization began in Athens before 1000BCE. Greek philosophy, democracy, and science have influenced Europe for nearly 2,000 years.

NORTH AMERICA

EUROPE

ASIA

SOUTH AMERICA

AFRICA

AUSTRALIA

Africa `7`
The ancient Egyptians established one of the earliest civilizations in North Africa in about 3000BCE. They built huge temples, cities and pyramids.

South America `6`
The Incas ruled a huge area from Ecuador to Chile c.1438–1532CE. They were expert engineers but did not write or use the wheel.

Polynesia `3`
In c.2500BCE, voyagers from southeast Asia began using boats to reach islands in Polynesia, a group of islands in the Pacific Ocean. It is thought that they used the stars and migrating birds to guide them.

Answers 1) Athens **2)** True **3)** In boats **4)** Democracy **5)** Horses **6)** The Incas **7)** The ancient Egyptians **8)** The Olmec **9)** Qin Shi Huangdi (he ruled 221–210BCE) **10)** Before 1000BCE

QUIZ FIVE
Sport and art

QUESTIONS:
Summer Olympics

Level 1
1. How many rings are there in the Olympic symbol?
2. Which Olympic sport features a 5m-long springy pole?
3. How often are the summer Olympic games held?
4. Do equestrian events use a horse, a bicycle or a pistol?
5. Which kind of swimming race is longer: a sprint or an endurance race?

Level 2
6. Is a marathon race 20km, 42km or 50km long?
7. What is the name of a competitor in a judo fight?
8. Which horse-based sport takes three days to complete?
9. What is the name of the building in which track cyclists compete?
10. Who set a world record of 6.14m for the pole vault?
11. What is the longest distance race in track athletics at the Olympics?
12. How many Olympics has Jeannie Longo-Ciprelli appeared at: three, four or six?
13. In which sport did Mark Spitz win seven gold medals in 1972?

Level 3
14. How long is a steeplechase race at the Olympics?
15. When was judo first included in the Olympics?
16. How many lengths of the pool do swimmers in the 1,500m race have to swim?
17. How much shorter is a woman's judo bout than a man's?
18. What fraction of the total gold medals for judo did Japan win in 2004?

FIND THE ANSWER:  Summer Olympics

First held in 1896, the modern summer Olympic Games is the biggest multi-sports event in the world. The games are watched by hundreds of millions of people on television all around the world. Thousands of athletes compete in sports as varied as shooting, high diving and fencing. Their aim is to be the best in the world and win a highly prized gold medal.

Olympic flag (1)
In 1913, the founder of the Olympics, Baron Pierre de Coubertin, unveiled the five-ring symbol of the Olympics.

Equestrian events (4) (8)
Equestrian events were introduced in 1912 for horses and riders. Horses race in showjumping around a course of obstacles. Eventing is held over three days.

Running (6) (11) (14)
Track athletics includes all the running and racewalking events. The shortest is the 100m sprint. The longest are the 42km marathon and 50km racewalk. Runners jump over hurdles in 100m, 110m and 400m races. There are barriers to clear in the 3,000m steeplechase.

showjumping

pistol shooting

running

swimming

Cycling (9) (12)
Events include mountain biking and track cycling in a velodrome. French woman Jeannie Longo-Ciprelli is famous for cycling in six Olympics.

Swimming (5) (13) (16)
In the 50m-long Olympic swimming pool the events range from 50m sprints to 1,500m endurance races. The US swimmer Mark Spitz won seven gold medals for swimming at the 1972 games.

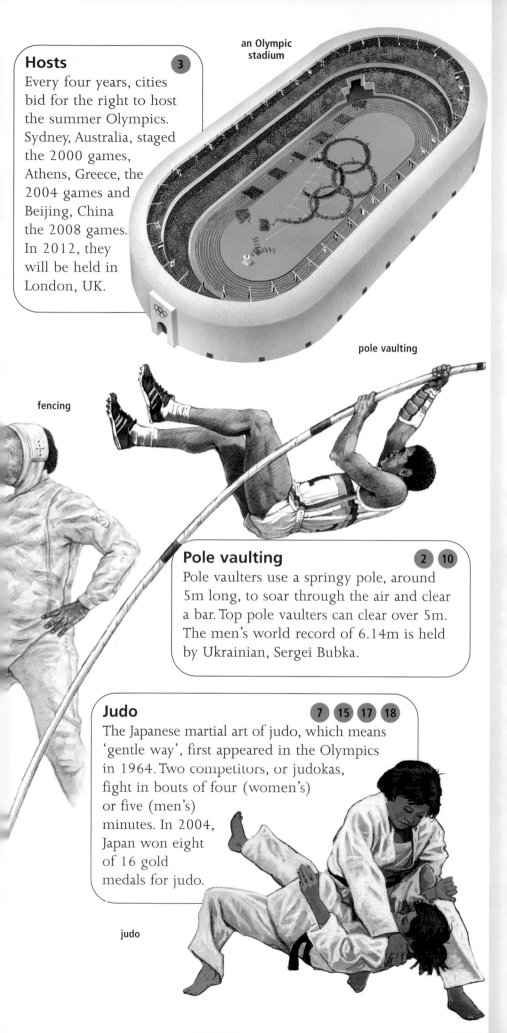

Hosts

3

Every four years, cities bid for the right to host the summer Olympics. Sydney, Australia, staged the 2000 games, Athens, Greece, the 2004 games and Beijing, China the 2008 games. In 2012, they will be held in London, UK.

an Olympic stadium

pole vaulting

fencing

Pole vaulting

2 **10**

Pole vaulters use a springy pole, around 5m long, to soar through the air and clear a bar. Top pole vaulters can clear over 5m. The men's world record of 6.14m is held by Ukrainian, Sergei Bubka.

Judo

7 **15** **17** **18**

The Japanese martial art of judo, which means 'gentle way', first appeared in the Olympics in 1964. Two competitors, or judokas, fight in bouts of four (women's) or five (men's) minutes. In 2004, Japan won eight of 16 gold medals for judo.

judo

QUESTIONS:
Gymnastics

Level 1

1. When do athletes warm up?
2. What are people who perform gymnastics called?
3. How many handles does a pommel horse have?
4. Are rings used only by men, or by both men and women?
5. What do some athletes dust their hands with to help with their grip?

Level 2

6. In gymnastics, how many events do female athletes compete in?
7. Did rhythmic gymnastics first appear in the Olympics in 1932, 1968 or 1984?
8. How many items of equipment are there in rhythmic gymnastics?
9. Was the first person to get the highest possible score in artistic gymnastics at the Olympics a man or a woman?
10. What is the highest possible mark given to a competitor for one routine: ten, 15 or 20?
11. What 'H' is a piece of rhythmic gymnastics equipment?
12. What are the two hoops hanging above the ground called?
13. What kind of gymnastics is performed to music?
14. How many panels of judges mark rhythmic gymnastics?

Level 3

15. How high are the parallel bars?
16. Who was the first person to get the highest possible score in artistic gymnastics at the Olympics?
17. Who invented the parallel bars?
18. From which gymnastics apparatus would a gymnast dismount?

Gymnastics

Gymnastics is a sport in which people perform a series of movements that require strength, balance and flexibility. Artistic gymnasts perform moves on apparatus such as the parallel bars, rings and the pommel horse. Rhythmic gymnastics is a combination of gymnastics moves and dance.

men's leather handguard

women's leather handguard

chalk

Get a grip 5

Many gymnasts dust their hands with chalk, which helps them get a strong grip on the apparatus they are using. Some also wear leather hand protectors to prevent sprains and injuries.

Pommel horse 2 3 18

The pommel horse has two handles on top. The gymnast (someone who performs gymnastics) carries out a series of swinging moves, before leaving the pommel horse and landing. This is called the dismount.

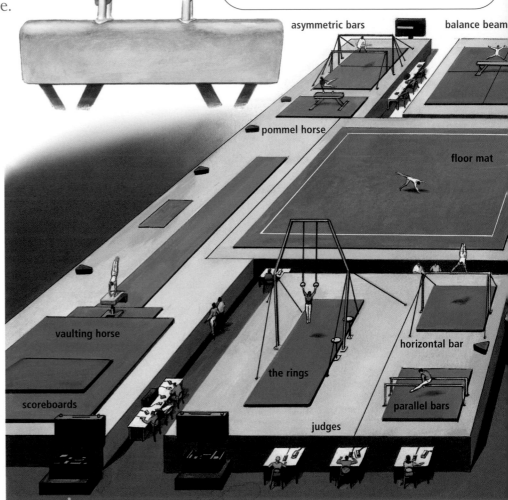

asymmetric bars

balance beam

pommel horse

floor mat

vaulting horse

horizontal bar

the rings

parallel bars

scoreboards

judges

Rings 4 12

This event is only for male gymnasts. The athlete swings on two rings, which hang 2.75m from a mat on the floor. They need great strength to perform their moves on the rings.

Judging 6 9 10 16

In artistic gymnastics, men are judged in six events, and women in four. In 1976, Nadia Comaneci became the first to achieve the highest score of ten.

Rhythmic gymnastics   7 13 14

Rhythmic gymnasts have been perfoming in the Olympics since 1984. Their routines are performed to music, last between 60 and 120 seconds and are marked by three panels of judges.

Equipment   8 11

Rhythmic gymnasts use five pieces of equipment in their routines: a pair of clubs, a ribbon, a rope, a ball and a hoop.

clubs

ball

rope

Parallel bars   15 17

Invented by Friedrich Jahn, the two flexible parallel bars stand 1.75m high and between 42 and 52cm apart. They are used by male gymnasts, who swing, then perform handstands and one-arm moves on them.

Warming up   1

Gymnasts always warm up before competing. The warm-up stretches their muscles so they perform their best, and helps prevent injuries from occurring.

QUESTIONS: Winter sports

Level 1

1. How many skis does a skier wear?
2. Do speed skaters race downhill, round a track or along a road?
3. Which country invented ice hockey?
4. Which is also known as cross-country skiing: Nordic or downhill?
5. What name is given to someone who teaches others to ski?

Level 2

6. In which winter sport do players try to hit a puck into a goal?
7. What is the front of a snowboard called?
8. Downhill skiing is part of the Winter Olympics. True or false?
9. What is the name of the sticks held in the hands of a skier?
10. In which winter sport can competitors reach a speed of 60km/h as they race around a track?
11. Are there six, nine or 11 players per side in ice hockey?
12. Do Nordic or slalom skiers race a zigzagging course?
13. What is the back of a snowboard called?
14. How many periods are there in an ice hockey game?
15. The biathlon involves rifle shooting and what sort of skiing?
16. In what year did snowboarding become an Olympic sport?

Level 3

17. Which can travel the fastest: speed skaters or downhill skiers?
18. What object fixes ski boots to skis?
19. Which skis are shorter and wider: Nordic skis or downhill skis?
20. What is the name of the player who guards a goal in ice hockey?

downhill skier
in action

Winter sports all involve snow or ice, and sometimes both. They can be lots of fun to try out, and most are also competitive sports. Many winter sports, such as skiing and skating, have developed out of people's need to travel through snow and ice. People have been ice skating, for example, for over 3,000 years.

Downhill skiing   8 12 17

Downhill skiing is one of the most exciting sports in the Winter Olympics. Skiers can sometimes reach speeds of over 130km/h in competition. Slalom skiing is a version of downhill skiing. Competitors must zigzag around a course as fast as possible.

Learning to ski   1 5 9 18

Millions of people learn to ski every year on gentle ski slopes or artificial dry slopes. Teachers are called ski instructors. Skiers wear special boots, which attach to their two skis with clips called bindings. They use ski poles to push themselves forwards.

Nordic skiing   4 15 19

Nordic, or cross-country, skiers travel long distances across gentle slopes and level surfaces. They use skis that are longer and narrower than downhill ones. In competitions, a top skier may complete a 15km course in less than 50 minutes. Some Nordic skiers also take part in the biathlon, which combines Nordic skiing and rifle shooting.

Nordic skiing in Finland

Snowboarding ⑦ ⑬ ⑯

Snowboarding became an Olympic sport in 1998. In freestyle snowboarding riders perform tricks similar to skateboarding. They press down on the back or tail of the board to lift the front or nose, and perform jumps and other exciting moves.

a snowboarder performs a trick

Ice hockey ③ ⑥ ⑪ ⑭ ⑳

Ice hockey was invented in Canada. The six-a-side teams skate on the ice and score points by hitting a puck past the goaltender into a goal. Ice hockey is played in three 20-minute-long periods.

Speed skating ② ⑩ ⑰

Skating can be fun – and a serious sport. Speed skaters race around icy tracks at speeds of 60km/h. Figure skaters are judged on their routines of skating moves.

skating in a city park

QUESTIONS:
Football

Level 1

1. What is the name given to the players who try to score goals?
2. Which player is allowed to touch the ball with their hands?
3. The warning card is yellow. True or false?
4. Challenging for the ball is known as passing, throwing in or tackling?
5. What is a football pitch usually made of?

Level 2

6. For what country did Pelé play?
7. Who has scored over 100 goals for his country: Wayne Rooney, Michael Ballack or Ali Daei?
8. What is the person in charge of a football match called?
9. How often did Pelé help win the World Cup?
10. How many players are in a football team?
11. What colour is the card that means the player is sent off the pitch?
12. In which city were the first full rules of football created?
13. Did Pelé score 478, 809 or 1,281 goals in his career?
14. Does Cristiano Ronaldo play for Portugal, France or Brazil?

Level 3

15. Which of the following parts of the body can a footballer use to control the ball: head, chest, arms, thigh, hands?
16. For what country did Ali Daei play?
17. What animal's bladder was used to make early footballs?
18. Which American woman has scored 158 goals for her country?

FIND THE ANSWER: Football

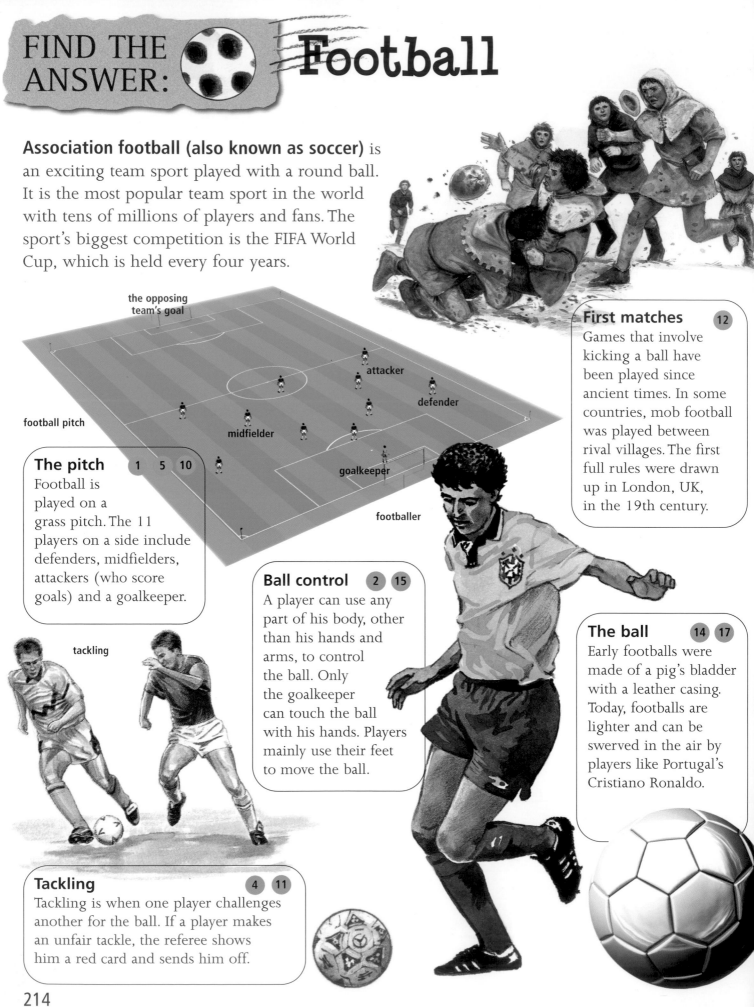

Association football (also known as soccer) is an exciting team sport played with a round ball. It is the most popular team sport in the world with tens of millions of players and fans. The sport's biggest competition is the FIFA World Cup, which is held every four years.

the opposing team's goal

attacker

defender

football pitch

midfielder

goalkeeper

footballer

First matches 12
Games that involve kicking a ball have been played since ancient times. In some countries, mob football was played between rival villages. The first full rules were drawn up in London, UK, in the 19th century.

The pitch 1 5 10
Football is played on a grass pitch. The 11 players on a side include defenders, midfielders, attackers (who score goals) and a goalkeeper.

Ball control 2 15
A player can use any part of his body, other than his hands and arms, to control the ball. Only the goalkeeper can touch the ball with his hands. Players mainly use their feet to move the ball.

The ball 14 17
Early footballs were made of a pig's bladder with a leather casing. Today, footballs are lighter and can be swerved in the air by players like Portugal's Cristiano Ronaldo.

tackling

Tackling 4 11
Tackling is when one player challenges another for the ball. If a player makes an unfair tackle, the referee shows him a red card and sends him off.

214

Scoring a goal

7 **16** **18**

To score a goal, a team must get the whole of the ball over their opponent's goal line. Iran's Ali Daei was the first male player to score over 100 goals for his country. Female striker Mia Hamm scored 158 goals for the USA during her career.

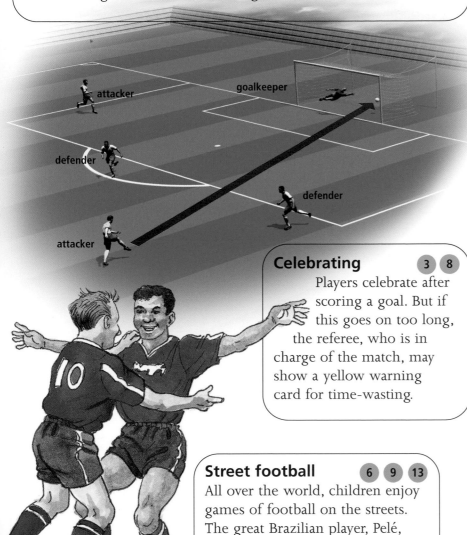

attacker

goalkeeper

defender

defender

attacker

Celebrating

3 **8**

Players celebrate after scoring a goal. But if this goes on too long, the referee, who is in charge of the match, may show a yellow warning card for time-wasting.

Street football

6 **9** **13**

All over the world, children enjoy games of football on the streets. The great Brazilian player, Pelé, began playing street football as a child. As an adult his team won the World Cup three times and he scored 1,281 goals himself.

QUESTIONS:
Art and painting

Level 1

1. The famous artist Michelangelo came from Italy. True or false?
2. What was Van Gogh's first name?
3. In what country are the famous Lascaux cave paintings?
4. Were sculptures, cave paintings or frescoes made on damp plaster?
5. The Lascaux cave paintings feature paintings of reindeer. True or false?

Level 2

6. What part of an egg was used by prehistoric cave painters?
7. Can you name either of the colours that were often used by the ancient Greeks to decorate their pottery?
8. Do artists painting frescoes have to work slowly or quickly?
9. Does tempera or oil paint produce richer colours?
10. Did Michelangelo paint a fresco on the doors, the walls or the ceiling of the Sistine Chapel?
11. From what was Michelangelo's sculpture of Moses carved?
12. Does oil paint or tempera paint dry more slowly?
13. What part of an egg was used to make tempera paints?

Level 3

14. *Blam!* is a famous Pop Art painting. Who painted it?
15. In what century did Michelangelo carve a sculpture of Moses?
16. How old was Van Gogh when he painted *Starry Night*?
17. In which decade did Pop Art first appear?
18. Are the prehistoric paintings in the Lascaux caves around 15,000, 16,000 or 17,000 years old?

Art and painting

Art is any piece of creative work that is used to portray images and express feelings. People have been making art for tens of thousands of years. Art is produced in many different forms, including photography, drawing and sculpture. Painting is one type of art that has been performed for at least 30,000 years.

Cave painting 3 5 18

The most famous early paintings were discovered in 1940 in the Lascaux caves in France. The lifelike animal paintings include horses, reindeer, oxen and bulls. They are about 17,000 years old.

Mixing paints 6 13

Prehistoric people made their own paints out of natural ingredients, such as earth, blood, plant juices and egg white. From about the 2nd century CE, artists began making 'tempera' paint by mixing pigments with egg yolk.

Decorative arts 7

Decorative arts include furniture, pottery, jewellery, metalware and glassware. Many civilizations have produced beautiful works of decorative art. The ancient Greeks, for example, were famous for their pottery. The pots were often painted in red or black with pictures of Greek heroes.

Oil painting 9 12

In the Renaissance (mid 1300s-1500s), painters crushed up coloured minerals and mixed them with oil to make oil paints. Oil paints produce richer colours and dry more slowly than tempera.

Frescoes
A fresco is a painting which is made on the damp plaster of a building. The plaster dries quickly, so the artist has to work fast. The Italian artist Michelangelo (1475–1564) painted a famous fresco on the ceiling of the Sistine Chapel in the Vatican in Rome, Italy.

Sculpture
A sculpture is a three-dimensional artistic work. Sculptures are made by carving stone, wood or other material. This marble sculpture of Moses was carved by Michelangelo in about 1513.

Van Gogh
The artist Vincent Van Gogh (1853–90) painted *Starry Night* (right) in 1889. He was famous for his expressive use of colour.

Pop Art
In the 1950s and 1960s Pop Art became fashionable. On the left is *Blam!* by the American artist Roy Lichtenstein (1923–97).

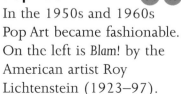

QUESTIONS: Ballet

Level 1
1. Do most ballet dancers start as children, teenagers or adults?
2. Do ballets take place in a rink, a court or in a theatre?
3. Do male ballet dancers wear make-up?
4. Is a tutu a ballet shoe, a skirt or a type of ballet move?

Level 2
5. What sort of musician often plays during ballet classes?
6. In *Swan Lake*, what part of the body does a ballerina move to look like wings?
7. Before a show, where do dancers put on their make-up?
8. A *port de bras* exercise involves the movement of what part of the body?
9. How many basic positions are there for the feet in ballet?
10. The heels touch together in which position: first, second or third?
11. ASK LAWNE can be rearranged to give the name of what ballet?
12. Why do dancers wear leg warmers when they practise?
13. What term means dancing on the tips of the toes?
14. In a ballet, what is the break between acts called?
15. Does a major ballet need as many as 30, 300 or 3,000 costumes?

Level 3
16. Which country does the ballet *Swan Lake* come from?
17. What term means the leading female dancer in a ballet company?
18. What 'O' is the name of a princess turned into a swan in *Swan Lake*?

FIND THE ANSWER:  Ballet

Ballet is a type of dance full of graceful and artistic movements. These are usually set to music and tell a story. Ballet began in Europe in the 16th and 17th centuries. Famous ballets include *The Nutcracker* and *The Sleeping Beauty*.

leg warmers

hairspray

hair grips

wrapover cardigan

ballet shoes

The ballerina 6 11 16 17 18
Prima Ballerina means 'first dancer' in Italian. It is the name given to the leading female dancer in a ballet company. This dancer is playing the lead part in the Russian ballet, *Swan Lake*. As Odette, a princess turned into a swan maiden, she stretches her neck and moves her arms to look like wings.

ballerina
in a tutu

Clothing 12
Ballet dancers wear special clothes when they practise. Leg warmers and a wrapover cardigan help keep their muscles warm, preventing strains and injuries.

Positions 9 10
Ballet dancers are taught five basic positions for their feet. In first position, the feet are turned out, with the two heels touching.

Practice 1 5 8
Most ballet dancers start classes when they are children. They learn the basic steps to music. Often a class has a pianist to play the music. The students in the class (left) are practising moving their arms in a *port de bras* exercise.

218

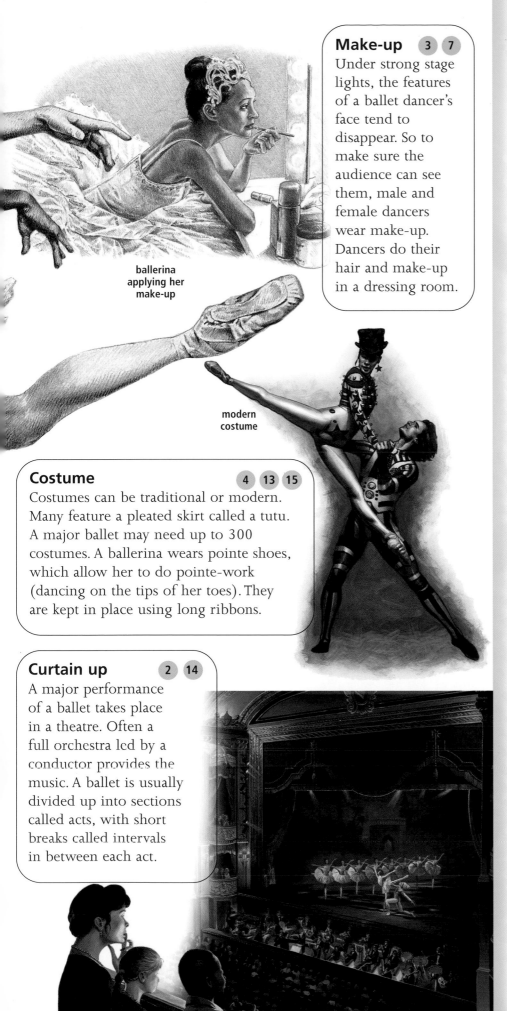

Make-up 3 7
Under strong stage lights, the features of a ballet dancer's face tend to disappear. So to make sure the audience can see them, male and female dancers wear make-up. Dancers do their hair and make-up in a dressing room.

ballerina applying her make-up

modern costume

Costume 4 13 15
Costumes can be traditional or modern. Many feature a pleated skirt called a tutu. A major ballet may need up to 300 costumes. A ballerina wears pointe shoes, which allow her to do pointe-work (dancing on the tips of her toes). They are kept in place using long ribbons.

Curtain up 2 14
A major performance of a ballet takes place in a theatre. Often a full orchestra led by a conductor provides the music. A ballet is usually divided up into sections called acts, with short breaks called intervals in between each act.

QUESTIONS:
Architecture

Level 1
1. Who built the Parthenon: the Greeks, Egyptians or Romans?
2. What is the name given to the giant buildings used to bury leaders (pharaohs) in ancient Egypt?
3. Were the first bricks made of mud and clay, or cement and gravel?
4. Are the pyramids of ancient Egypt made of mud, wood or stone?
5. Were the first bricks made solid by setting them on fire, letting them dry in the sun or freezing them?

Level 2
6. Which civilization invented concrete?
7. Was the Parthenon built of granite, cement or marble?
8. In which city is the Parthenon?
9. Why does Hardwick Hall have lots of windows?
10. Did the White House get water pipes or gas lighting installed first?
11. Did the Gothic style of architecture begin in Europe, Asia or Africa?
12. What is the name of the wooden strips that are filled in with daub?
13. Who built Hardwick Hall?

Level 3
14. What are the architect's detailed plans for a building called?
15. Which famous building did James Hoban rebuild?
16. The Parthenon was a temple for the worship of which goddess?
17. What is a flying buttress?
18. During which century did Gothic architecture first appear?

Architecture

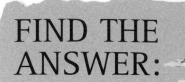

Egyptian pyramids

Architecture is the art of designing buildings and structures, such as bridges, houses and temples. Each building has its own purpose, but all architects aim for their buildings to last a long time, and to look good. Architects from different civilizations and historical eras have found many different ways of achieving this.

Greek temple

Parthenon 1 7 8 16
The ancient Greeks used stone and marble to build beautiful pillars and structures. An example is the Parthenon in Athens. It was built of marble in the 5th century BCE as a temple to the Greek goddess Athene.

Pyramids 2 4
The ancient Egyptians built enormous burial pyramids for their leaders (pharaohs). The largest of these, the Great Pyramid at Giza, was built over 4,500 years ago. It is made up of more than two million large stone blocks, each weighing two and a half tonnes.

Walls 12
In timber-framed buildings wooden strips called wattles formed a frame, filled in with daub – a mixture of straw, mud and dung.

Building materials 3 5
Over the years people have built with stone, wood, straw, leaves and grasses. The first bricks were made of mud and clay. These were left to dry and set hard in the sun.

building a house

Roman builders 6
The Romans used elements of Greek architecture, like the columns on this house. They were the first to design buildings with arches, and even invented concrete, which is still used today.

Church buildings (11) (17) (18)

A style of architecture called 'Gothic' was used for many churches in Europe between 1140 and 1500. A special side-support, called a flying buttress, allowed architects to build churches with very thin walls and large windows.

flying buttresses

Stately homes (9) (13)

A big house showed how rich and powerful a person was. Hardwick Hall in the UK, built by Bess of Hardwick, has lots of windows – a sign of wealth in the days when glass was very expensive.

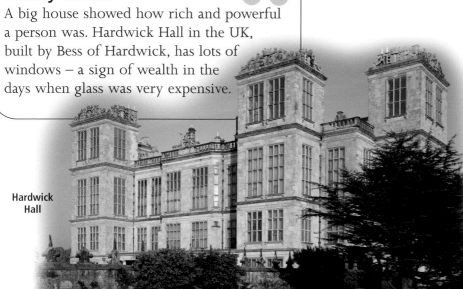

Hardwick Hall

The White House (10) (15)

The White House in Washington DC, USA, was started in 1792. It was burned down in 1814 but rebuilt by the architect James Hoban. Water pipes were fitted in 1833, followed by gas lighting (1848), a lift (1881) and electricity (1891).

Architects' plans (14)

Architects produce drawings and plans of their work to discuss with clients (the people paying them to build). Modern building plans are called blueprints.

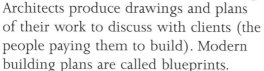

QUESTIONS:
Film and TV

Level 1

1. Were the first TV broadcasts black and white or colour?
2. What 'D' is the person in charge of the film-making process?
3. What name is given to someone who interviews people for the news?
4. What word describes people who play characters and appear in films?
5. What word describes the written-down version of a film?

Level 2

6. Who are the three people needed in a news team?
7. What word describes news reporting that is transmitted as the events unfold?
8. Was the first film with sound *Casablanca*, *The Jazz Singer* or *Snow White*?
9. WOOLY HOLD can be rearranged to give the name of what huge film industry based in the USA?
10. Near which big American city is this industry located?
11. What nickname is given to India's film industry?
12. What name is given to 24-hour news programmes?

Level 3

13. Was Telstar the name of an early television or a satellite?
14. In what year was the first 'talking' film made?
15. In 1962, what percentage of US homes had a television?
16. In what year was the first TV signal sent by satellite?
17. What word is used for sending programmes out from the TV station?
18. Which Asian country has one of the largest film industries in the world?

Film and TV

A film is made up of a number of photos, called frames, which are shown in a fast sequence to create moving images. Films are shown using projectors at cinemas, or they can be recorded on to videos or DVDs. Films can also be sent (transmitted) through the air or by a cable to people's television sets at home.

Film crew   8 14
Dozens of people work on the set of a film. Some help with the costumes, others build the scenery or operate equipment. To start with, films had no sound. The first 'talking' film with sound was *The Jazz Singer* in 1927.

Director   2 4 5
The person in charge of making a film is the director. The director works with the written-down version of the film (the script) and the people who play characters in the film (the actors).

Sets   9 10 11 18
A set is where a film is shot. It can be indoors or outside. Hollywood, near Los Angeles, USA, and Mumbai, in India are home to the world's two largest film industries. India's film industry is sometimes nicknamed Bollywood.

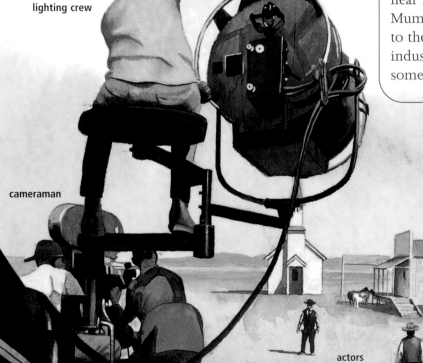

lighting crew

cameraman

actors

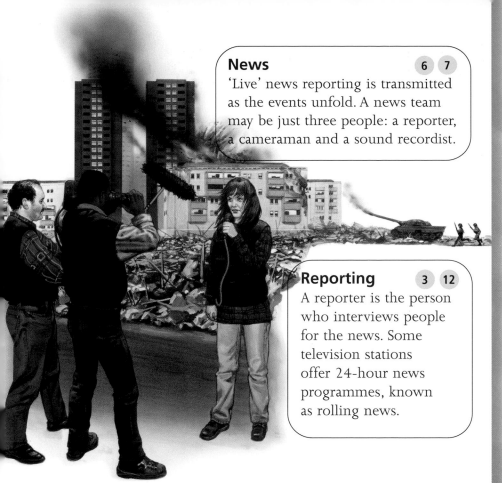

News 6 7

'Live' news reporting is transmitted as the events unfold. A news team may be just three people: a reporter, a cameraman and a sound recordist.

Reporting 3 12

A reporter is the person who interviews people for the news. Some television stations offer 24-hour news programmes, known as rolling news.

Studio 17

Many TV shows are filmed in a studio. A television camera uses a sensitive electronic tube to change light into electrical signals. These are then sent out to people's homes by transmitters. Sending out a programme is known as broadcasting.

Into the home 1 13 15 16

When television began in the 1930s the programmes were in black and white. The first colour sets were made in the USA in 1956. By 1962, 90 per cent of US homes had television sets. In the same year the first TV signal was sent by a satellite called Telstar. Today, many homes have satellite or cable television.

QUESTIONS:
Fairy tales

Level 1

1. Cinderella marries a prince. True or false?
2. Are Hansel and Gretel abandoned in the woods or in town?
3. Is Gretel, Cinderella or Sleeping Beauty woken up by a kiss from a prince?
4. Does the Pied Piper lure children away from town or get them to return to town?

Level 2

5. For how many years does Sleeping Beauty sleep: ten years, 50 years or 100 years?
6. In *Rumpelstiltskin*, is straw, palm leaves or sheep's wool spun into gold?
7. What 'G' is the witch's house made of in later versions of *Hansel & Gretel*?
8. What 'F' does the Pied Piper play to lure the children away?
9. Are there over 30, 340 or 560 versions of *Cinderella*?
10. What are mermaids: half men and half goats, half men and half fish, or half women and half fish?
11. Is Hamelin a German, French or Austrian town?
12. Are Hansel and Gretel the children of a miller, a prince or a woodcutter?
13. Who told the king that it is possible to spin gold: Rumpelstiltskin, the miller or his daughter?

Level 3

14. In the Chinese version of *Cinderella*, which 'W' finds the slipper?
15. Who wrote *The Little Mermaid*?
16. In which story does a fairy cast a spell?
17. In what year did the children really leave Hamelin?
18. When was the earliest version of *Cinderella* written?

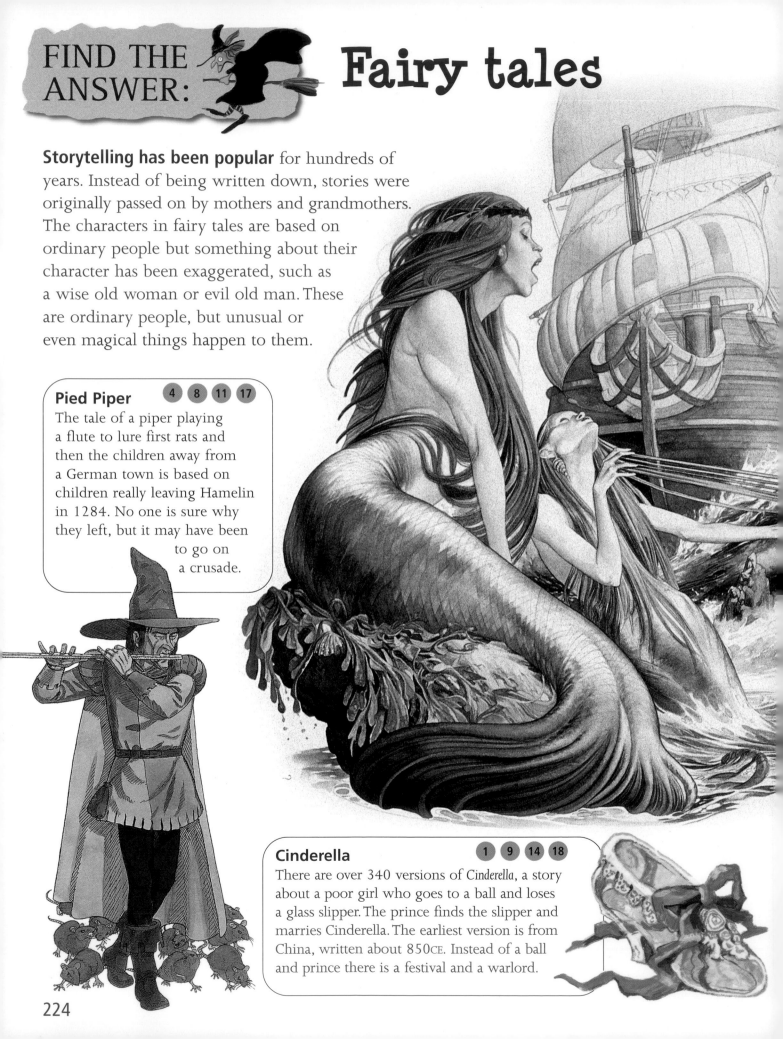

FIND THE ANSWER: Fairy tales

Storytelling has been popular for hundreds of years. Instead of being written down, stories were originally passed on by mothers and grandmothers. The characters in fairy tales are based on ordinary people but something about their character has been exaggerated, such as a wise old woman or evil old man. These are ordinary people, but unusual or even magical things happen to them.

Pied Piper   4 8 11 17

The tale of a piper playing a flute to lure first rats and then the children away from a German town is based on children really leaving Hamelin in 1284. No one is sure why they left, but it may have been to go on a crusade.

Cinderella   1 9 14 18

There are over 340 versions of *Cinderella*, a story about a poor girl who goes to a ball and loses a glass slipper. The prince finds the slipper and marries Cinderella. The earliest version is from China, written about 850CE. Instead of a ball and prince there is a festival and a warlord.

Rumpelstiltskin

The story of spinning straw into gold can be seen as a tale warning against bragging. A miller bragged to the king that his daughter could spin gold, but the daughter was punished for his lies.

Mermaids

Stories about mermaids, creatures that are half women and half fish, are told in many countries. In Hans Christian Andersen's well-known tale *The Little Mermaid*, a mermaid falls in love with a human prince.

Sleeping Beauty

There are different versions of the tale of fairies offering gifts to a princess. One fairy casts an evil spell on her, which involves a spindle used for spinning. In the best-known version, the princess pricks her finger on a spindle and sleeps for 100 years, until she is kissed by a prince.

Hansel & Gretel   12

The story of a woodcutter abandoning his children in the woods often happened for real in the Middle Ages, when food was often scarce. In the original story, the children find a witch's house, which was made of bread to attract children. In later versions, the house is made of gingerbread.

QUESTIONS:
Theatre

Level 1

1. Stage carpenters work with wood. True or false?
2. Stage hands are normally in charge of the actors' costumes. True or false?
3. Does a costume designer or set designer plan the layout of the stage?
4. Set builders build theatre scenery. True or false?
5. Is stage smoke a type of special effect?

Level 2

6. What 'C' is the name for the clothing that performers wear?
7. Does a costume designer work with a set designer?
8. Which 'D' cleans and mends the costumes?
9. Does the Metropolitan Opera House require 200, 500 or 1,000 staff to put on a performance?
10. Is the place where the audience sits called the wings, backstage or the auditorium?
11. On stage, what would a suitcase be considered: a set, costume or prop?
12. Are the sides of a stage out of the audience's view called the wings, upstage or front of house?
13. New York's Metropolitan Opera House is also known as what: The Op House, The Met or The Big Stage?
14. Rearrange AT BELL to name a type of performance that may need a dresser.

Level 3

15. Where are sets often assembled?
16. What is the largest number of people that can watch a single performance at New York's Metropolitan Opera House?
17. Which theatre staff sometimes help actors make quick costume changes?
18. Who uses scale models of the stage in their work?

Theatre

A theatre is where plays and other forms of entertainment, such as ballet or opera, are staged. A theatre can be as simple as a piece of ground outdoors or a huge and complex theatre building designed especially for staging plays. A major production requires a number of different staff, from the director and producer to stage hands.

A large theatre   9   10   13   16
New York's Metropolitan Opera House, known as the Met, is a big theatre. The auditorium – the place where the audience sits – can hold up to 3,800 people. Every time a performance is put on, the theatre employs about 1,000 people.

rehearsal space

Costumes   6   7
The clothes the performers wear are called costumes. They are designed carefully because fabric looks different on stage, under lights, than in daylight. The costume designer works with the lighting designer and set designer.

Set designers   3   18
The person who designs the layout of the stage and the scenery is called the set designer. A set designer often makes a scale model so others can see the design.

Set builders   1   4   15
The people who produce the scenery are known as set builders. Some may be stage carpenters working with wood. Others may be skilled scenery painters, plasterers or steel welders. A set is often built in a workshop, then assembled on the stage.

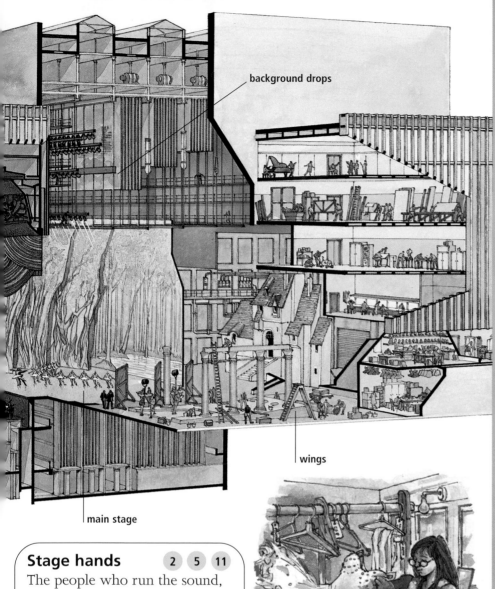

background drops

main stage

wings

Stage hands   2   5   11

The people who run the sound, lighting, scenery and special effects, such as stage smoke, during a play are stage hands. They are also responsible for props. These are objects used in the play, such as a suitcase or tray.

Dressers   8   12   14   17

The people who take care of the costumes for a play or ballet are called dressers. They keep the clothes clean and mend them if they are torn or damaged. Dressers also help the performers get dressed. They may need to help them make a quick change, sometimes in the wings (the sides of the stage, out of sight of the audience).

QUESTIONS:
Shakespeare

Level 1

1. *Macbeth* is a play about a figure from Scottish history. True or false?
2. Was Shakespeare's theatre called the Swan or the Globe?
3. *Hamlet* is a comedy play. True or false?
4. Did Shakespeare write a play called *Romeo and Juliet* or *Verona and Juliet*?

Level 2

5. Were people who watched a play from the pit called pitlings, groundlings or watchlings?
6. Was Shakespeare born in London, Stratford-upon-Avon or Paris?
7. What was the name of the uncovered part of the theatre where people stood to watch plays?
8. Richer people watched plays in the Globe in a covered area. True or false?
9. Could the Globe Theatre hold 500, 1,500 or 3,000 people?
10. Which 'M' is Shakespeare's bloodiest tragedy play?
11. Is the line 'To be, or not to be' from *Macbeth*, *Hamlet* or *Romeo and Juliet*?
12. Is *Romeo and Juliet* based on real lovers or a made-up tale?
13. The Globe Theatre was built close to which river in London?
14. Was *Hamlet* first performed in about 1550, 1600 or 1625?

Level 3

15. Where was the home of the real couple on whose story Shakespeare based *Romeo and Juliet*?
16. Which British king had a friendship with Shakespeare?
17. In what year was the Globe Theatre rebuilt after it had burned down?
18. By which year was Shakespeare recognized as a playwright?

FIND THE ANSWER: Shakespeare

The English writer William Shakespeare wrote plays, long poems, and shorter poems known as sonnets. During his life, he wrote dozens of famous comedies, tragedies and history plays, which are still popular today. They are performed in theatres around the world. Shakespeare is thought of as the greatest English playwright, and many of his plays have been turned into films.

The writer ⑥ ⑱

William Shakespeare (1564–1616) was born in Stratford-upon-Avon, UK. He moved to London, and by 1592 he became known as a playwright.

William Shakespeare

Macbeth ① ⑩ ⑯

Shakespeare's shortest, but bloodiest, tragedy play is *Macbeth*. It is based on a figure from Scottish history. The play reflects the author's friendship with King James I, who claimed Scottish lineage.

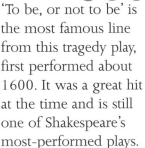

Hamlet ③ ⑪ ⑭

'To be, or not to be' is the most famous line from this tragedy play, first performed about 1600. It was a great hit at the time and is still one of Shakespeare's most-performed plays.

Romeo and Juliet ④ ⑫ ⑮

The tragedy of two lovers who died for each other is based on two real lovers in Verona, Italy, who died in 1303. Shakespeare turned the story into a play early in his career, about 1594–95.

The pit ⑦ ⑧

The area in front of the theatre stage was called the pit. It was uncovered and people had to stand there to watch the play. Richer people watched from seats covered by the roof.

The Globe ② ⑨ ⑬ ⑰

Shakespeare's original Globe Theatre opened in 1599 on the south bank of the River Thames in London, and held an audience of 3,000 people. Many of his best-known plays were performed there. It burned down in 1613 but was rebuilt the next year. In 1997, a replica of the Globe Theatre opened near the original site. People go there to watch Shakespeare's plays.

Groundlings ⑤

People who paid to watch plays in the pit were called groundlings. They paid an admission fee of one penny to watch a play in the pit.

QUESTIONS:
Famous ballets

Level 1

1. *The Nutcracker* features a nutcracker turned into a prince. True or false?
2. Is *Swan Lake* a difficult ballet to perform?
3. Was *Giselle* first performed in London or Paris?
4. Junior ballet dancers sometimes do solo performances. True or false?

Level 2

5. Is *The Firebird* based on a Shakespeare play or on Russian folk tales?
6. Who composed the music for the ballet *The Sleeping Beauty*: Tchaikovsky or Petipa?
7. Is *Giselle* still performed the same as in the first production?
8. In *The Firebird*, the dancer performing the part of the firebird often wears a plain costume. True or false?
9. Odile in *Swan Lake* is what type of creature?
10. Which 'P' roles are unsuitable for junior soloists?
11. Was the composer for *The Sleeping Beauty* Russian, French or American?
12. *The Nutcracker* is a popular production at what time of year?
13. Apart from Odile, what is one of the other characters seen in *Swan Lake*?

Level 3

14. What is the first name of the composer of the music for *The Firebird*?
15. In which year was the first production of *The Nutcracker*?
16. Puss in Boots makes an appearance in which ballet?
17. In which year was *Giselle* first performed?
18. Who choreographed the ballet *The Sleeping Beauty*?

FIND THE ANSWER:

Famous ballets

Ballets are set to music written by a composer, with the dance movements arranged by a choreographer. Many early ballets were produced in Russia. The Ballets Russes was a ballet company that toured Europe and the USA in the early 1900s, creating great interest in ballet.

Sleeping Beauty　⑥ ⑪ ⑱
The Russian composer Tchaikovsky wrote the music for *The Sleeping Beauty*. It was his first successful ballet. His success was largely due to his working with the choreographer Marius Petipa.

Nutcracker　① ⑫ ⑮
After working on *The Sleeping Beauty*, Tchaikovsky and Petipa created *The Nutcracker* in 1892, a ballet about a girl who dreams of a toy nutcracker turned into a prince. Today, it is often performed at Christmas time.

Puss in Boots　④ ⑩ ⑯
The main character of the fairy tale Puss in Boots – the cat who helps his master – makes an appearance in *The Sleeping Beauty* ballet. This light-hearted character and the White Cat are often danced by junior soloists who are not ready for principal, or main, roles.

Swan Lake　② ⑨ ⑬
Swan Lake is one of the most difficult ballets to perform. It includes the character Odile (a black swan maiden), a prince and an evil sorcerer.

Giselle

3 7 17

This French ballet was first performed in Paris in 1841. *Giselle* is one of the oldest ballets still performed, but changes have been made since the first production.

The Firebird

5 8 14

In 1910, the Russian composer Igor Stravinsky wrote the music for *The Firebird*, based on Russian folk tales about a magical bird. It was the first time that the Ballets Russes had music specially composed for them and it is one of Stravinsky's best works. The ballet features an energetic dance by the firebird wearing an elaborate costume.

QUESTIONS:
Basketball

Level 1

1. Children can play basketball. True or false?
2. Is Michael Jordan British or American?
3. A regular shot in basketball scores two points. True or false?
4. Are competition basketballs orange, yellow or green?

Level 2

5. How many metres off the ground is the basket: 2m, 3m or 5m?
6. In which year was basketball invented: 1891, 1911 or 1931?
7. A basketball weighs 600 to 650g, 700 to 750g, or 800 to 850g?
8. What 'H' is the line across the middle of a basketball court?
9. Rearrange CHAIN to spell the country that basketball player Yao Ming is from.
10. In what part of the basketball court can players stay with the ball for only three seconds: the key, the centre of the court or in the corners of the court?
11. How many panels make up a basketball: three, six or eight?
12. Are the balls used by children smaller, bigger or the same size as balls used by adults?
13. What type of basket was first used to play basketball: a basket for peaches, blueberries or tomatoes?

Level 3

14. How many metres wide is a basketball court?
15. By how many centimetres is Yao Ming taller than Michael Jordan?
16. Who invented basketball?
17. In basketball, what is the most points a single shot can score?
18. How much is a foul shot worth?

Basketball

Basketball is a fast-paced team sport, popular around the world. The ball is passed between team mates or dribbled by bouncing it along the floor. The aim of the game is to score points by shooting the ball through a basket, scoring one, two or three points. The team with the most points at the end of the game wins.

The first game 6 13 16

Since its invention by James Naismith in 1891, basketball has blossomed as a sport. At first players aimed a ball into a peach basket. Open nets were first used in 1903. Before then players retrieved the balls from the baskets.

The ball 4 7 11

A soccer ball was the first ball used to play basketball. Today's basketball used in competition is orange and made of eight panels. It weighs 600 to 650g.

basket

key

halfway line

Court 5 8 10 14

A basketball court is 28m long and 15m wide and the basket is 3m off the ground. The court is divided by a halfway line. Under each basket is an area called the key, where players can stay with the ball for only three seconds.

A child's game (1) (12)

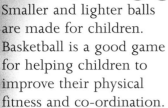

Smaller and lighter balls are made for children. Basketball is a good game for helping children to improve their physical fitness and co-ordination.

Scoring (3) (17) (18)

Two points are scored by making a successful regular shot. A long-distance shot is worth three points. Each foul shot is worth one point.

competing for the ball

Great heights (2) (9) (15)

Most professional basketball players are very tall, which gives them an advantage. Michael Jordan, a famous American player, is 1.98m tall. China's Yao Ming is 2.29m tall. You don't need to be tall to join in this sport, though.

QUESTIONS:
Horse and pony care

Level 1

1. Horses do not like being groomed. True or false?
2. Are horses sometimes massaged?
3. Is the seat a rider sits on called a bridle or a saddle?
4. Horses eat mostly hay and grass. True or false?
5. Horses are kept in buildings called what: stables or paddocks?

Level 2

6. What is the cloth that is used at the end of grooming called: a rubber glove, stable glove or stable rubber?
7. Is plaiting performed before or after clipping and grooming?
8. What type of 'C' comb can remove dried mud from a horse's body?
9. What 'M' name is given to the hair on a horse's neck?
10. Rearrange DIG BEND to give the name of something that is replaced in the stable every day.
11. How many times a day must a horse be fed: once, twice or three times?
12. Name one of two 'B' grains used in short feeds for horses.
13. Is a sponge, tack or saddle soap used to clean around a horse's eyes?
14. Can horses eat only small amounts of grains or large amounts?

Level 3

15. How much manure can an adult horse produce in a week?
16. What is the term used for putting a saddle and bridle on a horse?
17. What object containing horse food is hung up in a stable?
18. How many kilograms of hay can an adult horse eat in a day?

Horse and pony care

Owning a horse or pony is a lot of hard work. The owner must care for the horse, keeping it clean and well-fed, and exercising it regularly. Most horses and ponies live outside in a fenced-off area of field known as a paddock. When it is cold or wet, or when a horse is not well, it may stay inside in a stable. Some competition horses spend every night in a stable. Warm night rugs are put on horses and ponies during cold weather.

plaiting the mane

bridle

Plaiting   7 9
After clipping and grooming, a horse's mane – the hair on its neck – can be plaited, especially if it is going to a show. This makes it neat and tidy. A horse's tail can be plaited as well.

The stable   5 11 18
Horses kept in a stable, a building made to house horses, have to be fed at least twice a day. Daily tasks include grooming, exercising the horses, mucking out, and filling haynets and water buckets. An adult horse can eat 10kg of hay a day.

Mucking out   10 15
Keeping a horse's stable clean is called mucking out. An adult horse can produce 20kg of manure a day. Old bedding is removed with a garden fork and replaced with fresh bedding daily.

straw bedding

saddle

Tacking up   3 16
The saddle is the rider's seat and the bridle is the horse's headgear. Together these items are called tack. Putting them on a horse is called tacking up.

curry comb

Grooming ① ⑧ ⑬

Many tools are used to keep a horse's skin and coat clean and healthy. Most horses enjoy grooming. A rubber or plastic curry comb removes dried mud. A damp sponge cleans around a horse's eyes.

haynet

Feeds ④ ⑫ ⑭ ⑰

Hay and grass are called bulk feed and make up most of a horse's diet. Hay is hung in a haynet so the horse can eat when it likes. Horses can only eat a small amount of grains such as bran, oats and barley. These are short feeds.

short feed

stable rubber

clipping

Stable rubber ② ⑥

A cloth called a stable rubber is used at the end of grooming to remove any dust. It is also used to massage the horse's muscles.

QUESTIONS:
Martial arts

Level 1

1. Are martial artists often trained to use their skills to defend or to fight?
2. Tai chi movements are sharp and sudden. True or false?
3. Is karate a type of striking martial art?
4. Are throwing techniques and arm locks part of judo or kung fu?

Level 2

5. Does kickboxing, tai chi or karate combine boxing with kicking moves?
6. Does a kickboxer score points by striking with his hands, feet or both?
7. Training for karate is divided into forms and sparring. True or false?
8. From which 'J' country does kendo come from?
9. Which colour is usually the highest colour in the coloured belt system used in many martial arts: brown, black or purple?
10. Which qualities are required for success in the martial arts: discipline and self-control, or taking your own lead and being quick to respond?
11. Which 'K' is a form of martial art known for its kicks and open-hand techniques?
12. Which martial art is based on animal poses: tai chi, karate or kendo?
13. Which European country does the form of kickboxing called 'savate' come from: Italy, Spain or France?

Level 3

14. Why does the colour of a belt worn by a judo or karate student change?
15. What is the name of the sword used in kendo?
16. The teachings of which Buddhist led to the beginning of many martial arts?
17. Which martial art is based on jujutsu?

Martial arts

Martial arts are a collection of combat sports and skills. Many of these developed in different countries in Asia over centuries. Millions of people all over the world now enjoy martial arts as exercise. Others practise a martial art as a competitive sport or to learn self-defence.

Origin (16)

Many martial arts are based on teachings by Bodhidharma, a 5th-century Buddhist who visited the Shaolin Temple in China.

karate kick

Judo (4) (17)

Based on the ancient art of jujutsu, the sport of judo uses throwing techniques. In a bout, people grapple on the ground using arm locks, control holds and special choking techniques.

Karate (3) (7) (11)

A type of striking martial art, karate features kicks, punching, knee and elbow strikes, and open-hand techniques. Training is divided into the basics: forms – patterns using movements – and sparring with another person.

Training (1) (10)

Success in martial arts requires discipline. People practise for many hours. Martial artists are often trained to keep self-control all the time, using their skills to defend, not to fight.

blue belt

black belt

Belt colours (9) (14)

In many martial arts, the colour of a belt indicates a student's progress. A black belt is usually the highest colour. The colours and their order varies among schools.

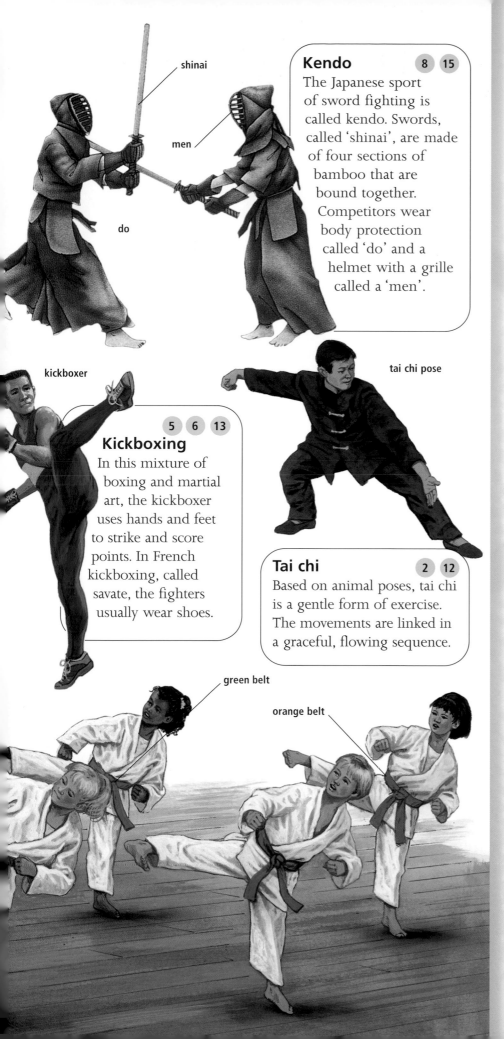

Kendo (8) (15)

The Japanese sport of sword fighting is called kendo. Swords, called 'shinai', are made of four sections of bamboo that are bound together. Competitors wear body protection called 'do' and a helmet with a grille called a 'men'.

shinai

men

do

kickboxer

tai chi pose

Kickboxing (5) (6) (13)

In this mixture of boxing and martial art, the kickboxer uses hands and feet to strike and score points. In French kickboxing, called savate, the fighters usually wear shoes.

Tai chi (2) (12)

Based on animal poses, tai chi is a gentle form of exercise. The movements are linked in a graceful, flowing sequence.

green belt

orange belt

QUESTIONS:
Motor racing

Level 1

1. A driver's helmet protects against what: ice, wind or fire?
2. Rearrange GEE INN to spell the name of a part of a car.
3. F1 cars are low and streamlined. True or false?
4. Does the team decide on a plan to win the race?

Level 2

5. Which 'M' is the name of the stewards who are in charge of fire safety?
6. How fast can an F1 pit crew change four wheels: seven seconds, 17 seconds or 37 seconds?
7. Many F1 drivers consider Silverstone to be one of the fastest F1 race tracks. True or false?
8. How many litres of petrol does an F1 car normally use to drive 100km: 25, 50 or 75?
9. What was the world land speed record for an F1 car set in 2006: 35km/h, 355km/h or 1,550km/h?
10. What are the three top NASCAR championships?
11. What is the important difference between ordinary tracksuits and the race suits worn by racing drivers?
12. What is the strong frame that makes up a NASCAR's structure made of?
13. The average speed over the entire racetrack of the Talladega Superspeedway is what: 160km/h, 303km/h or 354km/h?

Level 3

14. What must a driver do at a pit stop?
15. What are G-forces?
16. What do the pit crew do to an F1 car during a pit stop?
17. What is the advantage of starting a Formula One race with half-full fuel tanks?

Motor racing

back wing
or aerofoil

monocoque body
(made in one piece)

engine

open wheel

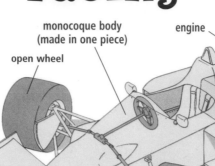

front wing

Motor racing is a popular sport that takes place round the world. Two of the most popular kinds are Formula One (F1, or first-class racing) and NASCAR. F1 began in 1950, and in 2006, 19 races were held on circuits (race tracks) worldwide. NASCAR, the National Association for Stock Car Auto Racing, was set up in 1948.

The car ② ③ ⑧ ⑫

Racing cars are low and streamlined. The powerful engine consumes about 75 litres of petrol per 100km. Each NASCAR vehicle is custom-built around a strong steel frame.

helmet

underwear

outer suit

glove

shoe

Race suits ① ⑤ ⑪

Drivers' race suits, shoes, gloves and underwear are fireproof – if the car catches fire, they protect the driver until track marshals use fire extinguishers. The strong, flexible helmets are also fireproof.

NASCAR ⑩ ⑬

NASCAR is now the USA's favourite motorsport, with more than 75 million fans. Races feature top speeds of more than 320km/h and close finishes. The big three competitions are the Busch Series, the Craftsman Truck Series and the Nextel Cup.

Strategy (4)(17)
To win, the team needs to have a plan. For example, half-full tanks will make the car lighter and faster, but full tanks will need fewer pit stops to refuel. The team decides which strategy is best.

refuelling

lollypop

fire safety

wheel changing

Pit stops (6)(14)(16)
F1 mechanics can change four wheels (faster than replacing worn tyres) and refuel in seven seconds. They also make repairs. The driver has to stop the car in an exact spot and wait for a signal before starting again.

Speed (7)(9)(15)
In 2006, Honda set a world land speed record of 355km/h for an F1 car. When racing, faster cars, such as Ferrari, exceed 300km/h. One of the fastest circuits is Silverstone, in the UK. During fast turns, drivers can suffer neck injuries from high G-forces (acceleration due to gravity).

ANSWERS

Did you get it right? Now you have finished *Train Your Brain*, you can turn over the pages to find the answers. Remember, with the help of a friend, you can also use the answer section for a quick quiz. Why not take it in turns, and see who gets the most right?

ANSWERS: The rainforest

Level 1

1. Are frogs reptiles or amphibians?
Answer: Amphibians

2. Are reptiles cold-blooded or warm-blooded?
Answer: Cold-blooded

3. What 'A' is the world's largest river?
Answer: The Amazon

4. How often does it usually rain in the rainforest: daily, weekly or monthly?
Answer: Daily

Level 2

5. In which continent does the cinchona tree grow?
Answer: South America

6. What type of animal is a boa?
Answer: A snake

7. Which plant has the largest flower in the world?
Answer: Rafflesia

8. In which part of the rainforest do most of its animals live?
Answer: The canopy

9. What do pitcher plants feed on?
Answer: Insects

10. What does the flower of the rafflesia plant smell like?
Answer: Rotten meat

11. GREEN STEM can be rearranged to give the name of which group of tall trees?
Answer: Emergents

12. Where in the world do poison dart frogs live?
Answer: South America

13. Is a bromeliad an animal or a plant?
Answer: A plant

14. A poison dart frog's skin has enough poison to kill a person. True or false?
Answer: True

15. Where does the Atlas moth live?
Answer: Southeast Asia

Level 3

16. Are snakes more closely related to frogs or lizards?
Answer: Lizards

17. How wide is the Amazon river at its mouth: more than 300km, more than 400km or more than 500km?
Answer: More than 300km

18. What illness is treated with quinine?
Answer: Malaria

19. What part of geckos' bodies gives them grip?
Answer: Their toes

20. Where do the plants known as epiphytes grow?
Answer: On other plants

ANSWERS: Ants

Level 1

1. Which have the stronger mandibles (jaws): worker or soldier ants?
Answer: Soldier ants

2. What 'Q' is the large ant that lays all the eggs in a colony?
Answer: The queen

3. Are aphids worms or insects?
Answer: They are insects

4. Are wood ants bigger or smaller than most other ants?
Answer: They are bigger

Level 2

5. Are there any ants that bring aphids into their nests?
Answer: Yes

6. Most ants build nests underground. True or false?
Answer: True

7. What do aphids feed on?
Answer: Plant sap

8. What is the name of the sugary substance that aphids produce?
Answer: Honeydew

9. Are honeypot ants most common in dry or wet places?
Answer: They are most common in dry places

10. Do leaf-cutter ants live in warm or cold forests?
Answer: They live in warm forests

11. Do wood ants ever bite people?
Answer: Yes

12. What type of substance can some ants fire at attackers?
Answer: Acid

13. What do wood ants build their nests from?
Answer: Pine needles

14. Do ants ever attack birds?
Answer: Yes

Level 3

15. Do leaf-cutter ants eat the leaves that they harvest?
Answer: No

16. How many different types of ant are there in a colony?
Answer: Three (queen, worker and soldier ants)

17. What does the word metamorphose mean?
Answer: Change shape

18. In what kind of forest do most wood ants live?
Answer: Pine forest

19. Do all of the workers in a honeypot ant colony store food in their bodies?
Answer: No

20. Name a continent in which both honeypot and leaf-cutter ants live.
Answer: North or South America

ANSWERS: Dinosaurs

Level 1

1. What did *Spinosaurus* have on its back: wings or a sail?
Answer: A sail

2. What 'S' was the largest stegosaur?
Answer: Stegosaurus

3. Which dinosaur had plates on its back: *Kentrosaurus* or *Tyrannosaurus rex*?
Answer: Kentrosaurus

4. Which had larger teeth: plant-eating or meat-eating dinosaurs?
Answer: Meat-eating dinosaurs

Level 2

5. *Tyrannosaurus rex* teeth could be more than 10cm long. True or false?
Answer: True

6. Do fossils take thousands or millions of years to form?
Answer: Millions of years

7. Did sauropods have long necks or short necks?
Answer: They had long necks

8. Did any dinosaurs have beaks?
Answer: Yes

9. What did *Styracosaurus* have on its nose?
Answer: A horn

10. What did male horned dinosaurs probably use their horns for, apart from defence?
Answer: To fight each other

11. Which are more common: scattered fossil bones or entire fossil skeletons?
Answer: Scattered fossil bones

12. What type of dinosaur was *Kentrosaurus*?
Answer: A stegosaur

13. How did a *Spinosaurus* cool down?
Answer: By pumping blood into its sail

14. Where can you see dinosaur bones on display?
Answer: At a museum

Level 3

15. What did *Tyrannosaurus rex* eat?
Answer: Meat

16. Which was bigger: *Seismosaurus* or *Stegosaurus*?
Answer: Seismosaurus

17. Are fossils made of bone or of minerals from rock?
Answer: Minerals from rock

18. *Styracosaurus* ate meat. True or false?
Answer: False

19. Is an *Apatosaurus* more closely related to a *Seismosaurus* or a *Styracosaurus*?
Answer: Apatosaurus and Seismosaurus are related

20. How many rows of plates did most stegosaurs have?
Answer: Two

ANSWERS: Snakes

Level 1

1. Are pythons snakes?
Answer: Yes

2. Do snakes have legs?
Answer: No

3. Can snakes see?
Answer: Yes

Level 2

4. Are there any snakes that eat eggs?
Answer: Yes

5. Which snakes have a hood that they raise when threatened?
Answer: Cobras

6. Where is a rattlesnake's rattle: in its mouth or on the end of its tail?
Answer: On the end of its tail

7. Are snakes vertebrates or invertebrates?
Answer: Vertebrates

8. What are snakes' skeletons made from?
Answer: Bone

9. Do snakes' eggs have hard or flexible shells?
Answer: Flexible shells

10. Are there any snakes that give birth to live young?
Answer: Yes

11. Rattlesnakes live in Africa. True or false?
Answer: False (they live in the Americas)

12. Do cobras have solid or hollow fangs?
Answer: Hollow fangs

13. Do anacondas grow to over 50cm long, over 3m long or over 8m long?
Answer: Over 8m long

14. Does camouflage make a snake harder or easier to see?
Answer: Harder to see

Level 3

15. What does a baby snake have on its snout to help it hatch?
Answer: An egg tooth

16. Why do snakes flick their tongues in and out?
Answer: To taste the air

17. How do snakes move?
Answer: By rippling muscles on the underside of their bodies

18. How do pythons kill their prey?
Answer: By constriction (squeezing)

19. What does the African egg-eating snake use to break eggs?
Answer: Spines sticking down from its backbone

ANSWERS: Sharks

Level 1

1. Are sharks fish or reptiles?
   Answer: Fish
2. The whale shark is the world's biggest fish. True or false?
   Answer: True
3. Do great white sharks eat lions or sea lions?
   Answer: Sea lions
4. Is a shark's egg case called a mermaid's purse or a sailor's purse?
   Answer: A mermaid's purse

Level 2

5. Do sharks have the same set of teeth all their lives?
   Answer: No
6. Do basking sharks live in warmer or cooler waters than whale sharks?
   Answer: Cooler
7. The biggest great white sharks can grow up to 6m long. True or false?
   Answer: True
8. What is the name given to the tiny sea creatures that are food for whale sharks?
   Answer: Plankton
9. Which is bigger: the basking or the great white shark?
   Answer: The basking shark
10. HE MADE HARM can be rearranged to give the name of which type of shark?
    Answer: Hammerhead
11. How heavy can a whale shark be: 11 tonnes, 21 tonnes or 31 tonnes?
    Answer: 21 tonnes
12. Do all sharks lay eggs?
    Answer: No (some give birth to live young)
13. The teeth of an individual shark are all the same shape. True or false?
    Answer: True
14. Which shark is more likely to attack people: the great white or the hammerhead?
    Answer: The great white
15. Do sharks ever resort to cannibalism (eating each other)?
    Answer: Yes

Level 3

16. What feature of a hammerhead makes it easier to follow a scent trail in the water?
    Answer: Its widely spaced nostrils
17. What is the largest type of fish seen off the UK?
    Answer: The basking shark
18. What is the largest shark to actively hunt prey?
    Answer: The great white

ANSWERS: Sea creatures

Level 1

1. How many tentacles does an octopus have?
   Answer: Eight
2. Most of a jellyfish's body is made up of air. True or false?
   Answer: False (it is mostly water)
3. What does SCUBA equipment help people to do?
   Answer: Breathe underwater
4. Are seahorses fish or molluscs?
   Answer: Fish

Level 2

5. What is the world's largest species of ray?
   Answer: The manta ray
6. Are there more than 100 types of shark in the world?
   Answer: Yes
7. How many tentacles does a squid have?
   Answer: Ten
8. What do squid eat: jellyfish, plankton or fish?
   Answer: Fish
9. What do jellyfish use to attack their prey?
   Answer: Stinging tentacles
10. Are squid invertebrates?
    Answer: Yes
11. Which ocean habitat is home to the most types of fish?
    Answer: Coral reefs
12. How long can divers stay underwater for: 10 minutes or more, 15 minutes or more or 20 minutes or more?
    Answer: 20 minutes or more
13. What do the tanks in SCUBA equipment contain?
    Answer: Compressed gas
14. Are sharks more closely related to squid or rays?
    Answer: Rays
15. Do squid spend most of their time in open water or on the seabed?
    Answer: In open water

Level 3

16. What 'P' leave behind the hard, stony cases we see in coral reefs?
    Answer: Polyps
17. To which of these creatures are corals most closely related: jellyfish, giant clams or sharks?
    Answer: Jellyfish
18. What word is used to describe a tail that can grip things?
    Answer: Prehensile

ANSWERS: Marine mammals

Level 1

1. What is the biggest animal on earth: the elephant or the blue whale?
Answer: The blue whale

2. Do seals eat fish or seaweed?
Answer: Fish

3. By what name are orcas more commonly known: killer whales or seals?
Answer: Killer whales

4. Baby harp seals are born with grey fur. True or false?
Answer: False

Level 2

5. Which use echolocation to find their prey: dolphins or walruses?
Answer: Dolphins

6. What 'K' are shrimp-like creatures that humpback whales eat?
Answer: Krill

7. Seals give birth in the sea. True or false?
Answer: False (they give birth on ice or land)

8. Do all walruses have tusks, or only the males?
Answer: All walruses have tusks

9. What 'P' is a group of killer whales known as?
Answer: A pod

10. Why are many large whales rare today?
Answer: Because in the past they were hunted

11. Which marine mammals sometimes kill and eat whales that are larger than they are?
Answer: Killer whales (orcas)

12. Do all whales eat large animals?
Answer: No (some eat small prey)

13. Which ocean surrounds the North Pole?
Answer: The Arctic ocean

14. What 'S' do walruses eat?
Answer: Shellfish

Level 3

15. Where on a whale would you find its baleen?
Answer: Inside its mouth

16. What 'C' is the name of the marine mammal group that contains whales and dolphins?
Answer: Cetaceans

17. Near which pole do walruses live: the North or the South Pole?
Answer: The North Pole

18. What part of a blue whale weighs as much as an elephant?
Answer: Its tongue

19. How long was the largest blue whale ever measured?
Answer: 33.5m long

ANSWERS: Sea birds

Level 1

1. Do puffins carry food in their mouths, their feet or their wings?
Answer: In their mouths

2. Do seagulls ever feed inland?
Answer: Yes

3. SNIFF UP can be rearranged to give the name of what sea birds?
Answer: Puffins

4. An albatross is a type of sea bird. True or false?
Answer: True

5. What 'F' is the main food of most sea birds?
Answer: Fish

Level 2

6. Some sea birds carry food for their chicks in their stomachs. True or false?
Answer: True

7. Why do cormorants stand with their wings open after hunting in the water?
Answer: To dry them out

8. Do puffins use their wings or feet to swim?
Answer: Their wings

9. Do boobies hunt by diving into the water from the air or by diving in from the surface?
Answer: By diving in from the air

10. Is a male frigate bird's throat-pouch red, yellow or blue?
Answer: Red

11. Do cormorants use their wings or feet to swim?
Answer: Their feet

12. Does oil float on water or does it sink?
Answer: It floats

13. Do frigate birds live in the tropics or near the North Pole?
Answer: In the tropics

Level 3

14. What 'G' is a sea bird that nests near the tops of cliffs?
Answer: The gannet

15. What does the word regurgitate mean?
Answer: Cough up

16. How do frigate birds get food?
Answer: By attacking other birds and stealing their food

17. Why do male frigate birds inflate their throat pouches with air?
Answer: To attract females

18. What 'T' is a word for warm air currents that frigate birds use to lift them into the air?
Answer: Thermals

ANSWERS:
Birds

Level 1

1. Do birds have teeth?
Answer: No

2. Birds are the only animals in the world that have feathers. True or false?
Answer: True

3. Do birds flap their wings when they are gliding?
Answer: No

4. Can swans fly?
Answer: Yes

Level 2

5. A NEST FILM can be rearranged to give the name of what parts of a feather?
Answer: Filaments

6. What is the world's largest bird?
Answer: The ostrich

7. Birds have elbow joints. True or false?
Answer: True

8. Are birds' bones solid or hollow?
Answer: Hollow

9. GLEAM UP can be rearranged to give what name for the feathers that cover a bird?
Answer: Plumage

10. Does a kestrel eat fruit, seeds or meat?
Answer: Meat

11. Which are usually more brightly coloured: male birds or female birds?
Answer: Male birds

12. Which 'H' means to stay still in mid-air?
Answer: Hover

13. Which has the longer beak: a curlew or a robin?
Answer: A curlew

14. How many times can hummingbirds flap their wings every second: seven times, 70 times or 700 times?
Answer: 70 times

Level 3

15. What is the chamber between a bird's mouth and its stomach called?
Answer: The crop

16. How many sections does a bird's stomach have?
Answer: Two

17. What do hummingbirds feed on?
Answer: Nectar

18. What 'R' is a large flightless bird?
Answer: Rhea

ANSWERS:
African herbivores

Level 1

1. Do zebras have spots or stripes?
Answer: Stripes

2. Are rhinos larger or smaller than rabbits?
Answer: Larger

3. Are zebras more closely related to horses or sheep?
Answer: Horses

4. Whereabouts on an elephant's body is its trunk?
Answer: On its face

Level 2

5. What is the world's largest land animal?
Answer: The elephant

6. What is the world's tallest land animal?
Answer: The giraffe

7. What 'B' is the word for a male elephant?
Answer: Bull

8. How can an elephant use its trunk to cool itself down?
Answer: By spraying itself with water

9. African elephants can weigh more than a tonne. True or false?
Answer: True

10. How tall do male giraffes grow: 3m, 6m or 10m?
Answer: 6m

11. Rhinos have excellent eyesight. True or false?
Answer: False (they have very poor eyesight)

12. Do giraffes feed mainly on grass, insects or leaves?
Answer: Leaves

13. Which African predator can kill elephants?
Answer: The lion

14. How many species (types) of zebra are there: three, five or seven?
Answer: Three

Level 3

15. What 'P' hunts elephants for their tusks?
Answer: Poacher

16. How many species (types) of rhino are there?
Answer: Five

17. What 'J' is a species of rhino that lives in Asia?
Answer: Javan

18. What are elephants' tusks made of?
Answer: Ivory

ANSWERS:
Lions

Level 1

1. What is the name for a female lion?
Answer: Lioness

2. RIP ED can be rearranged to give what name for a group of lions?
Answer: Pride

3. Which lions have manes: the males or the females?
Answer: The males

4. Do male or female lions make up most of the pride?
Answer: Females

5. Which are bigger: male or female lions?
Answer: Male lions

Level 2

6. Which are the last members of the pride to feed at a kill?
Answer: The cubs

7. Apart from hunting, what do the lionesses do in the pride?
Answer: Care for the young

8. Which members of a pride of lions do most of the hunting?
Answer: The females

9. Do female lions stay with or leave the pride when they grow up?
Answer: They stay

10. Do lions usually hunt in groups or on their own?
Answer: In groups

11. Do lions ever fight to the death?
Answer: Yes

12. How long do lion cubs stay hidden from the rest of the pride: eight days, eight weeks or eight months?
Answer: Eight weeks

13. What do lion cubs have on their coats that adult lions do not?
Answer: Spots

14. How many male lions usually lead a pride?
Answer: One

Level 3

15. What is the name of the area in which a pride of lions lives and hunts?
Answer: Territory

16. What do lions use to mark the borders of this area?
Answer: Urine, droppings and scratch marks

17. What do male lions do to keep others away?
Answer: They roar

18. How does a male lion take over a pride?
Answer: He challenges the established male

ANSWERS:
Polar animals

Level 1

1. Can penguins fly?
Answer: No

2. Can polar bears swim?
Answer: Yes

3. Polar bears can weigh over a tonne. True or false?
Answer: True

4. Do polar bears ever lie in wait for their prey?
Answer: Yes

5. Polar bears eat seals. True or false?
Answer: True

Level 2

6. In which season do migrating birds arrive in the polar regions?
Answer: Spring

7. Killer whales live in polar waters. True or false?
Answer: True

8. Why do some types of baby seal have white coats?
Answer: To hide them in the snow

9. Do polar bears live near to the North Pole or the South Pole?
Answer: The North Pole

10. Penguins live in the Antarctic. True or false?
Answer: True

11. ALE BUG can be rearranged to give the name of which whale that lives in Arctic waters?
Answer: Beluga

12. Which sense do polar bears use to find most of their prey: sight, hearing or smell?
Answer: Smell

13. How do penguins paddle themselves through the water: with their wings or with their feet?
Answer: With their wings

14. What is the world's largest kind of penguin?
Answer: The emperor penguin

Level 3

15. Which bird flies all the way from the Antarctic to the Arctic and back again every year?
Answer: The Arctic tern

16. How can people protect baby seals from humans hunting them for their fur?
Answer: By spraying them with harmless dye

17. Do narwhals live near to the North Pole or the South Pole?
Answer: Near to the North Pole

18. What word is used for keeping an egg warm until it hatches?
Answer: Incubating

ANSWERS: Farm animals

Level 1

1. Are dairy cows kept for their milk or their fur?
Answer: Their milk

2. Is a cockerel a male or a female chicken?
Answer: Male

3. What animal do farmers keep to hunt down rats and mice?
Answer: A cat

4. Which farm animals produce wool?
Answer: Sheep

Level 2

5. What 'K' is a baby goat?
Answer: Kid

6. Today, dairy cows are milked by hand. True or false?
Answer: False (they are milked by machine)

7. On which part of a cow are its teats?
Answer: On its udder

8. How many teats does a cow have?
Answer: Four

9. Which have larger crests on their heads: male or female chickens?
Answer: Male chickens

10. Which animal is needed to make butter?
Answer: A cow

11. EAGER FERN can be rearranged to give the name of what kind of chicken?
Answer: Free-range

12. Which farm animal does gammon come from?
Answer: Pigs

13. What 'L' is a meat from sheep?
Answer: Lamb

14. What 'F' is removed from a sheep by shearing it?
Answer: Fleece

Level 3

15. What is the smallest piglet in a litter called?
Answer: A runt

16. How many teats does a goat have?
Answer: Two

17. What is the most common kind of sheep dog in the UK?
Answer: The border collie

18. What is a male pig called?
Answer: A boar

19. What is the name for chickens that are kept in cages?
Answer: Battery chickens

ANSWERS: Horses

Level 1

1. What are baby horses called?
Answer: Foals

2. What do cowboys wear to shade them from the sun?
Answer: Wide-brimmed hats

3. In showjumping, do riders try to jump over obstacles or crash into them?
Answer: They try to jump over obstacles

4. Horses are used to pull ploughs. True or false?
Answer: True

5. What 'L' is the looped rope that cowboys use to catch cattle?
Answer: Lasso

6. Are ponies larger or smaller than horses?
Answer: Smaller

Level 2

7. Is an Exmoor a breed of pony or a breed of horse?
Answer: A breed of pony

8. What is the largest breed of horse?
Answer: The shire horse

9. What is the main difference between the skeleton of a horse and the skeleton of a human?
Answer: Horse skeletons have front legs instead of arms

10. When do male horses show their teeth and pull their lips back?
Answer: When they smell a female horse

11. HEN CARS can be rearranged to give the name of what large farms on which cowboys work?
Answer: Ranches

12. What is worn by jumping horses to protect their ankles from knocks?
Answer: Bandages

13. BANDY HURDS can be rearranged to give the name of what item, used for removing dirt from a horse's coat?
Answer: Dandy brush

Level 3

14. What 'C' is a type of pony from Iran?
Answer: A Caspian pony

15. How does a horse show aggression?
Answer: By holding its ears back

16. What is the name of the bones that make up a horse's spine?
Answer: Vertebrae

17. What kind of brush is used to brush away loose hair on a horse?
Answer: A rubber curry comb

18. What 'D' is a horse-riding sport, which tests obedience and rider control?
Answer: Dressage

ANSWERS: Cats

Level 1

1. What are baby cats called?
   Answer: Kittens
2. Is catnip a type of plant or a type of animal?
   Answer: A type of plant
3. Do cats creep up and pounce on their prey or chase it round and round until it is exhausted?
   Answer: They creep up and pounce
4. Do cat owners use brushes for grooming their cats or for feeding them?
   Answer: For grooming them
5. Can cats climb?
   Answer: Yes
6. Do young cats prefer playing with balls of wool or with knitting needles?
   Answer: With balls of wool
7. Are cats good at jumping?
   Answer: Yes

Level 2

8. Cats have claws. True or false?
   Answer: True
9. What is a scratching post for?
   Answer: Keeping the claws sharp
10. Do cats prefer to live on their own or in groups?
    Answer: On their own
11. For how long do a cat's eyes stay closed after it is born?
    Answer: A week
12. How often should cats be fed?
    Answer: At least once a day
13. Which fight more often: male cats or female cats?
    Answer: Male cats
14. What are male cats called?
    Answer: Tom cats
15. Why is it a good idea to use a special dish for feeding a cat?
    Answer: So that they come running when their owner approaches it

Level 3

16. What part of a cat's body can be retracted?
    Answer: Its claws
17. From which animal are domestic cats descended?
    Answer: The African wild cat
18. Why do cats spray and scent-mark things?
    Answer: To warn other cats to stay away from their territory

ANSWERS: Dogs

Level 1

1. What is a baby dog called?
   Answer: A puppy
2. Are most police dogs Alsatians or Dalmatians?
   Answer: Alsatians
3. Were pit bull terriers originally bred for fighting or fetching slippers?
   Answer: For fighting
4. Are most Labrador dogs friendly or aggressive?
   Answer: Friendly
5. The terrier is the largest breed of dog. True or false?
   Answer: False

Level 2

6. What is a group of related puppies, born at the same time, called?
   Answer: A litter
7. How long does it take for a puppy to grow into an adult: six months, a year or three years?
   Answer: A year
8. Which 'S' is a kind of dog often trained to be a sniffer dog?
   Answer: A spaniel
9. How might a hearing dog help a deaf owner?
   Answer: By alerting them if there is a knock on the door
10. If a dog wags its tail, is it happy or angry?
    Answer: Happy
11. Does a sad dog drop its tail or raise it?
    Answer: It drops it
12. Which wild animal is the ancestor of all domestic dogs?
    Answer: The wolf
13. EDGIER REVEL TORN can be rearranged to spell what breed of dog, often trained as guide dogs?
    Answer: Golden retriever
14. Which would make a better guard dog: a Rottweiler or a Labrador?
    Answer: A Rottweiler

Level 3

15. How long should you wait before giving away puppies to new owners?
    Answer: A few weeks
16. During which year of a dog's life is it easiest to train?
    Answer: Its first year
17. What is another word for cutting off a dog's tail?
    Answer: Docking
18. How can you tell when a dog is frightened?
    Answer: It holds its tail between its legs
19. What type of dog was bred to hunt large animals?
    Answer: Hounds

ANSWERS: Desert creatures

Level 1
1. What is a coyote: a wild dog or a wild cat?
Answer: A wild dog
2. What are the thorny devil and the gila monster: reptiles, birds or insects?
Answer: Reptiles
3. Desert foxes have large ears to help keep them cool. True or false?
Answer: True

Level 2
4. Some desert birds build their nests on cacti. True or false?
Answer: True
5. Desert birds of prey eat prickly plants. True or false?
Answer: False (they eat rodents, rabbits and snakes)
6. Which desert lizard is poisonous: the gila monster or the chameleon?
Answer: The gila monster
7. Which bird is not a desert bird of prey: the turkey vulture, lappet-faced vulture or kestrel?
Answer: Kestrel (it doesn't live in the desert)
8. What kind of fox lives in the desert: red fox, Arctic fox or fennec fox?
Answer: Fennec fox
9. Does the thorny devil collect dew from its body or from plants?
Answer: From its body
10. Which characteristics help desert hunters: swift movement, keen eyesight, claws, or all of the above?
Answer: All of the above
11. Does the Peruvian fox live in the Atacama desert in South America or the Sahara in North Africa?
Answer: The Atacama desert in South America
12. Which does the bobcat eat: rodents or coyotes?
Answer: Rodents

Level 3
13. Which type of lizard lives its whole life in a decaying cactus?
Answer: The yucca night lizard
14. Does the desert coyote weigh more or less than a coyote that lives in the mountains?
Answer: Less
15. Which feature of a bobcat helps its hearing?
Answer: The hairs on its ears
16. Which 'B' is a flying creature that eats the nectar found in cactus flowers?
Answer: A bat
17. What is another name for the Peruvian fox?
Answer: The Sechuran fox
18. Which 'G' lizard can live for months without food?
Answer: The gila monster

ANSWERS: Spiders

Level 1
1. Is the spider's body made up of two, three or eight parts?
Answer: Two parts
2. How many wings do spiders have: one pair, two pairs or none?
Answer: None
3. Spiders spin silk to make spider webs. True or false?
Answer: True
4. Most spiders have no eyes. True or false?
Answer: False (most have six or eight eyes)

Level 2
5. The trapdoor spider catches its prey in a web. True or false?
Answer: False (it catches prey with a trap)
6. What shape does an orb spider spin after it makes a frame: 'X', 'Y' or 'Z'?
Answer: 'Y'
7. A spider's silk-making organs are in its abdomen. True or false?
Answer: True
8. Are a spider's legs attached to the front part of its body or its abdomen?
Answer: The front part of its body
9. Can some spiders see only shadows and light?
Answer: Yes
10. How does a spider eat its prey: by chewing it, by turning its insides to liquid and sucking them out, or by eating it whole?
Answer: By turning its insides to liquid and sucking them out
11. In what 'A' part of the body are the organs a spider uses for digesting food?
Answer: The abdomen
12. Which spider is the largest in the world?
Answer: The goliath bird-eating spider
13. The goliath bird-eating spider eats only birds. True or false?
Answer: False (it usually eats insects, mice or lizards)

Level 3
14. A dry silk thread remains on the web when a spider finishes spinning. True or false?
Answer: False (it is removed)
15. What type of spiders are the wolf spider and tarantula?
Answer: Hunting spiders
16. What do a spider's hollow fangs hold?
Answer: Poison from venom glands
17. Is it thought that jumping spiders have good or poor eyesight?
Answer: Good eyesight
18. How does a bird-eating spider detect movement?
Answer: With the hairs on its body
19. How does a spider turn its prey's insides into liquid?
Answer: By injecting the prey with special juices

ANSWERS:
Bees

Level 1

1. Honey comes from which creatures: bats, bees or bears?
Answer: Bees

2. What 'D' are male honey bees called?
Answer: Drones

3. Wild honey bees build their own nest, called a hive. True or false?
Answer: True

4. Bees do not have an abdomen. True or false?
Answer: False

Level 2

5. Are a bee's wings attached to its thorax (the middle section of its body) or its head?
Answer: Its thorax

6. Worker bees collect pollen and nectar. True or false?
Answer: True

7. What 'N' is honey made from?
Answer: Nectar

8. What 'H' shape is a cell in a bee hive?
Answer: Hexagonal

9. Does a honey bee have two or three types of wings?
Answer: Two types (forewings and hind wings)

10. Do bees' eggs hatch in three days, one week or one month?
Answer: Three days

11. Bees have special glands that produce what: wax, oil or fat?
Answer: Wax

12. Some bees have a special 'honey stomach' for storing nectar. True or false?
Answer: True

13. What is the average number of flowers a bee will visit in a single trip: 5–10, 50–100, or 500–1,000 flowers?
Answer: 50–100

Level 3

14. Where do honey bees store pollen when collecting it?
Answer: In a pollen 'basket' on their hind legs

15. Name the special tube that bees use to suck nectar.
Answer: Proboscis

16. On average, how many eggs might a queen bee lay in one month?
Answer: 16,666

17. How is honey removed from a honey bee?
Answer: It is sucked out by a worker bee

18. Name a substance made by worker bees that is fed to future queen bees.
Answer: Royal jelly

19. What does a honey bee do when it finds a new supply of food?
Answer: It does a special 'dance'

ANSWERS:
Deadly creatures

Level 1

1. Some snakes are poisonous. True or false?
Answer: True

2. What do great white sharks hunt: seals, porpoises or both?
Answer: Both

3. Female black widow spiders are dangerous to people. True or false?
Answer: True

4. Which creature wraps its body around its victim to kill it: the boa constrictor snake or jellyfish?
Answer: Boa constrictor snake

Level 2

5. What 'T' do jellyfish have?
Answer: Tentacles

6. How does the crocodile kill its prey: by tossing it in the air or drowning it?
Answer: Drowning it

7. The cobra snake kills its prey by wrapping its body around it. True or false?
Answer: False (it uses a poisonous bite)

8. How do sharks find prey: by smell, by using special cells that sense movement, or both?
Answer: Both

9. What does the jellyfish eat: small fish, worms or both?
Answer: Small fish

10. How heavy is the great white shark: 200kg, 1,000kg or 2,000kg?
Answer: 2,000kg

11. Is the tiger shark considered safe or dangerous to people?
Answer: Dangerous (it is a fierce predator)

12. Does the crocodile hide from its prey?
Answer: Yes (under the water)

Level 3

13. What is another name for the box jellyfish?
Answer: Sea wasp

14. How many clusters of tentacles does the box jellyfish have?
Answer: Four

15. Which piranha fish is the most dangerous?
Answer: The red-bellied piranha

16. Which spider is the most dangerous?
Answer: The Brazilian wandering spider

17. The crocodile has what type of special feature to stay under the water?
Answer: Waterproof flaps to seal its eyes, ears, nostrils and throat

18. What 'B' does a piranha detect with a special sensory system?
Answer: Blood

ANSWERS: Frogs

Level 1
1. A baby frog is called a tadpole. True or false?
   Answer: True
2. Do flying frogs have feathers, like birds, or flaps of skin?
   Answer: Flaps of skin
3. Adult frogs have tails. True or false?
   Answer: False
4. Do frogs lay their eggs in water or in nests made in trees?
   Answer: In water

Level 2
5. Tadpoles have tails, gills and legs. True or false?
   Answer: False (they do not have legs)
6. How often do most frogs shed their skin: once a week, once a year or never?
   Answer: Once a week
7. How far can a flying frog glide: 2m, 12m or 22m?
   Answer: 12m
8. All frogs catch food with their tongues. True or false?
   Answer: False (some use their feet)
9. How many days does it take for a frog's eggs to hatch: 3–5 days, 3–25 days or 25–35 days?
   Answer: 3–25 days
10. FRET LOG can be rearranged to give the name of what stage of frog before it becomes an adult?
    Answer: Froglet
11. Are frogs' ears specially tuned in to hear the calls of predators or the calls of their own species?
    Answer: The calls of their own species
12. Would a frog puff its throat to call another frog, to scare a predator, or both?
    Answer: Both
13. What 'A' do tadpoles eat?
    Answer: Algae

Level 3
14. Where do poison dart frogs live?
    Answer: Tropical rainforests of Central and South America
15. Can a cricket frog jump twice its body length, ten times its body length or more than 30 times its body length?
    Answer: More than 30 times
16. What 'M' is the term used to describe the changes that a tadpole undergoes?
    Answer: Metamorphosis
17. Name a species of frog that guards its eggs from predators.
    Answer: Darwin's frog or poison dart frog (plus many other types of frog)
18. The poison from the poison dart frog is used by some tribesmen to do what?
    Answer: To hunt (they use the frogs' poison as a coating for their darts)
19. Give a reason why frogs need to keep their skin wet.
    Answer: To get oxygen

ANSWERS: Coral reef creatures

Level 1
1. Do most corals like warm, shallow water?
   Answer: Yes
2. Is the anemonefish one of the many species of fish that live in the coral reef?
   Answer: Yes
3. Starfish are not really fish. True or false?
   Answer: True
4. Do jellyfish have brains?
   Answer: No (they have a 'nerve net')

Level 2
5. Some fish are colourful or patterned so they can recognize each other. True or false?
   Answer: True
6. CLEAT NETS can be rearranged to give the name of what part of a jellyfish?
   Answer: Tentacles
7. What does a jellyfish's nerve net detect: touch or light?
   Answer: Touch
8. How many species of fish inhabit the coral reef: over 3,000, over 4,000 or over 5,000?
   Answer: Over 4,000
9. Which coral reef creature looks as harmless as a rock?
   Answer: The stonefish
10. Are brain coral and elkhorn types of hard coral or soft coral?
    Answer: Hard coral
11. What do corals use their tentacles for: to walk along the ocean floor, to feed themselves or to swim?
    Answer: To feed themselves
12. Do sea anemones protect anemonefish or eat them?
    Answer: They protect them

Level 3
13. What 'P' do corals eat?
    Answer: Plankton
14. What 'S' means 'life together'?
    Answer: Symbiosis
15. What is the name for a large group of jellyfish?
    Answer: A bloom
16. How many tentacles do soft corals have?
    Answer: Eight
17. What part of their body do most fish move to swim?
    Answer: Their tail
18. Which 'S' creature is an echinoderm?
    Answer: Starfish

ANSWERS: Dolphins and porpoises

Level 1

1. Is the bottle-nosed a type of dolphin, crab or lobster?
Answer: Dolphin

2. Most porpoises are smaller than dolphins. True or false?
Answer: True

3. What game do dolphins like to play: football, tennis or bow-riding?
Answer: Bow-riding

4. Which kind of animal is a dolphin: a mammal or a reptile?
Answer: A mammal

Level 2

5. Dolphins have a 'melon' in their head to help them find fish. True or false?
Answer: True (they use it for echolocation)

6. Do dolphins make clicks, whistles or both to communicate with each other?
Answer: Both

7. Why do porpoises swim upside down: to attract a mate or to eat their food?
Answer: To attract a mate

8. How fast does Dall's porpoise swim?
Answer: 55km/h

9. What 'S' do dolphins like to play with?
Answer: Seaweed

10. Does a porpoise or a dolphin have a triangular dorsal fin?
Answer: A porpoise

11. Where do female dolphins give birth to their babies: near the seabed or just below the surface of the water?
Answer: Just below the surface of the water

12. How many games are dolphins thought to play: more than three, more than 30 or more than 300?
Answer: More than 300

13. What is the function of a 'babysitter' dolphin?
Answer: To help the mother teach its young

14. Do female dolphins give birth to calves, kittens or pups?
Answer: Calves

Level 3

15. How many species of porpoises are there?
Answer: Six

16. Which species is the smallest porpoise?
Answer: The Vaquita

17. What is a dolphin's beak called?
Answer: A rostrum

18. What is bow-riding?
Answer: Surfing on the waves created by boats

19. What 'C' sound do dolphins use to learn about their surroundings and find fish?
Answer: A clicking sound

ANSWERS: Killer whales

Level 1

1. Do killer whales live in a family group called a pod?
Answer: Yes

2. Another name for the killer whale is the orca. True or false?
Answer: True

3. Do adult killer whales take care of their young or do they let their young take care of themselves?
Answer: Adults take care of their young

4. What is a whale jump called: a breach, a hop or a bungee?
Answer: A breach

Level 2

5. Is a killer whale also called a shark of the ocean or a wolf of the sea?
Answer: A wolf of the sea

6. How long is a male killer whale: up to 4m, 6m or 10m?
Answer: Up to 10m

7. Killer whales sometimes hunt young blue whales. True or false?
Answer: True

8. Why would a whale breach: to scare prey, warn of danger, attract a mate or all of the above?
Answer: All of the above

9. What 'C' and 'W' noises will a whale use to send messages to another whale?
Answer: Clicks and whistles

10. A clan is made up of several pods. True or false?
Answer: True

11. Does a killer whale poke its tail or head out of water when it is spyhopping?
Answer: Its head

12. Are killer whales mammals or large fish?
Answer: Mammals

13. Do killer whales protect injured and sick members of their pod, attack them or force them away?
Answer: They protect them

Level 3

14. What is a killer whale's cruising speed?
Answer: 10km/h

15. What is a lobtail?
Answer: A smack on the water with the tail

16. How much faster does a killer whale swim when it's hunting, not cruising?
Answer: 38km/h faster

17. LEAD CIT can be rearranged to give what name for the common calls shared by a whale pod?
Answer: Dialect

18. For how long can a whale hold itself up while spyhopping?
Answer: Up to 30 seconds

ANSWERS: Baleen whales

Level 1

1. Is the blue whale the largest mammal on earth?
Answer: Yes

2. What do baleen whales eat: birds or shrimp-like krill?
Answer: Shrimp-like krill

3. Whales never migrate with their young. True or false?
Answer: False

4. The blue whale is the loudest animal, much louder than humans. True or false?
Answer: True

Level 2

5. Only the blue whale has two blowholes. True or false?
Answer: False (all baleen whales have two blowholes)

6. The bowhead whale likes the warm waters of the Mediterranean sea. True or false?
Answer: False (it lives in Arctic waters)

7. The grey whale migrates along which coast of the USA: the eastern or the western coast?
Answer: The western coast

8. What are baleen plates used for: tossing fish, trapping krill or swimming?
Answer: Trapping krill

9. Do humpback whales use bubbles to trap krill?
Answer: Yes (they form a bubble netting)

10. Name one of two reasons why baleen whales migrate.
Answer: To breed or to feed

11. Why does the bowhead whale have a thick layer of blubber?
Answer: To keep it warm

12. How far can the grey whale migrate: 1,000km, 5,000km or 10,000km?
Answer: 10,000km

13. Rearrange FREET FIELDS to describe how a baleen whale eats.
Answer: Filter feeds

Level 3

14. How loud is a blue whale call?
Answer: Up to 188 decibels

15. Do humpback whales eat the food they catch by bubble netting on the seabed or at the surface?
Answer: At the surface

16. What percentage of its total length is the head of the bowhead whale?
Answer: 40 per cent

17. How many krill can a blue whale eat in a single day?
Answer: 4 million

ANSWERS: Birds of prey

Level 1

1. Which bird is the national bird of the USA: golden eagle, harpy eagle or bald eagle?
Answer: Bald eagle

2. Does the osprey live near water or in grasslands?
Answer: Near water

3. The peregrine falcon is faster than any other creature in the world. True or false?
Answer: True

4. What are talons: claws, wings or legs?
Answer: Claws

Level 2

5. How many species of falcon are there: about five, 35 or 75?
Answer: About 35

6. What kind of eagle is the South American harpy: a snake eagle, buzzard-like eagle or sea eagle?
Answer: Buzzard-like eagle

7. How fast can a peregrine falcon dive: 23km/h, 230km/h or 320km/h?
Answer: 320km/h

8. Which birds of prey have longer talons: those that catch rabbits or those that catch fish?
Answer: Those that catch fish

9. How many species of eagle are there: about 20, 40 or 60?
Answer: About 60

10. Which bird of prey has the largest wingspan?
Answer: The Andean condor

11. What is the world's largest eagle?
Answer: The South American harpy

12. What does the bald eagle eat: small animals, fish or both?
Answer: Both

13. What type of wings enables eagles and buzzards to soar for long periods: broad wings or long, tapered wings?
Answer: Broad wings

14. Is the kestrel a type of falcon or eagle?
Answer: Falcon

Level 3

15. Which wing shape allows birds to manoeuvre easily?
Answer: Short and round

16. The golden eagle is which type of eagle?
Answer: A booted eagle

17. What is unusual about the bottom of an osprey's feet?
Answer: They are covered with spiny scales for gripping prey

18. What happens to a bald eagle at three or four years of age?
Answer: It develops its white head and yellow beak

ANSWERS: Rats and mice

Level 1

1. To what animal group do rats and mice belong: rodents, insects or reptiles?
Answer: Rodents

2. Is the Swiss albino mouse the most common pet mouse?
Answer: Yes

3. The Norway rat is the most common rat in the world. True or false?
Answer: True

4. What disease were rats blamed for spreading: the plague, flu or colds?
Answer: The plague

Level 2

5. A mouse has lots of fur when it is born. True or false?
Answer: False (it has no fur)

6. The Norway rat killed off many black rats when it arrived in Europe. True or false?
Answer: True

7. Do some rats live in houses and other buildings?
Answer: Yes

8. Do dormice build nests or live in caves?
Answer: They build nests

9. Where did the Norway rat originate: Europe, Asia or Africa?
Answer: Asia

10. What 'I' are teeth that both rats and mice have?
Answer: Incisors

11. How many species of mice are there: less than ten, between ten and 100 or more than 100?
Answer: More than 100

12. What is another name for the Norway rat?
Answer: The brown rat

13. What 'H' do dormice do during the winter?
Answer: Hibernate

Level 3

14. What 'H' is one of the smallest types of mouse?
Answer: The harvest mouse

15. In which areas is the black rat more common than the brown rat?
Answer: Tropical areas

16. What does the Latin word *rodere* mean?
Answer: 'To gnaw'

17. How did the Norway rat arrive in North America?
Answer: On the ships of the new settlers

18. How fast can a mouse run?
Answer: Up to 13km/h

19. How many baby mice might a female mouse give birth to in a year?
Answer: About 40

ANSWERS: Bats

Level 1

1. Bats are flying mammals. True or false?
Answer: True

2. Vampire bats drink the blood of which animals: cattle, lizards or snails?
Answer: Cattle

3. Are a bat's bones light in weight to make flying easier?
Answer: Yes

Level 2

4. What are fruit bats sometimes called: flying cats, flying foxes or flying monkeys?
Answer: Flying foxes

5. All bats use echolocation to help them to find food. True or false?
Answer: False (some use their sense of smell)

6. Some baby bats can fly when they are only two weeks old. True or false?
Answer: True

7. What do bats use the clawed fingers on their wings for: climbing or hanging upside down?
Answer: For climbing

8. How many squeaks per second might a bat use during echolocation: two, 200 or 2 million?
Answer: 200

9. Which part of its body does a vampire use to detect heat?
Answer: A heat sensor

10. TURF BAITS can be rearranged to name which bats found in Asia, Africa and Oceania?
Answer: Fruit bats

11. Do bats have strong legs or weak legs?
Answer: Weak legs

12. What is the wingspan of the largest bat: 1.5m, 1.8m or 2.5m?
Answer: 1.8m

Level 3

13. Why does the vampire bat have fewer teeth than other bats?
Answer: It does not need to chew its food

14. What is another name for the bumblebee bat?
Answer: Kitti's hog-nosed bat

15. How do the fingers of fruit bats differ from other bats?
Answer: They also have a claw on the second fingers

16. What is the difference in wingspan between the smallest bat and the largest bat?
Answer: 165cm

17. How do some bats find fruit and nectar?
Answer: By using their sense of smell

18. Where can a flap of skin be found on a bat?
Answer: Between its legs and tail

ANSWERS: Big cats

Level 1

1. Lions hunt their prey in a group. True or false?
Answer: True

2. What is a group of lions called: a pride or school?
Answer: A pride

3. Do lions and tigers both roar?
Answer: Yes

4. All big cats are mammals. True or false?
Answer: True

5. What does a lion eat: zebras, penguins or lobsters?
Answer: Zebras

Level 2

6. The tiger, leopard, jaguar and lynx are all big cats. True or false?
Answer: False (the lynx is not a big cat)

7. How much can a tiger eat in one meal: 10kg, 40kg or 80kg of meat?
Answer: 40kg of meat

8. Which animal is the fastest on land: the jaguar, the lion or the cheetah?
Answer: The cheetah

9. Which cat is the largest: lion, tiger or cheetah?
Answer: Tiger

10. Rearrange ROD LEAP to name a big cat that feeds on impala, hares and birds.
Answer: Leopard

11. Each tiger has the same pattern of stripes on both sides of its body. True or false?
Answer: False (there is a different pattern on each side)

12. Which cat will hide its kill in a tree: a lion, tiger or leopard?
Answer: Leopard

13. Which is the only big cat that lives in the Americas: the cheetah, jaguar or ocelot?
Answer: Jaguar

14. Which 'S' describes the way lions and tigers hunt?
Answer: Stalking

Level 3

15. Which small tiger is native to Asia?
Answer: The Sumatran tiger

16. Which mammal group includes lions, tigers, leopards and jaguars?
Answer: Panthera

17. What two things help to hide a big cat when it is hunting?
Answer: Tall grass and the colouring of its fur

18. How far can a cheetah travel in just three strides?
Answer: 18m

19. Which is the only big cat that cannot fully retract its claws?
Answer: The cheetah

ANSWERS: Great apes

Level 1

1. Do chimps live together in groups?
Answer: Yes

2. What is an adult male gorilla called: a silverback, greyfront or bluetop?
Answer: Silverback

3. Chimps have calls to communicate with each other. True or false?
Answer: True

4. Because rainforests are being destroyed, are all of the great apes in danger of becoming extinct?
Answer: Yes

Level 2

5. Gorillas and chimps live in both Africa and Asia. True or false?
Answer: False (they live only in Africa; orang-utans live in Asia)

6. At what age do gorillas learn to 'knuckle walk': three weeks, nine months or nine years?
Answer: Nine months

7. The orang-utan is a sociable creature. True or false?
Answer: False (it lives alone after leaving its mother)

8. Is blackback another name for a young male gorilla, a young male orang-utan or a young male chimpanzee?
Answer: A young male gorilla

9. Which is an enemy of the gorilla: the leopard, tiger or jaguar?
Answer: The leopard

10. For how long will a juvenile male gorilla stay with his family: until he is three years old, eight years old or 11 years old?
Answer: Until he is 11 years old

11. How many gorillas do the largest wild groups contain: ten, 30 or 200?
Answer: 30

12. What feature identifies an adult male gorilla: a silver, black or brown patch of fur along its back?
Answer: A silver patch of fur

13. What is a gorilla group called: a clan, a troop or a family?
Answer: A troop

14. Where do orang-utans live: in trees, caves or tall grass?
Answer: In trees

Level 3

15. What 'B' is another word for a pygmy chimp?
Answer: Bonobo

16. How many nests can an orang-utan make over seven days?
Answer: 14

17. What do opposable thumbs allow a great ape to do?
Answer: Use tools

18. Which member of a gorilla group decides when it is time to move on?
Answer: The silverback

19. What do gorillas eat?
Answer: Mostly plant food, but they will also eat insects

ANSWERS: Bears

Level 1

1. Bears hibernate by going into a long sleep. True or false?
Answer: True

2. Where do polar bears live: the Arctic, the Antarctic or South America?
Answer: The Arctic

3. Are baby bears called kittens, pups or cubs?
Answer: Cubs

4. Where do mother bears give birth: underwater, by a lake or in a den?
Answer: In a den

5. Bears are sometimes scavengers. True or false?
Answer: True

Level 2

6. The grizzly bear is a type of brown bear. True or false?
Answer: True

7. For how long can a black bear hibernate: 50, 100 or 200 days?
Answer: 100 days

8. Is the sun bear, Kodiak bear or spectacled bear the smallest bear?
Answer: The sun bear

9. Does a polar bear have a 10cm layer, 30cm layer or 50cm layer of fat around its body?
Answer: A 10cm layer

10. At what age does a bear cub leave its mother: one year old, two years old or three years old?
Answer: At three years old

11. What 'S' do Alaskan brown bears love to eat?
Answer: Salmon

12. Where does the spectacled bear live: in mountains, deserts or tundra?
Answer: Mountains

Level 3

13. If a black bear weighs 180kg in spring, how much would it weigh at hibernation?
Answer: 360kg

14. What 'S' is a marine animal that is eaten by polar bears?
Answer: Seals

15. Name one of two main things cubs learn from their mother.
Answer: How to hunt or make shelters

16. What is an omnivore?
Answer: An animal that eats both plant foods and meat

17. Which bear is the largest bear?
Answer: The polar bear

18. Which bear eats bromeliad plants?
Answer: The spectacled bear

19. In the autumn, how many hours a week, on average, does a bear spend eating?
Answer: 140

ANSWERS: Pets

Level 1

1. Pet fish are kept in a tank called an aquarium. True or false?
Answer: True

2. Cats use their whiskers to find their way around at night. True or false?
Answer: True

3. Are rabbits fast runners or slow animals?
Answer: Fast runners

4. Is a cat with its tail held high happy or unhappy?
Answer: Happy

Level 2

5. Cavies are also called guinea pigs. True or false?
Answer: True

6. Do domestic cats have short hair, long hair or either kind?
Answer: Either kind

7. Are dogs most closely related to rabbits, foxes or wolves?
Answer: Wolves

8. Can a rabbit see almost 90 degrees, 180 degrees or 360 degrees?
Answer: Almost 360 degrees

9. Which is not a type of parrot: macaw, parakeet or quetzal?
Answer: Quetzal

10. What 'H' means an animal that eats plants?
Answer: Herbivore

11. The Abyssinian guinea pig has smooth, short hair. True or false?
Answer: False (it has a rough coat of swirls)

12. Which animal is also known as a desert rat: the guinea pig, the gerbil or the rabbit?
Answer: The gerbil

13. Rearrange DEER BURP to spell a word used to describe cats of a particular type.
Answer: Purebred

Level 3

14. What must a hamster do because its teeth grow all the time?
Answer: It gnaws on anything available

15. What ability is the African grey parrot known for?
Answer: Being one of the best mimics

16. What 'S' is another name for the golden hamster?
Answer: Syrian hamster

17. Pet fish owners need to make sure what 'T' in an aquarium is properly controlled to suit the type of fish?
Answer: The temperature

18. How many breeds of dog are there?
Answer: Over 400 breeds

19. Rabbits are most active during which times of day?
Answer: At dawn and dusk

20. In which states of the USA is it illegal to keep gerbils?
Answer: California and Hawaii

ANSWERS: Continents

Level 1
1. Where is the Nile?
Answer: In Africa

2. Which continent lies to the east of Europe?
Answer: Asia

3. Is Asia the second-most populated continent?
Answer: No (it is the most populated)

4. Is Central America part of North or South America?
Answer: North America

5. Which is the smallest continent?
Answer: Australia

Level 2
6. What is the world's largest country?
Answer: The Russian Federation

7. What divides Europe from Africa?
Answer: The Mediterranean sea

8. What population milestone was reached in 1802?
Answer: The world's population reached one billion

9. Is Sydney the capital city of Australia?
Answer: No (Canberra is the capital)

10. In which continent would you find the world's highest mountains?
Answer: Asia

11. What larger landmass contains Europe?
Answer: Eurasia

12. How many billion did the world's population reach in 1999: one, five, six or 11?
Answer: Six

13. Are the Andes on the east or west coast of South America?
Answer: On the west coast

Level 3
14. How much of the Amazon rainforest lies outside of Brazil?
Answer: 40 per cent

15. What are the names of the island groups of the South Pacific?
Answer: Melanesia, Micronesia and Polynesia

16. By how many million per year was the world's population increasing in 2004?
Answer: 75 million per year

17. How many countries are in Africa: 47, 52 or 53?
Answer: 53 countries

18. In which continent is the world's largest freshwater lake?
Answer: In North America

19. How long is the Andes mountain range?
Answer: 7,000km long

ANSWERS: The international community

Level 1
1. The United Nations was formed during World War I. True or false?
Answer: False (it was officially established just after World War II)

2. What does NATO stand for: the North Atlantic Treaty Organization or the North Antarctic Treaty Organization?
Answer: The North Atlantic Treaty Organization

3. All peacekeeping units are armed. True or false?
Answer: False (some are armed, some are unarmed)

4. What is the single currency of the European Union?
Answer: The euro

5. CRESS ROD can be rearranged to give the name of what organization that provides medical aid?
Answer: The Red Cross

Level 2
6. Why was NATO formed?
Answer: To ensure peace in its member states

7. What convention protects wounded soldiers and prisoners?
Answer: The Geneva Convention

8. In what city is the UN headquarters?
Answer: New York City

9. How many countries are in the UN?
Answer: 192

10. What treaty marked the beginning of the European union?
Answer: The Treaty of Paris

11. In what building do member nations of the UN meet?
Answer: The General Assembly Building

12. For what purpose can peacekeeping units use their weapons?
Answer: For self-defence

Level 3
13. In what year did the UN headquarters officially open?
Answer: 1951

14. What treaty led to the formation of the European Union?
Answer: The Maastricht Treaty

15. What is the full name of the Red Cross?
Answer: The International Committee of the Red Cross and the Red Crescent Movement

16. How much money was donated to buy land for the UN headquarters?
Answer: $8.5 million

17. What is the name of the central command of NATO's military forces?
Answer: SHAPE (Supreme Headquarters Allied Powers Europe)

18. Who first used the term 'United Nations'?
Answer: US President F D Roosevelt

ANSWERS: Flags

Level 1

1. What colours could a pirate flag be?
Answer: Red or black

2. Where are naval flags used: at sea or in space?
Answer: At sea

3. In what kind of sport is a black-and-white chequered flag used?
Answer: In auto and motorcycle racing

4. What kind of flag do explorers plant on lands they have discovered?
Answer: Their national flag

5. Which has the oldest national flag: Scotland or the USA?
Answer: Scotland

Level 2

6. Which sport uses flags: rugby, cycling, rowing or all three?
Answer: All three

7. What are naval flags called?
Answer: Signalling flags

8. What event prompted the redesign of the French flag?
Answer: The French revolution

9. Are signalling flags used alone, together or both?
Answer: Both alone and together

10. What is semaphore?
Answer: A signalling system using flags

11. How many US flags have been placed on the moon: four, five or six?
Answer: Six

12. Which colour is not used in naval flags: yellow, black or green?
Answer: Green

Level 3

13. What do referees use flags to indicate in an American football game?
Answer: An error

14. In semaphore, how is an 'R' signalled?
Answer: By holding both arms and flags straight out

15. On a pirate flag, what does an hour glass symbolize?
Answer: That time is running out

16. What colour flags are used in semaphore?
Answer: Red and yellow

17. In which century were pirate flags first used?
Answer: The 18th century

18. What displayed a US flag on Mars?
Answer: The Viking lander

ANSWERS: Natural wonders

Level 1

1. What is the tallest mountain in the world?
Answer: Everest

2. What is the tallest waterfall in the world?
Answer: Angel Falls

3. K2 is in Europe. True or false?
Answer: False (it is in Asia)

4. The Great Barrier Reef lies off the coast of which country?
Answer: Australia

5. The Great Barrier Reef can be seen from space. True or false?
Answer: True

6. Which is longer: the Grand Canyon or the Great Barrier Reef?
Answer: The Great Barrier Reef

Level 2

7. Who were the first people to reach the top of Mount Everest?
Answer: Edmund Hillary and Tenzing Norgay

8. How is the length of the Grand Canyon measured?
Answer: By the Colorado river

9. How many times higher is Angel Falls than Niagara Falls: 10, 15 or 20?
Answer: 15 times

10. What is the Hillary Step?
Answer: A steep section of Mount Everest

11. How old are the rocks in the Grand Canyon?
Answer: 2,000 million years old

12. In what continent is the widest waterfall in the world?
Answer: Asia

13. What is another name for *aurora borealis*?
Answer: The Northern Lights

Level 3

14. What causes the Northern Lights?
Answer: High-speed particles from the sun colliding with gas molecules

15. How much older are the Alps than the Himalayas?
Answer: 15 million years

16. How high is Mount Everest?
Answer: 8,850m high

17. What is the Latin name of the Southern Lights?
Answer: Aurora australis

18. What geographical feature is 10,783m wide?
Answer: Khône Falls

ANSWERS:
Coasts

Level 1
1. A tsunami is caused by the wind. True or false?
Answer: False

2. ACE VASE can be rearranged to give what name for a cavern in a cliff?
Answer: Sea cave

3. What is the wearing down of a headland called: erosion or erasure?
Answer: Erosion

4. What two materials do waves deposit on beaches?
Answer: Pebbles and sand

5. What 'W' causes waves?
Answer: The wind

6. HELLO BOW can be rearranged to give the name of what coastal feature?
Answer: Blow hole

Level 2
7. What is special about the Painted Cave?
Answer: It is the longest sea cave in the world

8. What does the word 'tsunami' mean?
Answer: Harbour wave

9. What causes water to gush through a blow hole?
Answer: Built-up air pressure

10. The fetch is the material deposited on a beach. True or false?
Answer: False

11. A stack is a mound of sand. True or false?
Answer: False

12. Is sea water acidic or alkaline?
Answer: Acidic

Level 3
13. Which is formed first: a cave or a blow hole?
Answer: A cave

14. How fast do tsunami waves move?
Answer: At over 700km/h

15. What coastal process do groynes prevent?
Answer: Longshore drift

16. On what island is the Painted Cave?
Answer: Santa Cruz Island, California, USA

17. How high can tsunamis be?
Answer: Up to 30m high

18. A stack is formed from which coastal feature?
Answer: An arch

ANSWERS:
Rivers

Level 1
1. What is the beginning of a river called?
Answer: The source

2. In what continent are the Great Lakes?
Answer: North America

3. Do waterfalls flow over a ledge of hard or soft rock?
Answer: Hard rock

4. What is the name of the process by which water moves between the land and sea and back again?
Answer: The water cycle

5. What is the name of the area of flat land on either side of a river?
Answer: A flood plain

Level 2
6. What 'R' is precipitation?
Answer: Rain

7. What kind of lakes are created by ice sheets?
Answer: Freshwater lakes

8. What is formed when a river floods shallow lakes or ponds?
Answer: A marsh

9. Do tributaries increase or decrease the water volume of a river?
Answer: Increase

10. What happens to evaporated water?
Answer: It condenses to form clouds

11. What other name is used for an estuary?
Answer: A harbour

12. Headwaters are the top of a waterfall. True or false?
Answer: False

13. What prevents water seepage in a marshland?
Answer: Granite, slate or quartz beneath

14. What forms at the bottom of a waterfall?
Answer: A plunge pool

Level 3
15. What 'Y' is a waterfall in the USA, created by a glacier?
Answer: Yosemite Falls, California, USA

16. What name is given to fertile land formed on a flood plain?
Answer: Alluvium

17. What can form from sediment in an estuary?
Answer: A delta

18. How was Lake Tanganyika formed?
Answer: By earth fault movements

ANSWERS: Deserts

Level 1

1. What 'D' is a sandy desert feature?
   Answer: Dune
2. Which animal is used to carry people and goods in the desert?
   Answer: The camel
3. Sand holds water. True or false?
   Answer: False
4. What plant with spines can survive in a desert?
   Answer: The cactus
5. What 'B' is the home of a meerkat?
   Answer: A burrow

Level 2

6. Is a Tuareg a type of sand dune or a member of a desert tribe?
   Answer: A member of a desert tribe
7. What type of sand dune forms when the wind blows in all directions?
   Answer: A star dune
8. What is a one-humped camel called?
   Answer: A dromedary
9. What is the name for wind carrying away fine sand?
   Answer: Deflation
10. What is the slope of a sand dune called?
    Answer: A slip face
11. Wind blowing in two different directions creates which type of sand dune?
    Answer: A linear dune
12. Is a hoodoo: a type of sand dune, a rock formation or a desert rodent?
    Answer: A rock formation
13. In which desert would you find a Tuareg?
    Answer: The Sahara desert

Level 3

14. What desert plant can be over 200 years old?
    Answer: The Saguaro cactus
15. What 'F' is a kind of fox that lives in the desert?
    Answer: The fennec fox
16. What is a barchan?
    Answer: A curved sand dune
17. What substance is formed by cemented sand and gravel?
    Answer: Calcrete
18. What features of a camel help it survive in deserts?
    Answer: It can go without water for several days, and has thick padded feet so that it can walk across hot sand without any pain

ANSWERS: The poles

Level 1

1. On which continent is the South Pole?
   Answer: Antarctica
2. The explorer Robert Scott reached the South Pole. True or false?
   Answer: True
3. LIE CRAG can be rearranged to give the name of what polar feature?
   Answer: Glacier
4. Icebergs are lumps of ice that have broken away from glaciers. True or false?
   Answer: True

Level 2

5. What is a hollow formed by melting blocks of ice called: a kettle hole or a sink hole?
   Answer: A kettle hole
6. How much of an iceberg is visible above the waterline?
   Answer: One-tenth
7. Who was the first person to reach the South Pole?
   Answer: Roald Amundsen
8. Why do glaciers shift?
   Answer: Because of the weight of ice and gravity
9. Today, most Inuit use dog sleds to travel over the Arctic ice. True or false?
   Answer: False
10. What imaginary line runs between the two poles?
    Answer: The axis on which the earth turns
11. What is a moraine?
    Answer: A ridge of rock left by a melting glacier
12. What language is spoken by the Inuit?
    Answer: Inuktitut
13. What 'P' is an item of clothing worn by Arctic people?
    Answer: A parka

Level 3

14. Do the Inuit live near to the North or the South Pole?
    Answer: The North Pole
15. In which year did a person reach the South Pole for the first time?
    Answer: 1911
16. Near which pole are flat-topped tabular icebergs found?
    Answer: The South Pole
17. When Scott and his crew fell into difficulties, how far would they have had to travel to safety?
    Answer: 17km
18. What Arctic people live in Greenland?
    Answer: The Kalaalit

ANSWERS: Africa

Level 1

1. Is Mount Kilimanjaro Africa's highest point?
   Answer: Yes
2. The Sahara is the largest desert in the world. True or false?
   Answer: True
3. Which 'N' in Africa is the longest river in the world?
   Answer: The Nile
4. Who built the pyramids: ancient Europeans, ancient Egyptians or ancient Americans?
   Answer: Ancient Egyptians

Level 2

5. The Serengeti is a sandy desert. True or false?
   Answer: False (it is a grassland)
6. Lake Tanganyika is the longest in the world. Is it also the deepest in Africa?
   Answer: Yes
7. Where does the Nile flow to: the Mediterranean sea, Red sea or Atlantic ocean?
   Answer: The Mediterranean sea
8. Is the Serengeti in Tanzania and Kenya or Botswana and South Africa?
   Answer: Tanzania and Kenya
9. What happens every year along the Nile: does the river dry up, stay the same or flood its banks?
   Answer: It floods its banks
10. How many blocks of stone make up the Great Pyramid: 23,000, 230,000 or 2,300,000?
    Answer: 2,300,000
11. What 'N' are people who live in the Sahara?
    Answer: Nomads
12. How many animals migrate in the Serengeti each year: almost 200,000, 2 million or 5 million?
    Answer: 2 million
13. Rearrange MAIN GOLF to name a bird that migrates to Lake Tanganyika.
    Answer: Flamingo

Level 3

14. How long is Lake Tanganyika?
    Answer: 670km long
15. Name the highest point on Mount Kilimanjaro.
    Answer: Kibo
16. For which 'C' pharaoh was the Great Pyramid built?
    Answer: Cheops
17. What is a stratovolcano?
    Answer: A volcano made of hardened lava and volcanic ash
18. How large is the Sahara?
    Answer: 9,000,000km^2

ANSWERS: The Middle East

Level 1

1. The Blue Mosque is in Istanbul. True or false?
   Answer: True
2. Do Muslims make pilgrimages to Mecca?
   Answer: Yes
3. Is the tallest hotel in the world in Dubai or Antarctica?
   Answer: Dubai
4. Minarets are tiny Islamic dancers. True or false?
   Answer: False (they are spiralling towers)

Level 2

5. Diriyah was the capital of which country: Saudi Arabia, Greece or Spain?
   Answer: Saudi Arabia
6. How many blue tiles are inside the Blue Mosque: over 200, over 2,000 or over 20,000?
   Answer: Over 20,000
7. Was the Blue Mosque completed in 3600BCE or 1616CE?
   Answer: 1616CE
8. Was Diriyah destroyed by a flood or an Egyptain-led army?
   Answer: An Egyptian-led army
9. Which is a servant in an Islamic mosque: the muezzin or the serf?
   Answer: The muezzin
10. In which 'S' country was the Krak des Chevaliers built?
    Answer: Syria
11. The Blue Mosque is also known as the Sultan Ahmed Mosque. True or false?
    Answer: True
12. What is a caliph: an Islamic leader or Jewish leader?
    Answer: An Islamic leader
13. What 'G' once covered the Dome of the Rock?
    Answer: Gold

Level 3

14. Who ordered the building of the Dome of the Rock?
    Answer: Abd al-Malik
15. Mecca is in which country?
    Answer: Saudi Arabia
16. What does Krak des Chevaliers mean?
    Answer: Fortress of the Knights
17. About how much higher than the Burj al-Arab will the Burj Dubai be?
    Answer: 489m higher
18. When were the Crusades?
    Answer: Between the 11th and 13th centuries

ANSWERS: Asia

Level 1

1. Mount Fuji is the tallest mountain in the world. True or false?
Answer: False (Mount Everest is the tallest)

2. Is the Taj Mahal in India, Croatia or Spain?
Answer: India

3. In building the Taj Mahal, over 1,000 elephants were used to haul marble. True or false?
Answer: True

4. Mount Fuji in Japan is a dormant volcano. True or false?
Answer: True

Level 2

5. Shah Jahan built the Taj Mahal for his favourite daughter. True or false?
Answer: False (he built it in memory of his wife)

6. What 'T' does 'wat' mean?
Answer: Temple

7. Where is the Potala Palace: Japan, Malaysia or Tibet?
Answer: Tibet

8. Which building was built in Kuala Lumpur, the capital of Malaysia: Angkor Wat, the Great Wall or Petronas Twin Towers?
Answer: Petronas Twin Towers

9. How many people climb Mount Fuji's summit to pray each year: 5,000, 50,000 or 500,000?
Answer: 500,000

10. When was Angkor Wat built: in the 11th, 12th or 13th century?
Answer: 12th century

11. The Sarawak Chamber is the world's largest cave chamber. True or false?
Answer: True

12. Name one of the first two people to reach the summit of Mount Everest.
Answer: Edmund Hillary or Tenzing Norgay

13. In which dynasty did the building of the Great Wall begin?
Answer: Qin dynasty

Level 3

14. For how many years did the Dalai Lamas use the Potala Palace as their winter home?
Answer: 311 years

15. Where can the Sarawak Chamber be found?
Answer: In Borneo, Malaysia

16. If Mount Fuji is 3,776m high, how much higher is Everest than Mount Fuji?
Answer: 5,072m

17. If the Petronas Twin Towers' skybridge is 170m high, how much taller are the towers themselves?
Answer: 282m higher

18. How long is the Great Wall of China?
Answer: About 6,300km

ANSWERS: Europe

Level 1

1. Where is Red Square: Paris or Moscow?
Answer: Moscow

2. Does the Channel Tunnel go under or over the English Channel?
Answer: Under

3. The Leaning Tower of Pisa was designed to lean. True or false?
Answer: False (but it began leaning during construction)

4. How many tracks are in the Channel Tunnel: one, two or three?
Answer: Three

Level 2

5. The Eisriesenwelt ice cave is the largest ice cave in the world. True or false?
Answer: True

6. Is the Guggenheim Museum in Paris, Bilbao or Salzburg?
Answer: Bilbao

7. Was the Eiffel Tower built in Paris to celebrate Bastille Day, the end of the Hundred Years' War or the Universal Exhibition?
Answer: The Universal Exhibition

8. Who commissioned the building of St Basil's Cathedral: Ivan the Terrible, Rasputin or Catherine the Great?
Answer: Ivan the Terrible

9. What does 'Eisriesenwelt' mean: tiny ice world, giant cave or giant ice world?
Answer: Giant ice world

10. Which famous Alpine mountain is pyramid-shaped?
Answer: The Matterhorn

11. What features appear on the top of St Basil's Cathedral?
Answer: Onion domes

12. How high is Mont Blanc: 4,808m, 5,808m or 7,808m?
Answer: 4,808m

13. What is a campanile: a bell tower, a dome or a steeple?
Answer: A bell tower

14. How much does the Eiffel Tower's structure weigh: about 5,330, 7,300 or 10,300 tonnes?
Answer: About 7,300 tonnes

Level 3

15. How long is the Channel Tunnel?
Answer: 50km

16. How long did it take to construct the Leaning Tower of Pisa?
Answer: 197 years

17. What forms the bottom of the Eiffel Tower?
Answer: A base held by four pillars

18. What material covers the curved panels in the Guggenheim Museum?
Answer: Titanium

ANSWERS: North America

Level 1

1. The Statue of Liberty is in Washington, D.C. True or false?
Answer: False (it is in New York Harbor)

2. How many falls is Niagara Falls made up of?
Answer: Three

3. The Grand Canyon is in Arizona. True or false?
Answer: True

4. Which is the world's tallest tree: the coast redwood or the Scots pine?
Answer: The coast redwood

5. Does the Golden Gate Bridge cross San Francisco Bay?
Answer: Yes

Level 2

6. Which US president's face is not carved on Mount Rushmore: Lincoln, Kennedy or Theodore Roosevelt?
Answer: Kennedy

7. How many main sections make up the Grand Canyon: three, five or seven?
Answer: Three (the South Rim, the North Rim and the Inner Canyon)

8. How many faces of US presidents were carved into Mount Rushmore: three, four or five?
Answer: Four

9. How high is the Statue of Liberty: 82.5m, 93.5m or 95m?
Answer: 93.5m

10. How old is the oldest giant sequoia: 1,000, 3,200 or 5,500 years old?
Answer: 3,200 years old

11. Do the vertical ribs on the Golden Gate Bridge stand out on a sunny day?
Answer: True

12. What 'S' on the Statue of Liberty's crown represent the world's seven seas and continents?
Answer: The spikes

13. Rearrange COWES TOAST to name where redwoods grow.
Answer: West Coast

Level 3

14. Why do the towers on the Golden Gate Bridge appear taller than they are?
Answer: The top of the towers are smaller than the base of the towers

15. What changes about the plants you can find as you go further down the Grand Canyon?
Answer: They become shorter and sparser

16. How much wider is Horseshoe Falls than American Falls?
Answer: 469m wider

17. How long did it take to carve the monument at Mount Rushmore?
Answer: 14 years

18. How long is the Golden Gate Bridge?
Answer: 2,737m

ANSWERS: South America

Level 1

1. Did the Incas build Machu Picchu in the Andes?
Answer: Yes

2. Angel Falls is the highest waterfall in the world. True or false?
Answer: True

3. The Amazon is the world's largest river, but not the longest. True or false?
Answer: True

4. Which city is famous for its beaches: Lima or Rio de Janeiro?
Answer: Rio de Janeiro

5. The llama is a kind of wild cat. True or false?
Answer: False (it is a camelid)

Level 2

6. Can a statue of Jesus be found at the top or base of Sugar Loaf Mountain in Brazil?
Answer: At the top of the mountain

7. What percentage of the earth's oxygen does the Amazon rainforest produce: two per cent, ten per cent or 20 per cent?
Answer: 20 per cent

8. Angel Falls is named after which American pilot?
Answer: James Crawford Angel

9. Machu Picchu was built in which century: the 13th, 14th or 15th?
Answer: 15th century

10. Is Lake Titicaca a freshwater lake or saltwater lake?
Answer: A freshwater lake

11. How many structures made up Machu Picchu: about ten, 100 or 200?
Answer: About 200

12. What 'A' in Argentina has fine fleece?
Answer: The alpaca

13. In the Quechua language, does Machu Picchu mean high mountain, old mountain or young mountain?
Answer: Old mountain

14. Can the source for the Amazon river be found in the Andes, Himalayas or Rocky mountains?
Answer: The Andes

Level 3

15. How long is the Amazon river?
Answer: 6,387km

16. Where can most of the remaining rainforests be found?
Answer: In the Amazon basin

17. What are the artificial islands in Lake Titicaca made from?
Answer: Reeds (totora reeds)

18. What material did the Incas use to build their structures?
Answer: Ashlar blocks

ANSWERS: Australia and Oceania

Level 1

1. Is Sydney Australia's largest city or one of its smaller cities?
Answer: Australia's largest city

2. Easter Island (or Rapa Nui) is home to statues carved by Polynesian settlers. True or false?
Answer: True

3. Does the kangaroo live in Australia?
Answer: Yes

4. Road trains are really trucks that pull trailers. True or false?
Answer: True

Level 2

5. Uluru in Australia is also called Ayers Rock. True or false?
Answer: True

6. How many statues are there on Easter Island (or Rapa Nui): 6, 60 or 600?
Answer: 600

7. Uluru is sacred to: British convicts, Australian Aborigines or marsupials?
Answer: Australian Aborigines

8. What is fitted to the front of an Australian road train: a roo bar, bull bar or marsupial bar?
Answer: A roo bar

9. What can be found on New Zealand's North Island: volcanoes, geysers, hot springs or all of the above?
Answer: All of the above

10. How long was the longest road train: 13 trailers, 33 trailers or 113 trailers?
Answer: 113 trailers

11. What 'F' are the Naracoorte Caves in Australia known for?
Answer: Fossils

12. Was Sydney founded as a new colony for sheep farmers, for sugar plantations or as a convict settlement?
Answer: As a convict settlement

Level 3

13. What is the name for the Easter Island (or Rapa Nui) statues?
Answer: Moai

14. What 'M' is a type of animal group, with the largest one living in Australia?
Answer: Marsupial

15. In what year did palaeontologists first visit Victoria Fossil Cave, one of the Naracoorte Caves in Australia?
Answer: 1969

16. Where was the Sydney Opera House built?
Answer: On Bennelong Point in Sydney Harbour

17. What is the Maori name for New Zealand?
Answer: Aotearoa

18. How far is Easter Island from South America?
Answer: About 4,000km

ANSWERS: Antarctica

Level 1

1. Penguins live in Antarctica. True or false?
Answer: True

2. How do people travel on the ice in Antarctica: by skidoo, car or bus?
Answer: By skidoo

3. There are permanent research stations in Antarctica. True or false?
Answer: True

4. What are groups of elephant seals called: harems or groupies?
Answer: Harems

5. A penguin is a bird. True or false?
Answer: True

Level 2

6. How many scientists live and work in Anatarctica during the summer: 400, 4,000, or 40,000?
Answer: 4,000

7. What does the Global Positioning System link to: the internet, mobile phones or satellites?
Answer: Satellites

8. Is the Lambert Glacier Antarctica's largest, smallest or youngest glacier?
Answer: Its largest glacier

9. How deep can an elephant seal dive: down to 15m, 150m or 1,500m?
Answer: Down to 1,500m

10. Why do whales migrate north: to breed, to feed or to follow ships?
Answer: To breed

11. When do whales migrate south: in the spring, summer, autumn or winter?
Answer: In summer

12. What is a Dornier 228: a plane, skidoo or bulldozer?
Answer: A plane

13. Ranulph Fiennes and Mike Stroud pulled their own sledges as they crossed Antarctica in 1993. True or false?
Answer: True

Level 3

14. What are rookeries?
Answer: Large penguin colonies

15. What is the name of earth's most southern point?
Answer: The South Pole

16. Which vehicle has tracks like a bulldozer?
Answer: The Hagglund

17. What might a beachmaster have in his harem?
Answer: Up to 50 cows

18. Why are special tents used by scientists?
Answer: To resist the strong, icy winds

ANSWERS: Exploring space

Level 1

1. The first living creature in space was a mouse. True or false?
Answer: False

2. Who was the first person on the Moon: Neil Armstrong, Nelly Armstrong or Norman Armstrong?
Answer: Neil Armstrong

3. ENVISION OUT can be rearranged to give the name of what group of republics?
Answer: The Soviet Union

4. What 'S' is an object that orbits Earth?
Answer: Satellite

Level 2

5. What 'L' was the name of the first living creature in space?
Answer: Laika

6. What 'S' was the first artificial satellite?
Answer: Sputnik

7. AN AIR RIG GUY can be rearranged to give the name of what astronaut, the first person to go into space?
Answer: Yuri Gagarin

8. In which year did people first walk on the Moon: 1959, 1969 or 1979?
Answer: 1969

9. In which year did a person first go into space: 1941, 1951 or 1961?
Answer: 1961

10. Who said 'That's one small step for man, one giant leap for mankind'?
Answer: Neil Armstrong

11. VAN OR RULER can be rearranged to give the name of what vehicle used on the surface of the moon?
Answer: Lunar rover

12. For how long did the first person to go into space stay there: 89 minutes, 89 hours or 89 days?
Answer: 89 minutes

Level 3

13. Which was the last *Apollo* mission to land people on the Moon?
Answer: Apollo 17

14. In what year did it reach the Moon?
Answer: 1972

15. What were Soviet astronauts called?
Answer: Cosmonauts

16. What 'V' was the first manned spacecraft?
Answer: Vostock 1

17. What was launched on 12 April 1981?
Answer: The first space shuttle

18. Where is the Baikonur Cosmodrome: in Kazakhstan, Ukraine or the Russian Federation?
Answer: Kazakhstan

ANSWERS: Solar System

Level 1

1. Which planet do people live on?
Answer: Earth

2. How many main planets are in the Solar System: five, eight or 15?
Answer: Eight

3. MY CURER can be rearranged to give the name of what planet?
Answer: Mercury

Level 2

4. On the part of a planet facing away from the Sun, is it night or day?
Answer: Night

5. How many planets in our Solar System have names beginning with the letter 'M'?
Answer: Two

6. Which planet is the nearest to the Sun?
Answer: Mercury

7. A GANG SITS can be rearranged to give the name of what group of large planets?
Answer: Gas giants

8. Which are the four rocky planets?
Answer: Mercury, Venus, Earth and Mars

9. The Sun is a star. True or false?
Answer: True

10. Are any planets in the Solar System bigger than the Sun?
Answer: No

11. Did the planets form at around the same time as the Sun or long before?
Answer: Around the same time

12. Which 'S' is a planet made mostly of hydrogen and helium?
Answer: Saturn

13. How long does the Earth take to circle the Sun: a day, a month or a year?
Answer: A year

14. What 'O' is the path planets take around the Sun?
Answer: Orbit

15. Which takes longer to circle the Sun: Earth or Pluto?
Answer: Pluto

16. How many planets in the Solar System have oceans of water?
Answer: One

Level 3

17. What 'N' is a swirling cloud of particles from which planets form?
Answer: Nebula

18. Which is farther from the Sun: Uranus or Saturn?
Answer: Uranus

19. Which is larger: Earth or Mars?
Answer: Earth

ANSWERS: Volcanoes and earthquakes

ANSWERS: Rocks and minerals

Level 1

1. Is the surface of the Earth made of solid or liquid rock?
   Answer: Solid rock
2. What is another name for the Earth's surface: the skin, crust or coat?
   Answer: The crust
3. RUIN POET can be rearranged to give what word for a volcano exploding?
   Answer: Eruption
4. A seismologist is a kind of earthquake. True or false?
   Answer: False (a seismologist is a scientist who studies earthquakes)

Level 2

5. What 'R' is the scale used to measure the strength of earthquakes?
   Answer: Richter
6. Which are thicker: continental plates or oceanic plates?
   Answer: Continental plates
7. Are most earthquakes strong enough to destroy buildings?
   Answer: No
8. How thick is the earth's mantle: 290km or 2,900km?
   Answer: 2,900km
9. Do ridges form where plates move together or where they move apart?
   Answer: Where they move apart
10. Earthquakes are common where plates slide past one another. True or false?
    Answer: True
11. Japan is situated where two plates meet. True or false?
    Answer: True
12. What 'L' is the molten rock released by a volcanic eruption?
    Answer: Lava
13. What 'F' is the force produced by plates sliding past each other?
    Answer: Friction
14. CUBOID NUTS can be rearranged to give the name of which kind of plate movement?
    Answer: Subduction
15. Volcanoes may occur where two plates are moving apart. True or false?
    Answer: True

Level 3

16. What is the most common substance in the Earth's core?
    Answer: Iron
17. Which makes up a greater proportion of the Earth: the crust or mantle?
    Answer: The mantle
18. On which plate do volcanoes occur when an oceanic plate and a continental plate meet?
    Answer: On the continental plate

Level 1

1. Emeralds are purple. True or false?
   Answer: False
2. What colour are rubies?
   Answer: Red
3. Gold is a metal. True or false?
   Answer: True
4. How many sides does a hexagon have: one, three or six?
   Answer: Six

Level 2

5. TEARING can be rearranged to give the name of what igneous rock, often used for building?
   Answer: Granite
6. Crystals form underground. True or false?
   Answer: True
7. Do sedimentary rocks form on the bottoms of seas, lakes and rivers or deep within the earth?
   Answer: On the bottoms of seas, lakes and rivers
8. What word is used for rocks which form under great pressure or heat: metamorphic, mathematic or metaphysical?
   Answer: Metamorphic
9. Is basalt an igneous or a sedimentary rock?
   Answer: Igneous
10. Gems are cut and polished to make gemstones. True or false?
    Answer: False (gemstones are cut and polished to make gems)
11. What 'C' is the substance from which diamond is formed?
    Answer: Carbon
12. Which are the most valuable: diamonds, emeralds or garnets?
    Answer: Diamonds
13. HIS PAPER can be rearranged to give the name of what valuable gemstone?
    Answer: Sapphire
14. A START can be rearranged to give what word for layers of rock?
    Answer: Strata

Level 3

15. In which country is the Giant's Causeway?
    Answer: Northern Ireland
16. What 'M' is molten rock, which cools to form igneous rocks?
    Answer: Magma
17. What is the name for a stone which has had its edges worn smooth by the action of water?
    Answer: A pebble
18. What 'E' cannot be broken down into any simpler substance?
    Answer: An element

ANSWERS: Weather

Level 1

1. Does weather happen in the atmosphere or under the sea?
Answer: In the atmosphere

2. Are clouds made of cotton wool or water vapour?
Answer: Water vapour

3. What 'O' is the gas we must breathe in order to live?
Answer: Oxygen

4. What 'L' is the word for an electrical charge released from a storm cloud?
Answer: Lightning

5. A weather balloon is a type of cloud. True or false?
Answer: False

Level 2

6. Where does the majority of the water vapour in clouds originally come from?
Answer: The sea

7. Does a weather vane measure wind speed or wind direction?
Answer: Wind direction

8. Which is usually associated with fine weather: high pressure or low pressure?
Answer: High pressure

9. What 'R' is sometimes formed as sunlight passes through raindrops?
Answer: A rainbow

10. Do rainbows appear when it rains or when there is no rain?
Answer: When it rains

11. Do raindrops become bigger or smaller as they fall through a cloud?
Answer: Bigger

12. What 'H' is a word for frozen raindrops?
Answer: Hail

13. Do clouds become cooler or hotter as they rise?
Answer: Cooler

14. REACH RUIN can be rearranged to give the name of what powerful storm?
Answer: Hurricane

15. RING TONE can be rearranged to give the name of what very common gas?
Answer: Nitrogen

Level 3

16. What is a scientist who studies the weather called?
Answer: A meteorologist

17. How many colours are there in a rainbow?
Answer: Seven

18. What 'S' do weather forecasters use to watch storms building up in the atmosphere?
Answer: Satellites

ANSWERS: Bones and muscles

Level 1

1. BELOW can be rearranged to give the name of what joint in the middle of the arm?
Answer: Elbow

2. Are there muscles in the human leg?
Answer: Yes

3. What 'S' is the name for all the bones in the body put together?
Answer: Skeleton

Level 2

4. Do people have joints in their fingers?
Answer: Yes

5. Muscles contain millions of cells called fibres. True or false?
Answer: True

6. What 'B' is a muscle in the arm that helps to raise the forearm?
Answer: The biceps

7. Which bones form a cage that protects the internal organs?
Answer: The ribs

8. What 'C' is the proper name for the gristle in human bodies?
Answer: Cartilage

9. Which bone links the legs to the backbone?
Answer: The pelvis

10. The patella is another name for which bone?
Answer: The kneecap

11. The muscles in the heart work automatically. True or false?
Answer: True

12. When a person raises their forearm does their triceps contract or relax?
Answer: Relax

13. How many bones are there in an adult's skull: two, 12 or 22?
Answer: 22

14. Do people have more muscles or more bones in their bodies?
Answer: More muscles

15. Is the shoulder joint a hinge joint or a ball-and-socket joint?
Answer: A ball-and-socket joint

16. What is the largest bone in the human body?
Answer: The thigh bone (femur)

17. Which is the name of the eight bones that, together, encase the brain?
Answer: The cranium

Level 3

18. The mandible is another name for which part of the body?
Answer: The lower jaw

19. In which part of the body is the smallest bone?
Answer: The ear

20. How many bones are there in the human skeleton?
Answer: 206

ANSWERS: Medicine

Level 1

1. What 'D' is the person people visit when they are feeling ill?
   Answer: Doctor
2. What vehicles take people to hospital: ambulances, fire engines or tractors?
   Answer: Ambulances
3. Are ambulances part of the emergency services?
   Answer: Yes
4. Do nurses work in hospitals or shops?
   Answer: In hospitals

Level 2

5. Broken bones mend themselves. True or false?
   Answer: True
6. What 'S' is used to listen to a person's heartbeat?
   Answer: Stethoscope
7. What does a thermometer measure?
   Answer: Temperature
8. Is intensive care given to people who are very ill or to people who are better, just before they leave hospital?
   Answer: People who are very ill
9. What 'S' is the word for a person who carries out operations?
   Answer: Surgeon
10. What 'T' means to replace a damaged body part with a new, healthy one?
    Answer: Transplant
11. Would you wear a plaster cast if you had flu or if you had a broken leg?
    Answer: If you had a broken leg
12. Rearrange A SCARED IMP to make the name of the people who look after patients on the way to hospital.
    Answer: Paramedics
13. A symptom is a kind of medicine. True or false?
    Answer: False
14. What 'S' is a large machine that looks inside people's bodies?
    Answer: Scanner

Level 3

15. What 'D' means 'to work out what is wrong with a patient'?
    Answer: Diagnose
16. What sort of injury can be treated by traction?
    Answer: A broken bone
17. What is used to transfer nutrients straight into a person's bloodstream?
    Answer: A drip
18. What 'M' is a kind of wave that scanners use to look inside a body?
    Answer: Magnetic

ANSWERS: Trains

Level 1

1. Which came first: steam engines or electric trains?
   Answer: Steam engines
2. Do all trains carry passengers?
   Answer: No
3. Is diesel a type of fuel or a type of food?
   Answer: A type of fuel
4. Who built the train that ran on the first-ever steam railway: Richard Trevithick, Richard Branson or Richard the Lionheart?
   Answer: Richard Trevithick
5. What 'C' was burned in steam engines?
   Answer: Coal

Level 2

6. Was the Wild West in Europe or in the USA?
   Answer: In the USA
7. Is steam created by heating water or by heating petrol?
   Answer: Heating water
8. Which country has bullet trains and super expresses?
   Answer: Japan
9. What 'R' was a famous steam engine built by George Stephenson?
   Answer: The Rocket
10. Which country has TGVs?
    Answer: France
11. Are there any trains that can go faster than 200km/h?
    Answer: Yes (Japanese bullet trains regularly run at over 300km/h)
12. What 'C' on Wild West trains was used for moving cattle off the line?
    Answer: Cowcatchers
13. Were steam trains cleaner or dirtier than modern trains?
    Answer: Dirtier

Level 3

14. In which country was the world's first-ever steam railway?
    Answer: Wales
15. In which century was the first railway to cross North America built?
    Answer: The 19th century
16. What 'F' is the word used for the goods carried by some trains?
    Answer: Freight
17. How long was the world's longest ever train: 5km, 6km or 7km?
    Answer: 6km
18. What 'P' were exploring settlers who travelled into the Wild West by train?
    Answer: Pioneers

ANSWERS: Early flight

Level 1

1. GIRDLE can be rearranged to give the name of what type of unpowered aircraft?
   Answer: Glider
2. The first manned flight was in a hot-air balloon. True or false?
   Answer: True
3. Is a dirigible a steerable airship or an Australian musical instrument?
   Answer: A steerable airship

Level 2

4. What 'H' is a type of aircraft with rotating blades?
   Answer: Helicopter
5. Which body of water was Louis Blériot first to fly across in 1909: the English Channel or Atlantic ocean?
   Answer: The English Channel
6. In which century did Otto Lilienthal make the first controlled glider flights: the 9th or 19th century?
   Answer: The 19th century
7. How many wings does a monoplane have: two or four?
   Answer: Two
8. Which 'G' is a country, home to Otto Lilienthal?
   Answer: Germany
9. Jean-François Pilâtre was the first man to fly. True or false?
   Answer: True
10. Was the first powered aeroplane flight in Europe or the USA?
    Answer: The USA
11. Which great 16th-century Italian artist and thinker designed a glider that was never built?
    Answer: Leonardo da Vinci
12. Which 'M' were brothers who built the first manned aircraft?
    Answer: Montgolfier

Level 3

13. What was the surname of Wilbur and Orville, who designed the first ever heavier-than-air powered aircraft?
    Answer: Wright
14. What was their aircraft called?
    Answer: The Wright Flyer
15. What did the first heavier-than-air powered aircraft use as fuel?
    Answer: Petrol
16. In which century did the first-ever manned aircraft take off: the 16th, 17th or 18th century?
    Answer: The 18th century
17. Who made the first-ever powered flight?
    Answer: Henri Giffard
18. What was his nationality?
    Answer: French

ANSWERS: Sailing

Level 1

1. Sailing boats use the wind to push them along. True or false?
   Answer: True
2. Are boats kept moored in a marina, a merino or a mariner?
   Answer: A marina
3. What kind of jackets do people wear to keep them afloat in the water?
   Answer: Life jackets
4. Do any sailing boats have engines?
   Answer: Yes
5. What suit keeps windsurfers warm?
   Answer: A wetsuit
6. A rudder is used to help a boat steer. True or false?
   Answer: True
7. What 'Y' is a large sailing boat used for pleasure?
   Answer: Yacht

Level 2

8. Which were invented first: square sails or triangular sails?
   Answer: Square sails
9. What 'P' is the left-hand side of a boat and a place where ships dock?
   Answer: Port
10. What is the word for the rear of a boat?
    Answer: The stern
11. BROAD ARTS can be rearranged to give what word for the right-hand side of a boat?
    Answer: Starboard
12. Boats with square sails can only go in the same direction as the wind. True or false?
    Answer: True
13. How many hulls do trimarans have?
    Answer: Three
14. What is a boat with two hulls called?
    Answer: A catamaran
15. What are small, open boats without cabins called?
    Answer: Dinghies
16. What 'W' are people who sail standing up on a board?
    Answer: Windsurfers

Level 3

17. What part of a boat helps keep it from tipping over?
    Answer: The keel
18. Which Mediterranean island was home to the sea-faring Minoans?
    Answer: Crete
19. When did ancient sailing ships use their oars?
    Answer: When they wanted to go forward against the wind

ANSWERS:
Submarines

Level 1

1. Does the word submarine literally mean 'under the sea' or 'above the mountains'?
   Answer: Under the sea
2. Is a torpedo a type of weapon or a running shoe?
   Answer: A type of weapon
3. What 'D' is the word for people who explore underwater?
   Answer: Divers
4. LATIN CAT can be rearranged to give the name of what ocean?
   Answer: Atlantic

Level 2

5. Which country's submarines were known as U-boats?
   Answer: Germany's
6. Are there any submarines that are driven by nuclear power?
   Answer: Yes
7. What is the name for the spinning objects that push submarines through the water?
   Answer: Propellers
8. Can submarines attack boats that are on the surface?
   Answer: Yes
9. Are research submarines called submersibles or submissives?
   Answer: Submersibles
10. What 'D' is a kind of fuel commonly used in submarines?
    Answer: Diesel
11. What is the name for the tanks that fill with seawater when a submarine descends?
    Answer: Ballast tanks
12. A bathyscaphe is a type of radar system. True or false?
    Answer: False
13. What do the letters ROV stand for?
    Answer: Remotely operated vehicle
14. SPICE ROPE can be rearranged to give the name of what device, used by submarine crews to see above the water?
    Answer: Periscope

Level 3

15. Where is the Mariana Trench, the deepest point on Earth?
    Answer: The Pacific ocean
16. What was the name of the bathyscaphe that first carried people to the bottom of the Mariana Trench?
    Answer: Trieste
17. What was the name of the manned submersible that first explored the wreck of the *Titanic*?
    Answer: Alvin
18. Which ocean liner was torpedoed and sunk by a German U-boat on 7 May 1915?
    Answer: RMS Lusitania

ANSWERS:
Household inventions

Level 1

1. Would you put bread in a toaster or a dishwasher?
   Answer: A toaster
2. What 'K' is used for heating water?
   Answer: Kettle
3. Is a Hoover a type of vacuum cleaner or a type of zip?
   Answer: A type of vacuum cleaner

Level 2

4. Which invention is usually credited to John Logie Baird?
   Answer: Television
5. SHARED WISH can be rearranged to give the name of what household appliance?
   Answer: Dishwasher
6. Did the automatic cut-out on an electric kettle appear in 1890, 1930 or 1989?
   Answer: 1930
7. Which was invented first: the electric washing machine or the dishwasher?
   Answer: The electric washing machine
8. Which household object is usually associated with Thomas Edison?
   Answer: The electric light bulb
9. People only started to use zips in the the 1940s. True or false?
   Answer: False
10. Which handy implement was invented by Laszlo Biro?
    Answer: The ball-point pen
11. The aero-foam extinguisher is used on what kind of fires?
    Answer: Gas and oil
12. SCOOPS RED ROOF can be rearranged to give the name of what kitchen appliance?
    Answer: Food processor
13. In which decade of the 20th century did microwave ovens first go on sale?
    Answer: The 1960s

Level 3

14. In what year was the first television picture transmitted?
    Answer: 1925
15. James Murray Spangler invented the first portable what?
    Answer: Vacuum cleaner
16. What did Alexandre Godefoy invent?
    Answer: The hairdryer
17. Which kitchen appliance was developed from an earlier invention called the magnetron?
    Answer: The microwave oven
18. Who invented the sewing machine?
    Answer: Elias Howe

ANSWERS:
Robots

Level 1
1. Are there robots that work in factories?
   Answer: Yes
2. Do robots ever get tired?
   Answer: No
3. Are there any robots that can work underwater?
   Answer: Yes
4. ODD SIR can be rearranged to give what name for robots such as R2-D2?
   Answer: Droids
5. Robots can only do one thing at a time. True or false?
   Answer: False

Level 2
6. Are there any robots that can play the piano?
   Answer: Yes
7. Which series of films starred the robot C-3PO?
   Answer: Star Wars
8. What 'C' is programmed with the information that is needed to make robots operate?
   Answer: Computer
9. LEWDING can be rearranged to give the name of what task performed by robots?
   Answer: Welding
10. Which have travelled farthest from earth: robots or humans?
    Answer: Robots
11. Solar panels are used to capture energy from which source?
    Answer: The sun
12. HOW TO CORD can be rearranged to give the name of what popular TV programme?
    Answer: Doctor Who
13. Which planet is currently being explored by robots?
    Answer: Mars
14. What 'M' is the word for doing more than one job at a time?
    Answer: Multitasking
15. Can robots be programmed to detonate bombs?
    Answer: Yes

Level 3
16. The word robot comes from which language?
    Answer: Czech
17. Which country developed the WABOT-2 robot?
    Answer: Japan
18. In what year was the animated film *Robots* released?
    Answer: 2005

ANSWERS:
Computers and gaming

Level 1
1. What 'I' is the network that links computers all over the world?
   Answer: The internet
2. Does PC stand for Perfect Computer or Personal Computer?
   Answer: Personal Computer
3. What is a computer that is small enough to fit in the hand called: a handbag, a handheld or a handshake?
   Answer: A handheld
4. What 'M' is a small furry animal, and a thing that attaches to a computer?
   Answer: A mouse
5. What is stored in MP3 files?
   Answer: Music

Level 2
6. Where were computer games played before people had home computers?
   Answer: In video arcades
7. Can people play computer games while they are on the move?
   Answer: Yes
8. What kind of computer is the word Mac short for?
   Answer: Macintosh
9. Do most handheld gaming machines take cartridges or discs?
   Answer: Cartridges
10. Is the information in a computer held in the hard drive, printer or mouse?
    Answer: In the hard drive
11. What 'B' is the computer equipment used to put information onto a CD?
    Answer: Burner
12. Is a computer keyboard a peripheral or a profiterole?
    Answer: A peripheral
13. What 'H' do you wear when playing a virtual-reality game?
    Answer: A headset
14. What 'V' is put in front of the word 'reality' to describe lifelike situations produced by computers?
    Answer: Virtual
15. TOP PAL can be rearranged to give what name for a portable computer?
    Answer: Laptop

Level 3
16. Which would you use to store data: a CD-RAM, a CD-REM or a CD-ROM?
    Answer: A CD-ROM
17. What connects a home computer to the internet?
    Answer: A telephone line
18. What kind of files would you put on to an iPod?
    Answer: MP3 files

ANSWERS: Telephones

Level 1

1. What 'T' is a written message sent by a mobile phone?
   Answer: Text
2. Were the first mobile phones bigger or smaller than mobile phones today?
   Answer: Bigger
3. Do most modern telephones have rotating dials or buttons?
   Answer: Buttons
4. Do mobile phones send messages using microwaves, water waves or Mexican waves?
   Answer: Microwaves
5. Are there mobile phones that can connect to the internet?
   Answer: Yes

Level 2

6. Did the world's first telephone have touch-tone dialling?
   Answer: No
7. In what century was the telephone invented: 9th, 19th or 21st?
   Answer: 19th
8. SAME CAR can be rearranged to spell what feature of some mobile phones?
   Answer: Cameras
9. HOME CUT PIE can be rearranged to spell what part of a telephone, that you speak into?
   Answer: Mouthpiece
10. What 'E' is the place where telephone calls are connected?
    Answer: Exchange
11. What name is given to people who used to connect the calls?
    Answer: Operators
12. How many names were in the first ever-telephone directory: 50, 500 or 5,000?
    Answer: 50
13. What 'T' was a kind of coded message used before telephones were invented?
    Answer: Telegram

Level 3

14. How did people generate the electricity to power early phones?
    Answer: By winding a handle on the side of the phone
15. Who invented the telephone?
    Answer: Alexander Graham Bell
16. In which country was Alexander Graham Bell born?
    Answer: Scotland
17. Who invented the carbon-granule microphone?
    Answer: Thomas Edison
18. Which was invented first: the fax or the telephone?
    Answer: The fax
19. In what year did rotating dials appear: 1886, 1896 or 1906?
    Answer: 1896

ANSWERS: Discoveries

Level 1

1. What type of food is said to have fallen on Isaac Newton's head, giving him the idea for his most famous theory?
   Answer: An apple
2. What 'W' turns around and around, allowing vehicles to move?
   Answer: A wheel
3. IT GRAVY can be rearranged to give the name of what force that pulls objects towards the ground?
   Answer: Gravity

Level 2

4. Which mathematician living in ancient Greece shouted 'Eureka' when he was in his bath?
   Answer: Archimedes
5. What nationality was Isaac Newton?
   Answer: English
6. In which century did the first cars with petrol engines appear?
   Answer: In the 19th century
7. Michael Faraday was an American scientist. True or false?
   Answer: False (he was English)
8. What 'S' was used to drive the earliest cars?
   Answer: Steam
9. Karl Benz was a pioneer of the motor car. True or false?
   Answer: True
10. SPICY HITS can be rearranged to give the name of what type of scientist?
    Answer: Physicist
11. Who came up with the theory of relativity?
    Answer: Albert Einstein
12. Was the wheel invented more than 3,000 years ago?
    Answer: Yes
13. What 'M' did Michael Faraday help us to understand better?
    Answer: Magnetism
14. What nationality was Nicolas Cugnot, who built the first car?
    Answer: French
15. By what three letters is deoxyribonucleic acid usually known?
    Answer: DNA

Level 3

16. In which modern country are the ruins of the city of Uruk?
    Answer: Iraq
17. Which two scientists are usually credited with discovering the double helix of deoxyribonucleic acid?
    Answer: Francis Crick and James Watson
18. In the formula $E = mc^2$, what does 'E' stand for?
    Answer: Energy

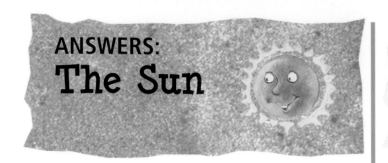

ANSWERS:
The Sun

ANSWERS:
The Moon

Level 1
1. The Sun has a core. True or false?
   Answer: True
2. While it is daytime in one part of the Earth can it be night-time in another part of the Earth?
   Answer: Yes
3. What 'S' is the name we give to the different times of year?
   Answer: The seasons
4. Rearrange RINSE US to spell the time of day when the Earth turns towards the Sun, and the Sun first appears above the horizon.
   Answer: Sunrise

Level 2
5. Energy released from the Sun affects electronic systems, such as telephone networks, on Earth. True or False?
   Answer: True
6. At sunset is the Earth turning towards or away from the Sun?
   Answer: Away from the Sun
7. Bright patches that appear in the Sun's corona are called solar prominences. True or false?
   Answer: False (they are called solar flares)
8. How long does a sunspot cycle usually last?
   Answer: ll years
9. What comes between the Earth and the Sun in a solar eclipse: the Moon, Mars or Venus?
   Answer: The Moon
10. What 'R' does the Earth do as it orbits around the Sun?
    Answer: The Earth rotates
11. What are magnetic storms on the Sun called: coronas, sunspots or eclipses?
    Answer: Sunspots
12. What 'H' does the Sun seem to sink below at sunset?
    Answer: The horizon
13. What is visible during a solar eclipse: sunspots, the Sun's corona or none of the above?
    Answer: The Sun's corona
14. Do the solstices occur when the Earth is most or least tilted on its axis?
    Answer: When it is most tilted

Level 3
15. How hot is the hottest part of the Sun?
    Answer: 15,000,000°C (at the core)
16. What 'T' is the dividing line between daytime and night-time?
    Answer: The terminator
17. How large can sunspots be?
    Answer: 50,000km in diameter
18. Name three things that are released from a build-up of energy in the Sun's corona.
    Answer: Radio waves, ultraviolet light and X-rays

Level 1
1. Does the Sun or the Earth light the moon?
   Answer: The Sun
2. The Moon doesn't have any gravity. True or false?
   Answer: False (it has one-sixth of the gravity produced by Earth)
3. Does the Moon orbit around the Earth or the Sun?
   Answer: The Earth
4. When the sea falls back from the shore it is low tide. True or false?
   Answer: True

Level 2
5. The new moon is sunny on the side we cannot see. True or false?
   Answer: True
6. There is a face of the Moon we never see. True or false?
   Answer: True
7. What 'G' causes tides?
   Answer: The Moon's gravity
8. Which type of tide occurs when the Moon is overhead: high tide or low tide?
   Answer: High tide
9. How long does the Moon take to orbit Earth: 24 hours, 27.3 days or 39.5 days?
   Answer: 27.3 days
10. Who was the first astronaut to set foot on the Moon: Al Shepard, Buzz Aldrin or Neil Armstrong?
    Answer: Neil Armstrong
11. Does the Earth's or the Sun's shadow pass over the Moon during a lunar eclipse?
    Answer: The Earth's shadow
12. Which 'W' means that the Moon is getting thinner?
    Answer: Waning
13. Are high tides higher or lower during spring tides?
    Answer: Higher
14. Do neap tides occur when the Earth, Moon and Sun are in line?
    Answer: No, they occur when the Earth, Moon and Sun shift apart

Level 3
15. What is the diameter of the Moon?
    Answer: 3,476km
16. How long does the Moon take to pass through all its phases?
    Answer: 29.3 days
17. Where are the Sun and Moon when there is a full moon?
    Answer: Opposite sides of Earth
18. When does a lunar eclipse occur?
    Answer: When the full moon passes exactly behind the Earth
19. What was the date of the first American Moon landing?
    Answer: 21 July, 1969

ANSWERS: Constellations

Level 1

1. You must always use binoculars or a telescope to see stars. True or false?
Answer: False (some stars can be seen with only your eyes)

2. The constellation Scorpius is also known as Scorpio. True or false?
Answer: True

3. How many halves can the celestial sky be split into: two or three?
Answer: Two

4. Can the Southern Cross be seen in the northern hemisphere?
Answer: No

5. Centaurus is a constellation named after a creature from Greek mythology. True or false?
Answer: True

Level 2

6. Pegasus is named after which animal from Greek mythology: a winged horse, bull or goat?
Answer: A winged horse

7. Columba is named after which bird sent from the Ark by Noah to look for land: a dove, pigeon or eagle?
Answer: A dove

8. Which constellation did sailors use to navigate in the southern hemisphere?
Answer: The Southern Cross

9. Rearrange BRUIN COLAS to name an instrument used for stargazing.
Answer: Binoculars

10. Which star is the brightest: Sirius, Orion or Cygnus?
Answer: Sirius, a star in the constellation of Canis Major

11. Which 'O' is the constellation with the largest number of bright stars?
Answer: Orion

12. Rearrange BEE GLUE SET to spell the name of the bright red star that marks Orion's shoulder.
Answer: Betelgeuse

13. Which 'C' is a southern constellation that can be seen in the northern hemisphere in February?
Answer: Columba

Level 3

14. What object does the constellation Libra depict?
Answer: A set of scales

15. What is the name of the 13th brightest star in the sky?
Answer: Antares, in the constellation of Scorpius

16. When in history do we know that the Southern Cross could be seen from the Middle East?
Answer: In Biblical times

17. Name the bright star that marks the tail of Cygnus.
Answer: Deneb

ANSWERS: Outer space

Level 1

1. Which can you find in outer space: a green hole, a black hole or an orange hole?
Answer: A black hole

2. Who was a famous astronomer: Rubble, Bubble or Hubble?
Answer: Hubble

3. The galaxy that contains Earth is called the Creamy Way. True or false?
Answer: False (it is called the Milky Way)

4. Does a star begin life in a nest or in a nebula?
Answer: In a nebula

Level 2

5. A galaxy is a large group of black holes. True or false?
Answer: False (it is a huge group of stars)

6. Stars usually last for billions of years. True or false?
Answer: True

7. Which is an American space agency: LASA, MASA or NASA?
Answer: NASA

8. When a nebula shrinks and condenses, does it heat up or cool down?
Answer: It heats up

9. Does the Milky Way appear to be pale, colourful or dark in the night sky?
Answer: Pale

10. Rearrange RAVEN SOUP to name a type of space explosion.
Answer: Supernova

11. How many galaxies are in the Local Group: about three, about 30 or about 300?
Answer: About 30

12. A nebula is a large star. True or false?
Answer: False (it is a cloud of dust and gas)

13. Is the Milky Way a large galaxy or a small galaxy?
Answer: A large galaxy

14. How many known types of galaxy are there: four, five or seven?
Answer: Four

15. Which forms first: a red giant or a white dwarf?
Answer: A red giant

Level 3

16. In which part of the Milky Way is Earth's solar system?
Answer: One of its arms

17. What do some scientists believe lies at the centre of our galaxy?
Answer: A giant black hole

18. What is the main gas in the Eagle Nebula?
Answer: Hydrogen

ANSWERS: Gold

Level 1

1. What 'Y' colour is gold?
   Answer: Yellow
2. Where in the USA was there a famous gold rush that began in 1848: California or Ohio?
   Answer: California
3. Gold is a hard metal. True or false?
   Answer: False (it is soft)
4. What is gold dust: chunks of gold or tiny particles of gold?
   Answer: Tiny particles of gold

Level 2

5. Rearrange GET GUNS to name the gold pieces found by mining.
   Answer: Nuggets
6. Were there gold rushes in the 19th century in South Africa, Russia or Japan?
   Answer: South Africa
7. Which 'O' is the word for rock that contains metals such as gold?
   Answer: Ore
8. Rearrange ANN PING to name a way of searching for gold in rivers using a wide pan.
   Answer: Panning
9. What 'G' do we call a person who can make jewellery from gold?
   Answer: A goldsmith
10. What 'I' is the word for the bars of gold that countries keep as part of their money reserves?
    Answer: Ingots
11. Exposing gold to air can make it dull. True or false?
    Answer: False
12. What 'P' is the name for someone who searches for gold?
    Answer: Prospector
13. Gold can be drawn out to make thin wire. True or false?
    Answer: True

Level 3

14. Which country is the world's largest gold producer?
    Answer: South Africa
15. What were used to wash gold pieces from river beds?
    Answer: Shallow metal pans
16. Where is the largest gold mine?
    Answer: In West Papua, Indonesia
17. For how long has gold been used as money?
    Answer: 4,000 years
18. What 'E' is a substance that cannot be broken down, such as gold?
    Answer: An element

ANSWERS: Caves

Level 1

1. Worms sometimes live in caves. True or false?
   Answer: True
2. Do bats or eagles roost in cave roofs?
   Answer: Bats
3. Do bacteria and insects feed on fungi or potatoes growing in caves?
   Answer: Fungi
4. Plants such as ferns and mosses cannot grow in a cave entrance. True or false?
   Answer: False

Level 2

5. Rearrange NOODLE WRAPS to name a big cat that shelters in caves in winter.
   Answer: Snow leopard
6. What is volcanic lava when it is red hot, soft and runny: molten, malted or moulded?
   Answer: Molten
7. Name one of two 'S' birds that nest on ledges in the ceiling of a cave's entrance.
   Answer: Swallows or swiftlets
8. Rearrange LEAST STIGMA to name the rock formations that grow up from a cave floor.
   Answer: Stalagmites
9. Fungi growing in caves need little light, water or nutrients. True or false?
   Answer: False (fungi need little light but they do need moisture and nutrients)
10. Do cockroaches or swallows feed on bat droppings in caves?
    Answer: Cockroaches
11. Which is the name of a zone of a cave system: the sunrise zone, twilight zone or midnight zone?
    Answer: Twilight zone
12. Which rock formations hang like icicles from cave roofs: stalagmites or stalactites?
    Answer: Stalactites
13. Name two 'S' types of creepy-crawly that can live in caves.
    Answer: Spiders and scorpions

Level 3

14. Which 'C' is a mineral that is formed when limestone is dissolved?
    Answer: Calcite
15. Temperatures remain constant in which cave zone?
    Answer: The dark zone
16. Underground rivers carve out what features?
    Answer: Tunnels and caves
17. What happened to the soft lava that once filled a lava tube?
    Answer: It drained or flowed away
18. Rearrange BLAME EMPIRE to form another word meaning 'watertight'
    Answer: Impermeable

ANSWERS:
Climate

Level 1

1. During a drought is there less or more rainfall than usual?
Answer: Less rainfall

2. What are clouds made of: water vapour or icy water?
Answer: Water vapour

3. Cirrus is the name for a type of cloud. True or false?
Answer: True

Level 2

4. Which 'S' is the largest desert in the world?
Answer: The Sahara desert

5. Which is a greenhouse gas: oxygen or carbon dioxide?
Answer: Carbon dioxide

6. In how many years do meteorologists think that all the glaciers could melt away: ten, 20 or 30?
Answer: 30 years

7. Is an arid climate hot and wet, hot and dry, or cold and icy?
Answer: Hot and dry

8. Where did scientists find a hole in the ozone layer: over Antarctica, the Arctic or both?
Answer: Both

9. How much rainfall do deserts receive in a year: less than 25cm, less than 50cm or more than 1m?
Answer: Less than 25cm

10. Which of these two cloud types brings rain: cirrus or cumulonimbus?
Answer: Cumulonimbus

11. Rearrange ACE GIRL to name a source of water entering rivers.
Answer: Glacier

12. What 'L's have been drying up in recent years?
Answer: Lakes

13. Are cumulus clouds wispy or puffy clouds?
Answer: Puffy clouds

14. How much of the land on Earth is desert: one-third, one-quarter or one-fifth?
Answer: One-third

Level 3

15. During a drought, why do crops die?
Answer: Because water supplies dry up

16. The ozone layer shields the Earth from what kind of harmful rays?
Answer: Ultraviolet rays

17. What never thaws in the tundra?
Answer: The soil

18. When did the recent drought in the Sahel, northern Africa, begin?
Answer: 1968

19. How high up in the atmosphere is the ozone layer?
Answer: 22km

ANSWERS:
Storms

Level 1

1. Lightning is a spark of electricity in a cloud. True or false?
Answer: True

2. Is a blizzard a snowstorm or a duststorm with strong winds?
Answer: A snowstorm with strong winds

3. Where do sandstorms happen: in deserts or rainforests?
Answer: In deserts

4. What time of year do thunderstorms usually happen: summer or winter?
Answer: Summer

Level 2

5. If a wave tips a lifeboat over, does it always sink?
Answer: No (modern lifeboats can flip upright)

6. Rearrange FIND LOGO into a word that describes what happens when seawater spills over on to dry land.
Answer: Flooding

7. How many people are killed by lightning in the USA every year: about 10, 100 or 1,000?
Answer: About 100

8. How many thunderstorms take place on Earth at any time: about 20, 200 or 2,000?
Answer: About 2,000

9. Electricity is made in what type of cloud: nimbostratus, cumulonimbus or cumulus?
Answer: Cumulonimbus

10. Lightning always takes the form of a long bright streak that follows a zigzag path. True or false?
Answer: False (lightning can be ball-shaped)

11. What 'M' is the word for a weather expert?
Answer: Meteorologist

12. What happens to a tree struck by lightning: does it get soggy, glow in the dark, or is it blown apart?
Answer: It is blown apart

13. What type of 'G' system can be found on lifeboats?
Answer: Global Positioning System

Level 3

14. A huge North Sea storm surge in 1953 hit which countries?
Answer: The UK and the Netherlands

15. What is thunder?
Answer: The vibrations made by heated air

16. What is the effect of warm air from the ground rising quickly into the cold atmosphere?
Answer: It can cause wind, rain and thunderstorms

17. What is a lightning rod?
Answer: A metal rod that directs lightning to the ground

18. How high can wind blow sand during a sandstorm?
Answer: 1,500m high

ANSWERS: Hurricanes and tornadoes

Level 1

1. Are planes ever flown into the centre of a hurricane?
Answer: Yes (to take measurements)

2. There is torrential rain during a hurricane. True or false?
Answer: True

3. Do hurricanes usually happen during the warmer or colder months?
Answer: The warmer months

4. Are hurricanes strong enough to lift up boats and trucks?
Answer: Yes

5. What is the term for studying storms up close: storm chasing, storm checking or storm charting?
Answer: Storm chasing

Level 2

6. Tornadoes are not much more than 10m in diameter. True or false?
Answer: False (they can be up to 1.5km wide)

7. What is the name of the truck used for studying storms up close?
Answer: A Doppler on wheels

8. Do hurricanes form over land or ocean?
Answer: Ocean (but they move to land)

9. Where is Tornado Alley: in China, India or the USA?
Answer: The USA

10. What 'D' is a kind of radar used to investigate storms?
Answer: Doppler

11. How many tornadoes can the USA have in a year: ten, 100 or more than 1,000?
Answer: More than 1,000

12. What is the minimum water temperature needed for a hurricane to form: 22°C, 27°C or 30°C?
Answer: 27°C

13. What 'R' equipment can be found on a weather-tracking plane?
Answer: Radar

14. Do hurricanes move faster or slower as they near land?
Answer: Faster

Level 3

15. What two things do weather-tracking aircraft measure about a hurricane?
Answer: Wind speed and pressure

16. Inside what type of cloud do tornadoes form?
Answer: Cumulonimbus (thunderclouds)

17. What are hurricane surges?
Answer: Huge waves that flood coasts

ANSWERS: Tsunamis

Level 1

1. A tsunami can travel thousands of kilometres. True or false?
Answer: True

2. A tsunami is only about 1m high when travelling across the ocean. True or false?
Answer: True

3. Can ships pass over tsunamis before they reach the coast?
Answer: Yes (the waves are small until they reach the coast)

4. A tsunami is one massive wave. True or false?
Answer: False (a tsunami is a train, or series, of waves)

5. Does a tsunami start on land or at sea?
Answer: At sea

Level 2

6. Rearrange HE ATE QUARK to name an undersea event that can cause a tsunami.
Answer: Earthquake

7. What 'A' is a rock hurtling in space, which may crash into the sea and set off a tsunami?
Answer: Asteroid

8. Tsunamis can be formed by rock slides. True or false?
Answer: True

9. What is the average height above sea level of a tsunami wave as it hits a coast: 3m, 45m or 500m?
Answer: 3m

10. There are usually two to four hours between two tsunami waves in a train. True or false?
Answer: False (it's usually 15–60 minutes between two waves)

11. How fast can a train of waves travel: 70km/h, 170km/h or 700km/h?
Answer: 700km/h

12. Do waves from tsunamis look curved or squarish when seen from the side?
Answer: Squarish (hurricane waves are curved)

13. Are mega-tsunami waves less than 4m, 14m or more than 40m high?
Answer: More than 40m

Level 3

14. Name the parts of the Earth's crust that move, causing an earthquake.
Answer: Tectonic plates

15. Why do tsunamis slow down as they approach a shore?
Answer: The seabed rising towards a coast slows it down

16. How many people were killed in the 2004 Indian ocean tsunami?
Answer: About 230,000

17. Which volcano in Indonesia erupted in 1883, causing massive waves that killed 36,000 people?
Answer: Krakatoa

18. What does the word 'wavelength' mean?
Answer: The distance between one wave and the next

ANSWERS:
The senses

Level 1

1. Which 'T' is the part of the mouth you use to taste food?
   Answer: The tongue
2. To smell something, you have to breathe the smell in through your nose. True or false?
   Answer: True
3. Do sensors in the ear send information about sound to the other ear or to the brain?
   Answer: The brain
4. If a person needs glasses, are the objects he sees without them focused or blurry?
   Answer: Blurry

Level 2

5. Rearrange FINEST GRIP to name a part of the body that is sensitive to touch.
   Answer: Fingertips
6. Does light enter the eye through the pupil, the lens or the retina?
   Answer: The pupil
7. Do sound waves first enter the ear through the outer ear, middle ear or inner ear?
   Answer: The outer ear
8. Rearrange LIBERAL to name a method that people can use to read with their fingertips.
   Answer: Braille
9. Is the middle ear made up of tiny bones, cilia or sensor cells?
   Answer: Tiny bones
10. Name four basic types of taste your tongue can detect.
    Answer: Sweet, salt, sour and bitter
11. Which 'C' is the word for the tiny hairs in the nose?
    Answer: Cilia
12. How many taste buds can be found on your tongue and throat: less than 100, 1,000 or up to 10,000?
    Answer: Up to 10,000
13. What 'G' would you wear to correct blurry vision?
    Answer: Glasses
14. Which part of the ear vibrates: the ear drum, middle ear or cochlea?
    Answer: Ear drum

Level 3

15. Where on your body are the sensors that detect temperature?
    Answer: All over the body, in the skin
16. Upside-down images form on which part of the eye?
    Answer: The retina
17. Rearrange CHEER TOP TROOPS into a word for cells in the retina.
    Answer: Photoreceptors
18. Do the sounds made by flutes have long wavelengths?
    Answer: No (they are high-pitched instruments so make sounds with short wavelengths)

ANSWERS:
Digestion

Level 1

1. Waste passes from the large intestine to the anus. True or false?
   Answer: True
2. What should you do when you feel thirsty: eat ice cream or drink water?
   Answer: Drink water
3. Where is saliva produced: in the mouth or liver?
   Answer: In the mouth
4. What 'T' rolls food into a ball before swallowing?
   Answer: The tongue

Level 2

5. Most sugars and fats are broken down in the large intestine. True or false?
   Answer: False (they are broken down in the small intestine)
6. Are finger-shaped villi found in the small intestine?
   Answer: Yes
7. Why do we need proteins: to prevent heart disease, provide energy or for body-building?
   Answer: For body-building (for strong bones and to build muscles)
8. Rearrange BOTCHED ARRAYS to name something in food.
   Answer: Carbohydrates
9. Is urine held in the stomach, bladder or lungs?
   Answer: The bladder
10. Where is bile stored: in the small intestine, stomach or gall bladder?
    Answer: Gall bladder
11. Does digestion in the stomach take one, two or four hours?
    Answer: Four hours
12. What 'B' is the name of the ball of food that is pushed down to the stomach when you swallow?
    Answer: Bolus
13. How long does digestion usually take in the intestines: eight, 20 or 30 hours?
    Answer: 20 hours
14. How much of our bodies is water: one-third, two-thirds or four-fifths?
    Answer: Two-thirds

Level 3

15. What role does saliva play in digestion?
    Answer: It starts the digestion of sugars
16. What are enzymes?
    Answer: Digestive chemicals that help break down proteins
17. What does bile do?
    Answer: It digests fats
18. What 'P' is the name for the muscle movements that push food down the oesophagus?
    Answer: Peristalsis

ANSWERS:
Inventors

Level 1

1. Is a telescope or a microscope used to see planets?
Answer: A telescope

2. Are microscopes used by scientists or musicians to carry out experiments?
Answer: Scientists

3. The Greek philosopher and scientist Aristotle studied plants and animals. True or false?
Answer: True

4. What is believed to have been the first writing instrument: a stylus made from reed or a pencil?
Answer: A stylus made from reed

Level 2

5. The other planets in the Solar System orbit the Earth. True or false?
Answer: False (all the planets orbit the Sun)

6. Rearrange MARINES US to name the ancient people who are believed to have invented the first writing system.
Answer: Sumerians

7. Which 'O' is a building where astronomers study the sky?
Answer: Observatory

8. When did Aristotle begin to study nature: about 3000BCE, 350BCE or 1350CE?
Answer: 350BCE

9. Who built the first telescope: Galileo or Isaac Newton?
Answer: Galileo

10. Rearrange REMOTE BAR to name a scientific instrument.
Answer: Barometer

11. Which scientist worked out the movement of planets: Aristotle, Galileo or Isaac Newton?
Answer: Isaac Newton

12. Which scientist studied plants and animals: Aristotle, Galileo or Isaac Newton?
Answer: Aristotle

13. Benjamin Franklin installed a lightning rod on his house. True or false?
Answer: True

14. Were the first writings made on clay, paper or plant leaves?
Answer: Clay

Level 3

15. In which year did Alexander Graham Bell first successfully try his telephone?
Answer: 1876

16. Who discovered that electricity has positive and negative charges?
Answer: Benjamin Franklin

17. Who made the first star maps?
Answer: Chinese astronomers

18. What shapes form the letters in cuneiform writing?
Answer: Triangles and lines

ANSWERS:
Cars

Level 1

1. What 'P' do most cars run on?
Answer: Petrol

2. The Ford Model-T was the first affordable car. True or false?
Answer: True

3. The Mini was originally designed for driving around where: in the city or in the countryside?
Answer: In the city

4. From where do solar-powered cars get energy?
Answer: The sun

Level 2

5. How many wheels did Karl Benz's Motorwagen have: two, three or four?
Answer: Three

6. Rearrange ARE RELAX to name a part found in a car.
Answer: Rear axle

7. What nationality was Henry Ford: British, American or Australian?
Answer: American

8. How many doors did the original Mini have?
Answer: Two

9. Which type of car is better for the environment: a petrol-powered car or solar-powered car?
Answer: A solar-powered car

10. What 'E' drives a car forward?
Answer: The engine

11. Was the Ford Model-T also known as Thin Lizzie, Tin Lizzie or Tin Dizzy?
Answer: Tin Lizzie

12. Which was the first vehicle to use a petrol-powered engine?
Answer: Karl Benz's Motorwagen

13. In which decade was the Mini introduced: the 1950s, 1960s or 1970s?
Answer: The 1950s

14. In 1914, a Ford Model-T could be assembled in 93 minutes. True or false?
Answer: True

15. Solar-powered cars can run all the time. True or false?
Answer: False (they may not run in bad weather)

Level 3

16. Is a propeller shaft a type of long rod, a series of gears or a type of steering mechanism?
Answer: A type of long rod

17. What 'A' means the way that air flows over a moving car?
Answer: Aerodynamics

18. What 'G' helps control the engine's speed?
Answer: The gearbox

ANSWERS: Motorcycles

ANSWERS: Aeroplanes

Level 1

1. Is the Lambretta a scooter?
Answer: Yes

2. A chopper is a motorcycle that was changed by chopping bits off its frame. True or false?
Answer: True

3. Rearrange EMPOD to name a very small type of motorcycle.
Answer: Moped

4. The first motorcycle was made in Germany. True or false?
Answer: True

Level 2

5. In racing, do motorcycles have the same or different engine capacities?
Answer: The same engine capacity

6. Are the handlebars on choppers higher or lower than on other motorcycles?
Answer: Higher

7. What 'S' is a bike that motocross racers use?
Answer: The scrambler

8. Was the Vespa introduced in 1946, 1956 or 1966?
Answer: 1946

9. What 'S' is the name for a motorcycle carriage with one wheel?
Answer: Sidecar

10. Did the Hildebrand brothers' 1889 trial motorcycle have a steam-driven or petrol-driven engine?
Answer: A steam-driven engine

11. Superbikes are not road bikes. True or false?
Answer: False (they are specially adapted road bikes)

12. Scramblers race for how long: 10 to 40 minutes or 1 to 2 hours?
Answer: 10 to 40 minutes

13. Is Harley Davidson known for scooters or choppers?
Answer: Choppers

Level 3

14. Name two of the three engine classes for Grand Prix motorcycle circuit racing.
Answer: 125cc, 250cc and MotoGP (up to 800cc)

15. In which year did Eric Oliver first win the World Motorcycle Sidecar Championship?
Answer: 1949

16. What 'P' is another word for a trial model?
Answer: A prototype

17. What was the top speed of the motorcycle made by the Hildebrand brothers and Alois Wolfmuller?
Answer: 40km/h

18. What is the name of the largest sidecar maker?
Answer: Watsonian-Squire

Level 1

1. Are the economy-class seats in an aeroplane usually in the back part of the cabin or the front?
Answer: The back part of the cabin

2. Do aircraft taxi or train as they move along the ground?
Answer: They taxi

3. Is cargo packed into containers before being loaded on a plane?
Answer: Yes

4. Rearrange NICER SOUPS to make a word that describes a really fast aircraft.
Answer: Supersonic

Level 2

5. At an airport, passengers might be driven in a bus to aircraft parked on the tarmac. True or false?
Answer: True

6. Which 'T' is the name of a building in an airport?
Answer: Terminal

7. What 'F' is the name of the part of an aeroplane where digital screens provide flight information?
Answer: The flight deck

8. Cargo decks can be found under the cabins. True or false?
Answer: True

9. What was the first wide-body jet plane: the Boeing 747 or the Airbus A380?
Answer: The Boeing 747

10. Do scissor trucks lift cargo containers into the cargo hold or lift passengers to the passenger cabins?
Answer: They lift cargo containers

11. Did Concorde fly from London, Paris, New York or all of the above?
Answer: All of the above

12. Which is quieter: the Boeing 747 or the Airbus A380?
Answer: The Airbus A380

13. What 'B' is the term used when a plane turns left or right in the air?
Answer: Bank

14. Where in an airport do passengers go when they want to board a plane?
Answer: The departure lounge (in the terminal building)

Level 3

15. What do flaps on the wings do when they are open?
Answer: They act like a brake

16. In which year did Concorde begin a passenger service?
Answer: 1976

17. What are the metal strips on the wings that make the plane turn called?
Answer: Ailerons

18. What is Mach 2.2 expressed as kilometres per hour?
Answer: 2,200km/h

ANSWERS: Ancient Egypt

Level 1
1. Which river flows through Egypt?
   Answer: The Nile
2. What did the ancient Egyptians call their leader?
   Answer: The pharaoh
3. Did Egyptians believe in life after death?
   Answer: Yes
4. What was made of wool or human hair?
   Answer: Wigs
5. What were Egyptian clothes made from?
   Answer: Linen

Level 2
6. What form of writing did the Egyptians use?
   Answer: Hieroglyphics
7. What was papyrus made from?
   Answer: Reed
8. What was usually buried with an Egyptian's body?
   Answer: Their clothes and furniture, and food and drink
9. How did the Egyptians usually decorate their coffins?
   Answer: With a portrait of the dead person
10. What was 'Opening the mouth'?
    Answer: A ceremony performed by priests at a dead pharaoh's tomb
11. What is the biggest pyramid called?
    Answer: The Great Pyramid of Giza
12. What flower was the symbol of the Nile?
    Answer: The lotus

Level 3
13. Which part of the body was used to measure a cubit: the leg, the foot or the forearm?
    Answer: The forearm
14. How did the Egyptians transport a pharaoh's body?
    Answer: In a funeral boat
15. What did Egyptians use to dry the body when embalming?
    Answer: Salt
16. What animal is associated with the Egyptian god of kings?
    Answer: The hawk
17. What did the priest say during a death ceremony?
    Answer: 'You live again, you live again forever'
18. For how long did the pharaohs rule Egypt?
    Answer: For 3,000 years
19. Who is buried in the Great Pyramid of Giza?
    Answer: The pharaoh Cheops

ANSWERS: Ancient Greece

Level 1
1. What 'M' is one of the seas around Greece?
   Answer: The Mediterrean sea
2. Who was the ruler of the Greek gods?
   Answer: Zeus
3. Where were the ancient Olympic games held?
   Answer: Olympia
4. Was the Trojan horse made of stone or wood?
   Answer: Wood
5. The Greeks had slaves. True or false?
   Answer: True

Level 2
6. A SPRAT can be rearranged to give the name of what Greek city-state?
   Answer: Sparta
7. What did women use to weave fabric for clothes?
   Answer: A loom
8. At about what age did women marry?
   Answer: 15 years old
9. Who hid inside the Trojan horse?
   Answer: Greek soldiers
10. SNOOD PIE can be rearranged to give the name of what Greek god?
    Answer: Poseidon
11. What material did the Greeks use to make bricks?
    Answer: Mud
12. How did wealthy Greeks travel on land: by horse or by carriage?
    Answer: By horse
13. The Greek empire included many islands. True or false?
    Answer: True
14. When travelling in Greece, people slept outside. True or false?
    Answer: True
15. Where were the gods said to live?
    Answer: On Mount Olympus

Level 3
16. In which modern country was the ancient city of Troy?
    Answer: Turkey
17. What did a winner receive at the Olympic games?
    Answer: A crown of olive leaves
18. What was a chiton?
    Answer: A basic woman's dress made of a single rectangle of cloth
19. Where in the home did the Greeks have an altar?
    Answer: In the courtyard
20. Who was the goddess of the home?
    Answer: Hestia

ANSWERS:
The Colosseum

Level 1

1. What famous gladiator led a revolt of slaves?
Answer: Spartacus

2. There were elephants in the Colosseum. True or false?
Answer: True

3. What signal did the crowd give for a gladiator to die?
Answer: Thumbs down

4. CUT ROSE can be rearranged to give the name of what type of gladiator?
Answer: Secutor

Level 2

5. In what part of the Colosseum were the gladiators and animals kept?
Answer: In underground chambers

6. Which emperor often fought at the Colosseum?
Answer: Commodus

7. What was a *bestiarius*?
Answer: A man trained to fight animals

8. What did a *retiarius* use to catch his opponent?
Answer: A net and a three-pronged spear

9. Who was thrown to the animals?
Answer: Christians, criminals and slaves

10. What kind of gladiator wore a helmet decorated with a fish?
Answer: A murmillo

11. How many years did it take to build the Colosseum: ten, 20 or 30?
Answer: ten

12. The *venationes* were Roman soldiers. True or false?
Answer: False

Level 3

13. What did a freed gladiator receive?
Answer: A bone tablet, inscribed with his name, and a gift of coins

14. How many people could attend games at the Colosseum?
Answer: 50,000 people

15. When were the first gladiator games held?
Answer: In 264BCE

16. How did the Colosseum get its name?
Answer: From the nearby colossus (statue) of Nero

17. How many times did Commodus fight at the Colosseum?
Answer: 735 times

18. How many animals were killed in the first celebrations at the Colosseum?
Answer: 5,000

ANSWERS:
Medieval life

Level 1

1. A banquet is a type of battle. True or false?
Answer: False (it is a feast)

2. People ate meals in the great hall. True or false?
Answer: True

3. Was a jongleur a person or a musical instrument?
Answer: A person

4. Who owned the land in medieval times?
Answer: The king

5. Who taught the children of noblemen: priests or servants?
Answer: Priests

Level 2

6. Who rented land from noblemen?
Answer: Knights and lords

7. What were jongleurs called in England?
Answer: Gleemen

8. What was the name of the system by which land was given out?
Answer: The feudal system

9. What was the centre of the castle called?
Answer: The keep

10. Where did important people sit during a banquet?
Answer: At the high table

11. How were castle floors kept warm?
Answer: They were covered with reeds

12. Where were medieval girls taught?
Answer: At home

13. What was the cup board for?
Answer: Displaying the lord's cups and plates

14. What was used to help rid the castle floor of bad smells?
Answer: Spices

Level 3

15. What language did sons of nobles learn?
Answer: Latin

16. Why did people like to hear music while they were eating?
Answer: They believed it aided digestion

17. Where did village boys learn trades?
Answer: At local guilds

18. What were trenchers?
Answer: Wooden boards that diners ate off

ANSWERS:
Knights

Level 1

1. What 'L' was a weapon used by knights on horseback?
Answer: A lance

2. What was a battering ram used for?
Answer: To weaken castle walls

3. RED GAG can be rearranged to give the name of what weapon, used by knights?
Answer: Dagger

4. Knights only ever fought on horseback. True or false?
Answer: False

Level 2

5. What did an esquire become during a dubbing ceremony?
Answer: A knight

6. What was a mace?
Answer: A heavy club

7. How did a jousting knight knock his opponent off his horse?
Answer: With a blunted lance

8. What kind of missiles did a mangonel shoot?
Answer: Rocks

9. Did a knight use a crossbow or a longbow?
Answer: He used both

10. Why did jousting begin?
Answer: As battle training

11. What weapon was used to shoot bolts at a castle?
Answer: A ballista

12. How could knights tell each other apart in battle?
Answer: By the coats of arms on their surcoats

13. What is a trebuchet?
Answer: A siege weapon used for hurling stones at castle walls

14. How could attackers force the defenders of a castle to surrender?
Answer: By starving them into surrender

Level 3

15. What was the name of the fee paid by knights who did not want to fight?
Answer: Scutage

16. What was a bevor?
Answer: A piece of armour that protected the knight's neck

17. How was an esquire dubbed?
Answer: His lord tapped him on the shoulder with the flat blade of his sword

18. By which century had knights begun wearing plated armour?
Answer: The 15th century

ANSWERS:
The Renaissance

Level 1

1. Does the word Renaissance mean 'rebirth' or 'revolting'?
Answer: It means 'rebirth'

2. BLAMER can be rearranged to give the name of what material, used by Renaissance sculptors?
Answer: Marble

3. Was Donatello a painter or a sculptor?
Answer: A sculptor

4. The lute is a musical instrument. True or false?
Answer: True

Level 2

5. Ghiberti was a Renaissance philosopher. True or false?
Answer: False

6. Where was block printing invented?
Answer: China

7. What was the lira da braccio used for?
Answer: For accompanying poems

8. What painting featured the ancient philosophers Plato and Aristotle?
Answer: The School of Athens

9. What was the first-ever mass-produced book?
Answer: A Bible

10. HARE PAL can be rearranged to give the name of what Renaissance artist?
Answer: Raphael

11. Of what nationality was Erasmus?
Answer: Dutch

12. Which two civilizations influenced Renaissance artists?
Answer: Greek and Roman

13. What is the name of the leather pad, which applied the ink in the first European printing press?
Answer: An inkball

14. What kind of philosophers thought that moral lessons could be learned from ancient texts?
Answer: Humanists

Level 3

15. What 'B' was a famous Renaissance architect?
Answer: Brunelleschi

16. In what year was the printing press invented in Europe?
Answer: 1440

17. The Renaissance lasted until which century?
Answer: The 17th century

18. Who invented the printing press in Europe?
Answer: Johannes Gutenberg

ANSWERS: Age of exploration

Level 1

1. Was Sir Francis Drake an Englishman or a Spaniard?
Answer: An Englishman

2. What was Columbus' largest ship called: the *Santa Maria*, the *Santa Anna* or the *Santa Barbara*?
Answer: The Santa Maria

3. Francisco Pizarro conquered the Incas. True or false?
Answer: True

4. From which country was Bartholomew Diaz?
Answer: Portugal

Level 2

5. Which did Magellan discover: the Indian ocean or the Pacific ocean?
Answer: The Pacific ocean

6. How many men were in the crew of Columbus' largest ship: 30, 40 or 60?
Answer: 40

7. Who sent Columbus to find a route to China?
Answer: The king of Spain

8. Did Diaz or da Gama sail around the southern tip of Africa?
Answer: Diaz

9. Who reached India in 1498?
Answer: Vasco da Gama

10. What was Zheng He the first to do?
Answer: Use a compass on a sea voyage

11. What were the names of Columbus' two caravels?
Answer: The Niña and the Pinta

12. What was a backstaff used for?
Answer: Measuring the angle of the sun

13. Why did Ferdinand Magellan not reach his final destination?
Answer: He was killed in the Philippines

14. What did Columbus believe he had reached?
Answer: The Far East

15. What part of the world did the Incas rule?
Answer: The western coast of South America (now Peru)

Level 3

16. On which island did Columbus land?
Answer: San Salvador

17. What was discovered in 1911?
Answer: Machu Picchu

18. What is a nao?
Answer: A merchant ship

19. When did a ship first sail all the way round the world?
Answer: 1522

ANSWERS: World War I

Level 1

1. What large machine was used for the first time in World War I?
Answer: The tank

2. What is a dogfight?
Answer: A battle in the air between two or more aircraft

3. What was the area between enemy trenches called?
Answer: No-man's-land

4. A grenade is a weapon. True or false?
Answer: True

Level 2

5. What kind of protection did soldiers have against gas?
Answer: Gas masks

6. For what purpose were horses used?
Answer: To haul ambulances and weaponry

7. Which 'J' was a major battle fought at sea?
Answer: The Battle of Jutland

8. Where was the Western Front?
Answer: In Belgium and France

9. What name is used for a trained marksman who tries to pick off lone soldiers?
Answer: A sniper

10. What weapon could be attached to a rifle?
Answer: A bayonet

11. How many lives were lost in the war: over 7.5 million, over 8.5 million or over 10 million?
Answer: Over 8.5 million

12. In which country is Jutland?
Answer: Denmark

13. What lined the tops of the trenches?
Answer: Sandbags

14. What weapons were fighter planes fitted with?
Answer: Machine guns

Level 3

15. In what year was poison gas first used?
Answer: 1915

16. Which model of tank was the first one strong enough to withstand anti-tank rifles?
Answer: The British Mark IV

17. What was the name given to the British soldiers who trained horses?
Answer: Roughriders

18. What German fighter plane was considered to be the best fighter plane of the war?
Answer: The Fokker D VII

ANSWERS: Ancient Egyptian daily life

Level 1
1. What animals did the Egyptians hunt: hippopotamuses, horses or hamsters?
Answer: Hippopotamuses

2. From what material did Egyptians build boats: plastic, plywood or papyrus?
Answer: Papyrus

3. Egyptians did not farm the land next to the River Nile. True or false?
Answer: False

4. Egyptians built houses out of mud bricks. True or false?
Answer: True

Level 2
5. Were Egyptian peasants ever beaten?
Answer: Yes

6. OH APRON can be rearranged to give what weapon used in hunting?
Answer: Harpoon

7. At what age did Egyptian children begin going to school: three, four or five?
Answer: Four

8. Egyptians drank beer. True or false?
Answer: True

9. When did the River Nile flood: spring, summer or winter?
Answer: Summer

10. Who baked bread in ancient Egypt: the men or the women?
Answer: The women

11. Only Egyptian boys went to school. True or false?
Answer: False

12. In what season did the Egyptian harvest take place?
Answer: Spring

13. What was a mertu: a type of person, a type of food or a type of house?
Answer: A type of person

14. What animals did the Egyptians use to help plough the land?
Answer: Oxen

15. What 'F' is used to make linen clothing?
Answer: Flax

Level 3
16. What did Egyptians call a team of five labourers?
Answer: A hand

17. What 'S' was an Egyptian hairstyle worn by children?
Answer: Side locks

18. What 'B' is a crop used by Egyptians to make a popular drink?
Answer: Barley

ANSWERS: Ancient Egyptian gods and goddesses

Level 1
1. Egyptians believed in magic. True or false?
Answer: True

2. Who was a ruler of the gods: Ma, Ra or Pa?
Answer: Ra

3. What name is given to evil magic: red, black or blue?
Answer: Black

4. Egyptians made statues of their gods. True or false?
Answer: True

Level 2
5. What was a 'coming forth': a birth, a death or a type of procession?
Answer: A type of procession

6. Only priests took part in daily rituals at the great temples. True or false?
Answer: True

7. ALE TUM can be rearranged to give the name of what item supposed to protect against magic?
Answer: Amulet

8. What kind of animal bit the god Ra: a tiger, a cobra or a spider?
Answer: A cobra

9. Anubis had the head of which animal: a snake, a jackal or a rhino?
Answer: A jackal

10. Was Amun a god of fire or of air?
Answer: A god of air

11. On what item of jewellery would an Egyptian wear a model of a hand?
Answer: A bracelet

12. Which god was guardian of the underworld?
Answer: Anubis

13. Who was the husband of Isis?
Answer: Osiris

Level 3
14. Who learned Ra's secret name?
Answer: Isis

15. What mask would priests wear when preparing a body for burial?
Answer: A jackal mask

16. Which Egyptian god had a name that meant 'The Hidden One'?
Answer: Amun

17. What 'K' is the location of a great temple to Amun?
Answer: Karnak

18. In which city was Amun originally worshipped?
Answer: Thebes

ANSWERS: Ancient Greek warfare

Level 1

1. What were Greek shields made of: linen, paper or wood?
Answer: Wood

2. REAPS can be rearranged to give what weapon used by the Greeks?
Answer: Spear

3. Where did the battle of Salamis take place: on land or at sea?
Answer: At sea

4. What did Greeks make helmets from: bronze, copper or aluminium?
Answer: Bronze

Level 2

5. The main tactic of Greek warships was to ram the enemy. True or false?
Answer: True

6. What was a phalanx: a weapon, a formation or an oar?
Answer: A formation

7. RIM TREE can be rearranged to give the name of what Greek warship?
Answer: Trireme

8. Spartans were Greeks. True or false?
Answer: True

9. At what age did boys start training in Sparta: seven, nine or 11?
Answer: Seven

10. What colour did Spartans use to paint on their shields: red or yellow?
Answer: Red

11. Who won the battle of Salamis: the Greeks or the Persians?
Answer: The Greeks

12. Rearrange I PASS to name a Greek shield.
Answer: Aspis

13. What 'H' was the most common kind of soldier in ancient Greece?
Answer: Hoplite

14. What part of the human body did a greave protect?
Answer: The shin

15. Who was Xerxes: a Persian king, a Spartan general or a Theban god?
Answer: A Persian king

Level 3

16. What letter did Spartans paint on their shields?
Answer: The letter 'L'

17. What did Spartans call their country?
Answer: Lacedaemonia

18. From what city were the Greeks who fought at Salamis?
Answer: Athens

19. What kind of weapon was a xiphos?
Answer: A type of sword

ANSWERS: Ancient Greek gods and goddesses

Level 1

1. What 'Z' was the king of the gods?
Answer: Zeus

2. The Greeks sacrificed bulls to the gods. True or false?
Answer: True

3. Was Aphrodite the goddess of love and beauty or of hatred and ugliness?
Answer: The goddess of love and beauty

Level 2

4. What 'A' was the Greek god of war?
Answer: Ares

5. What was the symbol of Athene: the owl, the eagle or the crow?
Answer: The owl

6. WORN RUDDLE can be rearranged to give the name of what place that Greeks went to after death?
Answer: The underworld

7. Was Asclepius the god of law or of medicine?
Answer: The god of medicine

8. Who was the Greek god of the sun: Artemis, Poseidon or Apollo?
Answer: Apollo

9. Who went to the Elysian Fields: those who had led good lives or those who had led bad lives?
Answer: Those who had led good lives

10. What 'L' was a gift of wine, poured onto an altar?
Answer: Libation

11. What 'S' was a river that the Greeks crossed when they died?
Answer: Styx

12. Athene was the goddess of hunting. True or false?
Answer: False

13. Where was the Panathenaea held?
Answer: In Athens

14. Rearrange STAR RUT to name a burning pit.
Answer: Tartarus

15. What animal appeared in the symbol of Asclepius: a snake, a spider or a scorpion?
Answer: A snake

16. What 'O' was a temple in which people could ask questions about the future?
Answer: An oracle

Level 3

17. What gift did Athene give to Athens?
Answer: The first olive tree

18. Who was the husband of Aphrodite?
Answer: The ugly god Hephaestos

19. Which temple in Athens contained a vast gold and ivory statue of Athene?
Answer: The Parthenon

ANSWERS: The Roman empire

Level 1

1. What could no one wear except the emperor: polka dots, purple or hats?
   Answer: Purple
2. The Romans built winding roads. True or false?
   Answer: False
3. SEA NET can be rearranged to give the name of what group of citizens?
   Answer: Senate

Level 2

4. What were aqueducts used to transport: water, men or food?
   Answer: Water
5. Was Rome founded by a pair of twins or a pair of lovers?
   Answer: A pair of twins
6. Which famous Roman was murdered: Hadrian, Augustus or Julius Caesar?
   Answer: Julius Caesar
7. What 'V' looted Rome?
   Answer: Vandals
8. The name Augustulus meant 'father of Augustus'. True or false?
   Answer: False
9. Augustus conquered the Dacians. True or false?
   Answer: False (Trajan did)
10. What was a toga: a crown, a shoe or a robe?
    Answer: A robe
11. How long is Zaghouan Aqueduct: more than 74km, more than 92km or more than 109km?
    Answer: More than 92km
12. Was Odoacer a German or a Greek?
    Answer: A German
13. SOUL RUM can be rearranged to give the name of what founder of Rome?
    Answer: Romulus
14. Julius Caesar was the first emperor. True or false?
    Answer: False (Augustus was)
15. Augustus was the son of Julius Caesar. True or false?
    Answer: False
16. Under which emperor was the empire at its largest: Nero, Trajan or Vespasian?
    Answer: Trajan

Level 3

17. Who was the first Christian emperor?
    Answer: Constantine
18. Who said 'I found Rome brick, and left it marble'?
    Answer: Augustus
19. Who killed himself so that Trajan would not capture him?
    Answer: The Dacian king Decebalus

ANSWERS: Roman warfare

Level 1

1. Roman soldiers fought together in formations. True or false?
   Answer: True
2. What was the symbol of the Roman army: a mouse, an eagle or a giraffe?
   Answer: An eagle
3. Would Roman soldiers be more likely to form a tiger, a tortoise or a toad?
   Answer: A tortoise

Level 2

4. What was an aquilifer: a general, a doctor or a standard bearer?
   Answer: A standard bearer
5. What 'L' was the name for a Roman foot soldier?
   Answer: A legionary
6. Was a ballista used to throw spears or rocks?
   Answer: Spears
7. COIN TUNER can be rearranged to give the name of what army officer?
   Answer: A centurion
8. What was an onager: a war machine, a soldier or a shield?
   Answer: A war machine
9. The Romans conquered the German tribes. True or false?
   Answer: False
10. What 'G' was a land conquered by Julius Caesar?
    Answer: Gaul
11. What name was given to soldiers from the provinces?
    Answer: Auxiliaries
12. TOE STUD can be rearranged to give the name of what formation?
    Answer: A testudo
13. Roughly how many men were there in a legion: 50, 500 or 5,000?
    Answer: 5,000 men
14. What 'P' was an empire to the east of Rome?
    Answer: The Parthian empire
15. How many years did an auxiliary have to spend in the army before they were given citizenship?
    Answer: 25 years

Level 3

16. How many soldiers were there in a century?
    Answer: 100
17. Who fought Julius Caesar in a great civil war?
    Answer: Pompey
18. Which Roman general was killed at the battle of Carrhae?
    Answer: Crassus

ANSWERS: The Aztecs

Level 1

1. The Aztecs sometimes demanded prisoners for human sacrifices. True or false?
Answer: True

2. What did scribes do: write things down or fight in battles?
Answer: Write things down

3. Most Aztec houses were made of concrete. True or false?
Answer: False

Level 2

4. The Aztecs had a team of men who collected household rubbish. True or false?
Answer: True

5. What does the name 'tlatoani' mean: speaker or listener?
Answer: Speaker

6. I BUTTER can be rearranged to give the name of what kind of payment made to the Aztecs?
Answer: Tribute

7. Where was the Aztec capital built: on Lake Texcoco, on Mount Texcoco or on the Texcoco river?
Answer: Lake Texcoco

8. The Aztec capital had no streets. True or false?
Answer: True

9. Who conquered the Aztecs: the Spanish, the French or the Portuguese?
Answer: The Spanish

10. The Aztec word 'hueyi' means 'small'. True or false?
Answer: False (it means 'great')

11. Aztec houses had no toilets. True or false?
Answer: False

12. A chinampa was a kind of floating house. True or false?
Answer: False (it was a floating garden)

13. What was a 'snake woman': a warrior, a doctor or an adviser?
Answer: An adviser

14. What 'G' did Aztecs use in writing?
Answer: Glyphs

15. How many days were there in the Aztec sacred calendar: 160, 260 or 360?
Answer: 260 days

Level 3

16. How many types of calendar did the Aztecs have?
Answer: Two

17. What was the Aztec capital city?
Answer: Tenochtitlán

ANSWERS: Aztec religion

Level 1

1. The Aztecs only sacrificed animals. True or false?
Answer: False

2. What did Aztecs use to make balls used in tlachtli: rubber, iron or wood?
Answer: Rubber

3. Was Huitzilopochtli the god of the sun or the god of the night?
Answer: The god of the sun

Level 2

4. Where did Aztecs perform sacrifices: on top of a temple, inside a temple or in front of a temple?
Answer: On top of a temple

5. What was the Aztec colour of sacrifice: red, yellow or blue?
Answer: Blue

6. Aztec priests shaved their hair off. True or false?
Answer: False (they grew it long)

7. What was cut out during sacrifice: the tongue, the liver or the heart?
Answer: The heart

8. Was Tlaloc the god of rain or the god of the moon?
Answer: The god of rain

9. Where did Huitzilopochtli have a shrine: in all temples or at the Great Temple in the capital city?
Answer: At the Great Temple in the capital city

10. Which Aztecs filed their teeth into points: warriors, priests or rulers?
Answer: Priests

11. How often did the Aztecs sacrifice to Huitzilopochtli: every hour, every day or every five years?
Answer: Every day

12. What was the penalty for losing a game of tlachtli?
Answer: Being offered as a sacrifice

13. How long did the Aztecs claim it took to sacrifice 84,400 victims: four days, four months or four years?
Answer: Four days

Level 3

14. BISON AID can be rearranged to give the name of what volcanic rock, used by the Aztecs to make knives?
Answer: Obsidian

15. Players in tlachtli could only use their hands. True or false?
Answer: False (they could not use their hands)

16. Which animal eating a snake was a sign to the Aztecs to build a city?
Answer: The eagle

17. What did Aztec priests use to paint their skin black?
Answer: Soot

ANSWERS: Summer Olympics

Level 1

1. How many rings are there in the Olympic symbol?
Answer: Five

2. Which Olympic sport features a 5m-long springy pole?
Answer: Pole vaulting

3. How often are the summer Olympic games held?
Answer: Every four years

4. Do equestrian events use a horse, a bicycle or a pistol?
Answer: A horse

5. Which kind of swimming race is longer: a sprint or an endurance race?
Answer: An endurance race

Level 2

6. Is a marathon race 20km, 42km or 50km long?
Answer: 42km

7. What is the name of a competitor in a judo fight?
Answer: A judoka

8. Which horse-based sport takes three days to complete?
Answer: Eventing

9. What is the name of the building in which track cyclists compete?
Answer: A velodrome

10. Who set a world record of 6.14m for the pole vault?
Answer: Sergei Bubka

11. What is the longest distance race in track athletics at the Olympics?
Answer: The 50km racewalk

12. How many Olympics has Jeannie Longo-Ciprelli appeared at: three, four or six?
Answer: Six

13. In which sport did Mark Spitz win seven gold medals in 1972?
Answer: Swimming

Level 3

14. How long is a steeplechase race at the Olympics?
Answer: 3,000m

15. When was judo first included in the Olympics?
Answer: 1964

16. How many lengths of the pool do swimmers in the 1,500m race have to swim?
Answer: 30

17. How much shorter is a woman's judo bout than a man's?
Answer: One minute

18. What fraction of the total gold medals for judo did Japan win in 2004?
Answer: Half

ANSWERS: Gymnastics

Level 1

1. When do athletes warm up?
Answer: Before competing

2. What are people who perform gymnastics called?
Answer: Gymnasts

3. How many handles does a pommel horse have?
Answer: Two

4. Are rings used only by men, or by both men and women?
Answer: Only by men

5. What do some athletes dust their hands with to help with their grip?
Answer: Chalk

Level 2

6. In gymnastics, how many events do female athletes compete in?
Answer: Four

7. Did rhythmic gymnastics first appear in the Olympics in 1932, 1968 or 1984?
Answer: 1984

8. How many items of equipment are there in rhythmic gymnastics?
Answer: Five

9. Was the first person to get the highest possible score in artistic gymnastics at the Olympics a man or a woman?
Answer: A woman

10. What is the highest possible mark given to a competitor for one routine: 10, 15, or 20?
Answer: 10

11. What 'H' is a piece of rhythmic gymnastics equipment?
Answer: Hoop

12. What are the two hoops hanging above the ground called?
Answer: Rings

13. What kind of gymnastics is performed to music?
Answer: Rhythmic gymnastics

14. How many panels of judges mark rhythmic gymnastics?
Answer: Three

Level 3

15. How high are the parallel bars?
Answer: 1.75m high

16. Who was the first person to get the highest possible score in artistic gymnastics at the Olympics?
Answer: Nadia Comaneci

17. Who invented the parallel bars?
Answer: Friedrich Jahn

18. From which gymnastics apparatus would a gymnast dismount?
Answer: The pommel horse

ANSWERS: Winter sports

Level 1

1. How many skis does a skier wear?
   Answer: Two
2. Do speed skaters race downhill, round a track or along a road?
   Answer: Round a track
3. Which country invented ice hockey?
   Answer: Canada
4. Which is also known as cross-country skiing: Nordic or downhill?
   Answer: Nordic skiing
5. What name is given to someone who teaches others to ski?
   Answer: Ski instructor

Level 2

6. In which winter sport do players try to hit a puck into a goal?
   Answer: Ice hockey
7. What is the front of a snowboard called?
   Answer: The nose
8. Downhill skiing is part of the winter Olympics. True or false?
   Answer: True
9. What is the name of the sticks held in the hands of a skier?
   Answer: Ski poles
10. In which winter sport can competitors reach a speed of 60km/h as they race around a track?
    Answer: Speed skating
11. Are there six, nine or 11 players per side in ice hockey?
    Answer: Six
12. Do Nordic or slalom skiers race a zigzagging course?
    Answer: Slalom skiers
13. What is the back of a snowboard called?
    Answer: The tail
14. How many periods are there in an ice hockey game?
    Answer: Three
15. The biathlon involves rifle shooting and what sort of skiing?
    Answer: Nordic skiing
16. In what year did snowboarding become an Olympic sport?
    Answer: 1998

Level 3

17. Which can travel the fastest: speed skaters or downhill skiers?
    Answer: Downhill skiers
18. What object fixes ski boots to skis?
    Answer: Bindings
19. Which skis are shorter and wider: Nordic skis or downhill skis?
    Answer: Downhill skis
20. What is the name of the player who guards a goal in ice hockey?
    Answer: The goaltender

ANSWERS: Football

Level 1

1. What is the name given to the players who try to score goals?
   Answer: Attackers
2. Which player is allowed to touch the ball with their hands?
   Answer: The goalkeeper
3. The warning card is yellow. True or false?
   Answer: True
4. Is challenging for the ball known as passing, throwing in or tackling?
   Answer: Tackling
5. What is a football pitch usually made of?
   Answer: Grass

Level 2

6. For what country did Pelé play?
   Answer: Brazil
7. Who has scored over 100 goals for his country: Wayne Rooney, Michael Ballack or Ali Daei?
   Answer: Ali Daei
8. What is the person in charge of a football match called?
   Answer: The referee
9. How often did Pelé help win the World Cup?
   Answer: Three times
10. How many players are in a football team?
    Answer: 11
11. What colour is the card that means the player is sent off the pitch?
    Answer: Red
12. In which city were the first full rules of football created?
    Answer: London
13. Did Pelé score 478, 809 or 1,281 goals in his career?
    Answer: 1,281
14. Does Cristiano Ronaldo play for Portugal, France or Brazil?
    Answer: Portugal

Level 3

15. Which of the following parts of the body can a footballer use to control the ball: head, chest, arms, thigh, hands?
    Answer: Head, chest, thigh
16. For what country did Ali Daei play?
    Answer: Iran
17. What animal's bladder was used to make early footballs?
    Answer: A pig's
18. Which American woman has scored 158 goals for her country?
    Answer: Mia Hamm

ANSWERS: Art and painting

Level 1

1. The famous artist Michelangelo came from Italy. True or false?
Answer: True

2. What was Van Gogh's first name?
Answer: Vincent

3. In what country are the famous Lascaux cave paintings?
Answer: France

4. Were sculptures, cave paintings or frescoes made on damp plaster?
Answer: Frescoes

5. The Lascaux cave paintings feature paintings of reindeer. True or false?
Answer: True

Level 2

6. What part of an egg was used by prehistoric cave painters?
Answer: The white

7. Can you name either of the colours that were often used by the ancient Greeks to decorate their pottery?
Answer: Red or black

8. Do artists painting frescoes have to work slowly or quickly?
Answer: Quickly

9. Does tempera or oil paint produce richer colours?
Answer: Oil paint

10. Did Michelangelo paint a fresco on the doors, the walls or the ceiling of the Sistine Chapel?
Answer: The ceiling

11. From what was Michelangelo's sculpture of Moses carved?
Answer: Marble

12. Does oil paint or tempera paint dry more slowly?
Answer: Oil paint

13. What part of an egg was used to make tempera paints?
Answer: The yolk

Level 3

14. *Blam!* is a famous Pop Art painting. Who painted it?
Answer: Roy Lichtenstein

15. In what century did Michelangelo carve a sculpture of Moses?
Answer: The 16th century

16. How old was Van Gogh when he painted *Starry Night*?
Answer: 36

17. In which decade did Pop Art first appear?
Answer: In the 1950s

18. Are the prehistoric paintings in the Lascaux caves around 15,000, 16,000 or 17,000 years old?
Answer: Around 17,000 years old

ANSWERS: Ballet

Level 1

1. Do most ballet dancers start as children, teenagers or adults?
Answer: As children

2. Do ballets take place in a rink, a court or in a theatre?
Answer: A theatre

3. Do male ballet dancers wear make-up?
Answer: Yes

4. Is a tutu a ballet shoe, a skirt or a type of ballet move?
Answer: A skirt

Level 2

5. What sort of musician often plays during ballet classes?
Answer: A pianist

6. In *Swan Lake*, what part of the body does a ballerina move to look like wings?
Answer: The arms

7. Before a show, where do dancers put on their make-up?
Answer: In the dressing room

8. A *port de bras* exercise involves the movement of what part of the body?
Answer: The arms

9. How many basic positions are there for the feet in ballet?
Answer: Five

10. The heels touch together in which position: first, second or third?
Answer: First

11. ASK LAWNE can be rearranged to give the name of what ballet?
Answer: Swan Lake

12. Why do dancers wear leg warmers when they practise?
Answer: To keep their muscles warm and prevent strains and injuries

13. What term means dancing on the tips of the toes?
Answer: Pointe-work

14. In a ballet, what is the break between acts called?
Answer: The interval

15. Does a major ballet need as many as 30, 300 or 3,000 costumes?
Answer: 300 costumes

Level 3

16. Which country does the ballet *Swan Lake* come from?
Answer: Russia

17. What term means the leading female dancer in a ballet company?
Answer: Prima Ballerina

18. What 'O' is the name of a princess turned into a swan in *Swan Lake*?
Answer: Odette

ANSWERS: Architecture

ANSWERS: Film and TV

Level 1

1. Who built the Parthenon: the Greeks, Egyptians or Romans?
Answer: The Greeks

2. What is the name given to the giant buildings used to bury leaders (pharaohs) in ancient Egypt?
Answer: Pyramids

3. Were the first bricks made of mud and clay, or cement and gravel?
Answer: Mud and clay

4. Are the pyramids of ancient Egypt made of mud, wood or stone?
Answer: Stone

5. Were the first bricks made solid by setting them on fire, letting them dry in the sun or freezing them?
Answer: Letting them dry in the sun

Level 2

6. Which civilization invented concrete?
Answer: The Romans

7. Was the Parthenon built of granite, cement or marble?
Answer: Marble

8. In which city is the Parthenon?
Answer: Athens

9. Why does Hardwick Hall have lots of windows?
Answer: As a sign of wealth

10. Did the White House get water pipes or gas lighting installed first?
Answer: Water pipes

11. Did the Gothic style of architecture begin in Europe, Asia or Africa?
Answer: Europe

12. What is the name of the wooden strips that are filled in with daub?
Answer: Wattles

13. Who built Hardwick Hall?
Answer: Bess of Hardwick

Level 3

14. What are the architect's detailed plans for a building called?
Answer: Blueprints

15. Which famous building did James Hoban rebuild?
Answer: The White House

16. The Parthenon was a temple for the worship of which goddess?
Answer: Athene

17. What is a flying buttress?
Answer: A special side-support

18. During which century did Gothic architecture first appear?
Answer: The 12th century

Level 1

1. Were the first TV broadcasts black and white or colour?
Answer: Black and white

2. What 'D' is the person in charge of the film-making process?
Answer: The director

3. What name is given to someone who interviews people for the news?
Answer: Reporter

4. What word describes people who play characters and appear in films?
Answer: Actors

5. What word describes the written-down version of a film?
Answer: The script

Level 2

6. Who are the three people needed in a news team?
Answer: Reporter, cameraman, sound recordist

7. What word describes news reporting that is transmitted as the events unfold?
Answer: Live

8. Was the first film with sound *Casablanca*, *The Jazz Singer* or *Snow White*?
Answer: The Jazz Singer

9. WOOLY HOLD can be rearranged to give the name of what huge film industry based in the USA?
Answer: Hollywood

10. Near which big American city is this industry located?
Answer: Los Angeles

11. What nickname is given to India's film industry?
Answer: Bollywood

12. What name is given to 24-hour news programmes?
Answer: Rolling news

Level 3

13. Was Telstar the name of an early television or a satellite?
Answer: A satellite

14. In what year was the first 'talking' film made?
Answer: 1927

15. In 1962, what percentage of US homes had a television?
Answer: 90 per cent

16. In what year was the first TV signal sent by satellite?
Answer: 1962

17. What word is used for sending programmes out from the TV station?
Answer: Broadcasting

18. Which Asian country has one of the largest film industries in the world?
Answer: India

ANSWERS: Fairy tales

Level 1

1. Cinderella marries a prince. True or false?
Answer: True

2. Are Hansel and Gretel abandoned in the woods or in town?
Answer: In the woods

3. Is Gretel, Cinderella or Sleeping Beauty woken up by a kiss from a prince?
Answer: Sleeping Beauty

4. Does the Pied Piper lure children away from town or get them to return to town?
Answer: He lures them away

Level 2

5. For how many years does Sleeping Beauty sleep: ten years, 50 years or 100 years?
Answer: 100 years

6. In *Rumpelstiltskin*, is straw, palm leaves or sheep's wool spun into gold?
Answer: Straw

7. What 'G' is the witch's house made of in later versions of *Hansel & Gretel*?
Answer: Gingerbread

8. What 'F' does the Pied Piper play to lure the children away?
Answer: A flute

9. Are there over 30, 340 or 560 versions of Cinderella?
Answer: Over 340

10. What are mermaids: half men and half goats, half men and half fish, or half women and half fish?
Answer: Half women and half fish

11. Is Hamelin a German, French or Austrian town?
Answer: A German town

12. Are Hansel and Gretel the children of a miller, a prince or a woodcutter?
Answer: A woodcutter

13. Who told the king that it is possible to spin gold: Rumpelstiltskin, the miller or his daughter?
Answer: The miller

Level 3

14. In the Chinese version of *Cinderella*, which 'W' finds the slipper?
Answer: A warlord

15. Who wrote *The Little Mermaid*?
Answer: Hans Christian Andersen

16. In which story does a fairy cast a spell?
Answer: Sleeping Beauty

17. In what year did the children really leave Hamelin?
Answer: 1284

18. When was the earliest version of Cinderella written?
Answer: About 850CE

ANSWERS: Theatre

Level 1

1. Stage carpenters work with wood. True or false?
Answer: True

2. Stage hands are normally in charge of the actors' costumes. True or false?
Answer: False (dressers are in charge of the costumes)

3. Does a costume designer or set designer plan the layout of the stage?
Answer: Set designer

4. Set builders build theatre scenery. True or false?
Answer: True

5. Is stage smoke a type of special effect?
Answer: Yes

Level 2

6. What 'C' is the name for the clothing that performers wear?
Answer: Costume

7. Does a costume designer work with a set designer?
Answer: Yes

8. Which 'D' cleans and mends the costumes?
Answer: The dresser

9. Does the Metropolitan Opera House require 200, 500 or 1,000 staff to put on a performance?
Answer: 1,000

10. Is the place where the audience sit called the wings, backstage or the auditorium?
Answer: The auditorium

11. On stage, what would a suitcase be considered: a set, costume or prop?
Answer: A prop

12. Are the sides of a stage out of the audience's view called the wings, upstage or front of house?
Answer: The wings

13. New York's Metropolitan Opera House is also known as what: The Op House, The Met or The Big Stage?
Answer: The Met

14. Rearrange AT BELL to name a type of performance that may need a dresser.
Answer: Ballet

Level 3

15. Where are sets often assembled?
Answer: On the stage

16. What is the largest number of people that can watch a single performance at New York's Metropolitan Opera House?
Answer: 3,800 people

17. Which theatre staff sometimes help actors make quick costume changes?
Answer: Dressers

18. Who uses scale models of the stage in their work?
Answer: The set designer

ANSWERS: Shakespeare

Level 1

1. *Macbeth* is a play about a figure from Scottish history. True or false?
Answer: True

2. Was Shakespeare's theatre called the Swan or the Globe?
Answer: The Globe

3. *Hamlet* is a comedy play. True or false?
Answer: False (it is a tragedy play)

4. Did Shakespeare write a play called *Romeo and Juliet* or *Verona and Juliet*?
Answer: Romeo and Juliet

Level 2

5. Were people who watched a play from the pit called pitlings, groundlings or watchlings?
Answer: Groundlings

6. Was Shakespeare born in London, Stratford-upon-Avon or Paris?
Answer: Stratford-upon-Avon

7. What was the name of the uncovered part of the theatre where people stood to watch plays?
Answer: The pit

8. Richer people watched plays in the Globe in a covered area. True or false?
Answer: True

9. Could the Globe Theatre hold 500, 1,500 or 3,000 people?
Answer: 3,000

10. Which 'M' is Shakespeare's bloodiest tragedy play?
Answer: Macbeth

11. Is the line 'To be, or not to be' from *Macbeth*, *Hamlet* or *Romeo and Juliet*?
Answer: Hamlet

12. Is *Romeo and Juliet* based on real lovers or a made-up tale?
Answer: Real lovers

13. The Globe Theatre was built close to which river in London?
Answer: The river Thames

14. Was *Hamlet* first performed about 1550, 1600 or 1625?
Answer: About 1600

Level 3

15. Where was the home of the real couple on whose story Shakespeare based *Romeo and Juliet*?
Answer: Verona, Italy

16. Which British king had a friendship with Shakespeare?
Answer: King James I

17. In what year was the Globe Theatre rebuilt after it had burned down?
Answer: 1614

18. By which year was Shakespeare recognized as a playwright?
Answer: 1592

ANSWERS: Famous ballets

Level 1

1. *The Nutcracker* features a nutcracker turned into a prince. True or false?
Answer: True

2. Is *Swan Lake* a difficult ballet to perform?
Answer: Yes

3. Was *Giselle* first performed in London or Paris?
Answer: Paris

4. Junior ballet dancers sometimes do solo performances. True or false?
Answer: True

Level 2

5. Is *The Firebird* based on a Shakespeare play or on Russian folk tales?
Answer: Russian folk tales

6. Who composed the music for the ballet *The Sleeping Beauty*: Tchaikovsky or Petipa?
Answer: Tchaikovsky

7. Is *Giselle* still performed the same as in the first production?
Answer: No (changes have been made since then)

8. In *The Firebird*, the dancer performing the part of the firebird often wears a plain costume. True or false?
Answer: False (the costume is usually elaborate)

9. Odile in *Swan Lake* is what type of creature?
Answer: A black swan maiden

10. Which 'P' roles are unsuitable for junior soloists?
Answer: Principal roles

11. Was the composer for *The Sleeping Beauty* Russian, French or American?
Answer: Russian

12. *The Nutcracker* is a popular production at what time of year?
Answer: Christmas time

13. Apart from Odile, what is one of the other characters seen in *Swan Lake*?
Answer: a prince or an evil sorcerer

Level 3

14. What is the first name of the composer of the music for *The Firebird*?
Answer: Igor (Stravinsky)

15. In which year was the first production of *The Nutcracker*?
Answer: 1892

16. Puss in Boots makes an appearance in which ballet?
Answer: Sleeping Beauty

17. In which year was *Giselle* first performed?
Answer: 1841

18. Who choreographed the ballet *The Sleeping Beauty*?
Answer: Marius Petipa

Basketball

Horse and pony care

Level 1

1. Children can play basketball. True or false?
Answer: True

2. Is Michael Jordan British or American?
Answer: American

3. A regular shot in basketball scores two points. True or false?
Answer: True

4. Are competition basketballs orange, yellow or green?
Answer: Orange

Level 2

5. How many metres off the ground is the basket: 2m, 3m or 5m?
Answer: 3m

6. In which year was basketball invented: 1891, 1911 or 1931?
Answer: 1891

7. A basketball weighs 600 to 650g, 700 to 750g, or 800 to 850g?
Answer: 600 to 650g

8. What 'H' is the line across the middle of a basketball court?
Answer: Halfway line

9. Rearrange CHAIN to spell the country that basketball player Yao Ming is from.
Answer: China

10. In what part of the basketball court can players stay with the ball for only three seconds: the key, the centre of the court or in the corners of the court?
Answer: The key

11. How many panels make up a basketball: three, six or eight?
Answer: Eight

12. Are the balls used by children smaller, bigger or the same size as balls used by adults?
Answer: Smaller

13. What type of basket was first used to play basketball: a basket for peaches, blueberries or tomatoes?
Answer: A peach basket

Level 3

14. How many metres wide is a basketball court?
Answer: 15m

15. By how many centimetres is Yao Ming taller than Michael Jordan?
Answer: 31cm

16. Who invented basketball?
Answer: James Naismith

17. In basketball, what is the most points a single shot can score?
Answer: Three points are awarded for a long-distance shot

18. How much is a foul shot worth?
Answer: *One point*

Level 1

1. Horses do not like being groomed. True or false?
Answer: False

2. Are horses sometimes massaged?
Answer: Yes

3. Is the seat a rider sits on called a bridle or a saddle?
Answer: A saddle

4. Horses eat mostly hay and grass. True or false?
Answer: True

5. Horses are kept in buildings called what: stables or paddocks?
Answer: Stables

Level 2

6. What is a cloth used at the end of grooming called: a rubber glove, stable glove or stable rubber?
Answer: Stable rubber

7. Is plaiting performed before or after clipping and grooming?
Answer: After

8. What type of 'C' comb can remove dried mud from a horse's body?
Answer: A curry comb

9. What 'M' name is given to the hair on a horse's neck?
Answer: Mane

10. Rearrange DIG BEND to give the name of something that is replaced in the stable every day.
Answer: Bedding

11. How many times a day must a horse be fed: once, twice or three times?
Answer: Twice

12. Name one of two 'B' grains used in short feeds for horses.
Answer: Barley and bran

13. Is a sponge, tack or saddle soap used to clean around a horse's eyes?
Answer: A sponge

14. Can horses eat only small amounts of grains or large amounts?
Answer: Small amounts (they have small stomachs)

Level 3

15. How much manure can an adult horse produce in a week?
Answer: Over 140kg

16. What is the term used for putting a saddle and bridle on a horse?
Answer: Tacking up

17. What object containing horse food is hung up in the stable?
Answer: A haynet

18. How many kilograms of hay can an adult horse eat in a day?
Answer: 10kg

ANSWERS: Martial arts

Level 1

1. Are martial artists often trained to use their skills to defend or to fight?
   Answer: To defend
2. Tai chi movements are sharp and sudden. True or false?
   Answer: False (they are flowing and slow)
3. Is karate a type of striking martial art?
   Answer: Yes
4. Are throwing techniques and arm locks part of judo or kung fu?
   Answer: Judo

Level 2

5. Does kickboxing, tai chi or karate combine boxing with kicking moves?
   Answer: Kickboxing
6. Does a kickboxer score points by striking with his hands, feet or both?
   Answer: Both
7. Training for karate is divided into forms and sparring. True or false?
   Answer: True
8. From which 'J' country does kendo come from?
   Answer: Japan
9. Which colour is usually the highest colour in the coloured belt system used in many martial arts: brown, black or purple?
   Answer: Black
10. Which qualities are required for success in the martial arts: discipline and self-control, or taking your own lead and being quick to respond?
    Answer: Discipline and self-control
11. Which 'K' is a form of martial art known for its kicks and open-hand techniques?
    Answer: Karate
12. Which martial art is based on animal poses: tai chi, karate or kendo?
    Answer: Tai chi
13. Which European country does the form of kickboxing called 'savate' come from: Italy, Spain or France?
    Answer: France

Level 3

14. Why does the colour of a belt worn by a judo or karate student change?
    Answer: To indicate a student's progress
15. What is the name of the sword used in kendo?
    Answer: Shinai
16. The teachings of which Buddhist led to the beginning of many martial arts?
    Answer: Bodhidharma
17. Which martial art is based on jujutsu?
    Answer: Judo

ANSWERS: Motor racing

Level 1

1. A driver's helmet protects against what: ice, wind or fire?
   Answer: Fire
2. Rearrange GEE INN to spell the name of a part of a car.
   Answer: Engine
3. F1 cars are low and streamlined. True or false?
   Answer: True
4. Does the team decide on a plan to win the race?
   Answer: Yes

Level 2

5. Which 'M' is the name of the stewards who are in charge of fire safety?
   Answer: Marshals
6. How fast can an F1 pit crew change four wheels: seven seconds, 17 seconds or 37 seconds?
   Answer: Seven seconds
7. Many F1 drivers consider Silverstone to be one of the fastest F1 race tracks. True or false?
   Answer: True
8. How many litres of petrol does an F1 car normally use to drive 100km: 25, 50 or 75?
   Answer: About 75 litres per 100km
9. What was the world land speed record for an F1 car set in 2006: 35km/h, 355km/h or 1,550km/h?
   Answer: 355km/h
10. What are the three top NASCAR championships?
    Answer: The Busch series, the Craftsman Truck series and the Nextel Cup
11. What is the important difference between ordinary tracksuits and the race suits worn by racing drivers?
    Answer: Race suits are fireproof
12. What is the strong frame that makes up a NASCAR's structure made of?
    Answer: Steel
13. The average speed over the entire racetrack of the Talladega Superspeedway is what: 160km/h, 303km/h or 354km/h?
    Answer: 303km/h

Level 3

14. What must a driver do at a pit stop?
    Answer: Stop the car in the exact spot and wait for a signal before going
15. What are G-forces?
    Answer: Acceleration forces caused by gravity
16. What do the pit crew do to an F1 car during a pit stop?
    Answer: They change the wheels, refuel and make repairs
17. What is the advantage of starting an F1 race with half-full fuel tanks?
    Answer: The car is lighter, so it will go faster

Glossary

A

Aboriginal people The original inhabitants of Australia.

abundance A very great quantity, more than enough of something.

accelerate Get faster.

acidic Of acid. Acids are chemical compounds that contain hydrogen and dissolve in water to produce hydrogen ions. Acids corrode most metals.

adapted Changed to suit a particular purpose or to fit particular needs. Desert creatures, for example, are adapted to survive in hot, dry conditions.

aerodynamics The way that the air and objects moving through the air interact.

afterlife Everlasting life after death. Most religions and cultures believe in some form of afterlife.

aggressive Hostile or attacking.

albino An animal or person with no pigment in their hair, skin or eyes, so that they are completely white and have pink eyes. There are many breeds of pet that are albinos.

alga (plural: algae) A single-celled plant usually found living in water.

alloy A mixture of two or more metals.

alluvium Fertile land occurring where sediment (fine particles) carried along by rivers are deposited.

amphibian A cold-blooded vertebrate animal, such as a frog, toad, newt or salamander, that spends most of its life on land but has to return to water to breed.

amphitheatre A place used for public performances and surrounded by tiers of seats. Ancient Greek amphitheatres are semicircular, while ancient Roman ones are circular.

amulet An object believed to bring luck or to protect its owner from harm.

anatomy The body structure of an animal or plant.

ancestor Referring to an animal, an early type of animal from which others have evolved.

ape One of a group of mammals that includes gorillas, chimpanzees, orang-utans and humans. Apes have gripping fingers and thumbs, and no tails.

aqueduct A channel that transports water. Often an aqueduct is a bridge that carries water across a valley.

arachnid A member of the group of invertebrate animals that includes spiders and scorpions. All arachnids have simple eyes and four pairs of legs.

archaeologist A scientist who studies the past using scientific analysis of material remains.

architecture Designing buildings and structures by planning attractive and practical designs and advising how to construct them.

Arctic The region around the North Pole, consisting of the Arctic Ocean and the tundra lands.

asteroid A spacerock orbiting the Sun. During the Earth's history, some asteroids have crashed into the Earth.

astronomer A scientist who studies the universe.

atmosphere The layer of gases around a planet or moon. Earth's atmosphere is made up of several layers, including the troposphere and the stratosphere.

auditorium The part of a theatre, concert hall or cinema where the audience sit or stand to hear and see the performance.

aurora A natural light show seen in the night sky in far northern and far southern regions of the Earth. Aurorae are caused by high-speed particles from the Sun colliding with gas molecules to produce light.

auxiliary The name for a type of soldier. In ancient Rome, auxiliaries were soldiers from the provinces, who fought in the Roman army but were not Roman citizens.

axis An imaginary line through the centre of a planet. The Earth spins on its axis.

Aztecs The peoples of what is now Mexico, who developed a vast empire between the 13th and 16th centuries CE.

B

baleen A tough, horny substance, made from the protein keratin, which makes up baleen plates. These plates are found in the mouths of baleen whales, and are used by the whales to filter food from sea water.

baleen whale A member of the group of whales that have baleen plates, including blue whales and humpback whales.

ballista A type of weapon, like a giant crossbow.

barometer An instrument that measures air pressure.

bat A flying mammal that is usually nocturnal. Bats have very long finger bones, between which skin is stretched to form wings.

Big Bang The name given to the explosion that scientists believe created our universe, space and time, about 13 billion years ago.

billion One thousand million (1,000,000,000).

bird A type of vertebrate animal. All birds have two legs, are covered with feathers, have beaks and lay eggs. Most birds can fly.

bird of prey A type of bird that hunts for its food. All birds of prey have strong talons, a curved beak and excellent eyesight. Eagles and owls are birds of prey.

black hole The remains of a star that has collapsed in on itself. Its gravity is so strong that it pulls everything towards it, even light.

blow hole A hole at the back of a sea cave that leads up to the headland above. Waves are forced up through the hole.

blowhole The breathing hole on the top of the head of a whale, dolphin or porpoise.

blubber A thick layer of fat just beneath a sea mammal's skin,

which helps it to keep warm and survive extreme cold.

blueprint A detailed plan or model.

Braille A system of writing for blind people, in which letters are represented by raised dots. They are read by touch.

breaching The word used to describe a whale jumping out of the water to breathe.

breed Produce young, have babies.

breed A variety of domestic or farm animal. There are hundreds of breeds of dogs and many breeds of horses, for example.

broadcasting The presentation or transmission of television, radio or internet programmes.

bromeliad A type of flowering plant, found especially in rainforests.

Buddhism A world religion based on the teachings of the Buddha (Siddhartha Gautama, an Indian prince who lived in the 6th century BCE).

C

cactus (plural: cacti) A type of plant that is adapted to life in desert conditions. Cacti store water in their fleshy stems, and many have spines.

caliph A type of Muslim leader.

calves Baby dolphins or cattle.

camouflage Colouring, patterns or markings that help an animal blend in with its surroundings, so that it is hard for predators or prey to see it. Soldiers also use camouflage to help stop themselves and their vehicles being seen by the enemy.

canyon A deep gorge.

capital The most important city of a country or region, where its government and administrative centre are found.

captivity Being imprisoned or caged. Animals in a zoo are in captivity.

carbohydrate A molecule, made up of carbon, hydrogen and oxygen atoms, that stores and transfers energy. Carbohydrates, also called sugars and starches, are an important part of the diet. Bread, potatoes and pasta are all high in carbohydrates.

cargo Goods carried in a ship or plane.

carnival A period of festivities, usually involving music, costume and dancing, especially in the period before Lent.

carnivore A type of animal that eats only meat.

cartilage A tough, flexible tissue, also called gristle. In animals with bony skeletons it covers bone ends in joints and helps support the body. Shark skeletons are made entirely of cartilage.

cathedral A large, important church.

cavalry Soldiers who fight on horseback.

cell One of the tiny living units from which all living organisms are made.

cephalopod A type of invertebrate animal with arms or tentacles and a well-developed nervous system. Octupuses and squid are cephalopods.

cetacean A type of marine mammal with a hairless body. Whales, dolphins and porpoises are cetaceans.

chivalry A code of behaviour that was an important part of medieval life. It usually refers to knights and the virtues they were expected to live up to, especially courage in battle, valour, fairness, godliness and graciousness towards women.

choreographer Someone who arranges sequences of dance movements to create dances or entire ballets.

Christian Someone who follows the teachings of Jesus Christ. Christianity spread from its early origins in Jerusalem's churches during the 1st century CE and developed further during the Roman empire. Today it is one of the major world religions.

climate The general weather conditions of a region or the whole Earth over a long period of time.

climate change The change to Earth's global or regional climate. Some climate change is natural, while the recent rapid increase in global temperature has been caused by human activity.

coast The part of the land that borders the sea.

cold-blooded An animal whose body temperature is the same as that of its surroundings. Fish, amphibians and reptiles are cold-blooded.

colony A group of the same type of animal, such as bats, that all live together.

committee A group of people who meet to discuss a particular topic or to do a particular job.

communication Passing information, for example through speaking, writing, sounds, body language or signals.

community A group of animals or people who share

the same environment, often sharing resources and establishing different roles for different community members.

composer Someone who writes music.

compressed Squeezed together, reduced in size.

condense Make smaller or denser. When a gas condenses, it becomes a liquid.

constellation A group of stars that appears in the sky in the form of a particular shape, such as a creature or a character from mythology.

continent A large land mass. Earth's seven continents are Asia, Africa, North America, South America, Antarctica, Europe and Australia.

continental drift The slow movement of Earth's continents over time.

convict Someone who has been found guilty of committing a crime.

coral reef An undersea community of marine organisms, such as corals, sponges and clams. Coral reefs are found in tropical waters and are home to many fish and other sea creatures.

core The metallic centre of the Earth, made of a molten outer core and solid inner core.

corona The outer atmosphere of the Sun or of any star.

country An area of land ruled by its own government.

crater A hollow on the surface of a planet or moon, caused by an object (for example an asteroid) crashing into it.

crust The outermost layer of a planet.

crystal A solid substance with a geometrical shape, straight edges and flat surfaces. Quartz is an example of a crystal.

cuneiform A style of writing on clay tablets developed in ancient Mesopotamia (modern-day Iraq) from around 3000BCE and thought to be the first writing. The word 'cuneiform' means 'wedge-shaped'.

currency The money officially in use in a country, such as the dollar in the USA, the pound in the UK or the euro in many European countries.

D

decaying Rotting away.

decibel Unit of loudness, measured in decibels (dB). Whispering is about 20dB, whereas a jet aircraft taking off makes a sound of about 130dB.

delicacy A food that is thought to be very rare, special or delicious.

delta A flat area of land, built up of material deposited by a river as it flows into the sea.

Deltas are usually roughly triangular in shape.

democracy A system of government by elected representatives of the people.

dependent Relying on something or someone else. For example, dogs are dependent on their owners looking after them.

deposit A layer of sediments such as sand, mud or gravel.

desert An area with very little rain or snow, and sparse vegetation.

diagnose Work out what illness a person has.

dialect A variety of speech used by people in a particular region. Some other mammals, such as whales and dolphins, also have dialects.

diameter The length of a straight line measured through the centre of a circle or sphere.

diesel A type of fuel, used in some cars, lorries, boats and trains.

diet The type and variety of food a person or animal eats every day.

digestion The breakdown of complex foods into simple nutrients that can be absorbed by the body.

dinosaur A member of a group of reptiles that lived from about 230 million years ago up until about 65 million years ago.

discipline Self-control. Discipline can mean a special kind of self-control learned through careful training, for example in martial arts.

dislocate Knock out of place.

diurnal Awake and active in the daytime.

DNA (deoxyribonucleic acid) The substance, found in the cell nuclei of all living things, that makes up genes and chromosomes. DNA is a code that contains the instructions needed to build and run cells, and to pass characteristics from parents to offspring.

dormant Inactive or asleep but not dead. A dormant animal is in a deep sleep – hibernating, for example. A dormant volcano is not active, and has not been active for a very long time, but may become active again in the future.

dorsal fin The vertical fin found on the back of all fish and some whales and dolphins.

domestic When referring to an animal, kept by or living with people rather than in the wild.

domesticated Tamed to live with humans.

dominant The strongest and most powerful in a group. For example, the strongest male

gorilla in a troop is called the dominant male.

drought A long period when rainfall is below the usual level.

dynasty Ruling royal family. An example is the Qin dynasty, emperors of China who ruled from 221BCE to 206BCE.

E

earthquake A large, sudden movement of the Earth's crust.

echinoderm A type of invertebrate animal that lives in oceans and seas. Sea stars, sea urchins, sea anemones and sea slugs are all echinoderms.

echo A sound wave that has reflected off a surface and is heard again after the original sound.

echolocation The way in which some animals, such as bats and dolphins, find their way around. They make sounds, then use the returning echoes to locate objects.

eclipse An effect that happens when one object in space is in the shadow of another. When the Moon covers the Sun and its shadow falls on Earth this is a solar eclipse. When the Earth's shadow covers the Moon it is a lunar eclipse.

electric charge A property of matter which causes electric forces between particles.

electricity The effect caused by the presence or movement of electrically charged particles.

electromagnet A piece of metal made into a powerful magnet by electricity passing through a coil of wire wound around it.

element A pure substance that cannot be broken down into simpler substances.

empire A number of different countries or peoples ruled by a single ruler or government.

endangered Describes a living thing that is threatened with extinction.

engineer Someone who designs or makes engines, machinery, computers or buildings.

environment An animal's or person's surroundings. In a general sense, the word is used to describe the natural world.

enzyme A type of protein, found in the body, that speeds up the rate of chemical reactions inside and outside cells.

epiphyte A type of plant that grows high up on other plants, instead of on the ground, to get a better share of light and water.

Equator The imaginary line drawn around the centre of the Earth at equal distance from the poles.

equestrian To do with the sport of horse riding.

erosion The gradual wearing down of rock by wind or water.

estuary The wide end of a river where it meets the sea.

EU (European Union) The group of countries that describes itself as a 'family of democratic European countries'. It started when six member states set up the European Commnity in 1952, and today the European Union has 27 member countries.

evaporate Change from a liquid into a gas. When water evaporates it becomes water vapour.

extinct Died out and disappeared forever.

F

fang A very sharp tooth found in some animals.

fault A fracture or crack in the Earth's crust where blocks of rock slip past each other.

feather A part of a bird's body, covering the skin. Birds have many different types of feathers. Some provide insulation from water and cold temperatures, while others help birds to fly. Birds are the only animals that have feathers.

fertile Capable of producing something. Fertile land is good for growing crops, and a fertile animal is capable of producing young.

feudal system The social system in medieval Europe. The king granted land to nobles in return for military services. Lords rented the land to knights and other lords. Peasants farmed the land.

fleece A sheep's woolly coat.

flexible Able to bend without breaking.

flipper A broad limb used for swimming, for example by penguins.

flood plain A flat, low-lying area near a river which is likely to flood often.

forest A large area covered with trees.

Formula One (F1) The highest class of motor racing. The word 'formula' refers to a set of rules which all cars and drivers must follow.

fossils The ancient remains of living things, preserved in rocks.

freight Another word for cargo or goods.

fresco A method of painting. Usually the picture is painted on plaster while it is still wet. Perhaps the most famous Renaissance fresco is the ceiling of the Sistine Chapel in Rome, painted by Michaelangelo.

freshwater Water that is fresh, like rain or river water, not salty like seawater.

friction The action of one object rubbing against another.

fungi A group of living things that are neither animals nor plants. The group includes mushrooms and other toadstools, and moulds.

G

G-force A measure of acceleration due to gravity on Earth. G-forces are the forces people feel while riding a rollercoaster. Positive G-forces are felt when the rollercoaster is travelling upwards, when riders feel as if they weigh more than they really do. The reverse happens when the rollercoaster is travelling downwards, and negative G-forces mean that the riders feel weightless.

galaxy A vast number of stars, gas and dust held together by gravity.

gill The organ used for breathing in water and taking oxygen from it. Fish and the young of amphibians have gills.

glacier A mass of ice, carrying rocks and soil, formed from densely packed snow which does not melt.

gladiator A professional fighter in ancient Rome. Gladiators were usually criminals or slaves.

gland An organ or tissue in the body that produces a particular substance, such as poison.

glyph A character or mark that makes up part of a writing system. Mayan writing uses glyphs.

Gothic A style of art (especially of architecture) popular in Europe from around 1140 to 1500CE. Many great cathedrals were built in the Gothic style. The style became fashionable again in the 19th century, when many buildings were designed in a way that imitated the Gothic.

GPS (Global Positioning System) A satellite system that aids navigation and map-making. GPS satellites in the Earth's orbit transmit signals, which are picked up by GPS receiving equipment, pinpointing the receiver's exact position on Earth.

gravity A physical force of attraction. The Sun's gravity pulls on Earth. Earth's gravity pulls on everything on Earth.

grenade A small bomb that is thrown by hand.

grooming Washing and smoothing the hair or feathers. Animals need to groom themselves to keep themselves clean, and some animals groom each other as part of social bonding. Grooming is also an important part of horse and pony care.

H

habitat The area where an animal lives, such as grassland, sea or rainforest.

harpoon A barbed dart or spear, used for killing fish or other water creatures. Ancient Egyptians used harpoons to hunt hippos.

headland An area of land surrounded by water on three sides.

helium A chemical element (symbol He). It is the second lightest and least reactive element. It is one of the noble gases.

hemisphere One half of a planet or moon. The Earth's two hemispheres are the northern hemisphere and the southern hemisphere.

herbivore A type of animal that eats only plants.

herds Large groups of animals. Groups of elephants, cattle and wildebeest are known as herds.

hibernation A period of deep sleep, which helps certain animals to survive winter.

hieroglyphics Picture-writing, as used by the ancient Egyptians.

honeycomb A network of hexagonal wax cells, made by honey bees, where they store their honey.

hoplite A foot soldier in an ancient Greek army.

horizon The line where earth and sky appear to meet.

horsepower A unit of power, used to measure the power of a car's engine, for example.

humanism A system of thought focusing on human rather than godly or spiritual matters. Humanism first developed in 15th-century Europe.

humidity The amount of moisture in the air.

hurricane A huge tropical storm.

hydrogen The lightest chemical element (symbol H), usually a colourless gas.

I

igneous rock A type of rock that forms when magma or lava cools and hardens. Granite and basalt are examples of igneous rock.

impermeable Something that does not allow liquid to pass through it. Certain rocks are impermeable, for example.

Incas People of the Inca civilization of South America, who lived in what is now Ecuador, Peru and Chile in the 15th and 16th century CE.

incisor One of the sharp-edged front teeth in the lower

and upper jaw of many animals (including people).

incubate Keep eggs warm until they hatch.

independent Not relying on others or controlled by others.

industry Any business or activity that produces goods or provides services for money. Mining, farming, steel-making, manufacture and banking are some examples of different industries.

insect A type of invertebrate with a three-part body and six legs. Most insects have wings and can fly. There are more than a million known species of insect.

intensive care Special medical care for dangerously-ill patients.

internet The network of telephone lines and servers that link computers around the world, allowing quick exchange of information.

intestine A long tube, part of the digestive system. Here, food is turned into a liquid and nutrients are absorbed into the bloodstream. The human intestine has two parts: the small intestine and the large intestine.

invertebrate A type of animal that has no backbone. Worms, insects, spiders, jellyfish and starfish are invertebrates.

Islam A religion based on submission to the will of God (Allah). It was founded by the prophet Muhammad, who was born in Mecca in about 570CE. It is one of the major world religions today.

J

joint A part of the skeleton where two or more bones meet. At most joints, the body can move or bend.

K

keel The bottom part of a ship, that supports its whole frame.

keratin A horny material found in horns, hair, nails and claws, fur, hooves, birds' beaks and feathers, reptiles' scales and whales' baleen plates.

Koran The most important holy book of Islam. Muslims believe that it is the literal word of Allah (God), as revealed to the prophet Muhammad.

krill Tiny animals that swim in large shoals on the surface of the sea.

L

larva The first stage in an insect's life cycle, after it has hatched from an egg. Caterpillars and grubs are types of larvae.

lava Molten (hot, liquid) rock that flows out of a planet or moon, e.g. during a volcanic eruption.

legionary An infantry soldier (foot soldier) in the army of ancient Rome.

lens The part of the eye that focuses light.

lightning A huge spark of electricity made in a cloud.

limb An arm or a leg.

litter A group of baby animals with the same mother, born at the same time.

liver A large organ that produces bile, breaks down amino acids in food, filters some poisons from the blood, and stores glycogen, minerals and vitamins.

longshore drift A geographical process by which sediment (mud, sand and pebbles) moves along a beach shore.

lunar Of the Moon.

lung A sac-like breathing organ found in mammals, birds, reptiles and adult amphibians.

M

mammal A type of warm-blooded vertebrate animal that has fur or hair, gives birth to live young and feeds its young on milk. Humans are mammals.

mandible Jaw or mouthparts.

mane Thick hair around a lion or horse's head and neck.

manipulate Handle, use or move into a particular position.

mantle The rocky middle layer of the Earth, between the core and the outer crust.

manufactured Made, especially in a factory.

marina A special harbour for pleasure-boats and yachts.

marine Of the sea.

marsh Low-lying wetland that is often flooded.

marsupial A type of mammal found mainly in Australia. Baby marsupials are born very underdeveloped and are usually carried in the mother's pouch. Kangaroos, wombats, wallabies and koalas are some examples of marsupials.

martial arts Activities, such as judo, karate and many others, based on ancient ways of fighting from countries including China and Japan. Today, most martial arts are practised as a sport or as self-defence, although ideas of mental discipline and meditation are still important.

mechanic A person who makes and repairs machinery.

medieval Relating to a period European history, from about the 5th to the 15th century CE.

merchant Trader, someone who buys and sells goods.

metamorphic rock A type of rock that forms when other rocks are exposed to great heat or pressure, or both. Marble and slate are examples of metamorphic rock.

metamorphosis Change of form, for example in the life cycles of some animals. Frogs undergo metamorphosis, changing in these stages: egg, tadpole, froglet, frog.

meteorologist A scientist who studies and forecasts the weather.

metropolis A city that is very large (with at least one million people living in its central area) and usually an important cultural centre.

microscope An instrument that magnifies very small objects to reveal details invisible to the naked eye.

microstate A tiny country. Europe has several microstates. These are Andorra, Monaco, San Marino, Liechtenstein and the smallest country in the world: the Vatican City.

microwave A particular type of electromagnetic wave with a very short wavelength.

middle ages The name often given to a period in history, stretching from approximately 1100 to 1460CE.

migration The annual journey made by some animals to find good weather, food or a place to breed.

military Of the armed forces.

million One thousand thousand (1,000,000).

mineral A type of naturally-occuring substance. Rocks are made up of minerals.

Minoans People of the Minoan civilization, who inhabited Crete from around 7000BCE to 1450BCE.

molar One of the strong, grinding back teeth found in the mouths of many mammals (including people).

molecule The smallest possible unit of a chemical. If a molecule is broken up into smaller sections it will no longer be the same chemical.

molten Melted, liquid.

mosque A place of worship for Muslims.

Muhammad A prophet, born in the city of Mecca in around 570CE, who founded Islam and is its most important prophet and holiest figure.

mummy A preserved human body. It may have been preserved deliberately, as in the case of ancient Egyptian mummies, or it may have been preserved naturally.

muscle The type of body tissue responsible for force and movement.

Muslim A follower of Islam.

N

NASCAR (the National Association of Stock Car Auto Racing) A motorsports organization in the USA or the type of motor racing organized by it. NASCAR is the second-most-watched sport in the USA.

native Describing an animal or plant, naturally living in the wild in a particular place. Describing people, the original inhabitants of a country.

NATO (North Atlantic Treaty Organization) A military alliance between certain countries of North America and Europe, established in 1949. Its headquarters are in Brussels, Belgium.

navigate To find the way and steer a ship or other vehicle.

navy A country's warships and their crews.

nebula A cloud of gas and dust in space.

nectar A sugary substance produced by plants. Many creatures feed on nectar, but only honey bees turn it into honey.

nerve A bundle of cells that carries information between the nervous system and the rest of the body.

nitrogen An element (symbol N). As a colourless, odourless gas, it makes up four-fifths of the Earth's atmosphere.

nocturnal Awake and active at night-time.

nomad A member of a community moving from place to place without settling in permanent homes.

nuclear power Energy generated by a nuclear reactor.

nucleus (plural: nuclei) A word meaning centre or core. The nucleus of an atom is the dense, central part containing protons and neutrons. The nucleus of a living cell is its control centre and contains the instructions it needs to work.

nunatak The exposed summit of a mountain that sticks out above a glacier.

O

observatory A building designed for observing space.

obsidian A naturally-occurring glass, usually dark green to black in colour. It can be used to make extremely sharp blades.

oesophagus The tube, part of the digestive system, which carries food from the throat to the stomach.

omnivore A type of animal that eats both plants and meat.

opaque Not transparent.

opera A type of theatrical production in which the story is told wholly or mainly through music and singing.

optic nerve The nerve that carries messages from the eye to the brain.

oracle Someone who predicts the future. The most famous ancient oracle was the ancient Greek oracle at Delphi, a priestess who operated from the Temple of Apollo at Delphi.

orbit The path a space object takes around another, bigger space object. The Moon orbits Earth and Earth orbits the Sun.

ore A solid mineral which contains a valuable metal and occurs naturally in the Earth's crust.

organ A body part, such as the lung or brain, that has a special function or functions.

organism Any individual living thing, such as an animal, plant or fungus.

oxygen An element (symbol O). Oxygen is a gas present in the Earth's atmosphere, vital for supporting life, and vital for combustion (burning).

ozone layer A layer of the gas ozone found in the Earth's upper atmosphere. It absorbs harmful ultraviolet radiation from the Sun.

P

packs Groups of animals that hunt together, such as wolves.

paddock The name for a field where a horse is kept.

paleontology The study of fossils. The study of dinosaurs is a part of paleontology.

pampas Fertile lowland plains in South America.

papyrus A thick, papery material made from a grass-like plant (also called papyrus) that was common in ancient Egypt. Ancient Egyptians used papyrus for writing on.

particle A very tiny thing or part of a thing. The word is often used as a general term to describe atoms or molecules, although it can mean any very tiny piece of something.

pelvis A basin-shaped bone that joins the legs to the lower part of the spine and supports the organs of the abdomen.

peristalsis The contractions of muscles in the walls of the digestive tube that push food through the tube.

pet An animal kept as a companion.

pharaoh A ruler in ancient Egypt.

pharmacist A person who is qualified to advise about and sell drugs and medicines.

philosopher A scientist or thinker who studies questions about knowledge itself.

photosphere The outer surface of a star.

pigment Paint, dye or any other substance that is used for colouring.

pilgrimage A journey undertaken for religious reasons, for example to a sacred place or shrine.

pioneer Someone who is one of the first people to do something or go somewhere.

plague A term used to describe any deadly and contagious disease, especially bubonic plague, a disease that killed over a third of the population of Europe in the 14th century CE.

plains Areas of lowland, usually fairly flat.

planet A large, round body, made of rock or gas, that orbits a star. In our Solar System there are eight main planets orbiting the Sun. There are also many other objects, including dwarf planets.

plankton Very tiny organisms that drift in the oceans and provide food for many larger organisms.

plate A section of the Earth's crust. Plates are solid and move slowly on top of the semi-molten mantle underneath them.

playwright Someone who writes plays.

plumage A bird's feathers, or the colour and pattern of its feathers.

poachers Illegal hunters.

pod A family group of whales, seals or dolphins.

poles The most northerly and most southerly points on Earth, the North Pole and South Pole.

pollen The male reproductive cells of a plant.

pollination The process by which plants are fertilized. Pollination occurs when pollen cells land on the female part of the flower, called the stigma, and form a pollen tube leading to the ovary. Pollination is necessary in order for fruit or seeds to develop.

pollution The release of poisonous substances into air or water.

population the number of people who live in a certain area, for example a city or country.

port A town with a harbour, usually an important place for trade.

predator An animal that hunts and kills other animals for food.

prehensile Capable of gripping. This word often describes tails.

prehistoric Relating to the time before written historical records exist.

president The elected ruler of an organization or country. The USA is an example of a country that has a president.

prey Animals that are hunted and killed by other animals.

pride A family group of lions.

priest A figure of religious authority. Many religions have priests, although often they are not called priests but have more specific names.

primate A type of mammal that includes lemurs, monkeys and apes (including humans). Primates have five fingers, fingernails and opposable thumbs.

proboscis The tube-shaped mouthparts of some kinds of insects, for example bees and butterflies.

projector A machine for displaying moving images by projecting them onto a screen. Projectors are used in cinemas to display films.

propeller Part of a ship or aeroplane that provides the driving mechanism by rotating blades around a central shaft.

prophet A holy person and/or someone who can see into the future.

protein A naturally-occurring chemical made up of amino acids. Proteins are the building blocks of cells and are essential to animal growth and repair. They can also be obtained from food and so are an important part of the diet.

prototype A trial model of something.

province A distinct area of a country or empire. In the Roman empire, countries that were conquered by Rome became Roman provinces.

pupil The circular opening in the centre of the iris that lets light into the eye.

QR

rainforest A thick forest with very tall trees. Rainforests grow in the tropics, where it is hot all the time and rains every day.

ray A type of fish, closely related to sharks.

referee An umpire or judge, especially in sport.

refugee Someone who is forced to flee from their home because of war, hunger or poverty. A refugee camp is a camp set up specially to house refugees until they can return home or find a permanent new home.

regurgitate Cough up.

relativity The theory that states that time, space and mass are not fixed but change relative to the position from which they are measured.

Renaissance The revival of art and literature and of interest in classical learning that happened in 14th–16th century Europe. The word 'Renaissance' means rebirth.

represent Stand for.

reproduction Making copies or new versions of something. When living things reproduce, they produce offspring (babies). In animals this is also known as breeding.

reptile A cold-blooded vertebrate animal, such as a snake or crocodile. Reptiles often have scaly skin. Some lay eggs and others give birth to live young.

republic A country which has no king or queen but is ruled by representatives of the people. France, Germany, the USA and Turkey are just a few examples of republics in the world today.

research Organized investigation or study.

retina The eyeball lining. It uses light to form images which are turned into signals and sent to the brain.

rib One of the bones that curve round and forward from the backbone.

ritual A set of actions performed for symbolic reasons. Religion involves many rituals, but rituals are not necessarily all religious.

rodent A small mammal, such as a mouse or rat, which has large front teeth for gnawing.

S

sacred Holy, religious.

sacrifice Destroying or going without something in order to achieve something good. In religious terms, sacrifice usually means an offering to the gods, for example the slaughter of animals or humans as an offering to the gods. In general terms it means suffering or going without for the sake of something good.

satellite An object that orbits a planet or moon. The Moon is a natural satellite of Earth. Telescopes in orbit around Earth are examples of man-made satellites.

scavenger An animal that feeds mainly on the dead remains of other animals.

scribe A person whose job it was to write things down, especially during times when not everyone was able to write.

scrubland A habitat where shrubs and grasses make up most of the vegetation.

SCUBA (Self Contained Underwater Breathing Apparatus) Swimming underwater while using breathing equipment.

sediment Materials, such as sand, mud and rock particles, that sink to the bottom of the sea or are deposited by wind, water or glaciers.

sedimentary rock A type of rock that forms when sediment is squeezed together over very long periods of time. Sandstone and limestone are examples of sedimentary rock.

seismologist A scientist who studies earthquakes.

semaphore A method and code of signalling, using flags held in different positions.

senate A law-making assembly, made up of people called senators, who vote on and pass laws. The first senate was in ancient Rome. Some modern countries, such as the USA and France, have senates based on the Roman model.

senses An organism's abilities to receive information from its surroundings and respond to this information. Senses include sight, hearing, touch, smell and taste.

sensor A device for detecting information about physical things, such as heat, light, movement or sounds. Animals and plants use special cells as sensors.

shoal A very large number of fish, swimming together.

siege The act of surrounding a town or fortress, cutting off its supply lines and attacking it.

skeleton The part of an animal's body that supports it and protects its internal organs. Vertebrates have internal skeletons, which are frameworks made of cartilage or bone. Invertebrates have external skeletons, which are hard body coverings, or no skeletons at all.

slave A person who is not free, but is owned by someone else and has to work for their owner for their whole life. Slaves earn no money, can be bought and sold, and are often treated harshly.

sniper A soldier who shoots at individuals one by one, from a hidden position.

social animals Animals that live in groups and have particular roles within a group. For example, gorillas live in family groups or troops. Bees live in colonies.

Solar System The Sun and all the objects that orbit it: eight main planets, over 140 moons, dwarf planets, spacerocks and comets.

solitary Alone.

solstice The longest (summer solstice) or shortest (winter solstice) day of the year, when the Earth's axis is most tilted.

sonnet A particular type of poem. A sonnet always has 14 lines, and follows certain rules about which of its lines rhyme with each other.

space shuttle A spacecraft designed to be used more than once. The first US space shuttle was launched in 1972, and since then there have been 115 missions.

species A particular type of animal or other living thing.

spyhopping The word used to describe a whale momentarily lifting the top half of its body out of the water, to breathe and to look around.

stable A building where horses are kept.

stalactite A pointed piece of limestone rock hanging down from the roof of a cave like an icicle.

stalagmite A pointed piece of limestone rock rising up from the floor of a cave.

stalking An animal following its prey very quietly so it can catch it.

star A ball of hot, bright gas in space.

stratum (plural: strata) A layer of sedimentary rock.

streamlined Shaped so that air or water flows smoothly around something, reducing drag. Many marine creatures and birds are well streamlined, and fast cars and planes are designed to be streamlined.

subduction When one of the Earth's plates slides underneath another.

submersible A type of submarine used for scientific and industrial work. Some are guided by remote control as they explore the oceans.

subtropical Of the subtropics – areas of the world further from the Equator than the tropics are, but not as far away as the temperate zones are. Winters in subtropical regions are fairly warm, and summers are hot.

Sumerians People who lived in parts of Mesopotamia (modern-day Iraq) from around 5000BCE to 2000BCE.

supersonic Faster than the speed of sound.

surgeon A type of doctor who performs operations.

suspension The system of springs supporting the chassis (framework) of a car.

symbiosis A relationship between two different types of organisms that is beneficial to both.

symptom A sign of something, such as of an illness. Symptons of the common cold, for example, include a fever, sore throat and runny nose.

T

talon A bird of prey's long, sharp, curved claw.

telescope An instrument that collects light from a distant object and turns that light into an image.

temperament Personality.

temperature How hot or cold something is, measured in degrees Celsius (°C).

temple A religious building where prayer and worship takes place. The word is used to describe religious buildings of many religions, including ancient Egyptian, ancient Greek, ancient Roman and Aztec buildings, as well as those of modern religions including Hinduism, Sikhism and Buddhism.

tentacle A long, flexible, arm-like part of the body of certain animals, such as octopuses and jellyfish, which is used for grasping things. Some animals use their tentacles to move or to sting their prey.

territory An area of land belonging to or controlled by someone or something. An animal's territory is the area it lives in, treats as its own and defends. A country's territory is the land it controls.

thermal A rising current of warm air, used by birds to gain height whilst flying or gliding.

thermometer An instrument that measures temperature.

thunder A loud rumbling or crashing sound casued when lighting heats air rapidly and the air vibrates.

thorax The middle section of an insect's three-part body, bearing the legs and wings

tissue A group of the same, or similar, types of cells in the body that work together to carry out a particular task.

tornado A powerful whirlwind.

tourist destination A place that is attractive to tourists and that has many visitors who visit it for this reason.

trade Buying and selling.

tragedy A play or other story that has a serious subject and a very sad ending. The first tragedies were performed in ancient Greece. They were also very popular during the 16th and 17th century, and Shakespeare wrote many fine tragedies. The word 'tragedy' is often also applied to very sad events in real life.

translucent Allowing some light to shine through it, but not completely transparent.

treaty A formal agreement between countries. Treaties are often set up after wars, to agree peace, but they can also be set up for many other reasons.

trebuchet A medieval war machine, used for launching stones at an enemy castle or fort.

trench A long, narrow ditch. During the First World War, much of the fighting occurred in the trenches, and millions of soldiers lived and died there.

tribe A kind of social group.

tributary A smaller river that flows into a larger river.

trireme An ancient Greek warship.

troop A group of gorillas.

tropical Relating to the tropics, which are hot regions of the Earth near the Equator.

tsunami A huge, long, high wave caused by an undersea earthquake.

tusk A long, pointed tooth that sticks out of the mouths of some animals, including walruses and elephants.

U

udder The part of a cow's body where milk is produced.

ultraviolet (UV) light A type of electromagnetic wave with a wavelength just shorter than that of visible light.

UN (United Nations) The world's largest international treaty organization, of which most nations are members. It was founded in 1945 and promotes peace and co-operation between nations. UN agencies act in areas including health, economic development and human rights.

underworld A place where, according to many religions and cultures, people are believed to go after they die. For example, in ancient Greek mythology, the Underworld is the land of the dead, ruled by the god Hades. Different religions and cultures have different beliefs about whether the underworld exists and what it is like.

unique One of a kind, with nothing else like it.

universe Everything that exists – all of space and everything in it.

V

vapour Droplets of water in the air.

vegetation Plants – the total plant cover in an area.

velodrome A sporting arena built specially for cycle races.

venom Poison.

vermin Animals that are a nuisance or danger to people, such as rats or cockroaches.

vertebra One of the bones that makes up the spine (backbone) of a vertebrate animal.

vertebrate A type of animal that has a backbone. Fish, amphibians, reptiles, birds and mammals (including people) are all vertebrates.

vertical Upright.

visual To do with sight. A visual message is a message you can see.

vitamin A type of chemical that is needed in minute amounts by the body and is found in certain foods. Fruit and vegetables, for example, are rich in many vitamins.

volcano An opening in the Earth's crust through which molten rock, hot gases and ash escape.

W

warm-blooded An animal that can keep its body at the same warm temperature all the time. Only birds and mammals are warm-blooded.

water cycle The continual flow of the Earth's water. Water vapour from the sea and land rises into the atmosphere, becoming clouds of rain, snow or hail, and then falls back to Earth.

wave A surge of energy travelling through water or air, or the ridge on the surface of a liquid created by that surge of energy.

wavelength The distance between a point on one wave and the same point on the next wave.

wax A type of oily substance. Beeswax is produced by bees and used by them to build their honeycombs. There are also man-made types of wax.

weather Atmospheric conditions: temperature, wetness, cloudiness and windiness.

Wild West The name given to the western United States of America in the time of the first settlers of the 19th century (e.g. cowboys and goldminers), before law and order was established.

wingspan The distance from tip to tip of a bird's or aircraft's wings.

XYZ

X-ray A type of radiation used to reveal things hidden beneath something else, such as bones in a person's body.

yacht A light, fast sailing ship used for racing or for pleasure-trips.

Index

Acknowledgements

The publisher would like to thank the following for permission to reproduce their material. Every care has been taken to trace copyright holders. However, if there have been unintentional omissions or failure to trace copyright holders, we apologize and will, if informed, endeavour to make corrections in any future edition.

b = bottom, c = centre, l = left, r = right, t = top

PHOTOGRAPHS
10cl Corbis/Michael Weber/zefa; 34br Kingfisher;
45b Corbis/John Hicks; 47t Corbis/Jose Fuste Raga;
49tl Corbis/Tibor Bognar; 54tr Corbis/L. Clarke;
63tr Corbis/Jeff Taflan/zefa; 63c Roger Ressmeyer/Corbis;
66bl NASA/ESA; 66br NASA; 75cr Corbis/Hulton-Deutsch Collection;
81b Corbis/Simon Marcus; 83c Corbis/Mark Seelen/zefa;
85tl Michael Freeman/Corbis; 87t Corbis/Fiat;
87b Fiat/Reuters/Corbis; 116l Lenfilm/The Kobal Collection;
116b 20th Century Fox/The Kobal Collection/Morton, Merrick;
126b Sutton